CONTENTS

Born to Code in C

Born to Code in C

Herbert Schildt

Osborne **McGraw-Hill**

Berkeley   New York   St. Louis   San Francisco
Auckland   Bogotá   Hamburg   London   Madrid
Mexico City   Milan   Montreal   New Delhi   Panama City
Paris   São Paulo   Singapore   Sydney
Tokyo   Toronto

Osborne **McGraw-Hill**
2600 Tenth Street
Berkeley, California 94710
U.S.A.

For information on translations and book distributors outside of the
U.S.A., please write to Osborne **McGraw-Hill** at the above address.

A complete list of trademarks appears on page 519.

Born to Code in C

234567890 DOC 89

ISBN 0-07-881468-5

This book is dedicated to Dennis Ritchie, the creator of the C language, and to programmers everywhere who were born to code in C.

This book is about C and C programmers. In its nine chapters you will find examples of C applied to a wide variety of applications. You will also find profiles of 14 of the world's finest C programmers. They describe how they discovered C, what their own personal design philosophies are, and how they approach programming.

These programmers were chosen because they were either instrumental to the advancement of the C language or because they have used C to create successful programs. I have attempted to present a representative cross-section of programmers. (Of course, it was not possible to include every worthy C programmer.)

In the process of writing the programmers' profiles, I noticed two traits common to all: drive and enthusiasm. Without fail, these are people who like their work. In fact, most would probably not refer to programming as work, but as a way of life. The creation of the programmer profiles was one of the most enjoyable writing tasks I have performed and I thank all who participated for their time and effort.

About This Book

The topic of each chapter was chosen because it met at least one of the following conditions: useful, interesting, unique, or fun. Chapter 1, the Little C Interpreter, is probably my favorite for one reason: it's just plain fun! Although language interpretation has several practical uses, I developed the Little C interpreter simply for the joy of doing it.

Chapter 2 explores icon-based interfaces. It includes a complete icon editor as well as an icon-based DOS interface as an example.

If you work (or play) in a DOS environment, you will find Chapters 3 and 4 particularly interesting and useful. Chapter 3 is about supercharging TSRs. You'll learn how to construct a memory-resident program that can perform sophisticated screen and disk I/O—and develop a full-featured TSR program in the process. Chapter 4 was very exciting to work on. It is a complete multitasking subsystem for DOS. It intercepts the computer's real-time clock interrupt and uses it to multitask individual parts of a C program. This is no toy—it really works!

Chapters 5 and 6 develop two useful subsystems: a screen editor and a database manager. These subsystems can be integrated into application programs as user-amenities.

Chapter 7 examines the creation of custom character fonts. It includes a complete font editor for creating characters and a custom character display subsystem. Custom character fonts can give your programs a unique appearance.

Chapter 8 looks at animation. It develops an animation editor with which you can define objects and their motion. It also develops an animation subsystem that can be included in your application programs. Mouse interfacing is also discussed.

Chapter 9 concludes the book with a look at controlling Epson (and compatible) printers. The Epson printers have many capabilities that are often overlooked. The chapter develops both text and graphics functions that take advantage of many of the Epson's more advanced features.

Who is this book for?

This book is for any C programmer. If you are just beginning, then you can use the programs "as is" until you become proficient. If you are an experienced programmer, you can use the functions and routines presented as starting points for your own applications.

Diskette Offer

There are many useful and interesting programs contained in this book. If you're like me, you probably would like to use them, but hate typing them into the computer. When I key in routines from a book it always seems that I type something wrong and spend hours trying to get the program to work. For this reason, I am offering the source code on diskette with all the functions and programs contained in this book for $24.95. Just fill in the order blank on the next page and mail it, along with your payment, to the address shown. Or, if you are in a hurry, just call (217) 586-4021 (the number of my consulting office) and place your order by telephone. (Visa and Mastercard accepted.)

HS

Mahomet, Illinois
March, 1989

Please send me _____ copies, at $24.95 each, of the programs in *Born to Code in C.* Foreign orders, please add $5 for shipping and handling.

Name_____

Address_____

City _____ State _____ Zip _____

Telephone_____

Diskette size (check one): 5 1/4" _____ 3 1/2"_____

Method of payment: check   Visa   MC

Credit card number: _____

Expiration date:_____

Signature:_____

Send to:_____

> Herbert Schildt
> RR 1, Box 130
> Mahomet, Il 61853

or phone: (217) 586-4021

Osborne/McGraw-Hill assumes NO responsibility for this offer. This is solely an offer of Herbert Schildt and not of Osborne/McGraw-Hill.

CHAPTER ONE

A C Interpreter

Language interpreters are fun! And what could be more fun for a C programmer than a C interpreter?

To begin this book I wanted a topic that would be of interest to virtually all C programmers. I also wanted the topic to be fresh, exciting, and useful. After rejecting many ideas, I finally decided upon the creation of the Little C interpreter. Here's why.

As valuable and important as compilers are, the creation of a compiler can be a difficult and lengthy process. In fact, just the creation of a compiler's run-time library is a large task in itself. By contrast, the creation of a language interpreter is an easier and more manageable task. Also, if correctly designed, the operation of an interpreter can be easier to understand than that of a comparable compiler. Beyond ease of development, language interpreters offer an interesting feature not found in compilers, an engine that actually executes the program. Remember, a *compiler* only translates your program's source code into a form that the computer can execute. However, an *interpreter* actually executes the program. It is this distinction that makes interpreters interesting.

1

Ralph Ryan
Project Manager of Microsoft C Version 3.0

Ralph Ryan has been very active in the C programming community. He was project manager for Microsoft's C, version 3.0, and then manager of Compiler Technology at Microsoft when version 4.0 was prepared. He coauthored (with Tom Plum) a C compiler test suite—Plum Hall Validation Suite—that became the industry standard. He has served on the ANSI standardization committee and is the author of a book about Microsoft's LAN Manager. These accomplishments are all the more impressive given that Ralph was first introduced to C only ten years ago, in 1979, when he was building general-purpose process-control systems. As Ralph puts it, "My prior professional experience had all been in FORTRAN or Assembler. But after learning C, I knew that there could be no going back."

As project manager of one of the most popular C compilers, Ralph is particularly proud of one innovation added by the Microsoft team to the 8086 (family) based C compilers: "The most important extensions we (Microsoft) added to C compilers for the 8086 family of processors were the **near** and **far** modifiers. These extensions let programmers take advantage of the Intel architecture to create high performance programs. No longer did a program have to be compiled for just one memory model. Instead, the programmer could control on a function-by-function and variable-by-variable basis how each element in the program would be treated."

Ralph has this to say about his personal design philosophy: "I resist the urge to plunge into coding until I have all of the details sketched out, usually into fairly low level pseudo-code. I gradually refine this into real code and add several debugging assertions as I go. In this way, I hope to minimize debugging and gain a more coherent design in the process."

Ralph gives this advice to C programmers: "C is a powerful tool. But, it is just a tool. Clarity and organization are the keys to creating great programs. Become a great programmer and you will get the most out of C."

Ralph left Microsoft after working there for over six years—a long time in the programming business. He is currently writing books about programming. He lives in Bellevue, Washington and when he isn't writing or programming, he enjoys playing in a local rock and roll band.

If you are like most C programmers, you use C not only for its power and flexibility but also because the language itself represents an almost intangible, formal beauty that can be appreciated for its own sake. In fact, C is often referred to as "elegant" because of its consistency and purity. Much has been written about the C language from the "outside looking in," but seldom has it been explored from the "inside." Therefore, what better way to begin this book than to create a C program that interprets a subset of the C language?

In the course of this chapter an interpreter is developed that can execute a subset of the ANSI C language. Not only is the interpreter functional, but it is also well-designed—you can easily enhance it, extend it, and even add features not found in ANSI C. If you haven't thought about how C really works, you will be pleasantly surprised to see how straightforward it is. The C language is one of the most theoretically consistent computer languages ever developed. By the time you finish this chapter, you will not only have a C interpreter that you can use and enlarge but you will also have gained considerable insight into the structure of the C language itself. If you're like me, you'll find the C interpreter presented here just plain fun to play with!

Note: The source code to the C interpreter presented in this chapter is fairly long, but don't be intimidated by it. If you read through the discussion, you will have no trouble understanding it and following its execution.

THE PRACTICAL IMPORTANCE OF INTERPRETERS

Although the Little C interpreter is interesting in and of itself, language interpreters do have some practical importance in computing.

As you probably know, C is generally a *compiled language*. The main reason for this is that C is a language used to produce commercially salable programs. Compiled code is desirable for commercial software products because it protects the privacy of the source, prevents the user from changing the source code, and allows the programs to make the most efficient use of the host computer, to name a few reasons. Frankly, compilers will always dominate commercial software development, as they should; however, any computer language can be compiled or interpreted. In fact, in recent years a few C interpreters have appeared on the market.

There are two traditional reasons for using a C interpreter. First, beginners to C sometimes find the (potentially) highly interactive environment of an interpreter preferable to a compiler (although this is changing since the introduction of C-integrated programming environments, such as Borland's Turbo C and Microsoft's QuickC).

The second reason is debugging. The advantage that an interpreter has over a compiler in debugging is that the contents of all variables can be known and changed at any time. Also, a C interpreter can provide trace facilities that are difficult to equal in a compiled environment.

Another practical use you might have for an interpreter is as the basis for a database *query language*. Virtually all database query languages are interpreted because of the nature of the task. Although using C as a query language would not be appropriate in most circumstances, many of the principles you learn here will be.

There is another reason that language interpreters are interesting: they are easy to modify, alter, or enhance. This means that if you want to create, experiment, and control your own language, it is easier to do so with an interpreter than a compiler. Interpreters make great language prototyping environments because you can change the way the language works and see the effects very quickly.

Interpreters are (relatively) easy to create, easy to modify, easy to understand, and, perhaps most important, fun to play with. For example, you can rework the interpreter presented in this chapter to execute your program backward—that is, executing from the closing brace of **main( )** and terminating when the opening brace is encountered. (I don't know why anyone would want to do this, but try getting a compiler to execute your code backward!) Or, you can add a special feature to C that you (and perhaps only you) have always wanted. The point is that while compilers absolutely make more sense when doing commercial software development, interpreters let you really have fun with the C language. It is in this spirit that this chapter was developed. I hope you will enjoy reading it as much as I enjoyed writing it!

THE LITTLE C SPECIFICATIONS

Despite the fact that ANSI C has only 32 *keywords* (built-in commands), C is a very rich and powerful language. It would take far more than a single chapter to fully describe and implement an interpreter for the entire C language. Instead, the Little C interpreter understands a fairly narrow subset of the language. However, this particular subset includes many of C's most important aspects. What to include in the subset was decided mostly by whether it fit one (or both) of these two criteria:

1. Is the feature fundamentally inseparable from the C language?

2. Is the feature necessary to demonstrate an important aspect of the language?

For example, features such as recursive functions and global and local variables meet both criteria. The Little C interpreter supports all three loop constructs (not because of the first criterion, but because of the second criterion). However, the **switch** statement is not implemented because it is neither necessary (nice, but not necessary) nor does it demonstrate anything that the **if** statement (which is implemented) does not. (Implementation of **switch** is left to you for entertainment!)

For these reasons, I implemented the following features in the Little C interpreter:

- Parameterized functions with local variables

- Recursion

- The **if** statement

- The **do-while**, **while**, and **for** loops

- Integer and character variables

- Global variables

- Integer and character constants

- String constants (limited implementation)

- The **return** statement, both with and without a value

- A limited number of standard library functions

- These operators: +, −, *, /, %, <, >, <=, >=, ==, !=, unary −, and unary +

- Functions returning integers

- Comments

Even though this list may seem short, it takes a relatively large amount of code to implement it. One reason for this is that a substantial "price of admission" must be paid when interpreting a structured language such as C.

One Important Little C Restriction

The source code for the Little C interpreter is quite long—longer, in fact, than I generally like to put in a chapter. In order to simplify and shorten the source code for Little C, I have imposed one small restriction on the C grammar: the targets of **if, while, do,** and **for** must be blocks of code surrounded by beginning and ending curly braces. You may not use a single statement. For example, Little C will not correctly interpret code such as this:

```
for(a=0; a<10; a=a+1)
  for(b=0; b<10; b=b+1)
    for(c=0; c<10; c=c+1)
      puts("hi");

if(...)
  if(...) statement;
```

Instead, you must write the code like this:

```
for(a=0; a<10; a=a+1) {
  for(b=0; b<10; b=b+1) {
    for(c=0; c<10; c=c+1) {
      puts("hi");
    }
  }
}

if(...) {
  if(...) {
    statement;
  }
}
```

This restriction makes it easier for the interpreter to find the end of the code that forms the target to one of these program control statements. However, since the objects of the program control statements are often blocks of code anyway, this restriction does not seem too harsh. (With a little effort, you can remove this restriction, if you like.)

INTERPRETING A STRUCTURED LANGUAGE

As you know, C is structured: it allows stand-alone subroutines with local variables. It also supports recursion. What you might find interesting is that in some areas, it is easier to write a compiler for a structured language than it is to write an interpreter for it. For example, when a compiler generates code to call a function, it simply pushes the calling arguments onto the system stack and executes a machine language CALL to the function. To return, the function puts the return value in the accumulator of the CPU, clears the stack, and executes a machine language RET. However, when an interpreter must "call" a function, it manually has to stop what it is doing, save its current state, find the location of the function, execute the function, save the return value, and return to the original point, restoring the old environment. (You will see an example of this in the interpreter that follows.) In essence, the interpreter must emulate the equivalent of a machine language CALL and RETURN. Also, while support for recursion is easy in a compiled language, it requires some effort in an interpreted one.

In my book *C: Power User's Guide* (Berkeley, Ca.: Osborne/McGraw-Hill, 1988) I introduced the subject of language interpreters by developing a small BASIC interpreter. In that book I stated that it is easier to interpret a language such as standard BASIC than C because BASIC was designed to be interpreted. What makes BASIC easy to interpret is that it is not structured. All variables are global and there are no stand-alone subroutines. I still stand by this statement; however, once you have created the support for functions, local variables, and recursion, the C language is actually easier to interpret than BASIC. This is because a language such as BASIC is full of exceptions at the theoretical level. For example, in BASIC the equal sign is an assignment operator in an assignment statement, but an equality operator in a relational statement. C has few of these inconsistencies.

AN INFORMAL THEORY OF C

Before we can begin to develop the C interpreter, it is necessary to understand how the C language is structured. If you have ever seen a formal specification for the C language (such as that found in the ANSI-standard specification), you know that it is quite long and filled with rather cryptic statements. Don't worry—we won't need to deal this formally with the C language to design our interpreter because most of the C language is so straightforward. While the formal specification of a language is necessary for the creation of a commercial compiler or interpreter, it is not needed for the creation of the Little C interpreter.[1] (Frankly, there isn't space in this chapter to explain how to understand the C formal syntax definition: it could fill a book!)

Although you do not need to be a language expert to implement and understand the Little C interpreter developed in this chapter, you will still need a basic understanding of how the C language is defined. For our purposes, the discussion that follows is sufficient. (Those of you who wish a more formal discussion may refer to the ANSI standard for C. Also, for an excellent theoretical introduction to languages, see *The Theory of Parsing, Translation, and Compiling*, Aho and Ullman, Englewood Cliffs, NJ: Prentice-Hall.)

To begin, all C programs consist of a collection of one or more functions, plus global variables (if any exist). A *function* is comprised of a function name, its parameter list, and the block of code associated with the function. A *block* begins with a {, is followed by one or more statements, and ends with a }. In C, a statement either begins with a C keyword, such as **if**, or it is an expression. (We will see what constitutes an expression in the next section.) Summarizing, we can write the following *transformations* (sometimes called *production rules*):

program → collection of functions (plus global variables)
function → function_specifier parameter-list code-block
code-block → { statement sequence }
statement → keyword, expression, or code-block

---

1. This chapter is designed to be understood by the widest variety of readers. It is not intended to be a formal introduction to the theory of structured languages in general or C in particular. As such, it intentionally simplifies a few concepts. However, as you will see, the creation of an interpreter for a subset of C does not require formal training in language theory.

All C programs begin with a call to **main( )** and end when either the last } or a **return** has been encountered in **main( )**—assuming that **exit( )** or **abort( )** has not been called elsewhere. Any other functions contained in the program must either be directly or indirectly called by **main( )**; hence, to execute a C program, simply begin at the start of the **main( )** function and stop when **main( )** ends. This is precisely what Little C does.

C Expressions

C expands the role of expressions relative to many other computer languages. In C, a statement is either a C keyword statement, such as **while** or **switch**, or it is an *expression*. For the sake of discussion, let's categorize all statements that begin with C keywords as *keyword statements*. Any statement in C that is not a keyword statement is, by definition, an expression. Therefore, in C the following statements are all expressions:

```
count = 100;                    /* line 1 */

sample = i / 22 * (c-10);       / * line 2 */

printf("this is an expression");/ * line 3 */
```

Let's look more closely at each of these expression statements. In C, the equal sign is an *assignment operator*. C does not treat the assignment operation the way a language such as BASIC would, for example. In BASIC, the value produced by the right side of the equal sign is assigned to the variable on the left. But, and this is important, in BASIC, the entire statement does not have a value. In C, the equal sign is an assignment operator and the value produced by the assignment operation is equal to that produced by the right side of the expression. Therefore, an assignment statement is actually an *assignment expression* in C; because it is an expression, it has a value. This is why it is legal to write expressions such as the following:

```
a = b = c = 100;

printf("%d", a=4+5);
```

The reason this works in C is that an *assignment* is an operation that produces a value.

Line 2 shows a more complex assignment.

In line 3, **printf( )** is called to output a string. In traditional C, all functions return values, whether explicitly specified or not. (The ANSI standard has added the type **void** to allow functions that do not return values to be so specified, but as far as we are concerned, this is a special case, which we can ignore relative to Little C.) Hence, a function call is an expression that returns a value—whether the value is actually assigned to something or not.

Evaluating Expressions

Before we can develop code that will correctly evaluate C expressions, you need to understand in more formal terms how expressions are defined. In virtually all computer languages, expressions are defined recursively using a set of production rules. The Little C interpreter supports the following operations: +, −, *, /, %, =, the relational operators (<, = =, > and so forth), and parentheses. Therefore, we can use these production rules to define Little C expressions:

expression → [assignment] [rvalue]
assignment → lvalue = rvalue
lvalue → variable
rvalue → part [rel-op part]
part → term [+term] [−term]
term → factor [*factor] [/factor] [%factor]
factor → part [rel-op part]
part → [+ or −] atom
atom → variable, constant, function, or (expression)

Here, *rel-op* refers to any of C's relational operators. The terms *lvalue* and *rvalue* refer to objects that can occur on the left side and right side of an assignment statement, respectively. One thing that you should be aware of is that the precedence of the operators is built into the production rules. The higher the precedence, the further down the list the operator will be.

To see how these rules let us evaluate a C expression, let's use this example:

```
count = 10 - 5 * 3;
```

First, we apply rule 1, which dissects the expression into these three parts:

count   =   10-5*3
 ↑   ↑   ↑

lvalue assignment operator rvalue

Since there are no relational operators in the "rvalue" part of the subexpression, the *term* production rule is invoked.

10 — 5*3
↑   ↑   ↑

term minus term

Of course, the second term is comprised of the following two factors: 5 and 3. These two factors are constants and represent the lowest level of the production rules. Next, we must begin moving back up the rules to compute the value of the expression. First, we multiply 5*3, which yields 15. Next, we subtract that value from 10, yielding −5. Finally, this value is assigned to **count** and is also the value of the entire expression.

The first thing we need to do to create the Little C interpreter is to construct the computerized equivalent of the expression evaluation we just performed in our minds.

THE EXPRESSION PARSER

The piece of code that reads and analyzes expressions is called an *expression parser*. Without a doubt, the expression parser is the single most important subsystem needed by the Little C interpreter. Because C defines expressions more broadly than do many other languages, a substantial amount of the code that constitutes a C program is actually executed by the expression parser.

There are several different ways to design an expression parser for C. Many commercial compilers use a *table-driven parser,* which is generally created by a parser-generator program. While table-driven parsers are generally faster than other methods, they are very hard to create by hand. For the Little C interpreter developed here, we will use a *recursive-descent parser,* which implements in logic the production rules discussed in the previous section.

A recursive-descent parser is essentially a collection of mutually recursive functions that process an expression. If the parser is used in a compiler, then it is used to generate the proper object code that corresponds to the source code. However, in an interpreter, the object of the parser is to evaluate a given expression. The parser used in this chapter expands upon that simple foundation. Most of the discussion that follows pertains to the use of the parser as support for a C interpreter.

Reducing the Source Code to Its Components

Fundamental to all interpreters (and compilers, for that matter) is a special function that reads the source code and returns the next logical symbol from it. For historical reasons, these logical symbols are generally referred to as *tokens.* Computer languages in general, and C in particular, define programs in terms of tokens. You can think of a token as an indivisible program unit. For example, the equality operator = = is a token. The two equal signs cannot be separated without changing the meaning. In the same vein, **if** is a token. Neither *i* nor *f* by itself has any meaning to C.

In the ANSI C standard, tokens are defined as belonging to one of these groups:

keywords   identifiers   constants
strings   operators   punctuation

The keywords are those tokens that make up the C language, such as **while**. *Identifiers* are the names of variables, functions, and user-types (not implemented by Little C). Constants and strings are self-explanatory, as are operators. Punctuation includes several items, such as semicolons, commas, braces, and parentheses. (Some of these are also operators, depending upon their use.) Given the statement

```
for(x=0; x<10; x=x+1) printf("hello %d", x);
```

the following tokens are produced, reading left to right:

Token	Category
for	keyword
(	punctuation
x	identifier
=	operator
0	constant
;	punctuation
x	identifier
<	operator
10	constant
;	punctuation
x	identifier
=	operator
x	identifier
+	operator
1	constant
)	punctuation
printf	identifier
(	punctuation
"hello %d"	string
,	punctuation
x	identifier
)	punctuation
;	punctuation

However, in order to make the interpretation of C easier, Little C categorizes tokens as shown here:

Token Type	Includes
delimiters	punctuation and operators
keywords	keywords
strings	quoted strings
identifiers	variable and function names
number	numeric constant
block	{ or }

The function that returns tokens from the source code for the Little C interpreter is called **get_token( )** and it is shown here:

```c
/* Get a token. */
get_token(void)
{

  register char *temp;

  token_type = 0; tok = 0;

  temp = token;
  *temp = '\0';

  /* skip over white space */
  while(iswhite(*prog) && *prog) ++prog;

  if(*prog=='\r') {
    ++prog;
    ++prog;
    /* skip over white space */
    while(iswhite(*prog) && *prog) ++prog;
  }

  if(*prog=='\0') { /* end of file */
    *token = '\0';
    tok = FINISHED;
    return(token_type=DELIMITER);
  }

  if(strchr("{}", *prog)) { /* block delimiters */
    *temp = *prog;
    temp++;
    *temp = '\0';
    prog++;
    return (token_type = BLOCK);
  }

  /* look for comments */
  if(*prog=='/')
    if(*(prog+1)=='*') { /* is a comment */
      prog += 2;
      do { /* find end of comment */
```

```c
      while(*prog!='*') prog++;
      prog++;
   } while (*prog!='/');
   prog++;
 }

if(strchr("!<>=", *prog)) { /* is or might be
                               a relation operator */
  switch(*prog) {
    case '=': if(*(prog+1)=='=') {
        prog++; prog++;
        *temp = EQ;
        temp++; *temp = EQ; temp++;
        *temp = '\0';
      }
      break;
    case '!': if(*(prog+1)=='=') {
        prog++; prog++;
        *temp = NE;
        temp++; *temp = NE; temp++;
        *temp = '\0';
      }
      break;
    case '<': if(*(prog+1)=='=') {
        prog++; prog++;
        *temp = LE; temp++; *temp = LE;
      }
      else {
        prog++;
        *temp = LT;
      }
      temp++;
      *temp = '\0';
      break;
    case '>': if(*(prog+1)=='=') {
        prog++; prog++;
        *temp = GE; temp++; *temp = GE;
      }
      else {
        prog++;
        *temp = GT;
      }
      temp++;
```

```
        *temp = '\0';
        break;
    }
    if(*token) return(token_type = DELIMITER);
}

if(strchr("+-*^/%=;(),'", *prog)){ /* delimiter */
  *temp = *prog;
  prog++; /* advance to next position */
  temp++;
  *temp = '\0';
  return (token_type=DELIMITER);
}

if(*prog=='"') { /* quoted string */
  prog++;
  while(*prog!='"'&& *prog!='\r') *temp++ = *prog++;
  if(*prog=='\r') sntx_err(SYNTAX);
  prog++; *temp = '\0';
  return(token_type=STRING);
}

if(isdigit(*prog)) { /* number */
  while(!isdelim(*prog)) *temp++ = *prog++;
  *temp = '\0';
  return(token_type = NUMBER);
}

if(isalpha(*prog)) { /* var or command */
  while(!isdelim(*prog)) *temp++ = *prog++;
  token_type=TEMP;
}

*temp = '\0';

/* see if a string is a command or a variable */
if(token_type==TEMP) {
  tok = look_up(token); /* convert to internal rep */
  if(tok) token_type = KEYWORD; /* is a keyword */
  else token_type = IDENTIFIER;
}
return token_type;
}
```

The **get_token( )** function uses the following global data and enumeration types:

```
char *prog;   /* points to current location in source code */
extern char *p_buf;   /* points to start of program buffer */

char token[80]; /* holds string representation of token */
char token_type; /* contains the type of token */
char tok; /* holds the internal representation of token if
             it is a keyword */

enum tok_types {DELIMITER, IDENTIFIER, NUMBER, KEYWORD, TEMP,
                STRING, BLOCK};

enum double_ops {LT=1, LE, GT, GE, EQ, NE};

/* These are the constants used to call sntx_err() when
   a syntax error occurs.  Add more if you like.
   NOTE: SYNTAX is a generic error message used when
   nothing else seems appropriate.
*/
enum error_msg
     {SYNTAX, UNBAL_PARENS, NO_EXP, EQUALS_EXPECTED,
      NOT_VAR, PARAM_ERR, SEMI_EXPECTED,
      UNBAL_BRACES, FUNC_UNDEF, TYPE_EXPECTED,
      NEST_FUNC, RET_NOCALL, PAREN_EXPECTED,
      WHILE_EXPECTED, QUOTE_EXPECTED, NOT_TEMP,
      TOO_MANY_LVARS};
```

The current location in the source code is pointed to by **prog**. The **p_buf** pointer is unchanged by the interpreter and always points to the start of the program being interpreted. The **get_token( )** function begins by skipping over all white space, including carriage returns and line feeds. Since no C token (except for a quoted string or character constant) contains a space, spaces must be bypassed. The **get_token( )** function also skips over comments. Next, the string representation of each token is placed into **token**, its type (as defined by the **tok_types** enumeration) is put into **token_type**, and, if the token is a keyword, its internal representation is assigned to **tok** via the **look_up( )** function (shown in the full parser listing that follows). The reason for the internal representation of keywords will be discussed later. As you can see by looking at get_token( ), it converts C's two-character relational operators into their corresponding enumeration value. Although not technically necessary, this step makes the parser easier to implement. Finally, if the parser encounters a syntax error, it calls the function **sntx_err( )** with an enumerated value that corresponds to the type of error found. The **sntx_err( )** function is also called by other routines in the interpreter whenever an error occurs. The **sntx_err( )** function is shown here:

```
/* display an error message */
void sntx_err(int error)
{
  char *p, *temp;
  register int i;
  int linecount = 0;

  static char *e[]= {
    "syntax error",
    "unbalanced parentheses",
    "no expression present",
    "equals sign expected",
    "not a variable",
    "parameter error",
    "semicolon expected",
    "unbalanced braces",
    "function undefined",
    "type specifier expected",
    "too many nested function calls",
    "return without call",
    "parentheses expected",
    "while expected",
    "closing quote expected",
    "not a string",
    "too many local variables"
  };
  printf("%s", e[error]);
  p = p_buf;
  while(p != prog) {   /* find line number of error */
    p++;
    if(*p == '\r') {
      linecount++;
    }
  }
}
```

```
    printf(" in line %d\n", linecount);

    temp = p;  /* display line with error */
    for(i=0; i<20 && p>p_buf && *p!='\n'; i++, p--);
    for(i=0; i<30 && p<=temp; i++, p++) printf("%c", *p);

    longjmp(e_buf, 1); /* return to safe point */
}
```

Notice that **sntx_err( )** also displays the line number in which the error was detected (which may be one line after the error actually occurred) and displays the line in which it occurred. Further, notice that **sntx_err( )** ends with a call to **longjmp( )**. Because syntax errors are frequently encountered in deeply nested or recursive routines, the easiest way to handle an error is to simply jump to a safe place. Although it is possible to set a global error flag and interrogate the flag at various points in each routine, this adds unnecessary additional overhead.

The Little C Recursive-Descent Parser

The entire code for the Little C recursive-descent parser is shown here, along with some necessary support functions, global data, and data types. This code, as shown, is designed to go into its own file. For the sake of discussion, call this file PARSER.C. (Because of its size, the Little C interpreter is spread among three separate files.) Enter this file now.

```
/* Recursive descent parser for integer expressions
   which may include variables and function calls.  */
#include "setjmp.h"
#include "math.h"
#include "ctype.h"
#include "stdlib.h"
#include "string.h"
#include "stdio.h"

#define NUM_FUNC         100
#define NUM_GLOBAL_VARS  100
#define NUM_LOCAL_VARS   200
#define ID_LEN           31
#define FUNC_CALLS       31
```

```
#define PROG_SIZE       10000
#define FOR_NEST        31

enum tok_types {DELIMITER, IDENTIFIER, NUMBER, KEYWORD, TEMP,
                STRING, BLOCK};

enum tokens {ARG, CHAR, INT, IF, ELSE, FOR, DO, WHILE, SWITCH,
                RETURN, EOL, FINISHED, END};

enum double_ops {LT=1, LE, GT, GE, EQ, NE};

/* These are the constants used to call sntx_err() when
   a syntax error occurs.  Add more if you like.
   NOTE: SYNTAX is a generic error message used when
   nothing else seems appropriate.
*/
enum error_msg
     {SYNTAX, UNBAL_PARENS, NO_EXP, EQUALS_EXPECTED,
      NOT_VAR, PARAM_ERR, SEMI_EXPECTED,
      UNBAL_BRACES, FUNC_UNDEF, TYPE_EXPECTED,
      NEST_FUNC, RET_NOCALL, PAREN_EXPECTED,
      WHILE_EXPECTED, QUOTE_EXPECTED, NOT_TEMP,
      TOO_MANY_LVARS};

extern char *prog;  /* current location in source code */
extern char *p_buf;  /* points to start of program buffer */
extern jmp_buf e_buf; /* hold environment for longjmp() */

/* An array of these structures will hold the info
   associated with global variables.
*/
extern struct var_type {
  char var_name[32];
  enum variable_type var_type;
  int value;
}  global_vars[NUM_GLOBAL_VARS];

/*  This is the function call stack. */
extern struct func_type {
  char func_name[32];
  char *loc;  /* location of function entry point in file */
} func_stack[NUM_FUNC];
```

```c
/* Keyword table */
extern struct commands {
  char command[20];
  char tok;
} table[];

/* "Standard library" functions are declared here so
   they can be put into the internal function table that
   follows.
*/
int call_getche(void), call_putch(void);
int call_puts(void), print(void), getnum(void);

struct intern_func_type {
  char *f_name; /* function name */
  int (* p)();  /* pointer to the function */
} intern_func[] = {
  "getche", call_getche,
  "putch", call_putch,
  "puts", call_puts,
  "print", print,
  "getnum", getnum,
  "", 0  /* null terminate the list */
};

extern char token[80]; /* string representation of token */
extern char token_type; /* contains type of token */
extern char tok; /* internal representation of token */

extern int ret_value; /* function return value */

void eval_exp(int *value), eval_exp1(int *value);
void eval_exp2(int *value);
void eval_exp3(int *value), eval_exp4(int *value);
void eval_exp5(int *value), atom(int *value);
void eval_exp0(int *value);
void sntx_err(int error), putback(void);
void assign_var(char *var_name, int value);
int isdelim(char c), look_up(char *s), iswhite(char c);
int find_var(char *s), get_token(void);
int internal_func(char *s);
int is_var(char *s);
char *find_func(char *name);
```

```
void call(void);

/* Entry point into parser. */
void eval_exp(int *value)
{
  get_token();
  if(!*token) {
    sntx_err(NO_EXP);
    return;
  }
  if(*token==';') {
    *value = 0; /* empty expression */
    return;
  }
  eval_exp0(value);
  putback(); /* return last token read to input stream */
}

/* Process an assignment expression */
void eval_exp0(int *value)
{
  char temp[ID_LEN];   /* holds name of var receiving
                           the assignment */
  register int temp_tok;

  if(token_type==IDENTIFIER) {
    if(is_var(token)) {   /* if a var, see if assignment */
      strcpy(temp, token);
      temp_tok = token_type;
      get_token();
      if(*token=='=') {   /* is an assignment */
        get_token();
        eval_exp0(value);   /* get value to assign */
        assign_var(temp, *value);   /* assign the value */
        return;
      }
      else {   /* not an assignment */
        putback();   /* restore original token */
        strcpy(token, temp);
        token_type = temp_tok;
      }
    }
  }
```

```
  eval_expl(value);
}

/* This array is used by eval_expl().  Because
   some compilers cannot initialize an array within a
   function it is defined, as a global variable.
*/
char relops[7] = {
  LT, LE, GT, GE, EQ, NE, 0
};

/* Process relational operators. */
void eval_expl(int *value)
{
  int partial_value;
  register char op;

  eval_exp2(value);
  op = *token;
  if(strchr(relops, op)) {
    get_token();
    eval_exp2(&partial_value);
    switch(op) {  /* perform the relational operation */
      case LT:
        *value = *value < partial_value;
        break;
      case LE:
        *value = *value <= partial_value;
        break;
      case GT:
        *value = *value > partial_value;
        break;
      case GE:
        *value = *value >= partial_value;
        break;
      case EQ:
        *value = *value == partial_value;
        break;
      case NE:
        *value = *value != partial_value;
        break;
    }
  }
```

```
}

/*  Add or subtract two terms. */
void eval_exp2(int *value)
{
  register char  op;
  int partial_value;

  eval_exp3(value);
  while((op = *token) == '+' || op == '-') {
    get_token();
    eval_exp3(&partial_value);
    switch(op) {  /* add or subtract */
      case '-':
        *value = *value - partial_value;
        break;
      case '+':
        *value = *value + partial_value;
        break;
    }
  }
}

/* Multiply or divide two factors. */
void eval_exp3(int *value)
{
  register char  op;
  int partial_value, t;

  eval_exp4(value);
  while((op = *token) == '*' || op == '/' || op == '%') {
    get_token();
    eval_exp4(&partial_value);
    switch(op) { /* mul, div, or modulus */
      case '*':
        *value = *value * partial_value;
        break;
      case '/':
        *value = (*value) / partial_value;
        break;
      case '%':
        t = (*value) / partial_value;
        *value = *value-(t * partial_value);
```

```
        break;
      }
    }
}

/* Is a unary + or -. */
void eval_exp4(int *value)
{
  register char  op;

  op = '\0';
  if(*token=='+' || *token=='-') {
    op = *token;
    get_token();
  }
  eval_exp5(value);
  if(op)
    if(op=='-') *value = -(*value);
}

/* Process parenthesized expression. */
void eval_exp5(int *value)
{
  if((*token == '(')) {
    get_token();
    eval_exp0(value);    /* get subexpression */
    if(*token != ')') sntx_err(PAREN_EXPECTED);
    get_token();
  }
  else
    atom(value);
}

/* Find value of number, variable or function. */
void atom(int *value)
{
  int i;

  switch(token_type) {
  case IDENTIFIER:
    i = internal_func(token);
    if(i!= -1) {  /* call "standard library" function */
      *value = (*intern_func[i].p)();
```

```
    }
    else
    if(find_func(token)){  /* call user-defined function */
      call();
      *value = ret_value;
    }
    else  *value = find_var(token);  /* get var's value */
    get_token();
    return;
  case NUMBER: /* is numeric constant */
    *value = atoi(token);
    get_token();
    return;
  case DELIMITER: /* see if character constant */
    if(*token=='\'') {
      *value = *prog;
      prog++;
      if(*prog!='\'') sntx_err(QUOTE_EXPECTED);
      prog++;
      get_token();
    }
    return;
  default:
    if(*token==')') return; /* process empty expression */
    else sntx_err(SYNTAX); /* syntax error */
  }
}

/* Display an error message. */
void sntx_err(int error)
{
  char *p, *temp;
  int linecount = 0;
  register int i;

  static char *e[]= {
    "syntax error",
    "unbalanced parentheses",
    "no expression present",
    "equals sign expected",
    "not a variable",
    "parameter error",
    "semicolon expected",
```

```
      "unbalanced braces",
      "function undefined",
      "type specifier expected",
      "too many nested function calls",
      "return without call",
      "parentheses expected",
      "while expected",
      "closing quote expected",
      "not a string",
      "too many local variables"
   };
   printf("%s", e[error]);
   p = p_buf;
   while(p != prog) {   /* find line number of error */
      p++;
      if(*p == '\r') {
         linecount++;
      }
   }
   printf(" in line %d\n", linecount);

   temp = p;
   for(i=0; i<20 && p>p_buf && *p!='\n'; i++, p--);
   for(i=0; i<30 && p<=temp; i++, p++) printf("%c", *p);

   longjmp(e_buf, 1); /* return to save point */
}

/* Get a token. */
get_token(void)
{

   register char *temp;

   token_type = 0; tok = 0;

   temp = token;
   *temp = '\0';

 /* skip over white space */
   while(iswhite(*prog) && *prog) ++prog;

   if(*prog=='\r') {
```

```
    ++prog;
    ++prog;
    /* skip over white space */
    while(iswhite(*prog) && *prog) ++prog;
  }

  if(*prog=='\0') { /* end of file */
    *token = '\0';
    tok = FINISHED;
    return(token_type=DELIMITER);
  }

  if(strchr("{}", *prog)) { /* block delimiters */
    *temp = *prog;
    temp++;
    *temp = '\0';
    prog++;
    return (token_type = BLOCK);
  }

  /* look for comments */
  if(*prog=='/')
    if(*(prog+1)=='*') { /* is a comment */
      prog += 2;
      do { /* find end of comment */
        while(*prog!='*') prog++;
        prog++;
      } while (*prog!='/');
      prog++;
    }

  if(strchr("!<>=", *prog)) { /* is or might be
                                 a relation operator */
    switch(*prog) {
      case '=': if(*(prog+1)=='=') {
          prog++; prog++;
          *temp = EQ;
          temp++; *temp = EQ; temp++;
          *temp = '\0';
        }
        break;
      case '!': if(*(prog+1)=='=') {
          prog++; prog++;
```

```
                       *temp = NE;
                       temp++; *temp = NE; temp++;
                       *temp = '\0';
                   }
                   break;
                case '<': if(*(prog+1)=='=') {
                       prog++; prog++;
                       *temp = LE; temp++; *temp = LE;
                   }
                   else {
                       prog++;
                       *temp = LT;
                   }
                   temp++;
                   *temp = '\0';
                   break;
                case '>': if(*(prog+1)=='=') {
                       prog++; prog++;
                       *temp = GE; temp++; *temp = GE;
                   }
                   else {
                       prog++;
                       *temp = GT;
                   }
                   temp++;
                   *temp = '\0';
                   break;
            }
            if(*token) return(token_type = DELIMITER);
    }

    if(strchr("+-*^/%=;(),'"", *prog)){ /* delimiter */
        *temp = *prog;
        prog++; /* advance to next position */
        temp++;
        *temp = '\0';
        return (token_type=DELIMITER);
    }

    if(*prog=='"') { /* quoted string */
        prog++;
        while(*prog!='"'&& *prog!='\r') *temp++ = *prog++;
        if(*prog=='\r') sntx_err(SYNTAX);
```

```
      prog++; *temp = '\0';
      return(token_type=STRING);
   }

   if(isdigit(*prog)) { /* number */
     while(!isdelim(*prog)) *temp++ = *prog++;
     *temp = '\0';
     return(token_type = NUMBER);
   }

   if(isalpha(*prog)) { /* var or command */
     while(!isdelim(*prog)) *temp++ = *prog++;
     token_type=TEMP;
   }

   *temp = '\0';

   /* see if a string is a command or a variable */
   if(token_type==TEMP) {
     tok = look_up(token); /* convert to internal rep */
     if(tok) token_type = KEYWORD; /* is a keyword */
     else token_type = IDENTIFIER;
   }
   return token_type;
}

/* Return a token to input stream. */
void putback(void)
{
  char *t;

  t = token;
  for(; *t; t++) prog--;
}

/* Look up a token's internal representation in the
   token table.
*/
look_up(char *s)
{
  register int i;
  char *p;
```

```
  /* convert to lowercase */
  p = s;
  while(*p){ *p = tolower(*p); p++; }

  /* see if token is in table */
  for(i=0; *table[i].command; i++)
      if(!strcmp(table[i].command, s)) return table[i].tok;
  return 0; /* unknown command */
}

/* Return index of internal library function or -1 if
   not found.
*/
internal_func(char *s)
{
  int i;

  for(i=0; intern_func[i].f_name[0]; i++) {
    if(!strcmp(intern_func[i].f_name, s))  return i;
  }
  return -1;
}

/* Return true if c is a delimiter. */
isdelim(char c)
{
  if(strchr(" !;,+-<>'/*%^=()", c) || c==9 ||
     c=='\r' || c==0) return 1;
  return 0;
}

/* Return 1 if c is space or tab. */
iswhite(char c)
{
  if(c==' ' || c=='\t') return 1;
  else return 0;
}
```

The functions that begin with **eval_exp** and the **atom( )** function implement the production rules for Little C expressions. To verify this, you might want to execute the parser mentally, using a simple expression.

For a detailed discussion of expression parsing, refer to *C: The Complete Reference* 2nd Edition by Herbert Schildt. (Berkeley,Ca.: Osborne/McGraw-Hill, 1989).

The **atom( )** function finds the value of an integer constant or variable, a function, or a character constant. There are two kinds of functions that may be present in the source code: user-defined or library. If a user-defined function is encountered, its code is executed by the interpreter in order to determine its value. (The calling of a function will be discussed in the next section.) However, if the function is a library function, then first its address is looked up by the **internal_func( )** function, and then it is accessed via its interface function. The library functions and the addresses of their interface functions are held in the **internal_func** array shown here:

```
/* "Standard library" functions are declared here so
   they can be put into the internal function table that
   follows.
*/
int call_getche(void), call_putch(void);
int call_puts(void), print(void), getnum(void);

struct intern_func_type {
  char *f_name; /* function name */
  int (* p)();  /* pointer to the function */
} intern_func[] = {
  "getche", call_getche,
  "putch", call_putch,
  "puts", call_puts,
  "print", print,
  "getnum", getnum,
  "", 0   /* null terminate the list */
};
```

As you can see, Little C knows only a few library functions, but you will soon see how easy it is to add any others that you might need. (The actual interface functions are contained in a separate file, which is discussed at the end of this chapter.)

One final point about the routines in the expression parser file: To correctly parse the C language occasionally requires what is called *one-token lookahead.* For example, in order for Little C to know that **count** is a function and not a variable, it must read both **count** and the parenthesis that follows it, shown on the next page.

```
alpha = count();
```

However, if the statement had read

```
alpha = count * 10;
```

then the second token (the *) would need to be returned to the input stream. For this reason, the expression parser file includes the **putback( )** function, which returns the last token to the input stream.

There may be functions in the expression parser file that you don't fully understand at this time, but their operation will become clear as you learn more about Little C.

THE LITTLE C INTERPRETER

In this section, the heart of the Little C interpreter is developed. Before jumping right into the actual code of the interpreter, it will help if you understand how an interpreter operates. In many ways, the code to the interpreter is easier to understand than the expression parser because, conceptually, the act of interpreting a C program can be summed up by the following algorithm:

```
while(tokens_present) {
   get_next_token;
   take_appropriate_action;
}
```

This algorithm may seem unbelievably simple when compared to the expression parser, but this really is exactly what all interpreters do! One thing to keep in mind is that the "take appropriate action" step may involve reading tokens from the input stream. To understand how the algorithm actually works, let's manually interpret the following C code fragment:

```
int a;

a = 10;

if(a<100)  printf("%d", a);
```

Robert Jervis
Creator of Turbo C

"Don't confuse being a C trivia expert with being a C expert," warns Robert Jervis. And he should know! As the creator of Turbo C, Robert Jervis ranks as one of the world's leading authorities on the C language. "Don't be lured by the power of the preprocessor, or other clever features of C, into writing difficult-to-understand code," continues Robert. If there is a single message that Robert wants to convey to C programmers it's "use the power of C, don't abuse it."

Robert claims his favorite C construct is the pointer. "Without C's pointer arithmetic capabilities, it is just Pascal with curly braces!" If you think about it, pointers exemplify exactly the type of feature that Robert is talking about when he warns about the misuse of C. Although powerful, pointers can be abused if not used carefully.

Given that Robert is the designer of Turbo C, one of the most popular C compilers in current use, I asked about his personal approach to a project. "Get it working—then get it fast and small. Simplicity of design is the most important feature of any great program. The details, no matter how numerous, must be arranged around a simple core." In Robert's view, a program is only as good as its weakest components.

Like many programmers, Robert was brought to C through UNIX. "UNIX is the granddaddy of C programs and it is what inspired me to write in C in the first place." Prior to his introduction to C, Robert had been using assembly code to create programs efficient enough to meet his needs. What he found in C was the flexibility of assembly programming without the burden. His drive for tight, efficient code is reflected in the object code generated by Turbo C.

Robert Jervis holds a B.S. in Mathematics from Florida International University. He has been a member of the ANSI C Standardization Committee since 1984.

Following the algorithm, read the first token, which is **int**. The appropriate action given this token is to read the next token in order to find out what the variable being declared is called (in this case **a**) and then to store it. The next token is the semicolon that ends the line. The appropriate action here is to ignore it. Next, go back and get another token. This token is **a**. Since the next line does not begin with a keyword, it must begin a C expression. Hence, the appropriate action is to evaluate the expression using the parser. This process eats up all the tokens in that line. Finally, we read the **if** token. This signals the beginning of an **if** statement. The appropriate action is to process the **if**. The sort of process described here takes place for any C program until the last token has been read. With this basic algorithm in mind, let's begin building the interpreter.

The Interpreter Prescan

Before the interpreter can actually start executing a program, a few clerical tasks must be performed. One characteristic of languages that were designed with interpretation rather than compilation in mind is that they begin execution at the top of the source code and end when the end of the source code is reached. This is the way BASIC works. However, C (or any other structured language) does not lend itself to this approach for two main reasons. First, all C programs begin execution at the **main( )** function. There is no requirement that **main( )** be the first function in the program; therefore, it is necessary that the location of the **main( )** function within the program's source code be known so that execution can begin at that point. (Remember also that global variables may precede **main( )**, so even if it is the first function, it is not necessarily the first line of code.) Some method must be devised to allow execution to begin at the right spot.

Another problem that must be overcome is that all global variables must be known and accounted for before **main( )** begins executing. Global variable declaration statements are never executed by the interpreter because they exist outside of all functions. (Remember: In C all executable code exists *inside* functions, so there is no reason for the Little C interpreter to go outside a function once execution has begun.)

Finally, in the interest of speed of execution, it is important (although not technically necessary) that the location of each function defined in the program be known so that a call to a function can be as fast as possible. If this step is not performed, a lengthy sequential search of the source code will be needed to find the entry point to a function each time it is called.

The solution to these problems is the *intepreter prescan*. Prescanners (or preprocessors, as they are sometimes called, although they have little resemblance to a C compiler's preprocessor) are used by all commercial interpreters regardless of what language they are interpreting. A prescanner reads the source code to the program before it is executed and performs whatever tasks can be done prior to execution. In our Little C interpreter, it performs two important jobs: first, it finds and records the location of all user-defined functions, including **main( )**; second, it finds and allocates space for all global variables. In the Little C intepreter, the function that performs the prescan is, strangely enough, called **prescan( )**. It is shown here:

```
/* Find the location of all functions in the program and
   store all global variables. */
void prescan(void)
{
  char *p;
  char temp[32];
  int brace = 0;   /* When 0, this var tells us that
                      current source position is outside
                      of any function. */

  p = prog;
  func_index = 0;
  do {
    while(brace) {   /* bypass code inside functions */
      get_token();
      if(*token=='{') brace++;
      if(*token=='}') brace--;
    }

    get_token();

    if(tok==CHAR || tok==INT) { /* is global var */
      putback();
      decl_global();
    }
    else if(token_type==IDENTIFIER) {
      strcpy(temp, token);
      get_token();
```

```
      if(*token=='(') {   /* must be assume a function */
        func_table[func_index].loc = prog;
        strcpy(func_table[func_index].func_name, temp);
        func_index++;
        while(*prog!=')') prog++;
        prog++;
        /* now prog points to opening curly
           brace of function */
      }
      else putback();
    }
    else if(*token=='{') brace++;
  } while(tok!=FINISHED);
  prog = p;
}
```

The **prescan( )** function works like this. Each time an opening curly brace is encountered, **brace** is incremented. Whenever a closing curly brace is read, **brace** is decremented. Therefore, whenever **brace** is greater than zero, the current token is being read from within a function. However, if **brace** equals zero when a variable is found, then it knows that it must be a global variable. By the same method, if a function name is encountered when **brace** equals zero, then it must be that function's definition.

   Global variables are stored in a global variable table called **global_vars** by **decl_global( )**, shown here:

```
/* An array of these structures will hold the info
   associated with global variables.
*/
struct var_type {
  char var_name[ID_LEN];
  int var_type;
  int value;
} global_vars[NUM_GLOBAL_VARS];

int gvar_index; /* index into global variable table */

/* Declare a global variable. */
void decl_global(void)
{
  get_token();  /* get type */
```

```
global_vars[gvar_index].var_type = tok;
global_vars[gvar_index].value = 0;   /* init to 0 */

do { /* process comma-separated list */
  get_token();   /* get name */
  strcpy(global_vars[gvar_index].var_name, token);
  get_token();
  gvar_index++;
} while(*token==',');
if(*token!=';') sntx_err(SEMI_EXPECTED);
}
```

The integer **gvar_index** will hold the location of the next free element in the array.

The location of each user-defined function is put into the **func_table** array, shown here:

```
struct func_type {
  char func_name[ID_LEN];
  char *loc;   /* location of entry point in file */
} func_table[NUM_FUNC];

int func_index; /* index into function table */
```

The **func_index** variable will hold the index of the next free location in the table.

The **main( )** Function

The **main( )** function to the Little C interpreter, shown here, loads the source code, initializes the global variables, calls **prescan( )**, "primes" the intepreter for the call to **main( )**, and then executes **call( )**, which begins execution of the program. The operation of the **call( )** function will be discussed shortly.

```
main(int argc, char *argv[])
{
  if(argc!=2) {
    printf("usage: littlec <filename>\n");
```

```
  exit(1);
}

/* allocate memory for the program */
if((p_buf=(char *) malloc(PROG_SIZE))==NULL) {
  printf("allocation failure");
  exit(1);
}

/* load the program to execute */
if(!load_program(p_buf, argv[1])) exit(1);

if(setjmp(e_buf)) exit(1); /* initialize long jump buffer */

/* set program pointer to start of program buffer */
prog = p_buf;
prescan(); /* find the location of all functions
              and global variables in the program */

gvar_index = 0;   /* initialize global variable index */
lvartos = 0;      /* initialize local variable stack index */
functos = 0;      /* initialize the CALL stack index */

/* setup call to main() */
prog = find_func("main");  /* find program starting point */
prog--; /* back up to opening ( */
strcpy(token, "main");
call();  /* start interpreting */
}
```

The **interp‗block( )** Function

The **interp‗block( )** function is the heart of the intepreter. It is the
function that decides what action to take based upon the next token in
the input stream. The function is designed to interpret one block of code
and then return. If the "block" consists of a single statement, then that
statement is interpreted and the function returns. By default,
interp‗block( ) interprets one statement and returns. However, if an
opening curly brace is read, then the flag **block** is set to 1 and the

function continues to interpret statements until a closing curly brace is read. The **interp_block( )** function is shown here:

```
/* Interpret a single statement or block of code.  When
   interp_block() returns from its initial call, the final
   brace (or a return) in main() has been encountered.
*/
void interp_block(void)
{
  int value;
  char block = 0;

  do {
    token_type = get_token();

    /* If interpreting single statement, return on
       first semicolon.
    */

    /* see what kind of token is up */
    if(token_type==IDENTIFIER) {
      /* Not a keyword, so process expression. */
        putback();  /* restore token to input stream for
                       further processing by eval_exp() */
        eval_exp(&value);  /* process the expression */
        if(*token!=';') sntx_err(SEMI_EXPECTED);
    }
    else if(token_type==BLOCK) { /* if block delimiter */
      if(*token=='{') /* is a block */
        block = 1; /* interpreting block, not statement */
      else return; /* is a }, so return */
    }
    else /* is keyword */
      switch(tok) {
        case CHAR:
        case INT:      /* declare local variables */
          putback();
          decl_local();
          break;
        case RETURN:  /* return from function call */
          func_ret();
          return;
        case IF:       /* process an if statement */
```

```
      exec_if();
      break;
   case ELSE:     /* process an else statement */
      find_eob(); /* find end of else block
                     and continue execution */
      break;
   case WHILE:    /* process a while loop */
      exec_while();
      break;
   case DO:       /* process a do-while loop */
      exec_do();
      break;
   case FOR: exec_for();
      break;
   case END:
      exit(0);
    }
  } while (tok != FINISHED && block);
}
```

Calls to functions like **exit( )** excepted, a C program ends when the last curly brace (or a **return**) in **main( )** is encountered—not necessarily the last line of source code. This is one reason that **interp_block( )** executes only a statement or a block of code, and not the entire program. Another reason is that, conceptually, C consists of blocks of code. Therefore, **interp_block( )** is called each time a new block of code is encountered. This includes both function calls as well as blocks begun by various C statements, such as **if**. This means that in the process of executing a program, the Little C interpreter may call **interp_block( )** recursively.

The **interp_block( )** function works like this. First, it reads the next token from the program. If the token is a semicolon and only a single statement is being interpreted, then the function returns. Otherwise, it checks to see if the token is an identifier; if so, the statement must be an expression, so the expression parser is called. Since the expression parser expects to read the first token in the expression itself, the token is returned to the input stream via a call to **putback( )**. When **eval_exp( )** returns, **token** will hold the last token read by the expression parser, which must be a semicolon if the statement is syntactically correct. If **token** does not contain a semicolon, an error is reported.

If the next token from the program is a curly brace, then either **block** is set to 1 in the case of an opening brace, or, if it is a closing brace, the function returns.

Finally, if the token is a keyword, the **switch** statement is executed, calling the appropriate routine to handle the statement. The reason that keywords are given integer equivalents by **get_token( )** is to support the **switch** instead of using a sequence of **if** statements and string comparisons (which are quite slow).

The keyword parser file is shown here. Before looking at the functions that actually execute C keyword statements individually, enter this code into a file called LITTLEC.C.

```
/* A Little C interpreter. */

#include "stdio.h"
#include "setjmp.h"
#include "math.h"
#include "ctype.h"
#include "stdlib.h"
#include "string.h"

#define NUM_FUNC          100
#define NUM_GLOBAL_VARS   100
#define NUM_LOCAL_VARS    200
#define NUM_BLOCK         100
#define ID_LEN            31
#define FUNC_CALLS        31
#define NUM_PARAMS        31
#define PROG_SIZE         10000
#define LOOP_NEST         31

enum tok_types {DELIMITER, IDENTIFIER, NUMBER, KEYWORD,
                TEMP, STRING, BLOCK};

/* add additional C keyword tokens here */
enum tokens {ARG, CHAR, INT, IF, ELSE, FOR, DO, WHILE,
             SWITCH, RETURN, EOL, FINISHED, END};

/* add additional double operators here (such as ->) */
enum double_ops {LT=1, LE, GT, GE, EQ, NE};

/* These are the constants used to call sntx_err() when
   a syntax error occurs.  Add more if you like.
   NOTE: SYNTAX is a generic error message used when
   nothing else seems appropriate.
*/
```

```
enum error_msg
     {SYNTAX, UNBAL_PARENS, NO_EXP, EQUALS_EXPECTED,
      NOT_VAR, PARAM_ERR, SEMI_EXPECTED,
      UNBAL_BRACES, FUNC_UNDEF, TYPE_EXPECTED,
      NEST_FUNC, RET_NOCALL, PAREN_EXPECTED,
      WHILE_EXPECTED, QUOTE_EXPECTED, NOT_TEMP,
      TOO_MANY_LVARS};

char *prog;  /* current location in source code */
char *p_buf; /* points to start of program buffer */
jmp_buf e_buf; /* hold environment for longjmp() */

/* An array of these structures will hold the info
   associated with global variables.
*/
struct var_type {
  char var_name[ID_LEN];
  int var_type;
  int value;
}  global_vars[NUM_GLOBAL_VARS];

struct var_type local_var_stack[NUM_LOCAL_VARS];

struct func_type {
  char func_name[ID_LEN];
  char *loc;  /* location of entry point in file */
} func_table[NUM_FUNC];

int call_stack[NUM_FUNC];

struct commands { /* keyword lookup table */
  char command[20];
  char tok;
} table[] = { /* Commands must be entered lowercase */
  "if", IF, /* in this table. */
  "else", ELSE,
  "for", FOR,
  "do", DO,
  "while", WHILE,
  "char", CHAR,
  "int", INT,
  "return", RETURN,
```

```
  "end", END,
  "", END   /* mark end of table */
};

char token[80];
char token_type, tok;

int functos;  /* index to top of function call stack */
int func_index; /* index into function table */
int gvar_index; /* index into global variable table */
int lvartos; /* index into local variable stack */

int ret_value; /* function return value */

void print(void), prescan(void);
void decl_global(void), call(void), putback(void);
void decl_local(void), local_push(struct var_type i);
void eval_exp(int *value), sntx_err(int error);
void exec_if(void), find_eob(void), exec_for(void);
void get_params(void), get_args(void);
void exec_while(void), func_push(int i), exec_do(void);
void assign_var(char *var_name, int value);
int load_program(char *p, char *fname), find_var(char *s);
void interp_block(void), func_ret(void);
int func_pop(void), is_var(char *s), get_token(void);
char *find_func(char *name);

main(int argc, char *argv[])
{
  if(argc!=2) {
    printf("usage: littlec <filename>\n");
    exit(1);
  }

  /* allocate memory for the program */
  if((p_buf=(char *) malloc(PROG_SIZE))==NULL) {
    printf("allocation failure");
    exit(1);
  }

  /* load the program to execute */
  if(!load_program(p_buf, argv[1])) exit(1);
```

```
   if(setjmp(e_buf)) exit(1); /* initialize long jump buffer */

   /* set program pointer to start of program buffer */
   prog = p_buf;
   prescan(); /* find the location of all functions
                  and global variables in the program */

   gvar_index = 0;   /* initialize global variable index */
   lvartos = 0;      /* initialize local variable stack index */
   functos = 0;      /* initialize the CALL stack index */

   /* setup call to main() */
   prog = find_func("main");  /* find program starting point */
   prog--; /* back up to opening ( */
   strcpy(token, "main");
   call();  /* call main() to start interpreting */
}

/* Interpret a single statement or block of code.  When
   interp_block() returns from its initial call, the final
   brace (or a return) in main() has been encountered.
*/
void interp_block(void)
{
  int value;
  char block = 0;

  do {
    token_type = get_token();

    /* If interpreting single statement, return on
       first semicolon.
    */

    /* see what kind of token is up */
    if(token_type==IDENTIFIER) {
      /* Not a keyword, so process expression. */
        putback();   /* restore token to input stream for
                        further processing by eval_exp() */
        eval_exp(&value);  /* process the expression */
        if(*token!=';') sntx_err(SEMI_EXPECTED);
    }
    else if(token_type==BLOCK) { /* if block delimiter */
```

```
        if(*token=='{') /* is a block */
          block = 1; /* interpreting block, not statement */
        else return; /* is a }, so return */
      }
      else /* is keyword */
        switch(tok) {
          case CHAR:
          case INT:      /* declare local variables */
            putback();
            decl_local();
            break;
          case RETURN:   /* return from function call */
            func_ret();
            return;
          case IF:       /* process an if statement */
            exec_if();
            break;
          case ELSE:     /* process an else statement */
            find_eob(); /* find end of else block
                           and continue execution */
            break;
          case WHILE:    /* process a while loop */
            exec_while();
            break;
          case DO:       /* process a do-while loop */
            exec_do();
            break;
          case FOR: exec_for();
            break;
          case END:
            exit(0);
        }
  } while (tok != FINISHED && block);
}

/* Load a program. */
load_program(char *p, char *fname)
{
  FILE *fp;
  int i=0;

  if((fp=fopen(fname, "rb"))==NULL) return 0;
```

```
    i = 0;
    do {
      *p = getc(fp);
      p++;  i++;
    } while(!feof(fp) && i<PROG_SIZE);
    *(p-2) = '\0'; /* null terminate the program */
    fclose(fp);
    return 1;
}

/* Find the location of all functions in the program
   and store global variables. */
void prescan(void)
{
  char *p;
  char temp[32];
  int brace = 0;   /* When 0, this var tells us that
                      current source position is outside
                      of any function. */

  p = prog;
  func_index = 0;
  do {
    while(brace) {   /* bypass code inside functions */
      get_token();
      if(*token=='{') brace++;
      if(*token=='}') brace--;
    }

    get_token();

    if(tok==CHAR || tok==INT) { /* is global var */
      putback();
      decl_global();
    }
    else if(token_type==IDENTIFIER) {
      strcpy(temp, token);
      get_token();
      if(*token=='(') {   /* must be assume a function */
        func_table[func_index].loc = prog;
        strcpy(func_table[func_index].func_name, temp);
        func_index++;
        while(*prog!=')') prog++;
```

```
        prog++;
        /* prog points to opening curly brace of function */
      }
      else putback();
    }
    else if(*token=='{') brace++;
  } while(tok!=FINISHED);
  prog = p;
}

/* Return the entry point of the specified function.
   Return NULL if not found.
*/
char *find_func(char *name)
{
  register int i;

  for(i=0; i<func_index; i++)
    if(!strcmp(name, func_table[i].func_name))
      return func_table[i].loc;

  return NULL;
}

/* Declare a global variable. */
void decl_global(void)
{
  get_token();   /* get type */

  global_vars[gvar_index].var_type = tok;
  global_vars[gvar_index].value = 0;   /* init to 0 */

  do { /* process comma-separated list */
    get_token();   /* get name */
    strcpy(global_vars[gvar_index].var_name, token);
    get_token();
    gvar_index++;
  } while(*token==',');
  if(*token!=';') sntx_err(SEMI_EXPECTED);
}

/* Declare a local variable. */
void decl_local(void)
```

```
{
  struct var_type i;

  get_token();  /* get type */

  i.var_type = tok;
  i.value = 0;   /* init to 0 */

  do { /* process comma-separated list */
    get_token(); /* get var name */
    strcpy(i.var_name, token);
    local_push(i);
    get_token();
  } while(*token==',');
  if(*token!=';') sntx_err(SEMI_EXPECTED);
}

/* Call a function. */
void call(void)
{
  char *loc, *temp;
  int lvartemp;

  loc = find_func(token); /* find entry point of function */
  if(loc==NULL)
    sntx_err(FUNC_UNDEF); /* function not defined */
  else {
    lvartemp = lvartos;  /* save local var stack index */
    get_args();  /* get function arguments */
    temp = prog; /* save return location */
    func_push(lvartemp);  /* save local var stack index */
    prog = loc;  /* reset prog to start of function */
    get_params(); /* load the function's parameters with
                      the values of the arguments */
    interp_block(); /* interpret the function */
    prog = temp; /* reset the program pointer */
    lvartos = func_pop(); /* reset the local var stack */
  }
}

/* Push the arguments to a function onto the local
   variable stack. */
void get_args(void)
```

```
{
  int value, count, temp[NUM_PARAMS];
  struct var_type i;

  count = 0;
  get_token();
  if(*token!='(') sntx_err(PAREN_EXPECTED);

  /* process a comma-separated list of values */
  do {
    eval_exp(&value);
    temp[count] = value;   /* save temporarily */
    get_token();
    count++;
  }while(*token==',');
  count--;
  /* now, push on local_var_stack in reverse order */
  for(; count>=0; count--) {
    i.value = temp[count];
    i.var_type = ARG;
    local_push(i);
  }
}

/* Get function parameters. */
void get_params(void)
{
  struct var_type *p;
  int i;

  i = lvartos-1;
  do { /* process comma-separated list of parameters */
    get_token();
    p = &local_var_stack[i];
    if(*token!=')') {
      if(tok!=INT && tok!=CHAR) sntx_err(TYPE_EXPECTED);
      p->var_type = token_type;
      get_token();

      /* link parameter name with argument already on
         local var stack */
      strcpy(p->var_name, token);
      get_token();
```

```
      i--;
    }
    else break;
  } while(*token==',');
  if(*token!=')') sntx_err(PAREN_EXPECTED);
}


/* Return from a function. */
void func_ret(void)
{
  int value;

  value = 0;
  /* get return value, if any */
  eval_exp(&value);

  ret_value = value;
}

/* Push local variable */
void local_push(struct var_type i)
{
  if(lvartos>NUM_LOCAL_VARS)
    sntx_err(TOO_MANY_LVARS);

  local_var_stack[lvartos] = i;
  lvartos++;
}

/* Pop index into local variable stack. */
func_pop(void)
{
  functos--;
  if(functos<0) sntx_err(RET_NOCALL);
  return(call_stack[functos]);
}

/* Push index of local variable stack. */
void func_push(int i)
{
  if(functos>NUM_FUNC)
    sntx_err(NEST_FUNC);
  call_stack[functos] = i;
```

```
    functos++;
}

/* Assign a value to a variable. */
void assign_var(char *var_name, int value)
{
  register int i;

  /* first, see if it's a local variable */
  for(i=lvartos-1; i>=call_stack[functos-1]; i--)  {
    if(!strcmp(local_var_stack[i].var_name, var_name)) {
      local_var_stack[i].value = value;
      return;
    }
  }
  if(i < call_stack[functos-1])
  /* if not local, try global var table */
    for(i=0; i<NUM_GLOBAL_VARS; i++)
      if(!strcmp(global_vars[i].var_name, var_name)) {
        global_vars[i].value = value;
        return;
      }
  sntx_err(NOT_VAR); /* variable not found */
}

/* Find the value of a variable. */
int find_var(char *s)
{
  register int i;

  /* first, see if it's a local variable */
  for(i=lvartos-1; i>=call_stack[functos-1]; i--)
    if(!strcmp(local_var_stack[i].var_name, token))
      return local_var_stack[i].value;

  /* otherwise, try global vars */
  for(i=0; i<NUM_GLOBAL_VARS; i++)
    if(!strcmp(global_vars[i].var_name, s))
      return global_vars[i].value;

  sntx_err(NOT_VAR); /* variable not found */
}
```

```c
/* Determine if an identifier is a variable. Return
   1 if variable is found; 0 otherwise.
*/
int is_var(char *s)
{
  register int i;

  /* first, see if it's a local variable */
  for(i=lvartos-1; i>=call_stack[functos-1]; i--)
    if(!strcmp(local_var_stack[i].var_name, token))
      return 1;

  /* otherwise, try global vars */
  for(i=0; i<NUM_GLOBAL_VARS; i++)
    if(!strcmp(global_vars[i].var_name, s))
      return 1;

  return 0;
}

/* Execute an IF statement. */
void exec_if(void)
{
  int cond;

  eval_exp(&cond); /* get left expression */

  if(cond) { /* is true so process target of IF */
    interp_block();
  }
  else { /* otherwise skip around IF block and
            process the ELSE, if present */
    find_eob(); /* find start of next line */
    get_token();

    if(tok!=ELSE) {
      putback();  /* restore token if
                     no ELSE is present */
      return;
    }
    interp_block();
  }
}
```

```
/* Execute a while loop. */
void exec_while(void)
{
  int cond;
  char *temp;

  putback();
  temp = prog;  /* save location of top of while loop */
  get_token();
  eval_exp(&cond);  /* check the conditional expression */
  if(cond) interp_block();  /* if true, interpret */
  else {  /* otherwise, skip around loop */
    find_eob();
    return;
  }
  prog = temp;  /* loop back to top */
}

/*Execute a do loop. */
void exec_do(void)
{
  int cond;
  char *temp;

  putback();
  temp = prog;  /* save location of top of do loop */

  get_token(); /* get start of loop */
  interp_block(); /* interpret loop */
  get_token();
  if(tok!=WHILE) sntx_err(WHILE_EXPECTED);
  eval_exp(&cond); /* check the loop condition */
  if(cond) prog = temp; /* if true loop; otherwise,
                           continue on */
}

/* Find the end of a block. */
void find_eob(void)
{
  int brace;

  get_token();
```

```
  brace = 1;
  do {
    get_token();
    if(*token=='{') brace++;
    else if(*token=='}') brace--;
  } while(brace);
}

/* Execute a while loop. */
void exec_for(void)
{
  int cond;
  char *temp, *temp2;
  int brace ;

  get_token();
  eval_exp(&cond);   /*initialization expression */
  if(*token!=';') sntx_err(SEMI_EXPECTED);
  prog++; /* get past the ; */
  temp = prog;
  for(;;) {
    eval_exp(&cond);   /* check the condition */
    if(*token!=';') sntx_err(SEMI_EXPECTED);
    prog++; /* get past the ; */
    temp2 = prog;

    /* find the start of the for block */
    brace = 1;
    while(brace) {
      get_token();
      if(*token=='(') brace++;
      if(*token==')') brace--;
    }

    if(cond) interp_block();   /* if true, interpret */
    else {   /* otherwise, skip around loop */
      find_eob();
      return;
    }
    prog = temp2;
    eval_exp(&cond); /* do the increment */
```

```
    prog = temp;   /* loop back to top */
  }
}
```

Handling Local Variables

When the interpreter encounters an **int** or **char** keyword, it calls
decl_local( ) to create storage for a local variable. As stated earlier, no
global variable declaration statement will be encountered by the interpreter once the program is executing, because only code within a function
is executed. Therefore, if a variable declaration statement is found, it must
be for a local variable (or a parameter, which will be discussed in the next
section). In structured languages, local variables are stored on a stack. If
the language is compiled, the system stack is generally used; however, in
an interpreted mode, the stack for local variables must be maintained by
the interpreter. The stack for local variables is held by the array
local_var_stack. Each time a local variable is encountered, its name,
type, and value (initially zero) are pushed onto the stack using
local_push( ). The global variable **lvartos** indexes the stack. (For reasons
that will become clear, there is no corresponding "pop" function. Instead,
the local variable stack is reset each time a function returns.) The
decl_local and **local_push( )** functions are shown here:

```
/* Declare a local variable. */
void decl_local(void)
{
  struct var_type i;

  get_token();   /* get type */

  i.var_type = tok;
  i.value = 0;   /* init to 0 */

  do { /* process comma-separated list */
    get_token(); /* get var name */
    strcpy(i.var_name, token);
    local_push(i);
    get_token();
  } while(*token==',');
```

```
  if(*token!=';') sntx_err(SEMI_EXPECTED);
}

/* Push local variable */
void local_push(struct var_type i)
{
  if(lvartos>NUM_LOCAL_VARS)
    sntx_err(TOO_MANY_LVARS);

  local_var_stack[lvartos] = i;
  lvartos++;
}
```

The **decl _ local( )** function first reads the type of the variable or variables being declared and assigns it an initial value of zero. Next, it enters a loop, which reads a comma-separated list of identifiers. Each time through the loop, the information about each variable is pushed onto the local variable stack. At the end, the final token is checked to make sure that it contains a semicolon.

Calling User-Defined Functions

Probably the most difficult part of implementing an interpreter for C is the execution of user-defined functions. Not only does the interpreter need to begin reading the source code at a different position and return to the calling routine after the function terminates, but it must also deal with these three tasks: the passing arguments, the allocation of parameters, and the return value of the function.

All function calls (except the initial call to **main( )**) take place through the expression parser from the **atom( )** function by a call to **call( )**. It is the **call( )** function that actually handles the details of calling a function. The **call( )** function is shown here, along with two support functions. Let's examine these functions closely.

```
/* Call a function. */
void call(void)
{
  char *loc, *temp;
  int lvartemp;
```

```
  loc = find_func(token); /* find entry point of function */
  if(loc==NULL)
    sntx_err(FUNC_UNDEF); /* function not defined */
  else {
    lvartemp = lvartos;  /* save local var stack index */
    get_args();  /* get function arguments */
    temp = prog; /* save return location */
    func_push(lvartemp);  /* save local var stack index */
    prog = loc;  /* reset prog to start of function */
    get_params(); /* load the function's parameters with
                     the values of the arguments */
    interp_block(); /* interpret the function */
    prog = temp; /* reset the program pointer */
    lvartos = func_pop(); /* reset the local var stack */
  }
}

/* Push the arguments to a function onto the local
   variable stack. */
void get_args(void)
{
  int value, count, temp[NUM_PARAMS];
  struct var_type i;

  count = 0;
  get_token();
  if(*token!='(') sntx_err(PAREN_EXPECTED);

  /* process a comma-separated list of values */
  do {
    eval_exp(&value);
    temp[count] = value;  /* save temporarily */
    get_token();
    count++;
  }while(*token==',');
  count--;
  /* now, push on local_var_stack in reverse order */
  for(; count>=0; count--) {
    i.value = temp[count];
    i.var_type = ARG;
    local_push(i);
  }
```

```
}

/* Get function parameters. */
void get_params(void)
{
  struct var_type *p;
  int i;

  i = lvartos-1;
  do { /* process comma-separated list of parameters */
    get_token();
    p = &local_var_stack[i];
    if(*token!=')') {
      if(tok!=INT && tok!=CHAR) sntx_err(TYPE_EXPECTED);
      p->var_type = token_type;
      get_token();

      /* link parameter name with argument already on
         local var stack */
      strcpy(p->var_name, token);
      get_token();
      i--;
    }
    else break;
  } while(*token==',');
  if(*token!=')') sntx_err(PAREN_EXPECTED);
}
```

The first thing that **call( )** does is find the location of the entry point in the source code to the specified function by calling **find _ func( )**. Next, it saves the current value of the local variable stack index, **lvartos**, into **lvartemp**; then it calls **get _ args( )** to process any function arguments. The **get _ args( )** function reads a comma-separated list of expressions and pushes them onto the local variable stack in reverse order. (The expressions are pushed in reverse order so that they can be more easily matched with their corresponding parameters.) When the values are pushed, they are not given names. The names of the parameters are given to them by the **get _ params( )** function, which will be discussed in a moment.

Once the function arguments have been processed, the current value of **prog** is saved in **temp**. This location is the return point of the function. Next, the value of **lvartemp** is pushed onto the function call stack. The routines **func _ push( )** and **func _ pop( )** maintain this stack. Its purpose is to store the value of **lvartos** each time a function is called. This value represents the starting point on the local variable stack for variables (and parameters) relative to the function being called. The value on the top of the function call stack is used to prevent a function from accessing any local variables other than those it declares.

The next two lines of code set the program pointer to the start of the function and link the name of its formal parameters with the values of the arguments already on the local variable stack with a call to **get_params( )**. The actual execution of the function is performed through a call to **interp_block( )**. When **interp_block( )** returns, the program pointer (**prog**) is reset to its return point and the local variable stack index is reset to its value before the function call. This final step effectively removes all of the function's local variables from the stack.

If the function being called contains a **return** statement, then **interp_block( )** calls **func_ret( )** prior to returning to **call( )**. This function processes any return value. It is shown here:

```
/* Return from a function. */
void func_ret(void)
{
  int value;

  value = 0;
  /* get return value, if any */
  eval_exp(&value);

  ret_value = value;
}
```

The variable **ret_value** is a global integer that holds the return value of a function. At first glance you might wonder why the local variable **value** is first assigned the return value of the function and then is assigned to **ret_value**. The reason is that functions can be recursive and **eval_exp( )** may need to call the same function in order to obtain its value.

Assigning Values to Variables

Let's return briefly to the expression parser. When an assignment statement is encountered, the value of the right side of the expression is computed and this value is assigned to the variable on the left using a call to **assign( )**. However, as you know, the C language is structured and supports global and local variables. Hence, given a program such as this:

```
int count;

main()
{
  int count;

  count = 100;

  f();
}

f()
{
  int count;

  count = 99;

}
```

how does the **assign( )** function know which variable is being assigned a value in each assignment? The answer is simple: first, in C, local variables take priority over global variables of the same name; second, local variables are not known outside their own function. To see how we can use these rules to resolve the above assignments, examine the **assign( )** function, shown here:

```
/* Assign a value to a variable. */
void assign_var(char *var_name, int value)
{
  register int i;

  /* first, see if it's a local variable */
  for(i=lvartos-1; i>=call_stack[functos-1]; i--)  {
    if(!strcmp(local_var_stack[i].var_name, var_name)) {
      local_var_stack[i].value = value;
      return;
    }
  }
```

```
  if(i < call_stack[functos-1])
  /* if not local, try global var table */
    for(i=0; i<NUM_GLOBAL_VARS; i++)
      if(!strcmp(global_vars[i].var_name, var_name)) {
        global_vars[i].value = value;
        return;
      }
  sntx_err(NOT_VAR); /* variable not found */
}
```

As explained in the previous section, each time a function is called, the current value of the local variable stack index (**lvartos**) is pushed onto the function **call_stack( )**. This means that any local variables (or parameters) defined by the function will be pushed onto the stack above that point. Therefore, the **assign( )** function first searches **local_var_stack**, beginning with the current top-of-stack value and stopping when the index reaches that value saved by the latest function call. This mechanism ensures that only those variables local to the function are examined. (It also helps support recursive functions because the current value of **lvartos** is saved each time a function is invoked.) Therefore, the line "count = 100;" in **main( )** causes **assign( )** to find the local variable **count** inside **main( )**. In **f( )**, **assign( )** finds its own **count** and does not find the one in **main( )**.

If no local variable matches the name of a variable, then the global variable list is searched.

Executing an **if** Statement

Now that the basic structure of the Little C intepreter is in place, it is time to add some control statements. Each time a keyword statement is encountered inside of **interp_block( )**, an appropriate function is called, which processes that statement. One of the easiest is the **if**. The **if** statement is processed by **exec_if( )**, shown here:

```
/* Execute an IF statement. */
void exec_if(void)
{
  int cond;
```

```
eval_exp(&cond); /* get left expression */

if(cond) { /* is true so process target of IF */
  interp_block();
}
else { /* otherwise skip around IF block and
          process the ELSE, if present */
  find_eob(); /* find start of next line */
  get_token();

  if(tok!=ELSE) {
    putback();  /* restore token if
                   no ELSE is present */
    return;
  }
  interp_block();
}
}
```

Let's look closely at this function.

The first thing the function does is to compute the value of the conditional expression by calling **eval_exp( )**. If the condition (**cond**) is true (non-zero) then the function calls **interp_block( )** recursively, allowing the **if** block to execute. If **cond** is false, then the function **find_eob( )** is called, which advances the program pointer to the location immediately after the end of the **if** block. If an **else** is present, the **else** is processed by **exec_if( )** and the **else** block is executed. Otherwise, execution simply begins with the next line of code.

If the **if** block executes and there is an **else** block present, there must be some way for the **else** block to be bypassed. This is accomplished in **interp_block( )** by simply calling **find_eob( )** to bypass the block when an **else** is encountered. Remember, the only time an **else** will be processed by **interp_block( )** (in a syntactically correct program) is when an **if** block was executed. When an **else** block executes, the **else** is processed by **exec_if( )**.

Processing a **while** Loop

A **while** loop, like the **if**, is quite easy to interpret. The function that actually performs this task, **exec_while( )**, is shown on the next page.

```
/* Execute a while loop. */
void exec_while(void)
{
  int cond;
  char *temp;

  putback();
  temp = prog;   /* save location of top of while loop */
  get_token();
  eval_exp(&cond);   /* check the conditional expression */
  if(cond) interp_block();   /* if true, interpret */
  else {   /* otherwise, skip around loop */
    find_eob();
    return;
  }
  prog = temp;   /* loop back to top */
}
```

The **exec_while( )** works like this. First, the **while** token is put back into
the input stream and the location of the **while** is saved into **temp**. This
address will be used to allow the interpreter to loop back to the top of the
while. Next, the **while** is reread to remove it from the input stream, and
eval_exp( ) is called to compute the value of the **while**'s conditional
expression. If the conditional expression is true, then **interp_block( )** is
called recursively to interpret the **while** block. When **interp_block( )**
returns, **prog** (the program pointer) is loaded with the location of the start
of the **while** loop and control returns to **interp_block( )**, where the entire
process repeats. If the conditional expression is false, then the end of the
while block is found and the function returns.

Processing a **do-while** Loop

A **do-while** loop is processed much like the **while**. When **interp_block( )**
encounters a **do** statement, it calls **exec_do( )**, shown here:

```
/*Execute a do loop. */
void exec_do(void)
{
  int cond;
  char *temp;
```

```
    putback();
    temp = prog;   /* save location of top of do loop */

    get_token(); /* get start of loop */
    interp_block(); /* interpret loop */
    get_token();
    if(tok!=WHILE) sntx_err(WHILE_EXPECTED);
    eval_exp(&cond); /* check the loop condition */
    if(cond) prog = temp; /* if true loop; otherwise, continue on */
}
```

The main difference between the **do-while** and the **while** loops is that the **do-while** always executes its block of code at least once because the conditional expression is at the bottom of the loop. Therefore, **exec_do( )** first saves the location of the top of the loop into **temp** and then calls **interp_block( )** recursively to interpret the block of code associated with the loop. When **interp_block( )** returns, the corresponding **while** is retrieved and the conditional expression is evaluated. If the condition is true, **prog** is reset to the top of the loop; otherwise, execution will continue on.

The **for** Loop

The interpretation of the **for** loop poses a more difficult challenge than the other constructs. Part of the reason for this is that the structure of the C **for** is definitely designed with compilation in mind. The main trouble is that the conditional expression of the **for** must be checked at the top of the loop, but the increment portion occurs at the bottom of the loop. Therefore, even though these two pieces of the **for** loop occur next to each other in the source code, their interpretation is separated by the block of code being iterated. However, with a little work, the **for** can be correctly interpreted.

When **interp_block( )** encounters a **for** statement, **exec_for( )** is called. This function is shown here:

```
/* Execute a for loop. */
void exec_for(void)
{
```

```
int cond;
char *temp, *temp2;
int brace ;

get_token();
eval_exp(&cond);   /*initialization expression */
if(*token!=';') sntx_err(SEMI_EXPECTED);
prog++; /* get past the ; */
temp = prog;
for(;;) {
  eval_exp(&cond);   /* check the condition */
  if(*token!=';') sntx_err(SEMI_EXPECTED);
  prog++; /* get past the ; */
  temp2 = prog;

  /* find the start of the for block */
  brace = 1;
  while(brace) {
    get_token();
    if(*token=='(') brace++;
    if(*token==')') brace--;
  }

  if(cond) interp_block();   /* if true, interpret */
  else {  /* otherwise, skip around loop */
    find_eob();
    return;
  }
  prog = temp2;
  eval_exp(&cond); /* do the increment */
  prog = temp;  /* loop back to top */
}
}
```

This function begins by processing the initialization expression in the **for**. The initialization portion of the **for** is executed only once and does not form part of the loop. Next, the program pointer is advanced to a point immediately after the semicolon that ends the initialization statement, and its value is assigned to **temp**. A loop is then established, which checks the conditional portion of the loop and assigns **temp2** a pointer to the start of the increment portion. The beginning of the loop code is found, and, finally, if the conditional expression is true, the loop block is interpreted.

Otherwise, the end of the block is found and execution continues on. When the recursive call to **interp_block( )** returns, the increment portion of the loop is executed, and the process repeats.

THE LITTLE C LIBRARY FUNCTIONS

Because the C programs executed by Little C are never compiled and linked, any library routines they use must be handled directly by Little C. The best way to do this is to create an interface function that Little C calls when a library function is encountered. This interface function sets up the call to the library function and handles any return values.

Because of space limitations, Little C contains only five "library" functions: **getche( )**, **putch( )**, **puts( )**, **print( )**, and **getnum( )**. Of these, only **puts( )**, which outputs a string to the screen, is described by the ANSI standard. The **getche( )** function is a common extension to C for interactive environments. It waits for and returns a key struck at the keyboard. Unlike most implementations of **getche( )**, it does not line-buffer input. This function is found in many compilers, such as TurboC, QuickC, and Lattice C. The **putch( )** is also defined by many compilers designed for use in an interactive environment. It outputs a single character argument to the console. It does not buffer output. The functions **getnum( )** and **print( )** are my own creations. The **getnum( )** returns the integer equivalent of a number entered at the keyboard. The **print( )** function is a very handy function that can output either a string or an integer argument to the screen. This is an example of a function that would be very difficult to implement in a compiled environment, but is easy to create for an interpreted one. The five library functions are shown here in their prototype forms.

```
int getche(void); /* read a character from keyboard and
return its value */
int putch(char ch); /* write a character to the screen */
int puts(char *s); /* write a string to the screen */
int getnum(void); /* read an integer from the keyboard and
                        return its value */
int print(char *s); /* write a string to the screen */
or
int print(int i); /* write an integer to the screen */
```

The Little C library routines are shown here. You should enter this file into your computer, calling it LCLIB.C.

```
/****** Internal Library Functions *******/

/* Add more of your own, here. */

#include "conio.h"  /* if your compiler does not
                        support this  header file,
                        remove it */
#include "stdio.h"
#include "stdlib.h"

extern char *prog; /* points to current location in program */
extern char token[80]; /* holds string representation of token */
extern char token_type; /* contains type of token */
extern char tok; /* holds the internal representation of token */

enum tok_types {DELIMITER, IDENTIFIER, NUMBER, COMMAND, STRING,
                QUOTE, VARIABLE, BLOCK, FUNCTION};

/* These are the constants used to call sntx_err() when
   a syntax error occurs.  Add more if you like.
   NOTE: SYNTAX is a generic error message used when
   nothing else seems appropriate.
*/
enum error_msg
     {SYNTAX, UNBAL_PARENS, NO_EXP, EQUALS_EXPECTED,
      NOT_VAR, PARAM_ERR, SEMI_EXPECTED,
      UNBAL_BRACES, FUNC_UNDEF, TYPE_EXPECTED,
      NEST_FUNC, RET_NOCALL, PAREN_EXPECTED,
      WHILE_EXPECTED, QUOTE_EXPECTED, NOT_STRING,
      TOO_MANY_LVARS};

int get_token(void);
void sntx_err(int error), eval_exp(int *result);
void putback(void);

/* Get a character from console.  (Use getchar() if
   your compiler does not support getche().) */
call_getche()
{
  char ch;
```

```
    ch = getche();
    while(*prog!=')') prog++;
    prog++;    /* advance to end of line */
    return ch;
}

/* Put a character to the display.  (Use putchar()
   if your compiler does not support putch().) */
call_putch()
{
    int value;

    eval_exp(&value);
    printf("%c", value);
    return value;
}

/* Call puts(). */
call_puts(void)
{
    get_token();
    if(*token!='(') sntx_err(PAREN_EXPECTED);
    get_token();
    if(token_type!=QUOTE) sntx_err(QUOTE_EXPECTED);
    puts(token);
    get_token();
    if(*token!=')') sntx_err(PAREN_EXPECTED);

    get_token();
    if(*token!=';') sntx_err(SEMI_EXPECTED);
    putback();
    return 0;
}

/* A built-in console output function. */
int print(void)
{
    int i;

    get_token();
    if(*token!='(')   sntx_err(PAREN_EXPECTED);

    get_token();
```

```
  if(token_type==QUOTE) { /* output a string */
    printf("%s ", token);
  }
  else {  /* output a number */
   putback();
   eval_exp(&i);
   printf("%d ", i);
  }

  get_token();

  if(*token!=')') sntx_err(PAREN_EXPECTED);

  get_token();
  if(*token!=';') sntx_err(SEMI_EXPECTED);
  putback();
  return 0;
}

/* Read an integer from the keyboard. */
getnum(void)
{
  char s[80];

  gets(s);
  while(*prog!=')') prog++;
  prog++;  /* advance to end of line */
  return atoi(s);
}
```

To add additional library functions, first enter their names and the addresses of their interface functions into the **internal_func( )** array. Next, following the lead of the functions shown previously, create appropriate interface functions.

COMPILING AND LINKING THE LITTLE C INTERPRETER

Once you have entered all three files that make up Little C, compile and link them together. If you use Turbo C, you can use a sequence such as the following.

```
tcc -c parser.c
tcc -c tclib.c
tcc littlec.c parser.obj tclib.obj
```

If you use Microsoft C, use this sequence:

```
cl -c parser.c
cl -c.tclib.c
cl littlec.c parser.obj tclib.obj
```

If you use a different C compiler, simply follow the instructions that come with it.

DEMONSTRATING LITTLE C

The following C programs demonstrate the features of Little C:

```
/* Little C Demonstration Program #1.

   This program demonstrates all features
   of C that are recognized by Little C.
*/

int i, j;    /* global vars */
char ch;

main()
{
  int i, j;  /* local vars */

  puts("Little C Demo Program.");

  print_alpha();

  do {
    puts("enter a number (0 to quit): ");
    i = getnum();
    if(i < 0 ) {
      puts("numbers must be positive, try again");
    }
```

```
    else {
      for(j = 0; j < i; j=j+1) {
        print(j);
        print("summed is");
        print(sum(j));
        puts("");
      }
    }
  } while(i!=0);
}

/* Sum the values between 0 and num. */
sum(int num)
{
  int running_sum;

  running_sum = 0;

  while(num) {
    running_sum = running_sum + num;
    num = num - 1;
  }
  return running_sum;
}

/* Print the alphabet. */
print_alpha()
{
  for(ch = 'A'; ch<='Z'; ch = ch + 1) {
    putch(ch);
  }
  puts("");
}


/* Nested loop example. */
main()
{
  int i, j, k;

  for(i = 0; i < 5; i = i + 1) {
    for(j = 0; j < 3; j = j + 1) {
      for(k = 3; k ; k = k - 1) {
```

```
            print(i);
            print(j);
            print(k);
            puts("");
        }
      }
    }
    puts("done");
}


/* Assigments as operations. */
main()
{
  int a, b;

  a = b = 10;

  print(a); print(b);
  while(a=a-1) {
    print(a);
    do {
        print(b);
    }while((b=b-1) > -10);
  }
}

/* This program demonstrates recursive functions. */
main()
{
 print(factr(7) * 2);
}

/* return the factorial of i */
factr(int i)
{
  if(i<2) {
    return 1;
  }
  else {
    return i * factr(i-1);
  }
}
```

```
/* A more rigorous example of function arguments. */
main()
{
  f2(10, f1(10, 20), 99);
}

f1(int a, int b)
{
  int count;

  print("in f1");

  count = a;
  do {
    print(count);
  } while(count=count-1);

  print(a); print(b);
  print(a*b);
  return a*b;
}

f2(int a, int x, int y)
{
  print(a); print(x);
  print(x / a);
  print(y*x);
}

/* The loop statements. */

main()
{
  int a;
  char ch;

  /* the while */
  puts("Enter a number: ");
  a = getnum();
  while(a) {
    print(a);
    print(a*a);
```

```
   puts("");
   a = a - 1;
 }

 /* the do-while */
 puts("enter characters, 'q' to quit");
 do {
   ch = getche();
 } while(ch!='q');

 /* the for */
 for(a=0; a<10; a = a + 1) {
   print(a);
 }
}
```

IMPROVING LITTLE C

The Little C interpreter presented in this chapter was designed with transparency of operation in mind. The goal was to develop an interpreter that could be easily understood with the least amount of effort. It was also designed in such a way that it could be easily expanded. As such, Little C is not particularly fast or efficient; however, the basic structure of the interpreter is correct, and you can increase its speed of execution by following these steps.

Virtually all commercial interpreters expand the role of the pre-scanner. The entire source program being interpreted is converted from its ASCII human-readable form into an internal form. In this internal form, all but quoted strings and constants are transformed into single-integer tokens, much the way that Little C converts the C keywords into single-integer tokens. It may have occurred to you that Little C performs a number of string comparisons. For example, each time a variable or function is searched for, several string comparisons take place. String comparisons are very costly in terms of time; however, if each token in the source program is converted into an integer, then much faster integer comparisons can be used. The conversion of the source program into an internal form is the *single most important change* you can make to Little C in order to improve its efficiency. Frankly, the increase in speed will be dramatic.

Another area of improvement, meaningful mostly for large programs, is the lookup routines for variables and functions. Even if you convert these items into integer tokens, the current approach to searching for them relies upon a sequential search. You could, however, substitute some other, faster method, such as a binary tree or some sort of hashing method.

As stated earlier, one restriction that Little C has relative to the full C grammar is that the objects of statements such as **if**—even if single statements—must be blocks of code enclosed between curly braces. The reason is that this greatly simplifies the **find_eob( )** function, which is used to find the end of a block of code after one of the control statements executes. The **find_eob( )** function simply looks for a matching closing curly brace to the one that starts the block. You might find it an interesting exercise to remove this restriction. One approach to this is to redesign **find_eob( )** so that it finds the end of a statement, expression, or block. Keep in mind, however, that you will need to use a different approach to finding the end of the **if**, **while**, **do-while**, and **for** statements when they are used as single statements.

EXPANDING LITTLE C

There are two general areas in which you can expand and enhance the Little C interpreter: C features and ancillary features. Some of these are discussed briefly in the following section.

Adding New C Features

There are two basic catagories of C statements you can add to Little C. The first is additional action statements, such as the **switch**, the **goto**, and the **break** and **continue** statements. You should have little trouble adding any of these if you study closely the way the statements that Little C does intepret are constructed.

The second category of C statement you can add is new data types. Little C already contains the basic "hooks" for additional data types. For example, the **var_type** structure already contains a field for the type of variable. To add other elementary types (for example, **float, double**, and **long**), simply increase the size of the **value** field to the size of the largest element you wish to hold.

Supporting pointers is no more difficult than supporting any other data type. However, you will need to add support for the pointer operators to the expression parser.

Once you have implemented pointers, arrays will be easy. Space for an array should be allocated dynamically using **malloc( )** and a pointer to the array should be stored in the **value** field of **var_type**.

The addition of structures and unions poses a slightly more difficult problem. The easist way to handle them is to use **malloc( )** to allocate space for them and simply use a pointer to the object in the **value** field of the **var_type** structure. (You will also need special code to handle the passing of structures and unions as parameters.)

To handle different return types for functions, add a **type** field to the **func_type** structure that defines what type of data a function returns.

One final thought—if you like to experiment with language constructs, don't be afraid to add a non-C extension. By far the most fun I've had with language interpreters is making them do things not specified by the language. If you want to add a Pascal-like **REPEAT-UNTIL** construct, for example, go ahead and do it! If something doesn't work the first time, try finding the problem by printing out what each token is as it is processed.

Adding Ancillary Features

Interpreters give you the opportunity to add several interesting and useful features. For example, you can add a trace facility that displays each token as it is executed. You can also add the ability to display the contents of each variable as the program executes.

Another feature you might want to add is an integrated editor so that you can "edit and go" instead of having to use a separate editor. You might want to try integrating the screen editor subsystem developed in Chapter 5, for example.

CHAPTER TWO

Icon-Based Interfaces

Several years ago, the introduction of Apple's Lisa and its progeny, the Macintosh, polarized programmers into two camps because of one special feature: the use of a visual operating system interface. The approach used by Apple was to display much of the functionality of the operating system on the screen.[1] This was accomplished partly by using small symbols, called *icons,* which represented certain operating system functions. Perhaps the most recognizable of these icons is the trash can. Programmers became polarized over Apple's icon-based interface not because it provided a visual representation of the system, but because it used pictures instead of words to represent system functions. Some programmers liked this approach; others could find no advantage to using icons instead of a simple text-based menu. Some even suggested that the meaning of some icons was not intuitive, but confusing, thus defeating the accessibility of the system. However, over the years, many programmers have come to believe that icon-based interfaces are valuable in many situations.

1. Icon-based interfaces were pioneered by Xerox at its PARC research laboratory.

Brad Silverberg
Vice President, Research and Development:
Borland International

I first spoke with Brad Silverberg early in 1987 when he and his team of progammers were putting the finishing touches on Borland's Turbo C. At the time, Turbo C was in beta testing and, as is the case with all beta test software, there were bugs to kill and anomalies to reconcile. It is not uncommon in the final weeks before a product's release for everyone connected with the project to get a little edgy—especially the head of research and development. However, the person I spoke with gave no indication of the pressure of the situation. Instead, I talked with a calm yet intense individual who held a clear vision of the compiler that was about to be released. Although he was genuinely interested in the minor bug I had found, I had the distinct feeling that this was a person who had everything well under control—that his vision of Turbo C was about to be realized. It was at this moment that I knew that Turbo C would be an enormous success.

Brad Silverberg is no newcomer to tough projects. As head of R & D at Borland, he has overseen the design and development of some of their best known products, including Turbo C, Turbo Pascal, SideKick, Quattro, Reflex, and Turbo Debugger. Prior to joining Borland, Brad worked at Apple on graphical user interfaces, word processing, and networks.

Brad discovered C in 1977 while working at the Stanford Research Institute. To understand why Brad stayed with C is best described in his own words: "C is compact, consistent, and easily mastered. It avoids excess generality. New features are added by writing new functions, not by inventing new syntax. I am amazed at how many of the right trade-offs Dennis Ritchie made when designing C."

In Brad's opinion, the creation of masterwork quality C programs relies on a deep understanding of the underlying data structures and algorithms used in the project. C is a language that lets you control the exact nature of the program because very little is hidden from you or taken out of your control. Brad also believes that a program is only as good as the pieces that comprise it. He says, "You must have the right building blocks at the core; they must be powerful and efficient." However, Brad offers one warning. "Use the language conservatively; don't become enamoured with the tricky things you can do. C is a language that demands discipline, but repays the careful programmer many times over."

Brad Silverberg holds a B.S. in Computer Science from Brown University (magna cum laude) and an M.S. in Computer Science from the University of Toronto. He lives with his wife and children in California. In his spare time he enjoys windsurfing, bicycling, and baseball.

In the years since Apple introduced icon-based interfaces for general consumption, they have become increasingly popular and are apparently here to stay. However, the implementation of some icon-based interfaces differs from that originally envisioned by Apple. For example, it is common for these interfaces to use both text menus and icons, intermixed. Some interfaces allow the user to bypass the icons altogether and use a command-line approach. The Apple interface assumes a mouse, but it is possible to construct an icon-based interface that does not require one. (No mouse is used in the icon-based interface developed here.)

This chapter discusses some of the theory behind icons and the interfaces based on them. The programs in this chapter are designed to run on an IBM PC or a compatible using DOS. However, if you use a different computer or operating system, you will need to change only the lowest-level video routines. This chapter develops an icon editor that lets you create your own icon images. Next, it develops a simple icon-based menu subsystem. Finally, a sample application is shown that uses icons to provide a visual DOS shell. If you want to add icon interfaces to your software, this chapter is for you.

Because icon-based interfaces require a graphics video mode, the chapter begins with a brief review of PC graphics. (If your computer does not have a graphics adapter, you will not be able to run the code in this chapter.)

Note: The examples in this chapter are compiler- and operating system-dependent. The reason for this is that the ANSI standard does not define any low-level screen control, graphics, or operating system interfacing functions. However, these types of functions must be used to create an icon-based interface. Although most compilers supply such functions, each compiler manufacturer takes a slightly different approach to these functions. The code in this chapter can be compiled for use by Turbo C or Microsoft C by defining either **TURBOC** or **MICROSOFTC** at the top of each program as indicated in the listings. This will cause the correct code for each compiler to be selected for conditional compilation. If you use a different compiler, you may have to make some slight modifications to the examples.

PC GRAPHICS

IBM PCs, ATs, PS/2s, and compatibles are capable of supporting several different video modes depending upon what type of video adapter is installed in the computer. For PCs and ATs, the video adapter is not built into the system and can be either a CGA, an EGA, or a monochrome adapter. Beginning with the PS/2 line, the VGA adapter is built in. The modes supported by each of these adapters are shown in Table 2-1. As the table shows, most of the video modes allow both text and graphics information to be displayed. The dimensions shown for text modes indicate the number of characters per row by the number of rows per screen. In graphics modes, the graphics dimensions represent the number of individual *pixels* (dots) per row and the number of rows per screen. In all modes, the upper left corner is location 0,0.

Table 2-1

The Most Common PC Screen Modes Available for the Various Video Adapter

Mode	Type	Graphics Dimensions	Text Dimensions	Adapter
0	text, b/w	n/a	40×25	CGA/EGA/VGA
1	text, 16 colors	n/a	40×25	CGA/EGA/VGA
2	text, b/w	n/a	80×25	CGA/EGA/VGA
3	text, 16 colors	n/a	80×25	CGA/EGA/VGA
4	graphics, 4 colors	320×200	40×25	CGA/EGA/VGA
5	graphics, 4 grey tones	320×200	40×25	CGA/EGA/VGA
6	graphics, 2 colors	640×200	80×25	CGA/EGA/VGA
7	text, b/w	n/a	80×25	monochrome
8	PCjr mode, not supported			
9	PCjr mode, not supported			
10	PCjr mode, not supported			
11	reserved			
12	reserved			
13	graphics, 16 colors	320×200	40×25	EGA/VGA
14	graphics, 16 colors	640×200	80×25	EGA/VGA
15	graphics, 2 colors	640×350	80×25	EGA/VGA
16	graphics, 16 colors	640×350	80×25	EGA/VGA
17	graphics, 2 colors	640×480	80×30	VGA
18	graphics, 16 colors	640×480	80×30	VGA
19	graphics, 256 colors	640×200	40×25	VGA

The routines in this chapter are designed to use EGA/VGA mode 16. The reason for this is easy to understand—it is the highest resolution commonly available. Because icons convey their information through the presentation of images, it is important to have fairly high resolution. (If you have a CGA, you can still use the code in this chapter, but you will need to change a few parameters.)

In mode 16, there are 16 different colors available for use. The colors are specified using the values 0 through 15. The default color associated with each value is shown in Table 2-2.

All the video adapters operate by mapping a reserved region of memory called the *video RAM* onto the screen. Information you want displayed must be written to the video RAM. Many video modes do not require all of the video RAM to display a screen full of information. These modes divide the video RAM into *pages*. By default, page 0 (the first page) is

Table 2-2

The Default Colors Available in Video Mode 16

Value	Color
0	black (that is, no color)
1	light blue
2	light green
3	light cyan
4	light red
5	light magenta
6	brown
7	low intensity white
8	gray
9	dark blue
10	dark green
11	dark cyan
12	dark red
13	dark magenta
14	yellow
15	high intensity white

used. However, it is possible to cause other pages to be displayed, although none of the routines created in this chapter uses this feature.

Although not defined by ANSI, most PC-based C compilers supply graphics functions. The exact nature, names, and uses of these functions, however, differ widely between compilers. Therefore, this chapter will develop the graphics functions it needs. These functions will be portable to virtually all PC-based compilers. However, you are free to use the graphics functions supplied with your compiler if you choose.

Only three graphics functions are needed to support an icon-based interface—set the video mode, read a pixel, and write a pixel. Let's look at these now.

Setting the Video Mode

Before you can use graphics, the video adapter must be set to the correct graphics mode. By far the easiest way to do this is to call the BIOS routine that sets the video mode. BIOS stands for Basic I/O System and comprises the lowest level I/O routines that you can access. The BIOS routines are reached via an interrupt. Generally, there are several subfunctions associated with each BIOS interrupt, and these subfunctions are specified by the value passed in the AH register. Other values needed by the BIOS routine are passed in other registers. The video mode is set using BIOS interrupt 16, function 0, with the desired mode passed in AL. To execute this routine, you must have a way to load the registers of the CPU and issue a software interrupt. For many DOS-based C compilers (including Microsoft C and Turbo C), the easiest way to do this is to use a function such as **int86( )**.

The **int86( )** function generates a software interrupt; it has this prototype:

```
int int86(int num, /* the interrupt number */
        union REGS *inregs, /* the input register values */
        union REGS *outregs /* the output register values */
)
```

The interrupt to generate is specified by **num**. You can specify the values of the registers at the time of the interrupt using **inregs**. Upon return,

outregs will hold the values of the registers as set by the ISR that handles the interrupt. The return value of **int86( )** is the value of the AX register.

The type **REGS** is supplied in the header **DOS.H**. The one shown here is defined by Turbo C. It is similar to the one defined by Microsoft C and other compilers.

```
/*
        Copyright (c) Borland International Inc. 1987
        All Rights Reserved.
*/

struct WORDREGS
        {
        unsigned int     ax, bx, cx, dx, si, di, cflag;
        };

struct BYTEREGS
        {
        unsigned char    al, ah, bl, bh, cl, ch, dl, dh;
        };

union   REGS    {
        struct  WORDREGS x;
        struct  BYTEREGS h;
        };
```

Notice that **REGS** is a union of two structures. Using the **WORD-REGS** structure allows you to access the registers of the CPU as 16-bit quantities. **BYTEREGS** gives you access to the individual 8-bit registers. For example, to access interrupt number 16, function number 5, you would use this code sequence:

```
union REGS in, out;

in.h.ah = 5;
int86(16, &in, &out);
```

Using **int86( )**, the **mode( )** function is shown in the following.

```
/* Set the video mode. */
void mode(int mode_code)
{
  union REGS r;

  r.h.al = mode_code;
  r.h.ah = 0;
  int86(0x10, &r, &r);
}
```

For example, to set the video adapter to mode 16, use this statement:

```
mode(16);
```

Reading and Writing Pixels Using BIOS

There are two common actions associated with graphics software: reading the value of a pixel from the screen and writing a value to a pixel on the screen. Both of these may be accomplished through BIOS functions. The values read or written to the screen essentially define the color of the pixel and, in some modes, its intensity.

To read the value of a pixel from the screen, use BIOS interrupt 16, function 13. The X coordinate of the pixel is specified in the CX register and the Y coordinate in the DX register. The video page, 0 in the programs in this chapter, is specified in the BH register. Upon return from the interrupt, the AL register contains the value of the specified pixel. The function **getpoint( )** is shown here:

```
/* Returns the value at the specified pixel. */
char getpoint(int x, int y)
{
  union REGS r;

  r.h.ah = 13;
  r.x.dx = y;
  r.x.cx = x;
  r.h.bh = 0;
```

```
   int86(16, &r, &r);
   return r.h.al;
}
```

To write a pixel, use BIOS interrupt 16, function 12. The color of the pixel is specified in the AL register. The X and Y coordinates of the pixel are specified in CX and DX, respectively. The video page, 0 for the programs in this chapter, is specified in BH. The **putpoint( )** function is shown here:

```
/* This version of putpoint() will work for all video
   adapters but is incredibly slow!
*/
void putpoint(int x, int y, int color)
{
  union REGS r;

  r.h.bh = 0;
  r.h.ah = 12;
  r.h.al = color;
  r.x.dx = y;
  r.x.cx = x;
  int86(16, &r, &r);
}
```

As the comment suggests, **putpoint( )** is very slow. This is because the BIOS routines that read and write pixels are very slow. They have the advantage of working for all video adapters and modes. However, the icon-based interface we will develop requires faster output routines for snappy performance. (For the purposes of this chapter, it is not important that the read-pixel routine run extremely fast.) For this reason, we will need to develop our own function that outputs values to the EGA/VGA video adapter directly.

Writing Directly to the EGA/VGA Video Adapter

As stated earlier, all video adapters map the contents of the video RAM onto the screen. For the original video adapters (the monochrome and the CGA) and the modes supported by them, this region of RAM was directly accessible to a program and it could be written *to* and read *from* just as in any other RAM in the system. However, the greater resolution modes of the EGA and VGA required more RAM than was set aside for this purpose. The solution developed by IBM was to divide the value of each pixel between four *bit planes,* each holding only a part of the total pixel color value, and each located at the same memory address. The EGA/VGA hardware swaps each plane in and out of the allocated memory space to compute the actual value displayed on the screen. For modes 13 through 16 video RAM starts at location A000:0000. This scheme is depicted in Figure 2-1.

Note: The EGA/VGA video adapters are fairly complex devices, and the discussion that follows presents only a brief description of a few of their features.

The EGA/VGA video RAM is not accessed directly by your program. Instead, for graphics modes, it is reached though the EGA/VGA adapter by writing to two ports. The first port, 0xC3E, is commonly referred to as the *index port.* The second, 0xC3F, is called the *value port.* The purpose of the index port is to determine the meaning of the information that will be subsequently passed in the value port. In essence, the value that is output to the index port selects a specific mode on the adapter. This mode determines the meaning of the value written to the value port.

The basic approach to outputting a color to a pixel is as follows. First, the address of the pixel is computed using this formula:

$$\text{pixel address} = \text{A000:0000} + (Y * 80) + X/8$$

This formula is derived from the fact that in mode 16, each row on the screen contains 640 pixels, and within each bit plane, one byte of memory holds 8 pixels. Thus, each row requires 80 bytes of memory (80 = 640/8). The address computed by this formula is then used to perform a "dummy read," which causes the EGA/VGA to load the contents of all four bit planes into an internal 32-bit register. The value actually read at the address is not used.

Next, a mask must be prepared that specifies which of the eight pixels at the address is being written to. This is done by setting the appropriate bit and clearing the rest.

A sequence of instructions can now be given to the EGA/VGA controller, which will cause the write operation to take place. The general procedure works this way: First, output the value of the function you will

Figure 2-1

How the EGA/VGA adapters construct a pixel

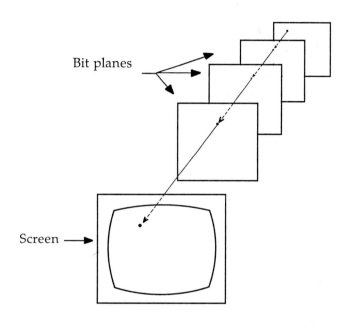

be using to the index port. For example, the function that receives the color you want to display is number 0. Therefore, to set the color, first output 0 to the index port and then the value of the color to the value port.

Once all the appropriate bits of information have been sent to the EGA/VGA controller, a dummy write causes the new values to be moved into the video RAM and, thus, output to the screen. In the function that follows, index 0 is used to load the color register, index 1 enables the write operation, index 3 determines how the output will be written, and index 8, using the mask, determines which pixel will be updated. The entire code for the hardware **putpoint( )** function is shown here. The global variable **egabase** is set elsewhere in the program to A000:0000. (The **putpoint( )** function shown here is adapted by permission from *Advanced*

Graphics in C, by Nelson Johnson (Berkeley, Ca.: Osborne/McGraw-Hill, 1987). This book is filled with a wealth of information about graphics and the EGA, and is recommended reading.)

```
/* This function sets the specified pixel to the
   specified color using an EGA/VGA video adapter.
   The value of the "how" parameter may be one of these:

   action        value

   overwrite     0
   XOR           0x18
   AND           8
   OR            0x10

*/
#define ENABLE 0x0F
#define INDEXREG 0x3CE
#define VALREG 0x3CF

/* Note: Borland does not document outp(), but it is
   in the library of Turbo C 2.0.  The documented function
   is called outport(), but it runs much slower.  However,
   in future versions you may need to use it instead.
   For this reason, the following conditional compilation
   directives have been included.
*/
#ifdef TURBOC
#define OUTINDEX(index, val) outp((INDEXREG), (index));\
                             outp((VALREG), (val));
#endif
#ifdef MICROSOFTC
#define OUTINDEX(index, val) outp((INDEXREG), (index));\
                             outp((VALREG), (val));
#endif

#define WIDTH 80L

/* These range values assume EGA mode 16 */
#define XMAX 639
#define YMAX 349
#define XMIN 0
#define YMIN 0
```

```
void putpoint(int x, int y, int color, int how)
{
  register unsigned char mask = 0x80;
  register char far *base;
  unsigned dummy;

  /* if you want range checking at this point, activate
     this line of code.  It will slow down the function
     however.
  */
  /*if(x<XMIN || x>XMAX || y<YMIN || y>YMAX) return;*/

  /* egabase is initialized elsewhere to 0xA000:0000 */
  base = (char far *) (egabase
        + ( (long) y * WIDTH + (long) x/8L ));

  mask >>= x % 8;

  /* This causes the memory READ necessary to
     load the EGA/VGA's internal registers.
  */
  dummy = *base;

  OUTINDEX(0, color);    /* load color */
  OUTINDEX(1, ENABLE);   /* enable write */
  OUTINDEX(3, how);      /* how written */
  OUTINDEX(8, mask);     /* which pixel */

  *base = 1;             /* dummy write */

  OUTINDEX(0, 0);        /* reset everything */
  OUTINDEX(1, 0);
  OUTINDEX(3, 0);
  OUTINDEX(8, 0xff);     /* enable all pixels */
}
```

As you can see by looking at the function, the **#ifdef** blocks are identical for both Turbo C and Microsoft C. The reason for this is indicated in the comment preceding the conditional compilation blocks. The function **outp( )** is not defined in the Turbo C manual but is available in version 2.0 and earlier. Turbo C documents the equivalent function **outport( )**, but when this is substituted, **putpoint( )** runs much slower.

However, since **outp( )** is not documented in Turbo C, it may go away on subsequent releases. Thus, you might need to change **outp( )** to **outport( )** inside the **TURBOC** conditional block.

The value of **how** determines how the color will be written to the screen. If **how** is 0, then the specified color overwrites the existing contents of the screen. If it is 8, the color is ANDed with the existing color. If **how** is 0x10, the color is ORed with the existing color. If **how** is 0x18, the color is XORed with the existing color.

Some Miscellaneous Screen Routines

Although not technically necessary for the creation of an icon-based interface, the examples in this chapter use three other screen functions: clear-to-end-of-line, clear-screen, and position-cursor. Since we are on the subject of screen control, let's look briefly at these functions.

The easiest way to clear the screen is to call BIOS interrupt 16, function 7, which scrolls the screen. Upon entry, this function expects the number of the upper left row in register CH, the upper left column in CL, the lower right row in DH, and the lower right column in DL. The row and column numbers are specified in units of lines and characters, not pixels. The video pages are specified in BH (0 for our purposes). The number of lines to scroll is specified in AL. However, if AL is 0, then the entire screen is cleared. This function works in all video modes. The **clrscr( )** function, which uses **int86( )** to generate the BIOS interrupt, is shown here:

```
/* Clear the screen. */
void clrscr(void)
{
  union REGS r;

  r.h.ah = 7;
  r.h.al = 0;   /* clear the screen */
  r.h.ch = 0;   /* upper left row */
  r.h.cl = 0;   /* upper left column */
  r.h.dh = 24;  /* lower right row */
  r.h.dl = 79;  /* lower left column */
```

```
  r.h.bh = 0;  /* use page 0 */
  int86(0x10, &r, &r);
}
```

To position the cursor, we can use another BIOS routine. This function affects only text written to the screen, not any graphics output. BIOS interrupt 16, function 2 positions the cursor to the X,Y character position specified in the DL and DH registers, respectively. The video page (0 for our purposes) is specified in BH. Remember, coordinates are specified in character, not pixel, units. The **gotoxy( )** function is shown here:

```
/* Send the cursor to x,y. */
void gotoxy(int x, int y)
{
  union REGS r;

  r.h.ah = 2; /* cursor addressing function */
  r.h.dl = x; /* column coordinate */
  r.h.dh = y; /* row coordinate */
  r.h.bh = 0; /* video page */
  int86(0x10, &r, &r);
}
```

An easy way to create a clear-to-end-of-line function is shown here:

```
/* Clears to end of line. */
void clr_eol(int x, int y)
{
    for(; x<80; x++) {
      gotoxy(x, y);
      printf(" ");
    }
}
```

CREATING ICONS

Before icons can be used they must be created. By far the easiest way to create an icon image is to use an *icon editor*. Most icon editors work in more or less the same way. They show an expanded view of the icon on the screen, which makes the editing process easier. Most also show the normal-sized icon image. The icon editor developed here uses the arrow keys to draw the icon, but some icon editors also allow the use of the mouse for input.

The examples in this chapter use two-color icons. This is the most common type of icon, although multicolor icons are certainly possible. As shown in the examples, the background color of the icon is blue and the foreground is white. This color scheme is easy to change, if you desire.

The icon-based interface uses video mode 16, which has 640 horizontal pixels and 350 vertical pixels. Although not technically necessary, most icons are (more or less) square as viewed on the screen. The dimension chosen for each icon in this chapter is 40 pixels across and 32 down. This makes the icon slightly taller than it is long, although it looks essentially square to the eye. The extra height makes it easier to include both text and an image within an icon. However, you can change the icon dimensions if you like.

The Icon Structure

Although an icon appears as a graphics image on the screen, the image is, in reality, only a part of its full purpose. Each icon has associated with it a structure that holds various bits of information related to the icon. Although the exact nature of the information associated with an icon varies somewhat between implementations, for the examples in this chapter the following information is linked with each icon: the graphical image of the icon, a pointer to the function that is called when the icon is selected, and the X,Y coordinate of the icon's position on the screen. Here is the structure used to hold each icon:

```
struct icon_type {
  unsigned char image[XDIM][YDIM];  /* icon image */
  void (*func)();  /* pointer to function associated
                      with each icon */
  int x, y;        /* X, Y Coordinates */
} icon;
```

The macros **XDIM** and **YDIM** specify the size, in pixels, of the icon. As stated earlier, they are defined as 40 and 32, respectively, for the examples, but you can change these if you wish.

Figure 2-2

A sample icon editor screen

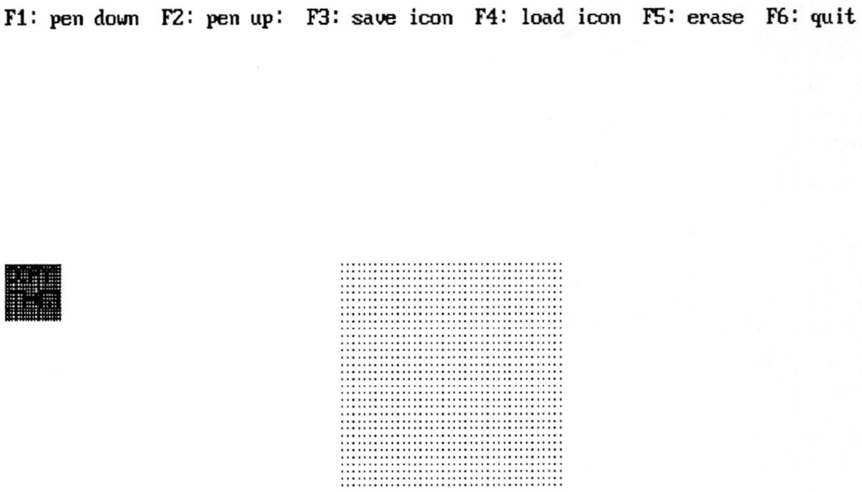

F1: pen down F2: pen up: F3: save icon F4: load icon F5: erase F6: quit

---

Notice the definition of **func**. This is defined as a pointer to a function that returns no value. Although neither **func( )** nor **x** or **y** will be given a value during the editing process, room for them is reserved inside the structure so that it will be available later, when the icon is used.

The Icon Editor

The entire icon editor program is shown here. You might want to enter the program into your computer at this time. A sample editor screen is shown in Figure 2-2. The details of its operation are discussed in the next section.

```
/* Icon Editor Program. */

#define TURBOC
```

```
/*  If you use MicrosoftC, define MICROSOFTC instead
    of TURBOC.  If you use a different compiler, see
    text.
*/

#include "stdio.h"
#include "dos.h"
#include "conio.h"
#include "bios.h"
#include "string.h"

#define IY 144
#define IX 240
#define XDIM 40
#define YDIM 32
#define XPAND 3

#define BCK_GND    9
#define FORE_GND  15
#define HIGHLIGHT 13

char getpoint(int x, int y), getkey(void);
void mode(int mode_code), gotoxy(int x, int y);
void clr_eol(int x, int y);
void palette(int pnum);
void display_grid(void),  edit_icon(void);
void display_icon(int x, int y);
void init_icon(void);
int save_icon(void), load_icon(char *fname);
void putpoint(int x, int y, int color, int how);

struct icon_type {
  unsigned char image[XDIM][YDIM];  /* icon image */
  void (*func)();  /* pointer to function associated
                      with each icon */
  int x, y;        /* X, Y Coordinates */
} icon;

char far *egabase;

void main(int argc, char *argv[])
{
```

```
  mode(16);

  /* Initialize the pointer to the EGA/VGA video
     RAM.
  */
#ifdef TURBOC
  egabase = (char far *) MK_FP(0xA000, 0000);
#endif
#ifdef MICROSOFTC
  egabase = (char far *) 0xA0000000;
#endif

  printf("F1: pen down  F2: pen up:  F3: save icon  ");
  printf("F4: load icon  F5: erase  F6: quit");

  init_icon();  /* initialize the icon */

  if(argc==2) load_icon(argv[1]);

  edit_icon();
  mode(2);
}

/* Display the expanded grid. */
void display_grid(void)
{
  register int x, y;

  for(y = IY; y<(IY+YDIM); y++)
    for(x = IX; x<(IX+XDIM); x++)
      putpoint(x+((x-IX)*XPAND), y+((y-IY)*XPAND),
               icon.image[x-IX][y-IY], 0);
}

/* Edit an icon.  This function displays an expanded
   grid to make editing easy.  It also displays the
   normal size version of the icon being edited. */
void edit_icon()
{
  register int x, y;
  char ch, pen, temp;

  x = IX; y = IY;  /* set x,y to upper left corner */
```

```
pen = BCK_GND;

display_icon(0, IY);
display_grid();
do {
  /* write pixel to grid */
  putpoint(x+((x-IX)*XPAND), y+((y-IY)*XPAND), pen, 0);

  /* save pixel color in icon image */
  icon.image[x-IX][y-IY] = pen;

  /* write pixel to icon */
  putpoint(x-IX, y, icon.image[x-IX][y-IY], 0);

  /* This code displays a dot that indicates the current
     position, waits for a keystroke and then replaces
     the original value.
  */
  temp = getpoint(x+((x-IX)*XPAND), y+((y-IY)*XPAND));
  putpoint(x+((x-IX)*XPAND), y+((y-IY)*XPAND),
           HIGHLIGHT, 0);
  ch = getkey();
  putpoint(x+((x-IX)*XPAND), y+((y-IY)*XPAND), temp, 0);

  switch(ch) {
    case 75: /* left */
      x--;
      break;
    case 77: /* right */
      x++;
      break;
    case 72: /* up */
      y--;
      break;
    case 80: /* down */
      y++;
      break;
    case 71: /* up left */
      x--; y--;
      break;
    case 73: /* up right */
      x++; y--;
      break;
```

```
        case 79: /* down left*/
          x--; y++;
          break;
        case 81: /* down right */
          x++; y++;
          break;
        case 59: pen = FORE_GND;   /* F1 - pen down */
          break;
        case 60: pen = BCK_GND;   /* F2 - pen up */
          break;
        case 61: save_icon();
          break;
        case 62: load_icon("");
          display_icon(0, IY);
          display_grid();
          break;
        case 63: init_icon();
          display_icon(0, IY);
          display_grid();
          break;
    }
    if(x < IX) x++;   if(x > IX+XDIM-1) x--;
    if(y < IY) y++;   if(y > IY+YDIM-1) y--;

  } while(ch != 64);
}

/* Displays the icon at specified X,Y. */
void display_icon(int startx, int starty)
{
  register int x, y;

  for(y = starty; y<starty+YDIM; y++)
    for(x = startx; x<startx+XDIM; x++)
      putpoint(x, y, icon.image[x-startx][y-starty], 0);
}

/* Initializes the icon. */
void init_icon()
{
  register int x, y;
```

```
    for(x= 0; x<XDIM; x++)
      for(y=0; y<YDIM; y++)
        icon.image[x][y] = BCK_GND;
}

/* Saves the icon. */
save_icon(void)
{
  FILE *fp;
  char fname[80];
  int result;

  gotoxy(0, 22);
  printf("save to: ");
  gets(fname);

  if((fp = fopen(fname, "wb"))==NULL) {
    printf("cannot open file");
    return 0;
  }

  fwrite(&icon, sizeof icon, 1, fp);

  if(ferror(fp)) result = 0;
  else result = 1;
  fclose(fp);
  clr_eol(0, 22);
  return result;
}

/* Loads the icon. */
load_icon(char *name)
{
+ FILE *fp;
  char fname[80];
  int result;

  if(!*name) {
    gotoxy(0, 22);
    printf("load from: ");
    gets(fname);
  }
```

```
  else strcpy(fname, name);

  if((fp = fopen(fname, "rb"))==NULL) {
    printf("cannot open file");
    return 0;
  }

  fread(&icon, sizeof icon, 1, fp);

  if(ferror(fp)) result = 0;
  else result = 1;
  fclose(fp);
  clr_eol(0, 22);
  return result;
}


/* Return the scan code of the key pressed.
   This function is compatible with Turbo C and
   Microsoft C (be sure to #define the appropriate
   symbol).  If you use a different compiler, consult
   the text.
*/
char getkey(void)
{
  union key {
    int i;
    char ch[2];
  } k;

#ifdef TURBOC
  k.i = bioskey(0);
#endif
#ifdef MICROSOFTC
  k.i = _bios_keybrd(0);
#endif
  return k.ch[1];
}

/* Set the video mode. */
void mode(int mode_code)
{
  union REGS r;
```

```
    r.h.al = mode_code;
    r.h.ah = 0;
    int86(0x10, &r, &r);
}

/* Send the cursor to x,y. */
void gotoxy(int x, int y)
{
  union REGS r;

  r.h.ah = 2; /* cursor addressing function */
  r.h.dl = x; /* column coordinate */
  r.h.dh = y; /* row coordinate */
  r.h.bh = 0; /* video page */
  int86(0x10, &r, &r);
}

/* Clears to end of line. */
void clr_eol(int x, int y)
{
   for(; x<80; x++) {
     gotoxy(x, y);
     printf(" ");
   }
}

/* Returns the value at the specified pixel. */
char getpoint(int x, int y)
{
  union REGS r;

  r.h.ah = 13;
  r.x.dx = y;
  r.x.cx = x;
  r.h.bh = 0;
  int86(16, &r, &r);
  return r.h.al;
}

/* This version of putpoint will work for all video
   adapters but is incredibly slow! */
```

```
*/
/*
void putpoint(int x, int y, int color, int how)
{
  union REGS r;

  if(how==0x18) color = color | 128;
  r.h.bh = 0;
  r.h.ah = 12;
  r.h.al = color;
  r.x.dx = y;
  r.x.cx = x;
  int86(16, &r, &r);
}
*/

/* This function sets the specified pixel to the
   specified color using an EGA/VGA video adapter.
   The value of how may be one of these:

     action         value

     overwrite      0
     XOR            0x18
     AND            8
     OR             0x10

*/
#define ENABLE 0x0F
#define INDEXREG 0x3CE
#define VALREG 0x3CF

/* Note: Borland does not document outp(), but it is
   in the library of Turbo C 2.0.  The documented function
   is called outport(), but it runs much slower.  However,
   in future versions you may need to use it instead.
   For this reason, the following conditional compilation
   directives have been included.
*/
#ifdef TURBOC
#define OUTINDEX(index, val) outp((INDEXREG), (index));\
                             outp((VALREG), (val));

#endif
#ifdef MICROSOFTC
```

```
#define OUTINDEX(index, val) outp((INDEXREG), (index));\
                             outp((VALREG), (val));
#endif

#define WIDTH 80L

/* These range values assume EGA mode 16 */
#define XMAX 639
#define YMAX 349
#define XMIN 0
#define YMIN 0

void putpoint(int x, int y, int color, int how)
{
   register unsigned char mask = 0x80;
   register char far *base;
   unsigned dummy;

   /* if you want range checking at this point, activate
      this line of code.  It will slow down the function
      however.
   */
   /*if(x<XMIN || x>XMAX || y<YMIN || y>YMAX) return;*/

   base = (char far *) (egabase
         + ( (long) y * WIDTH + (long) x/8L ));

   mask >>= x % 8;

   /* This causes the memory READ necessary to
      load the EGA/VGA's internal registers.
   */
   dummy = *base;

   OUTINDEX(0, color);
   OUTINDEX(1, ENABLE);
   OUTINDEX(3, how);
   OUTINDEX(8, mask);

   *base = 1;

   OUTINDEX(0, 0);
   OUTINDEX(1, 0);
```

```
  OUTINDEX(3, 0);
  OUTINDEX(8, 0xff);
}
```

How the Icon Editor Works

As Figure 2-2 shows, the icon editor presents two displays on the screen. The larger display is referred to, inside the program, as the *grid* (the smaller one is the icon). The grid is an expanded version of the actual image of the icon shown to its left. The expansion ratio is controlled by the value of **XPAND**. As the program is shown, this value is 3, but any value between 2 and 5 will work. The macros **IX** and **IY** specify the coordinates of the upper left corner of the grid.

The work of the program is performed mostly by **edit_icon( )**, which is reprinted here for your convenience. It begins by initializing **x** and **y** to the location of the upper left corner of the grid. Next, the initial value of **pen** is set to **BCK_GND**, the macro that represents the value of the background color. (This is blue, as the program is written.) Next, the grid and the icon are drawn. Unless an existing icon has been loaded from disk by specifying its name on the command line, both the icon and the grid will be filled entirely with the background color.

```
/* Edit an icon.  This function displays an expanded
   grid to make editing easy.  It also displays the
   normal size version of the icon being edited. */
void edit_icon()
{
  register int x, y;
  char ch, pen, temp;

  x = IX; y = IY;  /* set x,y to upper left corner */
  pen = BCK_GND;

  display_icon(0, IY);
  display_grid();
  do {
    /* write pixel to grid */
    putpoint(x+((x-IX)*XPAND), y+((y-IY)*XPAND), pen, 0);
```

```
/* save pixel color in icon image */
icon.image[x-IX][y-IY] = pen;

/* write pixel to icon */
putpoint(x-IX, y, icon.image[x-IX][y-IY], 0);

/* This code displays a dot that indicates the current
   position, waits for a keystroke and then replaces
   the original value.
*/
temp = getpoint(x+((x-IX)*XPAND), y+((y-IY)*XPAND));
putpoint(x+((x-IX)*XPAND), y+((y-IY)*XPAND),
         HIGHLIGHT, 0);
ch = getkey();
putpoint(x+((x-IX)*XPAND), y+((y-IY)*XPAND), temp, 0);

switch(ch) {
  case 75: /* left */
    x--;
    break;
  case 77: /* right */
    x++;
    break;
  case 72: /* up */
    y--;
    break;
  case 80: /* down */
    y++;
    break;
  case 71: /* up left */
    x--; y--;
    break;
  case 73: /* up right */
    x++; y--;
    break;
  case 79: /* down left*/
    x--; y++;
    break;
  case 81: /* down right */
    x++; y++;
    break;
  case 59: pen = FORE_GND;  /* F1 - pen down */
    break;
```

```
      case 60: pen = BCK_GND;   /* F2 - pen up */
        break;
      case 61: save_icon();
        break;
      case 62: load_icon("");
        display_icon(0, IY);
        display_grid();
        break;
      case 63: init_icon();
        display_icon(0, IY);
        display_grid();
        break;
    }
    if(x < IX) x++;   if(x > IX+XDIM-1) x--;
    if(y < IY) y++;   if(y > IY+YDIM-1) y--;

  } while(ch != 64);   /* F6 to quit */
}
```

Once the initializations have been completed, the main loop of **edit_icon( )** begins. It displays a small marker in the grid; this indicates the current position. (This marker is red, as the program is written.) Next, it reads a keystroke and takes appropriate action. For example, if the user presses an arrow key, the indicator is moved in the indicated direction. The code surrounding **getkey( )** is used to advance the indicator from point to point.

When the value of **pen** is **BCK_GND**, each pixel touched by the indicator is set to the background color. However, by pressing F1, the value of **pen** is changed to **FORE_GND**, and each pixel touched by the indicator is set to the foreground color. You can switch to the background color by pressing F2. As you draw points on the grid, each point is also displayed on the normal-sized icon image to the right. The reasons for showing both the grid and the icon is that the expanded view offered by the grid makes it much easier to actually draw an object, but the normal-sized icon image allows you to see exactly how the object will look in actual use.

The function **getkey( )** reads keystrokes from the keyboard but does not return their ASCII value. Instead, it returns their position-code equivalents. As you probably know, a PC keyboard does not generate the ASCII codes for the letters shown on the keys. In actuality, the keyboard has no "knowledge" of what characters are displayed on its keys. Instead, each time a key is pressed, the keyboard generates a value that corresponds to the key's position on the keyboard. This value is called a *scan code,* or occasionally, a *position code.*

You might be wondering why the keyboard generates scan codes instead of the actual ASCII characters that correspond to the keys. The answer is flexibility. By designing a keyboard in this way, it is possible to make it usable in the widest variety of situations. For example, many foreign languages use some characters that are different from those used in English. Also, the layout of the keyboard in some countries is slightly different than the keyboard layout in the U.S. Finally, some people prefer a keyboard layout called the Dvorak keyboard, which is supposed to increase typing efficiency. By generating scan codes instead of ASCII character codes it is possible for the operating system to translate those codes in any way it deems fit. In other words, a given scan code can be mapped onto whatever ASCII code equivalent is required by the situation.

Each time you press a key, the keyboard generates an interrupt in the main system unit and the scan code is latched into the computer. DOS contains a routine that translates this scan code into a character code. Once translated, both the scan code and the ASCII character code are put into the keyboard buffer, where they stay until the program requests keyboard information.

The PC keyboard contains several keys for which there are no ASCII character equivalents. For example, the arrow keys and the function keys have no ASCII key equivalents. When one of these keys is looked up in the character table, its corresponding character value is 0, which indicates that a non-ASCII key has been pressed. (No scan code has the value 0.) When the character code is 0, your program must examine the scan code to detemine which key was pressed.

Most high-level language keyboard-input functions discard the scan code and use only the character code. This means that it is generally impossible to use these functions to read special keys, such as the function or arrow keys. However, most PC-based C compilers include a special keyboard input function that returns both the scan code and the character code for each keypress. For example, in Turbo C this function is called **bioskey( )** and in Microsoft C the function is called **bios _ keybrd( )**. These functions simply call BIOS routines that return information about the keyboard. Both functions work the same way. If for some reason your compiler does not include a function of this type, you can use this one, which emulates Turbo C's **bioskey ( )** function. (It uses the BIOS keyboard interrupt 0x16, routines 0 through 2.)

```
/* Emulate bioskey(). */

unsigned bioskey(int mode)
{
  union REGS r;

  switch(mode) {
    case 0:  /* read scan keystroke */
      r.h.ah = 0;
      return int86(0x16, &r, &r);
    case 1:  /* is key waiting? */
      r.h.ah = 1;
      return int86(0x16, &r, &r);
    case 2:  /* return status */
      r.h.ah = 2;
      return int86(0x16, &r, &r);
  }
}
```

When **bioskey( )** or its equivalent function is called with an argument
of 0, it returns a 16-bit quantity that has the ASCII code stored in the
low-order byte and the scan code in the high-order byte. The **getkey( )**
function returns only the scan code because that is all that the icon editor
needs to know about. The **getkey( )** function is shown here:

```
/* Return the scan code of the key pressed.
   This function is compatible with Turbo C and
   Microsoft C (be sure to #define the appropriate
   symbol).  If you use a different compiler, consult
   the text.
*/
char getkey(void)
{
  union key {
    int i;
    char ch[2];
  } k;
#ifdef TURBOC
  k.i = bioskey(0);
#endif
#ifdef MICROSOFTC
```

```
  k.i = _bios_keybrd(0);
#endif
  return k.ch[1];
}
```

Saving and Loading Icon Images

To save an icon, press F3 and specify its filename. To load an icon, press F4. You can automatically load an icon by specifying its name on the command line when you execute the icon editor.

Now that you have seen how to create icons, it is time to move on to using them.

CREATING AN ICON MENU FUNCTION

When designing any type of icon-based interface, it is important to keep in mind that they are essentially menus. Hence, all icon-based interfaces share many common attributes. For example, they must display the currently active icons, wait for the user to select one, and take appropriate action when a selection is made.

The single most important function in an icon-based interface is the one that accepts the user's input. For the example in this chapter, this function is called **icon_menu( )**. It performs three main functions: First, it displays the icons that form the icon menu. Second, it allows the user to select one icon. Finally, it returns the user's selection to the calling routine. A pointer to an array of icons and the number of icons in the array must be passed to the function. Each icon is of type **icon_type**, which is the same as defined by the icon editor. The **icon_menu( )** function is shown here:

```
/* Display icon-based menu and return user's
   selection.  Must be passed a pointer to the
   icon array and the number of icons.
*/
icon_menu(struct icon_type *icons, int num)
{
  register int selection;
  char ch;
```

```
display_icons(icons, num);

gotoxy(0, 23);
printf("Arrow keys to move, ENTER, or F1 to select,");
printf(" F2 to move icon");
selection = 0;
for(;;) {
  invert_icon(icons[selection]);
  ch = getkey();
  display_icon(icons[selection]);
  switch(ch) {
    case 75: /* left */
      selection--;
      break;
    case 77: /* right */
      selection++;
      break;
    case 72: /* up */
      selection -= NUM_ACROSS;
      break;
    case 80: /* down */
      selection += NUM_ACROSS;
      break;
    case 60: /* F2: move an icon */
      move(&icons[selection]);
      clr_eol(0, 23);
      gotoxy(0, 23);
      printf("Arrow keys to move, ENTER (or F1) to select,");
      printf(" F2 to move icon");
      break;
    case 28: /* CR: */
    case 59: /* F1: make a selection */
      clr_eol(0, 23);
      return selection;
  }
  if(selection < 0) selection = num_icons-1;
  if(selection > num_icons-1) selection = 0;
  }
}
```

The **icon_menu( )** function works like this: First, it calls **display_icons( )** to display the icons in the array pointed to by **icons** on the screen. To do this, **display_icons( )** repeatedly calls **display_icon( )**. The **display_icon( )** function displays each icon at the X,Y location specified in its structure. (The position of each icon is determined elsewhere in a program that uses **icon_menu( )**.) These functions are shown here:

```
/* Display all icons.  Must be passed a pointer
   to the icon array and the number in the array.
*/
void display_icons(struct icon_type *icons,
                    register int num)
{
  register int i;

  for(i=0; i<num; i++)
    display_icon(icons[i]);
}

/* Display an icon at its X,Y location. */
void display_icon(struct icon_type icon)
{
  register int x, y;

  for(y = icon.y; y<icon.y+YDIM; y++)
    for(x = icon.x; x<icon.x+XDIM; x++)
      putpoint(x, y, icon.image[x-icon.x][y-icon.y], 0);
}
```

Next, **icon_menu( )** displays a prompting message and initializes **selection** to zero. After that, it enters its main loop. The **icon_menu( )** function highlights the currently active icon by reversing the icon's color scheme. In this case, it means turning blue to white and white to blue. This is done by using the **invert_icon( )** function. Next, it waits for a keypress and then redisplays the icon using its normal color scheme. If the key pressed was an arrow key, it moves to the next icon as indicated by the direction of the key. Because each icon carries with it its own screen coordinates, the **icon_menu( )** function does not need to worry about where the icon is on the screen; it simply increments or decrements **selection** by an appropriate amount. The macro **NUM_ACROSS** specifies the maximum number of icons that will appear on one horizontal line.

This value is used to determine how to increment or decrement **selection** when the user presses a DOWN or UP ARROW key.

To make a selection, the user simply presses ENTER or F1 when the highlight is on the desired icon. This causes the value of **selection** to be returned to the calling routine.

The user can dynamically move an icon about on the screen by pressing F2, which causes the **move( )** function to be called. This function will be discussed next.

DYNAMICALLY MOVING ICONS

Because each icon contains its screen coordinates, it is easy to change its position by changing the values of these coordinates. One way to do this is to let the user interactively move an icon about the screen. A good way to approach the interactive repositioning of icons is to use the arrow keys to "drag" the icon around the screen. This is the basic approach taken by the **move( )** function shown here, along with a support function called **box( )**.

```c
/* Reposition an icon.  It must be passed a
   pointer to the icon to reposition. */
void move(struct icon_type *icon)
{
  int x, y, oldx, oldy;
  char ch;

  clr_eol(0, 23);
  gotoxy(0, 23);
  printf("Arrow keys to move, F2 to accept, F1 to abort");
  x = oldx = icon->x;
  y = oldy = icon->y;
  do {
    /* outline the icon being moved */
    box(x, y, x+XDIM-1, y+YDIM-1, 0x18);
    ch = getkey();
    box(x, y, x+XDIM-1, y+YDIM-1, 0x18);
    switch(ch) {
      case 75: /* left */
        x -=5;
        break;
```

```
      case 77: /* right */
        x +=5;
        break;
      case 72: /* up */
        y -= 5;
        break;
      case 80: /* down */
        y +=5;
        break;
      case 71: /* left up */
        y -= 5;   x -= 5;
        break;
      case 73: /* right up */
        y -= 5;   x += 5;
        break;
      case 79: /* left down */
        y += 5;   x -= 5;
        break;
      case 81: /* right down */
        y += 5;   x += 5;
        break;
      case 59: return;   /* F1: abort */
    }
  } while(ch!=60);   /* F2: accept */
  icon->x = x;
  icon->y = y;

  /* erase old position */
  for(x=oldx; x<oldx+XDIM; x++)
    for(y=oldy; y<oldy+YDIM; y++)
      putpoint(x, y, 0, 0);

}


/* Draw a box in the foreground color. The
   how parameter determines how the box will
   be displayed on the screen, see putpoint()
   for details.
*/
void box(int startx, int starty,
         int endx, int endy, int how)
{
  register int x, y;
```

```
for(x=startx; x<endx; x++)
  putpoint(x, endy, FORE_GND, how);
for(y=starty; y<endy; y++)
  putpoint(endx, y, FORE_GND, how);
for(x=startx; x<endx; x++)
  putpoint(x, starty, FORE_GND, how);
for(y=starty; y<endy; y++)
  putpoint(startx, y, FORE_GND, how);
}
```

The **move( )** function must be passed a pointer to the icon that will be moved. The function then outlines the icon using the **box( )** function. Notice that **box( )** is called with the **how** parameter set to 0x18. This is the code used by **putpoint( )** to request that the screen output be XORed on the screen. The XOR-write feature has two benefits is this situation. First, it guarantees that the box will be visible, no matter what color it is passing over as it is moved. Second, by XORing the box on the screen a second time in the same screen position, the original contents of the screen will be restored. (Two XORs always produce the original value.) The reason that the entire icon is not dragged about the screen is that it takes too long to redraw it each time it is moved, causing a sluggish feel.

Once the box is in the desired position, pressing F2 moves the icon to that location. If you want to cancel the entire operation, press F1 and the icon's position will be unchanged.

Now that you have seen how the **icon_menu( )** and **move( )** functions operate, it is time to illustrate their use in a real application. The remainder of this chapter develops a simple, yet operational, icon-based DOS shell.

AN ICON-BASED DOS SHELL

An interesting application of an icon-based interface is found in a DOS shell. The one developed here can perform these seven DOS functions:

- run a program

- copy a file

- erase a file

- check the disk

- type a file

- display the DOS version number

- display the directory

There is also an icon that is used to terminate the shell. Each icon in the menu is linked to a function that performs the action suggested by the icon. Let's begin by examining these functions.

The Shell Functions

The easiest way to execute a DOS command from within a C program is to use the **system( )** function. This function is defined by the ANSI standard and should be part of the standard library provided with your C compiler. The **system( )** function has this prototype:

int system(const char *command);

This prototype is found in STDLIB.H. The **system( )** function passes to the operating system the string pointed to by *command*. The operating system (DOS in this case) executes the command as if it had been entered at the keyboard.

The only function that does not use **system( )** is **run( )**, which is used to run a program. This function must use **spawnl( )**, which is used to execute a program from within another. This function is not defined by the ANSI standard, but is found in most C compilers. It has this prototype:

int spawnl(int mode, char *progname, char *arg1,
          . . ., char *argN, NULL);

The *mode* parameter determines how the program specified by *progname* will be executed. If *mode* is **P_WAIT**, the parent program waits until the child program finishes and then it resumes execution. This is the mode used here. The strings pointed to by **arg1** through **argN** are any command-line parameters required by the program. By convention, the first argument also contains the program's name. The last argument to **spawnl( )** must be **NULL**.

The DOS functions supported by the icon-based shell are shown here:

```
/* List the current directory. */
void dir(void)
{
  char com[80], str[80];

  strcpy(com, "dir ");
  gotoxy(0, 10);
  printf("enter mask: ");
  gets(str);
  strcat(com, str);
  system(com);
}

/* Copy a file. */
void copy(void)
{
  char fname1[80], fname2[80];
  char com[80];

  strcpy(com, "copy ");
  gotoxy(0, 10);

  printf("From: ");
  gets(fname1);
  printf("To: ");
  gets(fname2);
  strcat(com, fname1);
  strcat(com, " ");
  strcat(com, fname2);
  system(com);
}

/* Erase a file. */
void erase(void)
{
```

```
  char fname[80];
  char com[80];

  gotoxy(0, 10);

  strcpy(com, "erase ");

  printf("File to erase: ");
  gets(fname);
  strcat(com, fname);
  printf("Sure? (y/n): ");
  if(tolower(getche())=='y') system(com);
}

/* Run a program. */
void run(void)
{
  char prog[80];

  gotoxy(0, 10);

  printf("enter program name: ");
  gets(prog);
  spawnl(P_WAIT, prog, prog, "");
}

/* Type a file. */
void type(void)
{
  char fname[80];
  char com[80];

  gotoxy(0, 10);

  strcpy(com, "type ");

  printf("File to type: ");
  gets(fname);
  strcat(com, fname);
  system(com);
}

/* Check the disk. */
void chkdsk(void)
```

```
{
  char com[80], str[80];

  strcpy(com, "chkdsk ");

  gotoxy(0, 10);

  printf("enter drive specifier: ");
  gets(str);
  strcat(com, str);
  system(com);
}

/* Display version number. */
void ver(void)
{
  gotoxy(0, 10);
  system("ver");
}

/* Return to the command line. */
void icon_end(void)
{
  mode(2);
  exit(0);
}
```

Initializing the Icon Structures

Before the **icon_menu( )** function can be used, each icon must be initialized. This consists of three operations: First, the image for each icon must be loaded. Second, its screen position must be determined. Third, the function that will be called when the icon is selected must be set. These initializations are performed by **main( )**, which is shown here, along with all global data, definitions, and prototypes.

```
#define IY 10
#define IX 10
#define XDIM 40
#define YDIM 32
#define NUM_ICONS 10
#define XPAND 3
```

```
#define ICON_X_SPACING 50
#define ICON_Y_SPACING 40
#define NUM_ACROSS   4

#define BCK_GND    9
#define FORE_GND  15
#define HIGHLIGHT 13

/* DOS system functions */
void dir(void), copy(void), erase(void), run(void);
void type(void), icon_end(void), chkdsk(void), ver(void);

struct icon_type {
  unsigned char image[XDIM][YDIM];  /* icon */
  void (*func)();  /* pointer to function associated
                      with each icon */
  int x, y;        /* X, Y Coordinates */
} icons[NUM_ICONS];

char *icon_files[] = {
  "copy.ico",
  "erase.ico",
  "dir.ico",
  "type.ico",
  "run.ico",
  "chkdsk.ico",
  "ver.ico",
  "end.ico",
  ""
};

void (*sys_funcs[])() = {
  copy, erase, dir, type, run, chkdsk, ver, icon_end
};

int num_icons;
char far *egabase;

char getkey(void);
void mode(int mode_code), gotoxy(int x, int y);
void clr_eol(int x, int y), clrscr(void);
void display_grid(void),  edit_icon(void);
```

```
int save_icon(void), load_icons(void);
void putpoint(int x, int y, int color, int how);
void box(int startx, int starty,
         int endx, int endy, int how);
void line(int startx, int starty,
         int endx, int endy, int how);
int icon_menu(struct icon_type *icons, int num);
void display_icons(struct icon_type *icons,
                   register int num);
void display_icon(struct icon_type icon);
void invert_icon(struct icon_type icon);
void move(struct icon_type *icon);

void main(void)
{
  register int i, j;
  int selection;

  mode(16);
#ifdef TURBOC
  egabase = (char far *) MK_FP(0xA000, 0000);
#endif
#ifdef MICROSOFTC
  egabase = (char far *) 0xA0000000;
#endif

  if((num_icons = load_icons())==0) exit(1);

  /* Compute X,Y positions for icons. This loop
     automatically positions the icons in
     rows, each row having NUM_ACROSS icons
     in it. */
  for(i=0, j=0; i<num_icons; i++, j++) {
    /* at end of row, reset X coordinate */
    if(!(j%NUM_ACROSS)) j=0;

    icons[i].x = j*ICON_X_SPACING+IX;
    icons[i].y = IY + (ICON_Y_SPACING * (i/NUM_ACROSS)) ;
  }

  /* initialize function fields */
  for(i=0; i<num_icons; i++)
    icons[i].func = sys_funcs[i];
```

```
for(;;) {
  box(0, 0, 210, 90, 0);
  selection = icon_menu(icons, num_icons);
  (*icons[selection].func)();
  printf("\npress ENTER to return to menu\n");
  getch();
  clrscr();
}
}
```

Remember, this code loads each icon's image using the filenames specified in the **icon_files** array. These images must have been previously created using the icon editor. You must be sure to store each image using the correct filename. If all of the icon files are not present, the shell will not execute. (If you purchase the companion disk, sample icon files will be included.)

As you can see, each time **icon_edit( )** returns a selection, this value is used to index the **icons** array to execute the function linked with the icon. The box around the icon menu is not necessary; you may remove it if you wish.

Figure 2-3

The default layout of the icon-based DOS shell

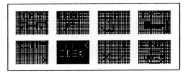

Arrow keys to move, ENTER (or F1) to select, F2 to move icon

Figure 2-4

The DOS shell after several icons have been moved

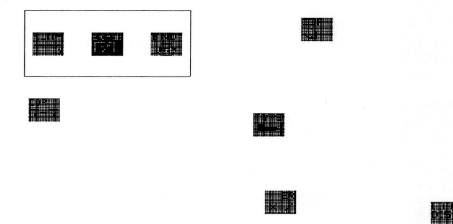

Arrow keys to move, ENTER (or F1) to select, F2 to move icon

The Entire Icon-Based DOS Shell Program

The entire icon-based DOS shell program is shown here. Figures 2-3 and 2-4 show how the icon-based shell appears in its default layout and after several of the icons have been moved. The icons shown in the figures are only suggestions; you can probably create better ones with little effort. The box around the icons is unnecessary and can be removed if you like.

```
/* Icon-based DOS Interface. */

#define TURBOC
/* If you use Microsoft C, #define MICROSOFTC
   instead of TURBOC.  If you have a different
   C compiler, see the text.
*/
```

```
#include "stdio.h"
#include "dos.h"
#include "conio.h"
#include "bios.h"
#include "stdlib.h"
#include "process.h"
#include "string.h"
#include "ctype.h"

#define IY 10
#define IX 10
#define XDIM 40
#define YDIM 32
#define NUM_ICONS 10
#define XPAND 3
#define ICON_X_SPACING 50
#define ICON_Y_SPACING 40
#define NUM_ACROSS  4

#define BCK_GND    9
#define FORE_GND 15
#define HIGHLIGHT 13

/* DOS system functions */
void dir(void), copy(void), erase(void), run(void);
void type(void), icon_end(void), chkdsk(void), ver(void);

struct icon_type {
  unsigned char image[XDIM][YDIM];  /* icon */
  void (*func)();  /* pointer to function associated
                      with each icon */
  int x, y;        /* X, Y Coordinates */
} icons[NUM_ICONS];

char *icon_files[] = {
  "copy.ico",
  "erase.ico",
  "dir.ico",
  "type.ico",
  "run.ico",
  "chkdsk.ico",
  "ver.ico",
  "end.ico",
```

```c
    " "
};

void (*sys_funcs[])() = {
  copy, erase, dir, type, run, chkdsk, ver, icon_end
};

int num_icons;
char far *egabase;

char getkey(void);
void mode(int mode_code), gotoxy(int x, int y);
void clr_eol(int x, int y), clrscr(void);
void display_grid(void),  edit_icon(void);
int save_icon(void), load_icons(void);
void putpoint(int x, int y, int color, int how);
void box(int startx, int starty,
         int endx, int endy, int how);
void line(int startx, int starty,
         int endx, int endy, int how);
int icon_menu(struct icon_type *icons, int num);
void display_icons(struct icon_type *icons,
                   register int num);
void display_icon(struct icon_type icon);
void invert_icon(struct icon_type icon);
void move(struct icon_type *icon);

void main(void)
{
  register int i, j;
  int selection;

  mode(16);
#ifdef TURBOC
  egabase = (char far *) MK_FP(0xA000, 0000);
#endif
#ifdef MICROSOFTC
  egabase = (char far *) 0xA0000000;
#endif

  if((num_icons = load_icons())==0) exit(1);

  /* Compute X,Y positions for icons. This loop
```

```
       automatically positions the icons in
       rows, each row having NUM_ACROSS icons
       in it. */
    for(i=0, j=0; i<num_icons; i++, j++) {
      /* at end of row, reset X coordinate */
      if(!(j%NUM_ACROSS)) j=0;

      icons[i].x = j*ICON_X_SPACING+IX;
      icons[i].y = IY + (ICON_Y_SPACING * (i/NUM_ACROSS)) ;
    }

    /* initialize function fields */
    for(i=0; i<num_icons; i++)
      icons[i].func = sys_funcs[i];

    for(;;) {
      box(0, 0, 210, 90, 0);
      selection = icon_menu(icons, num_icons);
      (*icons[selection].func)();
      printf("\npress ENTER to return to menu\n");
      getch();
      clrscr();
    }
}

/* Display icon-based menu and return user's
   selection.  Must be passed a pointer to the
   icon array and the number of icons.
*/
icon_menu(struct icon_type *icons, int num)
{
  register int selection;
  char ch;

  display_icons(icons, num);

  gotoxy(0, 23);
  printf("Arrow keys to move, ENTER (or F1) to select,");
  printf(" F2 to move icon");
  selection = 0;
  for(;;) {
    invert_icon(icons[selection]);
    ch = getkey();
```

```
      display_icon(icons[selection]);
      switch(ch) {
        case 75: /* left */
          selection--;
          break;
        case 77: /* right */
          selection++;
          break;
        case 72: /* up */
          selection -= NUM_ACROSS;
          break;
        case 80: /* down */
          selection += NUM_ACROSS;
          break;
        case 60: /* F2: move an icon */
          move(&icons[selection]);
          clr_eol(0, 23);
          gotoxy(0, 23);
          printf("Arrow keys to move, ENTER, or Fl to select,");
          printf(" F2 to move icon");
          break;
        case 28: /* CR: */
        case 59: /* Fl: make a selection */
          clr_eol(0, 23);
          return selection;
      }
      if(selection < 0) selection = num_icons-1;
      if(selection > num_icons-1) selection = 0;
    }
}

/* Reverse the colors on the specified icon.   This
   is used as a highlight.
*/
void invert_icon(struct icon_type icon)
{
  register int x, y;

  for(y = icon.y; y<icon.y+YDIM; y++)
    for(x = icon.x; x<icon.x+XDIM; x++)
      if(icon.image[x-icon.x][y-icon.y] == BCK_GND)
        putpoint(x, y, FORE_GND, 0);
      else
```

```
        putpoint(x, y, BCK_GND, 0);

}

/* Display an icon at its X,Y location. */
void display_icon(struct icon_type icon)
{
  register int x, y;

  for(y = icon.y; y<icon.y+YDIM; y++)
    for(x = icon.x; x<icon.x+XDIM; x++)
      putpoint(x, y, icon.image[x-icon.x][y-icon.y], 0);
}

/* Display all icons.  Must be passed a pointer
   to the icon array and the number in the array.
*/
void display_icons(struct icon_type *icons,
                   register int num)
{
  register int i;

  for(i=0; i<num; i++)
    display_icon(icons[i]);
}

/* Reposition an icon.  Must be passed a
   pointer to the icon to reposition. */
void move(struct icon_type *icon)
{
  int x, y, oldx, oldy;
  char ch;

  clr_eol(0, 23);
  gotoxy(0, 23);
  printf("Arrow keys to move, F2 to accept, F1 to abort");
  x = oldx = icon->x;
  y = oldy = icon->y;
  do {
    /* outline the icon being moved */
    box(x, y, x+XDIM-1, y+YDIM-1, 0x18);
    ch = getkey();
    box(x, y, x+XDIM-1, y+YDIM-1, 0x18);
```

```
    switch(ch) {
      case 75: /* left */
        x -=5;
        break;
      case 77: /* right */
        x +=5;
        break;
      case 72: /* up */
        y -= 5;
        break;
      case 80: /* down */
        y +=5;
        break;
      case 71: /* left up */
        y -= 5;   x -= 5;
        break;
      case 73: /* right up */
        y -= 5;   x += 5;
        break;
      case 79: /* left down */
        y += 5;   x -= 5;
        break;
      case 81: /* right down */
        y += 5;   x += 5;
        break;
      case 59: return;   /* F1: abort */
    }
  } while(ch!=60);   /* F2: accept */
  icon->x = x;
  icon->y = y;

  /* erase old position */
  for(x=oldx; x<oldx+XDIM; x++)
    for(y=oldy; y<oldy+YDIM; y++)
      putpoint(x, y, 0, 0);

}

/* Load the icons. */
load_icons()
{
  FILE *fp;
  register int i;
```

```
  for(i=0; (i<NUM_ICONS) && *icon_files[i]; i++) {
    if((fp = fopen(icon_files[i], "rb"))==NULL) {
      printf("cannot open file %s\n", icon_files[i]);
      return 0;
    }

    fread(&icons[i], sizeof (struct icon_type), 1, fp);

    if(ferror(fp)) break;
    fclose(fp);
  }

  return i;
}

/* Draw a box in the foreground color. The
   how parameter determines how the box will
   be displayed on the screen, see putpoint()
   for details.
*/
void box(int startx, int starty,
         int endx, int endy, int how)
{
  register int x, y;

  for(x=startx; x<endx; x++)
    putpoint(x, endy, FORE_GND, how);
  for(y=starty; y<endy; y++)
    putpoint(endx, y, FORE_GND, how);
  for(x=startx; x<endx; x++)
    putpoint(x, starty, FORE_GND, how);
  for(y=starty; y<endy; y++)
    putpoint(startx, y, FORE_GND, how);
}

/* List the current directory. */
void dir(void)
{
  char com[80], str[80];

  strcpy(com, "dir ");
  gotoxy(0, 10);
```

```c
  printf("enter mask: ");
  gets(str);
  strcat(com, str);
  system(com);
}

/* Copy a file. */
void copy(void)
{
  char fname1[80], fname2[80];
  char com[80];

  strcpy(com, "copy ");
  gotoxy(0, 10);

  printf("From: ");
  gets(fname1);
  printf("To: ");
  gets(fname2);
  strcat(com, fname1);
  strcat(com, " ");
  strcat(com, fname2);
  system(com);
}

/* Erase a file. */
void erase(void)
{
  char fname[80];
  char com[80];

  gotoxy(0, 10);

  strcpy(com, "erase ");

  printf("File to erase: ");
  gets(fname);
  strcat(com, fname);
  printf("Sure? (y/n): ");
  if(tolower(getche())=='y') system(com);
}

/* Run a program. */
```

```
void run(void)
{
  char prog[80];

  gotoxy(0, 10);

  printf("enter program name: ");
  gets(prog);
  spawnl(P_WAIT, prog, prog, "");
}

/* Type a file. */
void type(void)
{
  char fname[80];
  char com[80];

  gotoxy(0, 10);

  strcpy(com, "type ");

  printf("File to type: ");
  gets(fname);
  strcat(com, fname);
  system(com);
}

/* Check the disk. */
void chkdsk(void)
{
  char com[80], str[80];

  strcpy(com, "chkdsk ");

  gotoxy(0, 10);

  printf("enter drive specifier: ");
  gets(str);
  strcat(com, str);
  system(com);
}

/* Display version number. */
```

```
void ver(void)
{
  gotoxy(0, 10);
  system("ver");
}


/* Return to the command line. */
void icon_end(void)
{
  mode(2);
  exit(0);
}


/* Return the scan code of the key pressed.
   This function is compatible with Turbo C and
   Microsoft C (be sure to #define the appropriate
   symbol).  If you use a different compiler, consult
   the text.
*/
char getkey(void)
{
  union key {
    int i;
    char ch[2];
  } k;

#ifdef TURBOC
  k.i = bioskey(0);
#endif
#ifdef MICROSOFTC
  k.i = _bios_keybrd(0);
#endif
  return k.ch[1];
}


/* Set the video mode. */
void mode(int mode_code)
{
  union REGS r;

  r.h.al = mode_code;
  r.h.ah = 0;
```

```
  int86(0x10, &r, &r);
}

/* send the cursor to x,y */
void gotoxy(int x, int y)
{
  union REGS r;

  r.h.ah = 2; /* cursor addressing function */
  r.h.dl = x; /* column coordinate */
  r.h.dh = y; /* row coordinate */
  r.h.bh = 0; /* video page */
  int86(0x10, &r, &r);
}

/* Clear to end of specified line. */
void clr_eol(int x, int y)
{
    for(; x<80; x++) {
      gotoxy(x, y);
      printf(" ");
    }
}

/* Clear the screen. */
void clrscr(void)
{
  union REGS r;

  r.h.ah = 7;
  r.h.al = 0;
  r.h.ch = 0;
  r.h.cl = 0;
  r.h.dh = 24;
  r.h.dl = 79;
  r.h.bh = 0;
  int86(0x10, &r, &r);
}

/* This version of putpoint will work for all video
   adapters but is incredibly slow!
*/
/*
```

```
void putpoint(int x, int y, int color, int how)
{
  union REGS r;

  if(how==0x18) color = color | 128;
  r.h.bh = 0;
  r.h.ah = 12;
  r.h.al = color;
  r.x.dx = y;
  r.x.cx = x;
  int86(16, &r, &r);
}
*/

/* This function sets the specified pixel to the
   specified color using an EGA/VGA video adapter
   for modes 13 and greater.

   The value of how may be one of these:

   action       value

   overwrite      0
   XOR          0x18
   AND            8
   OR           0x10

*/
#define ENABLE 0x0F
#define INDEXREG 0x3CE
#define VALREG 0x3CF

/* Note: Borland does not document outp(), but it is
   in the library of Turbo C 2.0.  The documented function
   is called outport(), but it runs much slower.  However,
   in future versions you may need to use it instead.
   For this reason, the following conditional compilation
   directives have been included.
*/
#ifdef TURBOC
#define OUTINDEX(index, val) outp((INDEXREG), (index));\
                             outp((VALREG), (val));
#endif
```

```
#ifdef MICROSOFTC
#define OUTINDEX(index, val) outp((INDEXREG), (index));\
                                outp((VALREG), (val));

#endif


#define WIDTH 80L


/* These range values assume EGA mode 16 */
#define XMAX 639
#define YMAX 349
#define XMIN 0
#define YMIN 0

void putpoint(int x, int y, int color, int how)
{
   register unsigned char mask = 0x80;
   register char far *base;
   unsigned dummy;

   /* if you want range checking at this point, activate
      this line of code.  It will slow down the function
      however.
   */
   /*if(x<XMIN || x>XMAX || y<YMIN || y>YMAX) return;*/

   base = (char far *) (egabase
           + ( (long) y * WIDTH + (long) x/8L ));

   mask >>= x % 8;

   /* This causes the memory READ necessary to
      load the EGA/VGA's internal registers.
   */
   dummy = *base;

   OUTINDEX(0, color);
   OUTINDEX(1, ENABLE);
   OUTINDEX(3, how);
   OUTINDEX(8, mask);

   *base = 1;
```

```
    OUTINDEX(0, 0);
    OUTINDEX(1, 0);
    OUTINDEX(3, 0);
    OUTINDEX(8, 0xff);
}
```

Bjarne Stroustrup
Member of Technical Staff, AT&T, Bell Labs

The creator of C++, Bjarne Stroustrup, is already a legend in the world of C and C programming. He is also the author of *The C++ Programming Language* (Palo Alto, Ca: Addison-Wesley, © 1986). Bjarne holds a Ph.D. in Computer Science from Cambridge University, England.

Before coming to Bell Labs, Bjarne Stroustrup had used BCPL (a forerunner of C) for several years. At Bell, he began using C and in the process invented C++. If you are not familiar with C++, it is a powerful superset to C, which supports classes. Classes support data abstraction and object-oriented programming directly. As Bjarne puts it, "The notions of derived class and virtual function allow programs to be structured for clarity, extensibility, and ease of maintainance without loss of efficiency." Also, C++ allows operators to be overloaded, which means that you can define an operator in such a way that it will work with various types of data. Many people believe that C++ marks the future direction of C.

Given that C++ is a masterwork, I asked Bjarne what elements he thinks contribute most to the creation of masterwork programs. He answered, "Understanding the subject matter. The elegance of a design and the choice of data structures and algorithms are important style issues, but if you don't thoroughly understand the problem or cannot think of a clear solution, no programming style or language can help you."

Bjarne offers this advice to anyone who wants to become a great C programmer: "Read lots of code, in several languages. Concentrate on design. Throw at least the first version of any program away. Stick with it until you get it right."

Bjarne Stroustrup lives near Murray Hill, New Jersey, with his wife and two children.

CHAPTER THREE

Supercharging TSRs

At the time of this writing, DOS is the most widely used operating system in the world. With an installation base exceeding ten million systems, it is an environment that cannot be ignored. The success of DOS is due, in part, to the fact that it does what it is supposed to do—provide a single-user, single-tasking operating system for a personal computer. However, the one design flaw in DOS is the difficulty it has in supporting RAM-resident pop-up programs. RAM-resident programs are generally called *TSRs* because they use the DOS *terminate-and-stay-resident* function to stay resident in RAM. As you know, a TSR program remains suspended in RAM awaiting execution. Generally, what activates a pop-up TSR is a special *hot key* (a single key, designed to trigger a sequence of events when pressed). When it is executed, it interrupts the process currently executing. When the TSR terminates, the interrupted program resumes execution.

Frankly, it appears that the concept of TSR programs was overlooked when DOS was created, because there is virtually no documented support for them. However, over the years several undocumented, yet apparently

Jack Blevins
Manager of New Product Development,
Central Data Corporation

I have known Jack Blevins for several years. By day, Jack is the manager of new product development for Central Data Corporation, a leading manufacturer of Multibus system cards. But, in his spare time Jack is the archetypal hacker. Jack's personal projects range from constructing his own floppy disk controller (complete with a DOS interface written in C) to computerized card games. From time to time Jack will call and tell me about his latest after-hours endeavor. On one occasion, he told me that he had written a TSR program, which he calls "Hotkey," that has several interesting features. Since I'm always on the lookout for new ideas, I asked to see it. I was so impressed by it that many of the concepts and details he developed in Hotkey form the basis for the TSR program developed in this chapter.

Jack came to C, as many have, through necessity. Several years ago, when he was working for Gould Computer Systems Division, his job was to port UNIX to Gould hardware—and learn C in the process. Jack recalls, "I don't think I will ever forget the day that the UNIX copyright message appeared on the console for the first time, or the day the first test program ran!" After working with the internals of UNIX (which are written in C and described by many programmers as quite elegant), Jack was hooked and has been a C programmer ever since.

Although bringing up UNIX is no small task, Jack's real contribution to C programming has come in quite a different area: board-level, embedded code. He pioneered the use of C for the production of on-board code. As you might know, most cards that plug into a computer's bus have very sophisticated real-time software controlling their operation. By eliminating the use of assembly code, Jack's team has been able to produce higher-quality, real-time software in less time.

Jack is fairly unique in the world of computers: he is both a hardware and a software engineer. Often these two endeavors are at odds with each other. However, for Jack, the marriage of these two worlds is completely natural.

As a programmer, Jack demands one thing above all else when it comes to a program: It must perform its appointed task consistently and without failure. As Jack says, "For a program to succeed, it must work flawlessly. If it does not, it becomes part of the problem rather than part of the solution." In fact, his definition of a great program hinges on reliability: "A great program performs its task unerringly," a simple, yet excellent definition.

Jack Blevins holds a B.S. (EECS) and an M.S. (EE) from the University of Illinois (Urbana/Champaign). He is a frequent contributor to various computer magazines and writes a bimonthly column for *Supermicro Magazine.*

stable, features of DOS have been discovered, which, when used correctly, can allow a TSR to coexist with DOS. Although the use of the undocumented DOS features has been more or less universally accepted when writing TSR programs, there are various ways these features can be applied and various ways a TSR can be activated. There is still much debate as to what constitutes a "proper" TSR.

This chapter discusses the two most common undocumented features of DOS and explains the basic technology that makes TSR programs possible. However, its main focus is the development of a full-featured TSR application that provides the following functions:

- a pop-up help system

- a file list utility

- a directory list utility

- a number base converter

The pop-up help system can be used to provide help screens for any topic area you like. This application would make an excellent addition to any application program, and the presentation of the help information could be tailored to fit your specific needs. The other applications show various important aspects common to many pop-up TSR applications.

In my book *C: Power User's Guide,* (Berkeley, Ca.: Osborne/McGraw-Hill, 1988) the topic of TSRs was introduced with some simple applications. In this chapter you will see how to use both DOS and BIOS calls in your TSR programs and how to access disk files from a TSR application. You can think of this as *supercharging* your TSR applications.

The code in this chapter is written for Turbo C. Although most of the examples in this book are intended to be reasonably compiler-independent, this is not possible in this chapter for two reasons. First, creating a TSR program in C requires some special, non-ANSI standard features. Because these features are not defined by ANSI, they differ widely between compilers. Second, not all compilers provide equal support for TSR programs. Both Turbo C and Microsoft C, among others, offer excellent support for TSRs, but there is not sufficient room in one chapter to show examples using all compilers. If you do not have Turbo C, you should be able to generalize to your compiler. For example, converting to Microsoft C is basically a process of changing a few function names. One reason that Turbo C is used here is that it is possible to fully implement a functional TSR without the use of any assembly code. Other compilers may require some assembly language modules.

This chapter assumes that you have a basic knowledge of both DOS and its companion, BIOS. (If you don't, you can still try the TSR program, but be careful how you change it.)

One last point: this chapter discusses several technical issues related to TSR programs. However, you do not need to understand fully all these issues to use or modify the TSR program presented here. As long as you follow the lead of this TSR, you should have no trouble in developing your own.

WHY TSRS ARE SO TROUBLESOME

TSR programs are troublesome because DOS is not *reentrant*. This means that if DOS is doing something for one program, it may not be able to suspend that operation, do something for another program, and return to finish the job for the first. If DOS were reentrant, then virtually all TSR problems would disappear.

Given that DOS is not reentrant, support for TSR programs could still have been included cleanly by having DOS set only one flag when it is safe to interrupt it, and clear the flag when it can't be interrupted. As you will see, DOS does implement something similar, but in this case similar is not close enough! In reality, for a TSR to know that DOS can safely be interrupted requires, minimally, the examination of a flag and the interception of an interrupt.

A third problem with DOS and TSRs involves disk activity. DOS transfers disk information in the DTA (disk transfer area) allocated to each program. The default DTA is part of the PSP (program segment prefix) all programs have. When a TSR interrupts another program, it inherits the PSP of the other program. Therefore, if it performs any disk I/O, it runs the risk of overwriting information that is already in the other program's DTA. Hence, it is necessary for any TSR that accesses the disk to use its own DTA, perform the disk function, and then reset the DTA of the original program.

Another, different sort of problem with TSRs occurs when two or more attempt to exist together. Although a TSR may work correctly with DOS, it may not work well with another TSR. One potential trouble spot is that the hot keys used to activate one may also be used by the other.

A final problem with TSRs can occur when the program currently executing bypasses DOS (and even BIOS) for many functions. For example, it is possible for a program to perform its own disk I/O, bypassing both the DOS high-level functions and the BIOS low-level functions. If this happens, and your TSR is activated and attempts to perform a disk access, a nasty crash could occur. The problem of programs circumventing DOS and BIOS is the main reason why no TSR can be considered 100 percent safe in all situations. From a practical point of view, however, a TSR that follows the procedures described in this chapter will be reasonably safe to use.

TSRS AND INTERRUPTS

Virtually all TSR programs are activated by an *interrupt*. For interactive TSRs, a keystroke interrupt is commonly used. Before we can continue our discussion of TSRs, it is important that you know how interrupts for the 8086 family of processors operate. (Henceforth, the term *8086* will be used to encompass the entire 8086 family, which includes the 8086, 8088, 80186, 80286, 80386, and the 80486.)

The 8086 provides for 256 vectored interrupts. A *vectored interrupt* is an interrupt that is directed to its *interrupt service routine* (ISR) indirectly through an address held in a special location. The 8086 sets aside the first 1024 (1K) bytes of memory to hold the addresses of ISRs. This region is usually referred to as the *interrupt vector table*. Each address includes a segment and an offset portion and thus needs four bytes. (For a discussion of the 8086's segment/offset addressing, see Appendix A.) Therefore, the address of the ISR associated with interrupt 0 is location 0000:0000, the address of the ISR associated with interrupt 1 is 0000:0004, the ISR address of interrupt 2 is 0000:0008, and so on. For example, assume that the location of the ISR used by interrupt 2 is at 1000:0800. This address then would be stored in the interrupt vector table beginning at 0000:0008 and each time interrupt 2 was activated, the routine at 1000:0800 would be called.

Of the 256 available interrupts, a few are unused by DOS. For example, interrupt 0x64 is unused in all versions of DOS through version 4.0. We will use this unallocated interrupt as a flag that will indicate whether the TSR is already loaded or not.

All interrupt service routines must be written as FAR procedures. In general, they must also terminate with a *return from interrupt* instruction (IRET). Further, all ISRs must preserve all registers. This means that at startup, the ISR must PUSH each register and, upon exit, POP each register.

All TSR programs must intercept one or more interrupts and provide their own interrupt service routines for these functions. You will see how this is done, later in this chapter.

THE **interrupt** TYPE MODIFIER

Turbo C (and many other DOS-based compilers) provides one crucial element of support for TSRs, the **interrupt** function type modifier. When you declare a function to be of type **interrupt** it tells the compiler to automatically preserve all registers and to terminate the function with an IRET instruction. For Turbo C, an **interrupt** function is passed all registers as parameters. However, you can simply declare **interrupt** functions as **void** if you don't need the values of the registers. The ISRs developed in this chapter, for example, don't need them.

If your compiler does not include the **interrupt** type, then you must resort to an assembly language routine (or at least an assembly language interface) to handle the entry point to your TSR.

A QUICK LOOK AT THE PSP

The program segment prefix is used by all supercharged TSRs for two main reasons. First, it provides the disk transfer area (DTA). This region is located 0x80 bytes from the start of the PSP. Second, it contains the segment address of the block of memory that holds a program's environmental information. This address is located 0x2C bytes from the start of the PSP.

The PSP is also important to TSRs because it contains several other program-specific pieces of information. For this reason, some TSR applications will need to reset the PSP when they pop up, and restore it when they terminate.

Turbo C (and many other DOS-compatible C compilers) supplies a built-in variable called **_psp** that is a **far** pointer to the start of a program's PSP. The TSR developed in this chapter makes use of this variable to access the contents of the PSP.

THE BASIC DESIGN OF AN INTERACTIVE TSR

All TSRs consist of three major parts: the initialization part, the ISRs used to support and activate the TSR, and the actual transient application. Let's see what each piece consists of.

TSR Initialization

When a TSR program first begins executing, it performs three basic functions. First, it initializes anything that the application portion requires. For example, in the TSR developed in this chapter, the initialization part of the TSR loads the help file used by the pop-up help system. Since TSR pop-up applications are supposed to be fast, it makes no sense for the pop-up help system to reload this file each time it is activated. The second function that the initialization part of the TSR provides is the rerouting of various vectored interrupt addresses so that they point to the new routines provided by the TSR. Finally, the initialization part of the TSR terminates with a call to DOS function 0x31 that terminates the program but keeps it resident. Many C compilers provide their own functions for this. Turbo C calls this the **keep( )** function. (Microsoft's parallel function is called **_dos_keep( )**.) This function simply calls DOS function 0x31. The prototype for the **keep( )** function is shown here:

void keep(unsigned char status, unsigned mem_size);

The value of *status* is returned to DOS. The amount of RAM to allocate to the TSR is specified in paragraphs by *mem_size*. (A paragraph is 16 bytes.) If your compiler does not provide a function like **keep( )**, you can execute DOS function 0x31 with the return code in AL, and the size of the program (in paragraphs) in DX. (Most DOS-based compilers provide some mechanism to access the various DOS functions.)

Determining the exact amount of RAM to set aside for your TSR program can be tricky. Generally, there will be some instructions given with your compiler. Keep in mind that the amount of memory needed by your application is greater than the size of its .EXE file. For the application developed in this chapter, 64K is set aside. The reason this figure is used is that it should work for a TSR created by virtually any compiler.

If you cannot find instructions on how to compute the amount of RAM needed by your TSR, add the size of all the global data to the size of the .EXE file. Round up a few thousand bytes, and you should be safe. (If your TSR doesn't seem to run correctly, try increasing the amount of RAM you give it.)

The ISRs

Most pop-up TSRs are activated by pressing a special hot key. The way this hot key is intercepted is by replacing the keyboard input interrupt with one of your own that watches for this key. Since the TSR must intercept the hot key at the lowest level, it must replace the BIOS keyboard interrupt, which is interrupt 9, with its own, saving the address of the original interrupt 9 ISR.

Each time a key is pressed on the keyboard, interrupt 9 is generated. This causes your keyboard ISR to be called. The first thing your ISR must do is call the original keyboard input service. Next, your ISR must determine if the key that was pressed is the hot key. If so, the pop-up TSR application must be activated, provided that it is safe to do so. (How to determine whether it is safe to activate a TSR will be discussed shortly.) The hot key must also be removed from the input queue so that it does not become input to the interrupted application.

In addition to the keyboard interrupt, your TSRs will need to provide at least one other ISR, which is used to determine if DOS is safe to interrupt. Also, most interactive TSRs, including the one developed in this chapter, will need to intercept the timer interrupt (interrupt 8) to aid in the activation of the TSR. Finally, in some situations you may need to monitor the activity in a few other interrupts.

The Pop-Up Application

Once you have determined that DOS is safe to interrupt, you can activate the pop-up application. However, the pop-up application is still not free to execute like a normal program for several reasons. First, since the TSR is popping up, possibly during the execution of another application, it must provide a mechanism for saving the current contents of the screen and restoring them when the pop-up is terminated. Second, in general, the pop-up application cannot use C's dynamic allocation functions, such as **malloc( )**. This implies that functions like **printf( )** and **fopen( )** cannot be used, since they call **malloc( )** in the performance of their tasks. (Some compilers may differ in this regard, but this is generally true.) Hence, you will need to be careful about which standard C functions you use.

Although it is not strictly required, most pop-up TSRs operate through a *window* — that is, a portion of the screen. One advantage of this is that the user can still see part of the interrupted application. Since many TSRs are designed to provide support for other applications, this could be an important feature. Also, since the amount of memory and time it takes to save and restore a screen is proportional to the size of the screen saved, it is desirable to use a small window rather than the entire screen. Therefore, most pop-up TSRs must include windowing software to support their screen I/O. Even here, however, you may not be able to use "off the shelf" window routines because of the memory allocation problem. In addition, you will probably want the I/O routines to operate directly on the video RAM in order to obtain the fastest possible screen refreshes.

The TSR developed here includes a complete set of windowing routines. Although sufficient discussion is presented in this chapter to fully utilize these functions, further description of their derivation can be found in *C: Power User's Guide,* along with many additional functions which you might find helpful in developing your own TSRs.

WHEN IS DOS SAFE TO INTERRUPT?

Put simply, DOS is safe to interrupt when it isn't doing anything very important! For example, you can interrupt DOS when it is simply displaying the command prompt, but you shouldn't interrupt DOS when it is performing a disk access or writing to the screen. The problem is that there are no documented DOS features that allow you to determine when DOS is idle. Over the years, however, programmers have discovered two very important, yet undocumented, DOS functions that allow TSRs to know (at least most of the time) when DOS is safe to interrupt. These two features were evidently implemented to support the PRINT command, which provides background printing. I don't know why Microsoft chose not to document these features . Perhaps they simply didn't seem important at the time. Let's look at these two features now.

The DOS-Idle Interrupt

Whenever DOS is waiting for user input it essentially just loops. Part of this loop executes an interrupt 0x28 instruction, which has come to be known as the *DOS-idle* interrupt. Interrupt 0x28 is called repeatedly by the first 12 DOS functions. (These functions provide for character I/O.) Therefore, each time interrupt 0x28 is executed, it means that DOS is safe to interrupt. Hence, your TSR should intercept interrupt 0x28 and use it to pop up the TSR if the hot key has been pressed. However, the trouble is that DOS only executes interrupt 0x28 when it is using one of the character I/O functions. This means that some other mechanism must be used to know when DOS is safe when these functions are not being called. (Remember, many high-performance software packages bypass DOS and go directly to BIOS for console I/O, which means that interrupt 0x28 will never be called while these packages execute.) This trouble leads us to the second undocumented DOS feature: the *DOS-active flag*.

The DOS-Active Flag

When DOS is active, it sets a byte inside of itself to 1; when it becomes inactive, it resets this byte to 0. This byte is often called the DOS-active flag or sometimes the *inDOS* flag. The location of this flag can only be determined by using a second undocumented DOS function: 0x34. This function returns the segment of the DOS-active flag in the ES register and the offset in the BX registers. Before your TSR program pops up, it must interrogate the value of this flag. If it is 1, your TSR should not pop up. Instead, it must wait until this flag is 0.

The reason that the state of the DOS-active flag is insufficient in itself to indicate when a TSR can run is that it is set to 1 when the DOS prompt is displayed. (After all, DOS is active when displaying its prompt.) This is the reason that you must monitor the interrupt 0x28 as well.

THE TIMER INTERRUPT

As you will see, the *timer interrupt* is used to help activate the TSR developed in this chapter. On IBM PCs and compatibles, the system clock causes interrupt 8 to be executed every 18.2 seconds. We will use this interrupt to check the state of DOS. When DOS is safe, and a hot key has been pressed, the TSR will pop up.

TSRS AND GRAPHICS MODES

Although there is no fundamental reason why you cannot use pop-up TSR programs when the computer is in a graphics mode, it may be better (and is easier) to wait until the computer is in a text mode. The reasons for this are as follows. First, there are only a few text modes. The most common are video mode 2 (80-column black and white), mode 3 (80-column color text), and mode 7 (80-column monochrome). However, there are several different graphics modes. Further, in the 80-column text modes, 4,000 bytes of memory are required to hold the contents of the screen, no matter which 80-column mode is being used. This means that when the TSR is activated, in the worst case, your pop-up application need supply a buffer of only 4,000 bytes to save the entire text screen. Each graphics mode, however, requires substantially more memory; different graphics modes require differing amounts of RAM to hold an entire screen. Therefore, to allow a pop-up in a graphics mode means that your TSR will have to allocate enough memory to hold the worst case storage requirements for the screen, which can be as large as 64K. Also, the time it takes to store and restore the old screen will be noticeably longer to the user in the higher resolution graphics modes. For these reasons, the TSR examples developed in this chapter will pop up only when the computer is in a text mode. However, keep in mind that this is not a fundamental limitation of TSRs.

ACCESSING THE VIDEO RAM

For a TSR application to pop up quickly enough to satisfy the desires of most users, it should completely bypass all DOS and BIOS video functions, and, instead, write its output directly to the video RAM. Doing this allows characters to be put on the screen very quickly. Let's see what this involves.

The characters that are displayed on the screen are held in RAM reserved on the display adapters. The location of the monochrome memory is B000:0000 and the CGA/EGA/VGA video RAM starts at B800:0000. Although the CGA, EGA, and VGA function differently in some modes, they are the same in mode 2 or 3.

Each character displayed on the screen requires two adjacent bytes of video memory. The first byte holds the actual character, the second holds its *screen attribute*. For color adapters the attribute byte is interpreted as shown in Table 3-1. If you have a CGA, EGA, or VGA the default mode is 3, and the characters are displayed with an attribute byte value of 7. This turns the three foreground colors on, producing white. To produce reverse video, the foreground bits are turned off and the three background bits are turned on, producing a value of 70H.

The monochrome adapter recognizes the blinking and intensity bits. Fortunately, it is designed to interpret an attribute of 7 as normal and 70H as reverse video. Also, the value 1 produces underlined characters.

Each adapter actually has four times as much memory as it needs to display text in 80-column mode. The reason for this is twofold. First, the extra memory is needed for graphics (except in the monochrome adapter, of course). The second is to allow multiple screens to be held in RAM and then simply switched in when needed. Each region of memory is called a *video page* and the effect of switching the active video page is quite

---

Table 3-1

The Text Video Attribute Byte

Bit	Binary Value	Meaning When Set
0	1	blue foreground
1	2	green foreground
2	4	red foreground
3	8	low intensity
4	16	blue background
5	32	green background
6	64	red background
7	128	blinking character

dramatic. By default, page 0 is used when DOS initializes, and virtually all applications use page 0. For this reason it will be used in the routines in this chapter. However, you can use other pages if you desire.

To determine the location of the video RAM, you must know what video mode is currently in use. (Remember, the monochrome adapter has its video RAM at B000:0000, while the others have theirs at B800:0000.) Fortunately, there is an easy way to do this. The ROM-BIOS interrupt 16, function 15, returns the current video mode. As was stated earlier, the routines developed in this chapter require that the mode be either 2, 3, or 7. Modes 2 and 3 can only be used by the CGA, EGA, and VGA, and they cannot use mode 7: only the monochrome adapter can. Therefore, if the current video mode is 7, then there is a monochrome adapter in use; otherwise, it is either a CGA, EGA, or VGA. Once the video mode is known, your program can set a global variable equal to the starting point of the appropriate location.

Once a pointer to the start of the video RAM has been obtained, it is a simple matter to use it to read or write characters to or from the video RAM. Remember, the video memory requires two bytes for each character, one for the character itself and one for its attribute. Also, the character byte is first and the attribute is second. Therefore, it takes 160 bytes for each line on the screen. Hence, to find the address of a specific character position, you must use this formula:

address = address of adapter + X*160 + Y*2

SOME SPECIAL TURBO C FUNCTIONS

The TSR program uses some special Turbo C-specific functions, although many compilers have their own equivalents. These functions are **int86( )**, **int86x( )**, **getvect( )**, **setvect( )**, and **freemem( )**. Before continuing, a short discussion of these will help avoid confusion.

The **int86( )** function generates a software interrupt. It takes this general form:

```
int int86(int num, /* the interrupt number */
        union REGS *inregs, /* the input register values */
        union REGS *outregs /* the output register values */
)
```

The interrupt to generate is specified by *num*. You can specify the values of the registers at the time of the interrupt using *inregs*. Upon return, *outregs* will hold the values of the registers as set by the ISR that handles the interrupt. The return value of **int86( )** is the value of the AX register.

The type **REGS** is supplied in the header DOS.H. The one shown here is defined by Turbo C; however, it is similar to the one defined by Microsoft C and other compilers.

```
/*
        Copyright (c) Borland International Inc. 1987
        All Rights Reserved.
*/

struct WORDREGS
        {
        unsigned int    ax, bx, cx, dx, si, di, cflag;
        };

struct BYTEREGS
        {
        unsigned char   al, ah, bl, bh, cl, ch, dl, dh;
        };

union   REGS    {
        struct  WORDREGS x;
        struct  BYTEREGS h;
        };
```

As you can see, **REGS** is a union of two structures. Using the **WORD-REGS** structure allows you to access the registers of the CPU as 16-bit quantities. **BYTEREGS** gives you access to the individual 8-bit registers. For example, to access interrupt number 16, function number 5, you would use this code sequence:

```
union REGS in, out;

in.h.ah = 5;
int86(16, &in, &out);
```

A variation of **int86( )** is **int86x( )**, which also loads the values of the segment registers into a structure of type **SREGS,** which is its third argument.

The **getvect( )** and **setvect( )** functions are used to read and set, respectively, an address in the interrupt vector table given the number of the interrupt. Their prototypes are

void interrupt *getvect(int int_num);

void setvect(int int_num, void interrupt (*ISR)( ));

Here, *ISR* is a pointer to the new interrupt service routine. Its address will be installed in *int_num*'s vector table location.

For example, to return the address of the ISR that is used by interrupt 5, use this statement:

```
addr = getvect(5);
```

To set interrupt 5's ISR to the address of a function called **newint5( )**, use this statement:

```
setvect(5, newint5);
```

The **freemem( )** function is used to free memory previously allocated by DOS. This function translates to a call to DOS, function 0x49. Its only argument is the segment of the memory to free.

CREATING A TSR APPLICATION

Now that the theoretical groundwork has been laid, it is time to develop an actual, working example. The example not only provides real TSR applications that you can use, but also serves as a skeleton from which you may construct your own TSR programs. From this point on, the TSR example will be referred to as the *SCTSR* (Supercharged TSR).

Initializing the SCTSR

Most of the initialization portion of the SCTSR is contained in **main( )**, shown here. Take a close look at it now.

```c
main()
{
  union REGS r;
  struct SREGS s;

  if(!load_help()) {  /* load the help file */
    /* You may want to take other action here. */
    exit(1);
  }

  /* see if already loaded */
  old_int64 = getvect(0x64); /* unused interrupt */
  if(!old_int64) setvect(0x64, 1); /* set a flag */
  else {
    printf("TSR already loaded");
    exit(0);
  }

  /* obtain the dos_active flag address */
  r.h.ah = 0x34;
  int86x(0x21, &r, &r, &s);
  dos_active = MK_FP(s.es, r.x.bx);

  /* get old ISR addresses */
  old_key = getvect(9); /* keystroke int */
  old_int28 = getvect(0x28);  /* int 28 */
  old_int8 = getvect(8);  /* timer interrupt */

  /* re-route interrupt vectors to our handlers */
  setvect(9, tsr_keystroke);
  setvect(0x28, dos_idle);
  setvect(8, new_int8);

  printf("SC-TSR installed\n");
  printf("F1: help    F2: file list    F3: directory");
  printf("    F4: base converter\n");

  key = 0;
  set_vid_mem();  /* get address of video memory */

  /* initialize all windows */
  make_tsrwindow(0, " Help ('quit' to exit, 'topics' for topics) ",
              0, 0, 79, 24, BORDER);
```

```
make_tsrwindow(1, " File Lister ", 0, 0, 79, 16, BORDER);
make_tsrwindow(2, " Directory ", 0, 0, 79, 12, BORDER);
make_tsrwindow(3, " Base Converter ", 0, 0, 50, 3, BORDER);

keep(0, 4000); /* terminate and stay resident */
}
```

The first thing that **main( )** does is to call the **load_help( )** function. This function reads in a help file of your own creation and sets up various pointers into it. This function will be discussed when the pop-up help system is discussed. However, one point is important and must be made now: since the loading of the help file can fail (for example, it may not be in the current directory), it must be performed before any other initialization functions are performed. For example, you should not reset an interrupt vector until all tasks that could possibly fail have been performed. You cannot "half-install" a TSR!

The next few lines of code are there to prevent the SCTSR from being loaded more than once. Although it is not technically wrong to load a TSR more than once, it is not a good idea because it uses up the system's memory. As mentioned, interrupt 0x64 is not used for any other purpose, so we can use the memory reserved for it in the interrupt vector table as a flag. Before the SCTSR redirects any interrupts it checks the value of interrupt 0x64's address vector. If this vector is 0, then the SCTSR assumes that this is the first time it is being loaded and it sets this value to 1. However, if it finds this vector to be set to 1, then it assumes that the SCTSR is already loaded and exits before redirecting any interrupts. (Remember, if the program exits after redirecting the interrupt vectors but before calling DOS function 0x49 to stay resident, then each time a redirected interrupt is executing, it will be jumping into nowhere!)

The **main( )** function next determines the location of the DOS-active flag using a call to DOS function 0x34. Once the values of ES and BX have been loaded, a **far** pointer is constructed using Turbo C's **MK_PF( )** function. This pointer is then stored in the DOS-active flag.

Next, the location of the original ISRs for interrupts 8, 9, and 0x28 are saved using Turbo C's **getvect( )** function. The substitute ISRs will use these addresses to call the original ones. When you write a TSR, you must make sure that you link your replacement ISR with the original ones because, as is the case with the keyboard interrupt and timer interrupts, the original ISRs may provide a crucial service. Also, if there is more than one TSR present in the system, you must make sure that you provide an unbroken chain between them. Finally, if you deactivate the TSR, you must replace the addresses of your ISRs with the original ones.

Once the addresses of the original ISRs for interrupts 8, 9, and 0x28 have been saved, the addresses of our new routines can be installed using Turbo C's **setvect( )** function. The name of the new keyboard function is **tsr_keystroke( )**, the new timer function is called **new_int8( )**, and the new interrupt 0x28 handler is called **dos_idle( )**. Once this step has been accomplished, the new interrupt handlers are, in fact, active, so you must make sure that any initialization necessary to their functioning has been performed prior to this point.

In Turbo C, the pointers to the original ISRs are declared as follows:

```
void interrupt (*old_int28)();
void interrupt (*old_key)();
void interuupt (*old_int8());
```

If you are using a different compiler, a somewhat different syntax may be required.

The next line of code initializes the value of the global variable **key**, which is used to pass key codes to the **dos_idle( )** and **new_int8( )** functions. (You will see it in action shortly.) After that, the function **set_vid_mem( )** is called to set the global **far** pointer **vid_mem** to point to the start of the video memory used for text output. This function is shown here along with the **video_mode( )** function.

```
/* Set the vid_mem pointer to the start of video
   memory.
*/
void set_vid_mem(void)
{
  int vmode;

  vmode = video_mode();
  if((vmode!=2) && (vmode!=3) && (vmode!=7)) {
    printf("video must be in 80 column text mode");
    exit(1);
  }
  /* set proper address of video RAM */
  if(vmode==7) vid_mem = (char far *) MK_FP(0xB000, 0000);
  else vid_mem = (char far *) MK_FP(0xB800, 0000);
```

```
}

/* Returns the current video mode. */
video_mode(void)
{
  union REGS r;

  r.h.ah = 15;  /* get video mode */
  return int86(0x10, &r, &r) & 255;
}
```

The SCTSR has four distinct pop-up functions; hence, the next section of code in **main( )** initializes four distinct windows. The operation of **make_tsrwindow( )** will be discussed later in this chapter. Although the windowing system allows you to create windows "on the fly," in the interest of maintaining a snappy response to a pop-up request, all windows are created during initialization.

Finally, the SCTSR terminates with a call to **keep( )**, which is Turbo C's function that executes the DOS terminate-and-stay-resident function. After this, control returns to the command prompt.

The **tsr_keystroke( )** ISR

The **tsr_keystroke( )** function is shown here:

```
/* This is the function that intercepts the keystroke
   interrupt (int 9). */
void interrupt tsr_keystroke(void)
{
  int far *t2 = (int far *) 1050;   /* address head pointer */
  char far *t = (char far *) 1050; /* address head pointer */

  (*old_key)();   /* first, call old keystroke ISR */

  if(*t != *(t+2)) {/* if not empty */
    t += *t-30+5; /* advance to the character position */
    if(*t>=59 && *t <=63) {
      switch(*t) {  /* see what is in scan code */
        case 59:  /* F1 - help */
          key = 1;
```

```
      break;
    case 60:  /* F2 - file list */
      key = 2;
      break;
    case 61:  /* F3 - directory */
      key = 3;
      break;
    case 62:  /* F4 - dec to hex */
      key = 4;
      break;
    case 63: /* F5 - detache tsr */
      key = 5;
      break;
  }
  *(t2+1) = *t2;  /* zero buffer */
    }
  }
}
```

The first thing the function does is call the original keyboard ISR. The reason for this is easy to understand: the original keyboard ISR actually reads the key from the keyboard and puts it into the keyboard buffer. There is no reason for our replacement ISR to perform these functions. Once the keystroke is in the buffer, the **tsr_keystroke( )** function takes over and determines if a hot key has been hit. Although not technically necessary, this function dos not use any BIOS or DOS functions to read the key from the buffer. Instead, it directly interrogates the keyboard buffer. How and why it does this is the subject of the next section.

The Keystroke Character Buffer

As you know, standard versions of DOS buffer up to 15 characters entered at the keyboard, which allows typeahead. Each time a key is pressed, an interrupt 9 is generated. The keystroke input ISR reads the character from the port and places it in the buffer. When you call a DOS or BIOS keyboard character input function, only the contents of the buffer are examined, not the actual port. Therefore, it is possible for your routines to examine directly the contents of the keystroke buffer in a fashion similar to the BIOS and DOS routines, thus allowing your TSR entry function to determine whether a hot key has been pressed.

The keystroke input buffer is located at 0000:041E (1054 in decimal). Because all keystrokes generate a 16-bit scan code, 30 bytes are needed for the 15 characters. However, 32 bytes are actually used because the scan code for the carriage return key is automatically appended to the end of the buffer.

The buffer is organized as a circular queue, which is accessed through a head pointer and a tail pointer. The head pointer points to the character last typed. The tail pointer points to the next character to be returned by an input request by DOS or BIOS. The head pointer is stored at location 0000:041A (1050 in decimal) and the tail pointer at 0000:041C (1052 in decimal). The values of the head and tail pointers are actually indexes into the queue, which means that their values are the index of the current position plus 30. (This is because of the way the 8086 processes indirect addressing.) The values of the head and tail pointers are the same when the queue is empty.

The reason that **tsr_keystroke( )** examines the keyboard buffer and does not call one of the standard input functions is twofold. First, it is faster to examine the key buffer directly than it is to use an operating system call. If a computer has several TSRs running in it, sluggish response could result. Second, this approach gives you the ability to modify the contents of the key buffer. Although not needed by the SCTSR, changing the contents of the buffer may be valuable to other applications.

The SCTSR uses the function keys F1 through F5 for its hot keys. You will probably want to change these to something like ALT-F1 through ALT-F9 for actual use so that you don't lose the DOS command line editing functions associated with these keys. For testing and experimentation, however, it is simply easier to press one key than two! The scan code for F1 is 59, for F2 is 60, and so on. These values are encoded into the global variable **key** beginning with 1. The reason for encoding the key rather than using its scan code is that you can change the hot key by changing only one line of code.

If a hot key has been pressed, you will want to remove it from the keystroke buffer. The fastest way to do this is to set the head pointer equal to the tail pointer, as is done in **tsr_keystroke( )**.

Notice one important point about **tsr_keystroke( )**: it does not, itself, actually activate the TSR. The reason for this is simple: some application software cannot be interrupted during the keystroke interrupt. For example, attempting to activate a TSR from the keystroke interrupt while the

Turbo C integrated environment is active can lead to a system crash. (Frankly, I'm not sure why this should be the case, but I have proved it to myself several times!) This is the reason that the timer interrupt is used to activate the TSR during those times when the DOS-idle interrupt is not being called.

The **new _ int8( )** Interrupt

The function that intercepts the timer interrupt is quite simple. First, it calls the old timer routine. This is important; failing to call the original timer ISR will cause your system to crash. Next, **new _ int8( )** checks to see if DOS is idle, if **busy** is cleared, and if a hot key is waiting in **key**. If these conditions have been met, then the TSR is popped up by calling **activate _ sctsr( )**.

The global variable **busy** is used to ensure that the TSR is not activated while it is already active. As stated earlier, DOS is not reentrant. Further, the stack-switching scheme is not reentrant, so a second activation while the first activation of the TSR is still executing will crash the system and must be prevented. The value of **busy** is set by **activate _ sctsr( )** when the TSR is activated and cleared upon exit. In this way, secondary activations are prevented.

The **new _ int8( )** interrupt is shown here along with the global variable **busy**.

```
/* busy is set to 1 when the program is active, 0 otherwise */
char busy = 0;

/* New interrupt 8. */
void interrupt new_int8(void)
{
  (*old_int8)();
  if(!*dos_active && !busy && key)
      activate_sctsr();
}
```

The **dos _ idle( )** ISR

The **dos _ idle( )** ISR is virtually the same as **new _ int8( )**. It first calls the original interrupt 0x28 ISR and then, if **busy** is cleared and a hot key is waiting, the TSR is popped up. The **dos _ idle( )** function is shown here.

```
/* This function intercepts int 0x28  (the dos-idle
   interrupt).
*/
void interrupt dos_idle(void)
{
  (*old_int28)();  /* call old int 0x28 ISR */
  if(!busy && key) activate_sctsr();
}
```

The **activate _ sctsr( )** Function

The entry point to the TSR utilities is through **activate _ sctsr( )**. This
function calls the function associated with the hot key pressed. However,
before this is done, **activate _ sctsr( )** has one very important job: it must
reset the stack to one defined by the TSR. The reason for this is very
simple. When an interrupt is executed, DOS automatically switches to one
of its very small internal stacks. This internal stack is just barely large
enough to hold the two **far** pointers declared in **tsr _ keystroke( )** plus the
overhead created by the interrupt. It is far too small to support the stack
requirements of the TSR applications. For this reason, **activate _ sctsr( )**
must reassign the stack upon entry and then reset it upon exit. This
process once again requires the use of Turbo C's built-in register variables.
If your compiler does not include this feature, then you must use some
assembly code to accomplish the stack switching. The SCTSR stack is held
in an unsigned character array called **stack** which is 0x2000 bytes long.
The **activate _ sctsr( )** function is shown here:

```
/* Pop up the SCTSR. */
void activate_sctsr(void)
{
  /* setup TSR stack */
  disable();  /* disable interrupts */
    ss = _SS;
    sp = _SP;
    _SS = _DS;
    _SP = (unsigned) &stack[STK_SIZE-2];
  enable();   /* enable interrupts */

  /* check video mode - don't popup if not in
     an 80-column text mode
```

```
*/
video = video_mode();
if(!busy && (video==7 || video==3 || video==2)) {
  busy = !busy;  /* don't allow a second activation */
  switch(key) {
    case 1: do_help();
      break;
    case 2: do_filelist();
      break;
    case 3: dirlist();
      break;
    case 4: dectohex();
      break;
  }
  busy = !busy;
}
if(key==5){ /* deactivating TSR */
  cursor_pos();   /* get current cursor position */
  write_string(old_col, old_row, "SC-TSR deactivated",
            NORM_VID);
}

/* restore old stack */
disable();
  _SP = sp;
  _SS = ss;
enable();

if(key==5) {  /* reset old ISR routines and free memory */
  setvect(8, old_int8);
  setvect(9, old_key);
  setvect(0x28, old_int28);
  setvect(0x64, old_int64);
  freemem(_psp);  /* free program block */
} else  key = 0;
}
```

Notice that the stack switching is preceded by a call to **disable( )**. This Turbo C function disables interrupts. Until the entire stack switch is accomplished, no interrupts may occur. If they do, the stack may not be set correctly. Once the stack has been changed, interrupts are enabled using a call to **enable( )**. If your compiler does not have **disable( )** and **enable( )**, you will need to use their assembly language code equivalent instructions: CLI and STI.

Next, **activate_sctsr( )** finds out which video mode is currently in use. This value will be used to make sure that the TSR is not activated in a graphics mode.

Assuming the video mode is correct and the TSR is not currently active, the next thing that **activate_sctsr( )** does is to call the function associated with the hot key. The value of **key** will be zero unless a hot key has been pressed. If the F5 key has been pressed, the TSR is deactivated. The deactivation sequence is a little tricky because the stack must be restored to its original value before the original interrupt routines are restored. However, the deactivation message must be displayed prior to the stack change. This is why there are two comparisons for **key==5**.

The function **cursor_pos( )** assigns to the global variables **old_col** and **old_row** the current value of the cursor. These values are then used by **write_string( )** to output a string to the console. The **write_string( )** function is a low-level routine included in the windowing system.

At the end of **activate_sctsr( )**, the value of **key** is reset to 0.

A QUICK TOUR OF THE WINDOWING SYSTEM

Before looking at the SCTSR's applications, a short discussion of its windowing system is necessary.

The windowing functions used by the SCTSR were developed in my book *C: Power User's Guide* over the course of three chapters. They are used by the TSR applications to provide a safe and rapid method of displaying information on the screen. They also provide functions for saving and restoring the original screen. It is far beyond the scope of this chapter to discuss in detail the derivation or operation of the window functions. However, you should have no trouble understanding them. The quick sketch given here will be sufficient for you to use them; plus, the source code to the window functions is fully documented.

The windowing system is based upon a structure of type **window_frame**. An array of these structures, called **frame**, holds the information about each window in the system. The **window_frame** structure is shown on the next page.

```
struct window_frame {
  int startx, endx, starty, endy; /* corners of window */
  int curx, cury; /* current cursor position in window */
  unsigned char *p; /* pointer to buffer */
  char *header; /* header message */
  int border; /* border on/off */
  int active; /* on screen yes/no */
} frame[MAX_FRAME];
```

The value for the macro **MAX_FRAME** must be large enough to hold the number of windows defined by the system. For the SCTSR this value is 4.

Before a window can be used, it must be defined using a call to **make_tsrwindow( )**. The prototype for the **make_tsrwindow( )** function is shown here:

```
make_tsrwindow(
               int num, /* window number */
               char *header, /* header text */
               int startx, int starty, /* upper left corner */
               int endx, int endy, /* lower right corner */
               int border /* no border if 0 */
)
```

All windows are accessed via their window number specified in *num*. A window's size is defined by its dimensions, and no text can be written outside of a window. If you like, you can give a window a title by specifying it as a string in the **header** field. To give a window a border, make sure that **border** is non-zero. In the windowing system, the upper left corner is location 0, 0.

Keep in mind that **make_tsrwindow( )** only defines a window. Before you can output to a window, you must call **tsrwindow( )** with the number of the window you wish to activate. The **tsrwindow( )** function automatically saves the portion of the screen used by the window into a global character array called **wp**. (The SCTSR only allows one window to be active at a time. If more than one were to be active, then multiple video buffers would be required.) To remove a window and restore the original contents of the screen, use **deactivate( )**. This function takes as its only argument the number of the window that is being removed.

The remainder of the window functions provide support for console I/O. For example, **tsrwindow_gets( )** inputs a string in the specified window. To position the cursor at a specific location within a window, use the **tsrwindow_xy( )** function. All cursor position requests are relative to the window, not the screen. Keep in mind one simple rule: All of the functions that begin with **tsrwindow** take as their first argument the number of the window being used. After reading about the TSR applications, you should have no trouble using the windowing system.

THE SCTSR POP-UP APPLICATIONS

The SCTSR has four pop-up applications: the generic help system, a file list function, a directory list function, and a hexadecimal-to-decimal, decimal-to-hexadecimal number base converter. Let's look at each in turn.

The Help System

Of the four pop-up applications, perhaps the most interesting from a commercial point of view is the help system, which is activated by pressing F1. Two things make the help system exciting. First, it can be used to provide whatever type of help is relevant to your needs, because it is driven by a help file, which is loaded when the SCTSR initializes. For example, if you provide an accounting package for veterinarians, then you could create a custom, pop-up help system tailored specifically for your software. The second thing that makes the help system exciting is that it can read the word on the screen at the current cursor position when it activates and automatically provide help about that topic. For example, if the DOS command COPY was in the help database, then the user could simply type COPY at the command line and press F1, causing the help information about COPY to appear. You will see how this is accomplished shortly.

Before you can look at the functions that support the help system, you need to know how the help file is organized. As the program is written, the help file must be called TSRHELP.DAT (although you can change this if you like). The help file required by the help system is a straight ASCII file. The only restrictions are that the name of each help topic consists of one word, that each topic is preceded by a ^ (caret), and that there is at least one space or newline after the topic and the help information related to that topic. For example, the fragment in Figure 3-1 shows part of a help file for DOS. In this fragment, the topics are APPEND, ASSIGN, ATTRIB, BACKUP, and BREAK because they are the words preceded by a ^.

Figure 3-1

Sample help file for DOS

```
^APPEND
The external APPEND command is used to join one directory to
another.  If directory B is joined to A, it will appear to
the  user that directory A contains all of A's and B's
files.  APPEND is executed the first time using one of the
following two forms:

     APPEND path1[;path2;..pathN]

or

     APPEND [/X] [/E]

 The first form uses APPEND's default method of operation,
in  which files with extensions of .EXE, .COM, or .BAT are
not appended.  The second form only applies when APPEND is
first installed.

^ASSIGN
The external ASSIGN command is used to redirect
input/output (I/O operations) from one disk drive to
another. It takes the general form

     ASSIGN drive1=drive2 [drive3=drive4 ...]

For example, to reverse the assignments of drives A and B,
you could use the following command:

ASSIGN A=B B=A

Now all I/O operations for A will go to B, and all I/O
operations for B will be redirected to A.
```

Figure 3-1 continued

Sample help file for DOS

^ATTRIB
The external ATTRIB command is used to set or examine the
archive and read-only file attributes. It takes the
general form

        ATTRIB [+R] [-R] [+A] [-A] [file-name] [/S]

where file-name is the name of the file(s) that will have its
attributes set or examined. Wildcard characters are
allowed. +R turns on the read-only attribute, while -R
turns it off. The +A turns on the archive attribute, while
-A turns it off. If one of these is not present, the
current state of the file attributes is displayed. The /S
option tells ATTRIB to process files in the current
directory and any subdirectories.

^BACKUP
The external BACKUP command is used primarily to back up the
contents of a fixed disk by copying it to several floppy
diskettes. Used in this way, it takes the general form

        BACKUP source-drive[file-name] target-drive [/A] [/D:date]
                [/F] [/L] [/M] [/S] [/T:time]

The file-name may include wildcard characters.

^BREAK
The internal BREAK command tells DOS to check more
frequently for the CTRL-BREAK key combination, which is
used to cancel commands. It takes the general form

        BREAK [ON]
or
        BREAK [OFF]

Though setting BREAK to ON may seem tempting, it is usually
not a good idea because it slows down the execution of all
commands and programs.

The **main( )** function loads the help file via a call to **load _ help( )**, which is shown here, along with some necessary global data.

```
#define HELP_SIZE 75
#define KEY        0
#define MSG        1
#define HELP_BUF_SIZE 32000

char *help_index[HELP_SIZE][2]; /* indexes the help file */
char help_buf[HELP_BUF_SIZE];   /* holds the help file */

/* Load the help file. This file must be called
   TSRHELP.DAT.   See text for details.
*/
load_help(void)
{
  FILE *fp;
  char *p, ch;
  int i;

  p = help_buf;

  if((fp = fopen("TSRHELP.DAT", "r"))==NULL) {
    printf("cannot open TSRHELP.DAT");
    return 0;
  }

  ch = getc(fp);
  for(i=0; i<HELP_SIZE && !feof(fp); i++) {
    if(ch != '^') {
      printf("TSRHELP.DAT corrupted - use backup");
      fclose(fp);
      return 0;
    }
    if(p > help_buf+HELP_BUF_SIZE) {
      printf("Help file too big");
      fclose(fp);
      return 0;
    }

    help_index[i][KEY] = p;   /* pointer to keywords */

    while((*p=tolower(getc(fp)))!='\n') p++;   /* read keyword */
    *p = '\0'; /* null terminate the keyword */
```

```
    p++;

    help_index[i][MSG] = p;   /* pointer to help msg */

    while((*p=getc(fp))!='^' && !feof(fp)) p++; /* read msg */
    ch = *p;
    *p = '\0'; /* null terminate the message */
    p++;
  }
  fclose(fp);
  return 1;
}
```

This function reads TSRHELP.DAT into the global character array called **help_buf**. While the file is being read, a two-dimensional array of character pointers called **help_index** is initialized as follows. Index 0 of the first dimension points to the topic; index 1 points to the start of the message that describes that topic. Once the file has been read, the location of all topics and their associated help information is recorded in **help_index**.

The pop-up help application is provided by the **do_help( )** function, shown here:

```
/* This is the help function.  (See text for
   details.)
*/
void do_help(void)
{
  char str[80];
  int i;

  /* See if a topic is located at the current cursor
     position. */
  read_at_cursor(str);
  cursor_pos();  /* save old cursor coordinates */

  tsrwindow(0); /* activate window */
  tsrwindow_xy(0, 1, 1);
  tsrwindow_puts(0, "Topic: ");
  if(*str) tsrwindow_puts(0, str);
  for(;;) {
```

```
    if(!strcmp("quit", str)) break;
    tsrwindow_xy(0, 1, 3);

    if(!strcmp("topics", str))
      /* show help topics */
      for(i=0; help_index[i][KEY]; i++) {
        if(!(i%6)) tsrwindow_puts(0, "\n");
        tsrwindow_puts(0, help_index[i][KEY]);
        tsrwindow_puts(0, "  ");
      }
    else {
      for(i=0; help_index[i][KEY]; i++)
        /* lookup topic and display message if found */
        if(!strcmp(help_index[i][KEY], str)) {
          tsrwindow_puts(0, help_index[i][MSG]);
          break;
        }

      if(!help_index[i][KEY]) tsrwindow_puts(0, "Not found.");
    }
    tsrwindow_xy(0, 8, 1);
    while(!bioskey(1)) ;  /* wait for keystroke */
    tsrwindow_cls(0);
    tsrwindow_xy(0, 1, 1);
    tsrwindow_puts(0, "Topic: ");
    tsrwindow_gets(0, str);
  }
  deactivate(0);  /* close window */
  gotoxy(old_col, old_row); /* restore old cursor position */
}
```

When **do_help( )** begins executing, it first reads any word that may be at the current cursor position by calling **read_at_cursor( )**. This function is shown here:

```
/* Read the word that is at the current cursor location. */
void read_at_cursor(char *str)
{
  int x;
  char far *p;
  union REGS i, o;
```

```
i.h.bh = 0;
i.h.ah = 3;
int86(16, &i, &o);   /* get current cursor position */

p = vid_mem + (o.h.dh * 160) + (o.h.dl * 2 );

/* look for a word to the right of cursor */
for(x=0; *p && p<vid_mem+VID_SIZE && x<78; x++) {
  if(isspace(*p) || strchr("(!,;{ }<>", *p)) break;
  *str = *p;
  p += 2; str++;
}
*str = NULL;
if(!x) { /* no word to the right, check left */
  p -= 2;
  while(!isspace(*p) && !strchr("(,;{ }[]<>", *p))
        p -= 2;
  p += 2;
  for(x=0; *p && p>=vid_mem && x<78; x++) {
    if(isspace(*p) || strchr("(!,;{ }[]<>", *p)) break;
    *str = *p;
    p += 2; str++;
  }
  *str = NULL;
}
}
```

The **read_at_cursor( )** function works like this. First, the current cursor position is obtained by calling DOS function 3, using the default video page (0). The pointer **p** is then set equal to the location corresponding to this cursor position in the video RAM. Next, the function checks to see if there is a word beginning at and extending to the right of the current cursor position. If there is, this word is read off the screen and put into the string pointed to by **str**. Notice that a word is delimited by white space as well as various other characters. (You can change the delimiters to suit your needs.) If no word is found to the right, then the function looks to the left by scanning backward to the next delimiter and reading that word. Here are some examples. (The cursor location is indicated by the up arrow.)

Example	Word Found
This is an if ↑	if
This is an if ↑	an
A > COPY_↑	COPY
A > COPY ↑	Y
A > ↑	< no topic found >

If no topic is found at the current cursor location, **do‿help( )** will request one.

Once the topic, if any, is read from the cursor position, the coordinates of the cursor are saved by calling **cursor‿pos( )**. Because the pop-up routines will be positioning the cursor for their own purposes, you must restore the original cursor position when the pop up terminates.

Next, **do‿help( )** searches for the specified topic using the indexes constructed by **load‿help( )**. If a match is found, the corresponding help information is displayed. The function continues to loop, prompting for new topics. To exit the help system, type **quit**. You can obtain a list of all topics in the help database by typing **topics** when prompted for a topic.

As the help system is currently constructed, it can only display one screen of information about a topic. However, you might find it an interesting project to change this to allow multiple screens.

The File List Utility

The file list utility illustrates how you can access disk files in a TSR pop-up application. Although the actual listing of the file is trivial, the use of disk files in TSRs is a little more complicated than you might expect for two reasons. First, as mentioned earlier, when an application pops up, the DTA is not reset automatically. Instead, the disk transfer address of the previously executing program is still in effect. This means that if the pop-up application accesses a disk file, the contents of the other application's data might be (actually, probably *will* be) affected. Therefore, it is necessary to give the pop-up application a DTA separate from that used by the preempted program. To do this, you can use Turbo C's **getdta( )**

and **setdta( )** functions. (If your compiler does not have equivalent functions, you can call DOS functions 0x2F and 0x1A, respectively.) As stated, the default DTA is located at offset 0x80 in the program's PSP. Hence, this sequence of code resets the DTA to the TSR's default DTA.

```
char far *old_dta;

old_dta = getdta();  /* get the dta  */
setdta(MK_FP(_psp, 0x80)); /* make TSR's dta current */
```

The value of **old _ dta** is used to reset the DTA to the value used by the interrupted program when the TSR terminates.

The second complication found in performing disk accesses is that, for most compilers, you cannot use C's buffered I/O system. That is, functions like **fopen( )**, **fread( )**, and **fwrite( )** will not work in a TSR because they all use C's dynamic memory allocation system. Most implementations of C's dynamic memory system will not function in a TSR; hence, you must use the UNIX-like functions **open( )**, **close( )**, **read( )**, and **write( )**. These functions are generally translated directly into equivalent DOS calls. Some compilers, like Turbo C, provide special versions of these functions, beginning with an underscore, which are guaranteed to be direct calls to DOS. If your compiler makes such a distinction, be sure to use these functions.

The file list function is shown here. It displays the contents of a text file, one window at a time. Each time you press a key, it displays the next page. To stop viewing the file, type **q**. It also recognizes the PGUP, PGDN, HOME, and END keys. Each time you press PGUP, the file pointer is moved 512 bytes backward. Pressing HOME repositions the file pointer to the top of the file. Pressing END positions the file pointer 512 bytes from the end of the file. PGDN displays the next window full of text.

```
/* List a file. */
void do_filelist(void)
{
  int fd;  /* file descriptor */
  int numbytes, cr;
  char fname[80];
  char ch;
  union inkey {
    char ch[2];
    int i;
  } c;
```

```
char far *old_dta;
long fpos, oldpos;

cursor_pos();  /* save old cursor coordinates */
old_dta = getdta();  /* get dta using a Turbo C function */
setdta(MK_FP(_psp, 0x80));  /* make TSR's dta current */

tsrwindow(1);  /* activate window */

tsrwindow_xy(1, 0, 0);
tsrwindow_puts(1, "enter name: ");
tsrwindow_gets(1, fname);

if((fd = _open(fname, O_RDONLY)) < 0) {
  tsrwindow_puts(1, "cannot open file");
  deactivate(1);
  setdta(old_dta);  /* restore old dta */
  gotoxy(old_col, old_row);
  return;
}

do {
  cr = 0;
  tsrwindow_xy(1, 0, 0);
  tsrwindow_cleol(1);
  tsrwindow_puts(1, fname);
  tsrwindow_puts(1, ":");
  tsrwindow_xy(1, 0, 1);
  oldpos = tell(fd);
  do {
    numbytes = _read(fd, &ch, 1);
    tsrwindow_putchar(1, ch);
    if(ch=='\n') cr++;
  }while(numbytes && cr<frame[1].endy-2);
  c.i = tsrwindow_getche(1);
  tsrwindow_cls(1);
  switch(c.ch[1]) {
    case 71:  /* home: top of file */
      lseek(fd, 0L, SEEK_SET);
      break;
    case 73: /* pgup: previous page */
      fpos = oldpos - 512L;
```

```
        if(fpos<0L) fpos = 0L;
        lseek(fd, fpos, SEEK_SET);
        break;
      case 81: /* pgdn: next page */
        break;
      case 79: /* end */
        lseek(fd, -512L, SEEK_END);
        break;
    }
  } while(tolower(c.ch[0]!='q'));

  _close(fd); /* close file */
  deactivate(1); /* close window */
  setdta(old_dta); /* reset old dta */
  gotoxy(old_col, old_row); /* restore old cursor position */
}
```

The Directory Utility

The directory utility displays the current working directory. Because it accesses the disk, it also must reset the DTA. The directory list is obtained through calls to Turbo C's **findfirst( )** and **findnext( )** functions. These functions are the equivalent of DOS functions 0x4E and 0x4F. (Most DOS-based compilers have similar functions.) To call **findfirst( )**, specify the name of the file you want to find as the first parameter. This name can include wildcard characters. Hence, to find all files, use *.*. The next parameter is a pointer to a structure that will receive the information about the first file that matches the name. The information about each file is put in a Turbo C structure of type **ffblk**, which contains not only the filename, but other information as well. You might want to refer to your user manual for details. The final parameter is the attribute. Using zero matches all "normal" files. The prototypes for **findfirst( )** and **findnext( )** are shown here:

```
int findfirst(const char *fname, struct ffblk *info,
            int attr);
```

```
int findnext(struct ffblk *info);
```

Both **findfirst( )** and **findnext( )** return 0 if a match is found, −1 if no further matches are present. The directory entries are displayed six across.

```
/* List the current directory. */
void dirlist(void)
{
  struct ffblk f;
  register int done, i;
  int cr, len;
  char ch;
  char far *old_dta;

  cursor_pos();  /* save old cursor coordinates */

  old_dta = getdta();  /* get dta using a Turbo C function */
  setdta(MK_FP(_psp, 0x80)); /* make TSR's dta current */

  tsrwindow(2);  /* activate window */

  /* find first match */
  done = findfirst("*.*", &f, 0);
  i = 1;
  do {
    cr = 0;
    tsrwindow_cls(2);
    while(!done) {
      tsrwindow_puts(2, f.ff_name);
      for(len=strlen(f.ff_name); len<14; len++)
        tsrwindow_puts(2, " ");
      i++;
      done = findnext(&f); /* find next match */
      if(!(i%6)) { /* print six across */
        tsrwindow_puts(2, "\n");
        i = 1;
        cr++;
        if(cr == frame[2].endy-1) break;
      }
    }
    ch = tsrwindow_getche(2);
  } while(!done && tolower(ch) != 'q');
  deactivate(2);  /* close window */
  setdta(old_dta); /* reset old dta */
  gotoxy(old_col, old_row); /* restore old cursor position */
}
```

The Base Converter Utility

The simplest of the pop-up utilities is the number base converter, shown here. Its operation is straightfoward and you should have no trouble understanding it. One point of interest is that it uses **sscanf( )** and **sprintf( )**. As stated earlier, you generally cannot use any of the formatted I/O functions of C because they use C's dynamic allocation system. However, these two functions are called with the output buffer as a parameter and don't need to use the dynamic allocation system. (While this is true for Turbo C, other implementations may differ; so, if you encounter problems using **sscanf( )** or **sprintf( )**, remove them from your code.)

```c
/* Base converter: hex to dec, dec to hex. */
void dectohex(void)
{
  char str[80], out[80], ch;
  int num;

  cursor_pos();  /* save old cursor coordinates */
  tsrwindow(3);  /* activate window */
  tsrwindow_puts(3, "(1) hex to dec (2) dec to hex");
  ch = tsrwindow_getche(3);
  tsrwindow_puts(3, "\n");
  if(ch == '1') {
    tsrwindow_puts(3, "enter hex: ");
    tsrwindow_gets(3, str);
    sscanf(str, "%x", &num);
    tsrwindow_puts(3, " dec: ");
    sprintf(out, "%d", num);
  }
  else {
    tsrwindow_puts(3, "enter dec: ");
    tsrwindow_gets(3, str);
    sscanf(str, "%d", &num);
    tsrwindow_puts(3, " hex: ");
    sprintf(out, "%X", num);
  }
  tsrwindow_puts(3, out);
  tsrwindow_getche(3);
  deactivate(3);  /* close window */
  gotoxy(old_col, old_row); /* restore old cursor position */
}
```

Jesper Boelsmand
Cocreator of TopSpeed C and TopSpeed C++

Jesper Boelsmand is the cocreator (along with George Barwood) of the JPI TopSpeed C and C++ compilers. He holds an M.S. degree from the Technical University of Denmark.

Jesper's approach to program design is governed by two main principles. "First, you must have in mind a solid overview of the entire project before you begin to code a single routine. If you don't, you will spend much time trying to patch together disconnected bits and pieces. Second, once you begin coding, elegance and simplicity are the key. If your program begins to get 'ugly,' try again (and again, if necessary). The creation of quality programs takes a combination of talent, skill, and hard work. It is a good idea to mimic modern software-engineering practices, such as modular design. Also, you should use full-function prototyping; it will reduce the debugging time."

Jesper believes that C++ is the future of C. "It has the benefit of allowing you to compile your existing C programs, while allowing you to utilize some of C++'s exciting features. It is easy to convert a C program into a C++ program because C++ is essentially a superset of C. C++ reflects a somewhat more formal and modern approach to C and presents the programmer with a safer environment. This added safety is especially important in large programming projects. However, there is no doubt that C will continue to be used for many years."

I asked Jesper if he could define one feature of C that he thought was particularly important. "One thing I find very useful is C's ability to pass variable length arguments to functions, such as **printf( )**. Of the mainstream procedural languages, this feature is unique to C and increases its power significantly."

Like many Europeans, Jesper is also keenly interested in the Modula-2 language. (As you probably know, Modula-2 is Professor Wirth's much improved successor to Pascal.) "Basically, you can express the same things in Modula-2 as you do in C. The main difference is that Modula-2 provides a more controlled environment that can reduce the debugging task."

Jesper Boelsmand currently lives in London, England.

THE ENTIRE SCTSR PROGRAM LISTING

The entire listing for the Supercharged TSR is shown here:

```
/* Terminate-and-Stay-Resident utilities.
*/
#include "stdio.h"
#include "stdlib.h"
#include "string.h"
#include "dos.h"
#include "ctype.h"
#include "fcntl.h"
#include "dir.h"
#include "conio.h"
#include "bios.h"
#include "io.h"

#define BORDER 1
#define MAX_FRAME 4
#define REV_VID 0x70
#define NORM_VID 7
#define BKSP 8
#define VID_SIZE 4000
#define STK_SIZE 0x2000

#define HELP_SIZE 75
#define KEY         0
#define MSG         1
#define HELP_BUF_SIZE 32000

/* window function prototypes */
void save_video(int num), restore_video(int num);
void write_string(int x, int y, char *p, int attrib);
void write_char(int x, int y, char ch, int attrib);
void display_header(int num), draw_border(int num);
void tsrwindow_gets(int num , char *s);
void tsrwindow_cleol(int num), tsrwindow(int num);
void tsrwindow_cls(int num),  set_vid_mem(void);
int make_tsrwindow(int num, char *header, int startx,
                   int starty, int endx, int endy,
                   int border);
int tsrwindow_xy(int num, int x, int y);
int tsrwindow_puts(int num, char *str);
```

```
void deactivate(int num);
int video_mode(void), tsrwindow_putchar(int num, char ch);
int tsrwindow_getche(int num);

/* TSR function prototypes */
int load_help(void);
void read_at_cursor(char *str);
void do_help(void), cursor_pos(void);
void activate_sctsr(void);
void interrupt tsr_keystroke(void);
void interrupt dos_idle(void);
void interrupt new_int8(void);
void interrupt (*old_int28)();
void interrupt (*old_int8)();
void interrupt (*old_key)();
void interrupt (*old_int64)();
void do_filelist(void), dirlist(void), dectohex(void);

char far *vid_mem;
char video;

struct window_frame {
  int startx, endx, starty, endy; /* corners of window */
  int curx, cury; /* current cursor position in window */
  unsigned char *p; /* pointer to buffer */
  char *header; /* header message */
  int border; /* border on/off */
  int active; /* on screen yes/no */
} frame[MAX_FRAME];

char wp[VID_SIZE]; /* buffer to hold contents of the screen
                      when saved by save_video() */

/* busy is set to 1 when the program is active, 0 otherwise */
char busy = 0;

char *help_index[HELP_SIZE][2];

char help_buf[HELP_BUF_SIZE];  /* holds the help file */

unsigned char stack[STK_SIZE];
unsigned int sp, ss;
```

```
int old_row, old_col;
int key;
char far *dos_active;

main()
{
  union REGS r;
  struct SREGS s;

  if(!load_help()) {  /* load the help file */
    /* You may want to take other action here. */
    exit(1);
  }

  /* see if already loaded */
  old_int64 = getvect(0x64); /* unused interrupt */
  if(!old_int64) setvect(0x64, 1); /* set a flag */
  else {
    printf("TSR already loaded");
    exit(0);
  }

  /* obtain the dos_active flag address */
  r.h.ah = 0x34;
  int86x(0x21, &r, &r, &s);
  dos_active = MK_FP(s.es, r.x.bx);

  /* get old ISR addresses */
  old_key = getvect(9); /* keystroke int */
  old_int28 = getvect(0x28);  /* int 28 */
  old_int8 = getvect(8);  /* timer interrupt */

  /* re-route interrupt vectors to our handlers */
  setvect(9, tsr_keystroke);
  setvect(0x28, dos_idle);
  setvect(8, new_int8);

  printf("SC-TSR installed\n");
  printf("F1: help    F2: file list    F3: directory");
  printf("    F4: base converter\n");

  key = 0;
```

```
  set_vid_mem();  /* get address of video memory */

  /* initialize all windows */
  make_tsrwindow(0, " Help ('quit' to exit, 'topics' for topics) ",
             0, 0, 79, 24, BORDER);
  make_tsrwindow(1, " File Lister ", 0, 0, 79, 16, BORDER);
  make_tsrwindow(2, " Directory ", 0, 0, 79, 12, BORDER);
  make_tsrwindow(3, " Base Converter ", 0, 0, 50, 3, BORDER);

  keep(0, 4000); /* terminate and stay resident */
}


/* This is the function that intercepts the keystroke
   interrupt (int 9). */
void interrupt tsr_keystroke(void)
{
  int far *t2 = (int far *) 1050;  /* address head pointer */
  char far *t = (char far *) 1050; /* address head pointer */

  (*old_key)();  /* first, call old keystroke ISR */

  if(*t != *(t+2)) {/* if not empty */
    t += *t-30+5; /* advance to the character position */
    if(*t>=59 && *t <=63) {
      switch(*t) {  /* see what is in scan code */
        case 59:  /* F1 - help */
          key = 1;
          break;
        case 60:  /* F2 - file list */
          key = 2;
          break;
        case 61:  /* F3 - directory */
          key = 3;
          break;
        case 62:  /* F4 - dec to hex */
          key = 4;
          break;
        case 63: /* F5 - detach tsr */
          key = 5;
          break;
      }
      *(t2+1) = *t2;  /* zero buffer */
    }
```

```c
  }
}

/* New interrupt 8. */
void interrupt new_int8(void)
{
  (*old_int8)();
  if(!*dos_active && !busy && key)
      activate_sctsr();
}

/* This function intercepts int 0x28  (the dos-idle
   interrupt).
*/
void interrupt dos_idle(void)
{
  (*old_int28)();  /* call old int 0x28 ISR */
  if(!busy && key) activate_sctsr();
}

/* Pop up the SCTSR. */
void activate_sctsr(void)
{
  /* set up TSR stack */
  disable();  /* disable interrupts */
    ss = _SS;
    sp = _SP;
    _SS = _DS;
    _SP = (unsigned) &stack[STK_SIZE-2];
  enable();    /* enable interrupts */

  /* check video mode - don't pop up if not in
     an 80-column text mode
  */
  video = video_mode();
  if(!busy && (video==7 || video==3 || video==2)) {
    busy = !busy;  /* don't allow a second activation */
    switch(key) {
      case 1: do_help();
        break;
      case 2: do_filelist();
        break;
      case 3: dirlist();
```

```
          break;
        case 4: dectohex();
          break;
    }
    busy = !busy;
  }
  if(key==5){ /* deactivating TSR */
    cursor_pos();   /* get current cursor position */
    write_string(old_col, old_row, "SC-TSR deactivated",
                 NORM_VID);
  }

  /* restore old stack */
  disable();
    _SP = sp;
    _SS = ss;
  enable();

  if(key==5) {   /* reset old ISR routines and free memory */
    setvect(8, old_int8);
    setvect(9, old_key);
    setvect(0x28, old_int28);
    setvect(0x64, old_int64);
    freemem(_psp);  /* free program block */
  } else  key = 0;
}

/* This is the help function.  (See text for
   details.)
*/
void do_help(void)
{
  char str[80];
  int i;

  /* See if a topic is located at the current cursor
     position. */
  read_at_cursor(str);
  cursor_pos();  /* save old cursor coordinates */

  tsrwindow(0);  /* activate window */
  tsrwindow_xy(0, 1, 1);
  tsrwindow_puts(0, "Topic: ");
  if(*str) tsrwindow_puts(0, str);
```

```
    for(;;) {
      if(!strcmp("quit", str)) break;
      tsrwindow_xy(0, 1, 3);

      if(!strcmp("topics", str))
        /* show help topics */
        for(i=0; help_index[i][KEY]; i++) {
          if(!(i%6)) tsrwindow_puts(0, "\n");
          tsrwindow_puts(0, help_index[i][KEY]);
          tsrwindow_puts(0, "   ");
        }
      else {
        for(i=0; help_index[i][KEY]; i++)
          /* lookup topic and display message if found */
          if(!strcmp(help_index[i][KEY], str)) {
            tsrwindow_puts(0, help_index[i][MSG]);
            break;
          }

        if(!help_index[i][KEY]) tsrwindow_puts(0, "Not found.");
      }
      tsrwindow_xy(0, 8, 1);
      while(!bioskey(1)) ;   /* wait for keystroke */
      tsrwindow_cls(0);
      tsrwindow_xy(0, 1, 1);
      tsrwindow_puts(0, "Topic: ");
      tsrwindow_gets(0, str);
    }
    deactivate(0);   /* close window */
    gotoxy(old_col, old_row); /* restore old cursor position */
}

/* List a file. */
void do_filelist(void)
{
  int fd;  /* file descriptor */
  int numbytes, cr;
  char fname[80];
  char ch;
  union inkey {
    char ch[2];
    int i;
  } c;
```

```c
char far *old_dta;
long fpos, oldpos;

cursor_pos();   /* save old cursor coordinates */
old_dta = getdta();   /* get dta using a Turbo C function */
setdta(MK_FP(_psp, 0x80)); /* make TSR's dta current */

tsrwindow(1);   /* activate window */

tsrwindow_xy(1, 0, 0);
tsrwindow_puts(1, "enter name: ");
tsrwindow_gets(1, fname);

if((fd = _open(fname, O_RDONLY)) < 0) {
  tsrwindow_puts(1, "cannot open file");
  deactivate(1);
  setdta(old_dta);   /* restore old dta */
  gotoxy(old_col, old_row);
  return;
}

do {
  cr = 0;
  tsrwindow_xy(1, 0, 0);
  tsrwindow_cleol(1);
  tsrwindow_puts(1, fname);
  tsrwindow_puts(1, ":");
  tsrwindow_xy(1, 0, 1);
  oldpos = tell(fd);
  do {
    numbytes = _read(fd, &ch, 1);
    tsrwindow_putchar(1, ch);
    if(ch=='\n') cr++;
  }while(numbytes && cr<frame[1].endy-2);
  c.i = tsrwindow_getche(1);
  tsrwindow_cls(1);
  switch(c.ch[1]) {
    case 71:  /* home: top of file */
      lseek(fd, 0L, SEEK_SET);
      break;
    case 73: /* pgup: previous page */
      fpos = oldpos - 512L;
```

```
          if(fpos<0L) fpos = 0L;
          lseek(fd, fpos, SEEK_SET);
          break;
        case 81: /* pgdn: next page */
          break;
        case 79: /* end */
          lseek(fd, -512L, SEEK_END);
          break;
    }
  } while(tolower(c.ch[0]!='q'));

  _close(fd); /* close file */
  deactivate(1); /* close window */
  setdta(old_dta); /* reset old dta */
  gotoxy(old_col, old_row); /* restore old cursor position */
}

/* List the current directory. */
void dirlist(void)
{
  struct ffblk f;
  register int done, i;
  int cr, len;
  char ch;
  char far *old_dta;

  cursor_pos();  /* save old cursor coordinates */

  old_dta = getdta();  /* get dta using a Turbo C function */
  setdta(MK_FP(_psp, 0x80)); /* make TSR's dta current */

  tsrwindow(2);  /* activate window */

  /* find first match */
  done = findfirst("*.*", &f, 0);
  i = 1;
  do {
    cr = 0;
    tsrwindow_cls(2);
    while(!done) {
      tsrwindow_puts(2, f.ff_name);
      for(len=strlen(f.ff_name); len<14; len++)
        tsrwindow_puts(2, " ");
```

```
      i++;
      done = findnext(&f); /* find next match */
      if(!(i%6)) { /* print six across */
        tsrwindow_puts(2, "\n");
        i = 1;
        cr++;
        if(cr == frame[2].endy-1) break;
      }
    }
    ch = tsrwindow_getche(2);
  } while(!done && tolower(ch) != 'q');
  deactivate(2);  /* close window */
  setdta(old_dta); /* reset old dta */
  gotoxy(old_col, old_row); /* restore old cursor position */
}

/* Base converter: hex to dec, dec to hex. */
void dectohex(void)
{
  char str[80], out[80], ch;
  int num;

  cursor_pos();  /* save old cursor coordinates */
  tsrwindow(3);  /* activate window */
  tsrwindow_puts(3, "(1) hex to dec (2) dec to hex");
  ch = tsrwindow_getche(3);
  tsrwindow_puts(3, "\n");
  if(ch == '1') {
    tsrwindow_puts(3, "enter hex: ");
    tsrwindow_gets(3, str);
    sscanf(str, "%x", &num);
    tsrwindow_puts(3, " dec: ");
    sprintf(out, "%d", num);
  }
  else {
    tsrwindow_puts(3, "enter dec: ");
    tsrwindow_gets(3, str);
    sscanf(str, "%d", &num);
    tsrwindow_puts(3, " hex: ");
    sprintf(out, "%X", num);
  }
  tsrwindow_puts(3, out);
  tsrwindow_getche(3);
```

```
    deactivate(3);  /* close window */
    gotoxy(old_col, old_row); /* restore old cursor position */
}

/* Load the help file. This file must be called
     TSRHELP.DAT.   See text for details.
*/
load_help(void)
{
  FILE *fp;
  char *p, ch;
  int i;

  p = help_buf;

  if((fp = fopen("TSRHELP.DAT", "r"))==NULL) {
    printf("cannot open TSRHELP.DAT");
    return 0;
  }

  ch = getc(fp);
  for(i=0; i<HELP_SIZE && !feof(fp); i++) {
    if(ch != '^') {
      printf("TSRHELP.DAT corrupted - use backup");
      fclose(fp);
      return 0;
    }
    if(p > help_buf+HELP_BUF_SIZE) {
      printf("Help file too big");
      fclose(fp);
      return 0;
    }

    help_index[i][KEY] = p;  /* pointer to keywords */

    while((*p=tolower(getc(fp)))!='\n') p++;  /* read keyword */
    *p = '\0'; /* null terminate the keyword */

    p++;

    help_index[i][MSG] = p;  /* pointer to help msg */

    while((*p=getc(fp))!='^' && !feof(fp)) p++; /* read msg */
```

```
    ch = *p;
    *p = '\0'; /* null terminate the message */
    p++;
  }
  fclose(fp);
  return 1;
}

/* Set the vid_mem pointer to the start of video
   memory.
*/
void set_vid_mem(void)
{
  int vmode;

  vmode = video_mode();
  if((vmode!=2) && (vmode!=3) && (vmode!=7)) {
    printf("video must be in 80 column text mode");
    exit(1);
  }
  /* set proper address of video RAM */
  if(vmode==7) vid_mem = (char far *) MK_FP(0xB000, 0000);
  else vid_mem = (char far *) MK_FP(0xB800, 0000);
}

/* Read the word that is at the current cursor location. */
void read_at_cursor(char *str)
{
  int x;
  char far *p;
  union REGS i, o;

  i.h.bh = 0;
  i.h.ah = 3;
  int86(16, &i, &o);

  p = vid_mem + (o.h.dh * 160) + (o.h.dl * 2 );

  /* look for a word to the right of cursor */
  for(x=0; *p && p<vid_mem+VID_SIZE && x<78; x++) {
    if(isspace(*p) || strchr("(!,;{}<>", *p)) break;
    *str = *p;
```

```
      p += 2; str++;
    }
    *str = NULL;
    if(!x) { /* no word to the right, check left */
      p -= 2;
      while(!isspace(*p) && !strchr("(,;{}[]<>", *p))
            p -= 2;
      p += 2;
      for(x=0; *p && p>=vid_mem && x<78; x++) {
        if(isspace(*p) || strchr("(!,;{}[]<>", *p)) break;
        *str = *p;
        p += 2; str++;
      }
      *str = NULL;
    }
}

/* Read and save cursor coordinates. */
void cursor_pos(void)
{
  union REGS i, o;

  i.h.bh = 0;
  i.h.ah = 3;
  int86(16, &i, &o);

  old_row = o.h.dh;
  old_col = o.h.dl;
}

/* Send cursor to specified X,Y (0,0 is upper
   left corner). */
void gotoxy(int x, int y)
{
  union REGS i;

  i.h.dh = y;
  i.h.dl = x;
  i.h.ah = 2;
  i.h.bh = 0;
  int86(16, &i, &i);
}
```

```
/*****************************************************/
/* Window functions

   These functions are adapted from those developed in
   "C: Power User's Guide," Herbert Schildt,
   Osborne/McGraw-Hill, 1987.  Details of their operation
   are found there.
*/
/*****************************************************/

/* Display a pull-down window. */
void tsrwindow(int num) /* window number */
{
  /* get active window */
  if(!frame[num].active) { /* not currently in use */
    save_video(num);        /* save the current screen */
    frame[num].active = 1; /* set active flag */
  }

  if(frame[num].border) draw_border(num);
  display_header(num); /* display the window */
}

/* Construct a pull-down window frame
   1 is returned if window frame can be constructed;
   otherwise 0 is returned.
*/
make_tsrwindow(
             int num, /* window number */
             char *header, /* header text */
             int startx, int starty, /* upper left corner */
             int endx, int endy, /* lower right corner */
             int border /* no border if 0 */
)
{
  if(num>MAX_FRAME) {
    tsrwindow_puts(0, "Too many windows\n");
    return 0;
  }

  if((startx>78) || (startx<0) || (starty>24) || (starty<0)) {
    tsrwindow_puts(0, "range error");
    return 0;
```

```
  }

  if((endx>79) || (endy>25)) {
    tsrwindow_puts(0, "window won't fit");
    return 0;
  }

  /* construct the frame */
  frame[num].startx = startx; frame[num].endx = endx;
  frame[num].starty = starty; frame[num].endy = endy;
  frame[num].p = wp;
  frame[num].header = header;
  frame[num].border = border;
  frame[num].active = 0;
  frame[num].curx = 0; frame[num].cury = 0;
  return 1;
}

/* Deactivate a window and remove it from the screen. */
void deactivate(int num)
{
  /* reset the cursor position to upper left corner */
  frame[num].curx = 0;
  frame[num].cury = 0;
  restore_video(num);
}

/* Display the header message in its proper location. */
void display_header(int num)
{
  register int x, len;

  x = frame[num].startx;

  /* Calculate the correct starting position to center
     the header message--if negative, message won't
     fit.
  */
  len = strlen(frame[num].header);
  len = (frame[num].endx - x - len) / 2;
  if(len<0) return; /* don't display it */
  x = x +len;
```

```
  write_string(x, frame[num].starty,
               frame[num].header, NORM_VID);
}

/* Draw a border around the window. */
void draw_border(int num)
{
  register int i;
  char far *v, far *t;

  v = vid_mem;
  t = v;
  for(i=frame[num].starty+1; i<frame[num].endy; i++) {
     v += (i*160) + frame[num].startx*2;
     *v++ = 179;
     *v = NORM_VID;
     v = t;
     v += (i*160) + frame[num].endx*2;
     *v++ = 179;
     *v = NORM_VID;
     v = t;
  }
  for(i=frame[num].startx+1; i<frame[num].endx; i++) {
     v += (frame[num].starty*160) + i*2;
     *v++ = 196;
     *v = NORM_VID;
     v = t;
     v += (frame[num].endy*160) + i*2;
     *v++ = 196;
     *v = NORM_VID;
     v = t;
  }
  write_char(frame[num].startx, frame[num].starty, 218, NORM_VID);
  write_char(frame[num].startx, frame[num].endy, 192, NORM_VID);
  write_char(frame[num].endx, frame[num].starty, 191, NORM_VID);
  write_char(frame[num].endx, frame[num].endy, 217, NORM_VID);
}

/* Write a string at the current cursor position
   in the specified window.
   Returns 0 if window not active;
   1 otherwise.
*/
```

```
tsrwindow_puts(int num, char *str)
{
   /* make sure window is active */
  if(!frame[num].active) return 0;

  for( ; *str;  str++)
    tsrwindow_putchar(num, *str);
  return 1;
}

/* Write a character at the current cursor position
   in the specified window.
   Returns 0 if window not active;
   1 otherwise.
*/
tsrwindow_putchar(int num, char ch)
{
   int x, y;
  char far *v;

  /* make sure window is active */
  if(!frame[num].active) return 0;

  x = frame[num].curx + frame[num].startx + 1;
  y = frame[num].cury + frame[num].starty + 1;

  v = vid_mem;
  v += (y*160) + x*2; /* compute the address */
  if(y>=frame[num].endy) {
    return 1;
  }
  if(x>=frame[num].endx) {
    return 1;
  }

  if(ch=='\n') { /* newline char */
    y++;
    x = frame[num].startx+1;
    v = vid_mem;
    v += (y*160) + x*2; /* compute the address */
    frame[num].cury++;  /* increment Y */
    frame[num].curx = 0; /* reset X */
  }
```

```
  else if(ch=='\r') return 1;
  else {
    frame[num].curx++;
    *v++ = ch;   /* write the character */
    *v++ = NORM_VID;     /* normal video attribute */
  }
  tsrwindow_xy(num, frame[num].curx, frame[num].cury);
  return 1;
}

/* Position cursor in a window at specified location.
   Returns 0 if out of range;
   non-zero otherwise.
*/
tsrwindow_xy(int num, int x, int y)
{
  if(x<0 || x+frame[num].startx>=frame[num].endx-1)
    return 0;
  if(y<0 || y+frame[num].starty>=frame[num].endy-1)
    return 0;
  frame[num].curx = x;
  frame[num].cury = y;
  gotoxy(x+1, y+1);
  return 1;
}

/* Read a string from a window. */
void tsrwindow_gets(int num, char *s)
{
  char ch, *temp;

  temp = s;
  for(;;) {
    ch = tsrwindow_getche(num);
    switch(ch) {
      case '\r':  /* the ENTER key is pressed */
        *s='\0';
        return;
      case BKSP: /* backspace */
        if(s>temp) {
          s--;
          frame[num].curx--;
          if(frame[num].curx<0) frame[num].curx = 0;
```

```
        tsrwindow_xy(num, frame[num].curx, frame[num].cury);
          write_char(frame[num].startx+ frame[num].curx+1,
        frame[num].starty+frame[num].cury+1, ' ', NORM_VID);
      }
      break;
    default: *s = ch;
      s++;
    }
  }
}

/* Input keystrokes inside a window.
   Returns full 16-bit scan code.
*/
tsrwindow_getche(int num)
{
  union inkey {
    char ch[2];
    int i;
  } c;

  if(!frame[num].active) return 0; /* window not active */

  tsrwindow_xy(num, frame[num].curx, frame[num].cury);

  c.i = bioskey(0);    /* read the key */

  if(c.ch[0]) {
    switch(c.ch[0]) {
      case '\r': /* the ENTER key is pressed */
        break;
      case BKSP: /* backspace */
        break;
      default:
        if(frame[num].curx+frame[num].startx < frame[num].endx-1) {
        write_char(frame[num].startx+ frame[num].curx+1,
          frame[num].starty+frame[num].cury+1, c.ch[0], NORM_VID);
          frame[num].curx++;
        }
    }
    if(frame[num].curx < 0) frame[num].curx = 0;
    if(frame[num].curx+frame[num].startx > frame[num].endx-2)
      frame[num].curx--;
```

```
      tsrwindow_xy(num, frame[num].curx, frame[num].cury);
  }
  return c.i;
}

/* Clear to end of line. */
void tsrwindow_cleol(int num)
{
  register int i, x, y;

  x = frame[num].curx;
  y = frame[num].cury;
  tsrwindow_xy(num, frame[num].curx, frame[num].cury);

  for(i=frame[num].curx; i<frame[num].endx-1; i++)
    tsrwindow_putchar(num,' ');
  tsrwindow_xy(num, x, y);
}

void tsrwindow_cls(int num)
{
  register int i, j;
  char far *v;

  for(i=frame[num].starty+1; i<frame[num].endy; i++)
    for(j=frame[num].startx+1; j<frame[num].endx; j++) {
      v = vid_mem;
      v += (i*160) + j*2;
      *v++ = ' ';  /* write a space */
      *v++ = NORM_VID;
    }
  frame[num].curx = 0;
  frame[num].cury = 0;
}

/*****************************************************
 Low-level video functions.
 ****************************************************/

/* Display a string with specified attribute. */
void write_string(int x, int y, char *p, int attrib)
{
  char far *v;
```

```
  v = vid_mem;
  v += (y*160) + x*2; /* compute the address */
  for(; *p; ) {
    *v++ = *p++;  /* write the character */
    *v++ = attrib;    /* write the attribute */
  }
}

/* Write character with specified attribute. */
void write_char(int x, int y, char ch, int attrib)
{
  char far *v;

  v = vid_mem;
  v += (y*160) + x*2;
  *v++ = ch;  /* write the character */
  *v = attrib;    /* write the attribute */
}

/* Save a portion of the screen. */
void save_video(int num)
{
  register int i,j;
  char *buf_ptr;
  char far *v, far *t;

  buf_ptr = frame[num].p;
  v = vid_mem;
  for(i=frame[num].startx; i<frame[num].endx+1; i++)
    for(j=frame[num].starty; j<frame[num].endy+1; j++) {
      t = (v + (j*160) + i*2);
      *buf_ptr++ = *t++;
      *buf_ptr++ = *t;
      *(t-1) = ' ';  /* clear the window */
    }
}

/* Restore a portion of the screen. */
void restore_video(int num)
{
  register int i,j;
  char far *v, far *t;
```

```
  char *buf_ptr;

  buf_ptr = frame[num].p;
  v = vid_mem;
  t = v;
  for(i=frame[num].startx; i<frame[num].endx+1; i++)
    for(j=frame[num].starty; j<frame[num].endy+1; j++) {
      v = t;
      v += (j*160) + i*2;
      *v++ = *buf_ptr++;   /* write the character */
      *v = *buf_ptr++;     /* write the attribute */
    }
  frame[num].active = 0; /* restore_video */
}

/* Returns the current video mode. */
video_mode(void)
{
  union REGS r;

  r.h.ah = 15;   /* get video mode */
  return int86(0x10, &r, &r) & 255;
}
```

SOME OTHER CONSIDERATIONS

The SCTSR works fine on my systems, which include an early XT, an AT clone, and a Model 60 and with the software I use (mostly compilers and editors). It will probably work fine for you, too; however, if you experience some problems, here are a couple of things you might try.

Because some programs bypass DOS for much of their disk and screen I/O, some TSR programs watch for calls to interrupts 0x10 (BIOS screen routines) and 0x13 (BIOS disk I/O). These TSRs will not pop up while one of these interrupts is active. The SCTSR does not monitor these interrupts; however, in demanding situations, you may need to.

As stated earlier, the SCTSR program relies upon the clock interrupt (INT 8) to trigger the pop-up application when interrupt 0x28 is not being called. Frankly, I don't like this approach because it degrades the overall system performance. However, popping up during a keyboard interrupt can cause problems when used with some application programs (the

Turbo C integrated environment, for example), and the clock appears to be the only safe way to activate the TSR in these situations. You might want to experiment using the keyboard interrupt to activate the TSR for your specific environment. If you experience no troubles, this approach will avoid slowing down your system.

CHAPTER FOUR

A Multitasking Kernel for DOS

If there is one single programming trait common to all C programmers it must be a tendency to want to take full control of the way the computer executes their programs. This chapter explores an exciting example, the creation of a multitasking subsystem.

When the term *multitasking* is used, one immediately thinks of operating systems such as OS/2, UNIX, or some large, mainframe OS. Traditionally, if multiple tasks were to be run on one system, it was the operating system that managed and scheduled the tasks, making sure that all tasks got some slice of the CPU's time. (For the rest of this chapter, the term *task* will refer to an individual unit of execution.) However, there is another approach to multitasking in which various pieces of a single program are multitasked without aid from the supporting operating system. To accomplish this, the program must include a multitasking subsystem, often referred to as a *multitasking kernel* or *multitasking executive*.

The multitasking kernel as presented in this chapter requires the use of Turbo C and is designed to run under DOS. Turbo C is necessary because it includes the **interrupt** type modifer, which makes possible the

Tom Green
Development Engineer, Central Data Corporation

Tom Green writes programs that very few people are aware of, yet thousands of people use every day. The programs that he writes control circuit cards used in Multibus-based computers. Tom jokingly refers to board-level programming as a "high-risk adventure" and is the first to admit that not every C programmer would like to have his job. The code that he writes executes in a real-time, multitasking environment and it must be downloaded and run on the host circuit card for testing. Compounding the difficulty of the job, Tom often must write software for a new chip, such as a DMA controller. This means poring over the technical specifications, which often lack examples and are poorly written. As Tom puts it, "The software I work with often involves the control of new chips. Bringing up new hardware generally requires much experimentation and does not often lend itself to textbook approaches. Sometimes you just have to try things until you get it right."

As one might guess, Tom is a person who likes challenges. In fact, his recreational programming often rivals what others do for a living. For example, one day he and a co-worker were discussing the possibility of creating an entire multitasking kernel using only C—no assembly code. By the end of their discussion, he had the germ of an idea. As Tom put it, "That evening I went home and started experimenting. Within a few evenings of work, I had developed a fully operational multitasking subsystem entirely in C. This is the kind of stuff that keeps programming fresh." In fact, most of the central concepts used in the multitasking system developed in this chapter were first worked out by Tom.

When I asked Tom for the most important piece of advice he had to offer other C programmers, he responded, "Knowing what code your compiler produces for various statements. If you understand how your compiler generates code, you will be better able to write highly efficient, optimized programs."

I asked Tom what he thought lay ahead for C. "C++ is the real future of C. I think the concept of objects as implemented in C++ fits very well with many other programming paradigms in common use. I think the maturing of C compilers and related tools in the DOS environment has strengthened C's position over the last couple of years. C is not as easy to learn as some other languages, but its power and flexibility make it the best choice for systems programming and most other tasks."

Tom Green lives with his wife and son in Illinois. Even when not programming, he is seldom far from a computer because his hobby is playing MIDI (Musical Instrument Digital Interface) synthesizers.

creation of interrupt service routines in C. Turbo C also includes the register psuedo-variables, which eliminate the need for any assembly code. If you do not use Turbo C, then you will almost surely need to use some assembly code to create a multitasking subsystem. (However, following the lead shown here, you should have little trouble.) Also, the code in this chapter must be compiled using a small data model. (The default *small* model works fine.) The approach to multitasking presented here can be generalized to virtually any environment, so even if you don't use DOS, it can still act as a guide.

The explanation of how the multitasking kernel works assumes that you have a working knowledge of the 8086 family of processors. If you don't, don't worry! You will still be able to use the multitasking system. If you haven't read Chapter 3 yet, you might want to skim at least the sections on interrupts because much of that information is applicable to this chapter.

One last point: The multitasking kernel developed in this chapter supports true, time-sliced multitasking. It intercepts the computer's timer and switches tasks with each clock tick. This multitasking subsystem is not a toy, but a powerful tool that can be used to enhance the performance of your programs.

TWO VIEWS OF MULTITASKING

There are actually two main approaches to multitasking: process-based and thread-based. A *process-based* multitasking system is capable of running two or more entire processes at one time. (For most practical purposes, a process is a program.) If you have used UNIX, Windows, or a mainframe operating system, process-based multitasking is familiar to you. In environments like these, for example, you can run an editor, a compiler, and a database at the same time. The advantage of process-based multitasking is that it allows more than one program to share the CPU. This is important when more than one person wants to use the system. However, process-based multitasking does not improve the execution time of any single process. In fact, because the CPU is being shared, all processes running in the system will run slower than in a single-tasking environment.

The multitasking kernel we will develop does not support process-based multitasking. Instead, it uses a *thread-based* approach. In a thread-based multitasking environment it is possible to run two or more pieces of a single process simultaneously. For practical purposes, you can think of a thread as being similar to a function or set of related functions. (The term *thread* is derived from the phrase "thread of execution.") For example, one part of a database program may process user input while another part sorts the database, while yet a third part executes a query. Unlike process-based multitasking, a thread-based multitasking system can be used to improve the run time of the entire program. The reason for this is simple to understand: since many programs spend much time waiting for something to happen—waiting for input, for example—much time is wasted in a single-tasking environment. In many programs, this wasted time can be put to good use. Some operating systems, such as OS/2, actually use a combination of process and thread-based multitasking. However, the multitasking system developed in this chapter uses only thread-based multitasking.

HOW MULTITASKING IS ACCOMPLISHED

No matter which type of multitasking system is used, the process of task switching is essentially the same. Before we can develop the multitasking kernel, some theory is in order. (If you are already familiar with task switching, feel free to skip ahead.)

The Scheduler

All true multitasking systems have one thing in common: a routine that switches execution from one task to another. This routine is sometimes referred to as the *scheduler*. In virtually all multitasking situations, the scheduler is executed as the result of an interrupt caused by the system clock. There are two basic approaches to scheduling tasks. The first is quite simple and is called *time slicing*. In time slicing's simplest form (the one we will use) tasks are organized in a circular queue. Each time the clock interrupt occurs, the scheduler suspends execution of the currently executing task and resumes the next one in the queue. Thus, tasks are executed in a round-robin fashion. A second approach to multitasking is called *priority-based scheduling*. In this method, the task with the highest priority will be allowed to run. If that task cannot run (perhaps it is waiting for input, for example), then a task of lower priority can run. Generally, in priority-based systems, tasks with equal priorities are executed in round-robin fashion. Many commercial multitasking systems provide a hybrid approach, which combines time slicing with priorities.

Each Task Needs Its Own Stack

One of the most fundamental points to understand about multitasking is that each task must have its own stack. There are two reasons for this. First, the stack is used to accomplish a task switch (as described in the next section); second, it is used as storage for a task's local variables.

How Task Switching Is Accomplished

No matter which approach to multitasking is taken, the basic methodology of effecting a task switch is the same. Simply put, a task switch is accomplished by calling a routine that resets the stack pointer from the old task's stack to the new task's stack. When the routine returns, the new task's instruction pointer (IP) is popped off the stack, and the new task automatically begins execution. The multitasking kernel developed in this chapter uses the timer interrupt to activate a task switch. Therefore, to understand the mechanics of task switching, you must begin by examining what happens when an interrupt service routine (ISR) is executed.

Note: Since the multitasking kernel in this chapter is written for the 8086 family of processors, the discussion that follows is written from that perspective.

When an interrupt occurs two things happen. First, the Flags register is pushed onto the stack. Next, the CS (code segment) is pushed, followed by the instruction pointer (IP). Finally, the segment address of the interrupt service routine is loaded into the CS register and the offset is loaded into the IP register. This causes the ISR to begin executing. When the interrupt returns, the CS, IP, and Flags registers are popped automatically. Thus, after the interrupt returns and the CPU begins processing instructions again, the IP automatically points to the next instruction of the

interrupted program, and execution resumes. A program that is interrupted has no knowledge that it has been interrupted. To the program it
will seem as though it never happened.

Given the fact that an interrupt causes the currently executing program to be stopped, an ISR to be executed, and then the program to be
resumed, it is a relatively small step to making an interrupt service routine
switch tasks. To do this, the routine performs two jobs. First, it saves all
registers, except the stack pointer (SP) and stack segment (SS) registers,
onto the stack. (The SP and SS registers are saved elsewhere.) Second, it
changes the value of the SS and SP registers *to point to the stack of another
task*. Thus, when the ISR returns, the registers are popped from the new
task's stack, making the state of the machine reflect the new task. Since
the IP is one of the registers popped, the new task (rather than the old)
will resume execution.

To make sure that the task-switching process is completely clear, let's
work through an example. Assume that there are two tasks residing in the
system called A and B, and that task A is currently executing. When the
scheduler is activated via an interrupt, the state of task A is saved on its
stack, the stack pointer is set to the top of B's stack, and the scheduler
returns. By returning, the scheduler causes the previous state of B to be
popped off the stack and B begins executing. When the scheduler is
activated again, the state of B is saved, the stack pointer is reset to the top
of A's stack, and the scheduler returns, restoring A's state in the process.
The key concept is that each time the stack pointer is switched and the
scheduler returns, the old value of the instruction pointer is popped, thus
causing execution to resume in a new task.

Initializing the Stack

While reading the foregoing discussion this question may have occurred
to you: How does a task begin executing for the first time since, prior to
execution, its stack will be empty? That is, a new task will not have
anything in its stack to restore. The answer is that, before a task is run, it
must have its stack initialized in such a way that when its first time-slice
occurs, the values popped from the stack cause it to start executing from
its beginning. To accomplish this, its stack must be initialized to contain
the correct register values and the instruction pointer must point to the

first instruction in the program. As you will soon see, the means of accomplishing this relies upon the use of some special Turbo C features.

THE REENTRANCY REQUIREMENT

Any function that may be shared by two or more tasks must be fully reentrant, or access to it must be serialized. A reentrant function is one that uses no global or **static** data. The reason functions must be reentrant if they might be shared by two or more tasks is easy to understand by using an example. Assume that there are two functions, A and B, currently executing, and A has just called a non-reentrant function called F, which uses a global variable called V. Assume also that F has not yet terminated when A is suspended and B resumes execution. Now, if at this point B also calls F, then the value of V will be changed to reflect B's invocation of F. Thus, when B's time slice is used up and A resumes execution, V will not have the same value it did before A was suspended. Depending upon what A is doing, the change in V could mean disaster.

This is particularly important because DOS is not reentrant. Hence, any function, including C's library functions, that accesses DOS is not reentrant.

If a function cannot be made reentrant, then access to it must be serialized; that is, it must be used by one — and only one — task at a time. How serialization is accomplished is discussed later in this chapter.

THE **interrupt** TYPE MODIFIER

Turbo C (and many other DOS-based compilers) provides one crucial element of support for interrupt service routines: the **interrupt** function type modifier. When you declare a function to be of type **interrupt**, it tells the compiler to automatically preserve all registers (except SP and SS) and to terminate the function with an IRET instruction. (If your compiler does not include the **interrupt** type, then you must resort to an assembly language routine, or at least an assembly language interface, to handle the entry point to an interrupt routine.)

Since we must initialize each task's stack, it is imperative that we know exactly how the **interrupt** modifier causes the registers to be saved. (The information that follows is valid for versions of Turbo C through 2.0. (If you have a later version, you will want to double-check the discussion that follows with your user manual if you encounter any troubles.) Turbo C executes this series of instructions each time an **interrupt** function is entered.

```
push ax
push bx
push cx
push dx
push es
push ds
push si
push di
push bp
```

As stated earlier, the 8086 automatically pushes the Flags, CS, and IP registers when an interrupt occurs. Therefore, upon entry to an **interrupt** function, the stack will look like that shown in Figure 4-1. We will make use of the arrangement of the stack in an **interrupt** function to initalize a task's stack for execution.

Figure 4-1

The stack after entering an interrupt function

BP ◀— top of stack
DI
SI
DS
ES
DX
CX
BS
AX
IP
CS
FLAGS

A SIMPLE TWO-TASK MODEL

Before implementing a full-featured multitasking kernel, a minimal two-task system will be created. This "bare-bones" model is developed first because it clearly illustrates the basic mechanics of task initialization and task switching. Once you understand these basic principles, they will be used to create the full-featured multitasking subsystem.

The Task Control Structure

A multitasking system must store various pieces of information about each task. For the simple, dual-task system, this information consists of the following three items: the task's stack segment, its stack pointer, and a pointer to the task's stack region. This information is most easily kept in a structure. The dual-task model uses the following array of structures to store information about the tasks.

```
struct task_struct {
  unsigned sp;
  unsigned ss;
  unsigned char *stck;
} tasks[2];
```

Initializing a Task

Before a task can be executed, it must be initialized. The initialization performs two things: it allocates space for the task's stack and it creates a register image at the top of the stack, which will be used to begin the task's execution. The function that does this, **make_task( )**, is shown here. Let's take a close look at it.

```
/* Define a new task. */
void make_task(task_type task, unsigned stck_size,
               unsigned id)
{
  struct int_regs *r;

  disable();
    tasks[id].stck = malloc(stck_size +
                     sizeof(struct int_regs));
```

```
      r = (struct int_regs *) tasks[id].stck +
          stck_size - sizeof(struct int_regs);

      /* initialize task stack */
      tasks[id].sp = FP_OFF((struct int_regs far *) r);
      tasks[id].ss = FP_SEG((struct int_regs far *) r);

      /* set up task code segment and IP */
      r->cs = FP_SEG(task);
      r->ip = FP_OFF(task);

      /* set up DS and ES segments */
      r->ds = _DS;
      r->es = _ES;

      /* enable interrupts - see text */
      r->flags = r->flags | 0x200;
    enable();
}
```

The **make_task( )** function is called with three parameters. The first is a **far** pointer to the function that serves as the entry point to the task. The type **task_type** is defined this way:

```
typedef int (far *task_type) (void);
```

You do not need to actually declare the function(s) that you multitask as being **far,** but you will need to cast them as **task_type** when you call **make_task( )**. The second parameter specifies the size of the stack for the task. Although the amount of stack used by a task varies widely, 1024 bytes are probably sufficient for nonrecursive tasks performing no disk I/O. If a task is using disk I/O, you will want to allow *at least* 4096 bytes. The last parameter to **make_task( )** specifies the task's ID number. For the dual-task model, the only valid IDs are 0 and 1.

The first line of code in the function allocates space for the task's stack. Once the stack has been allocated, it must be made to contain a register image, which will be used to start the task executing. To make this job easier, the following structure type is used.

```
typedef struct int_regs {
  unsigned bp;
  unsigned di;
  unsigned si;
  unsigned ds;
  unsigned es;
  unsigned dx;
  unsigned cx;
  unsigned bx;
  unsigned ax;
  unsigned ip;
  unsigned cs;
  unsigned flags;
} ;
```

This structure is organized exactly the way the stack is organized when an **interrupt** function is called. The second line of code in **make_task( )** sets the pointer **r** equal to the start of the register image. Using this pointer, the initial values of the SP, SS, CS, IP, DS, ES, and Flags registers can be properly set. Let's examine the how and why of each register initialization.

The segment and offset of the stack region are stored in the task's SS and SP registers, respectively. The segment is obtained using **FP_SEG( )**, and the offset is found using **FP_OFF( )**. These are Turbo C-specific functions, which return the segment and offset of a **far** address. If you are using a different compiler, you may have similar functions at your disposal. If not, you must use some assembly code to accomplish the same thing.

The instruction pointer is set to the offset address of the first instruction of the task and the code segment is set to the segment of the task.

The values of the DS and ES registers are the same as those currently used by the program as long as you are compiling for a small data model. These values are obtained using Turbo C's built-in register variables **_DS** and **_ES**. If you are not using Turbo C, you will need to use some assembly code to obtain these values.

Finally, the Flags register is initialized to 0x200. This value causes bit 9 to be turned on. When this bit is set, interrupts are enabled. This step is important because interrupts must be enabled when the task begins execution. The reason that interrupts are disabled before the initialization process takes place is to ensure that no task switch occurs before the task is fully initialized.

Intercepting the Timer and Starting Task Switching

If you have read Chapter 3, then you know that all PCs and compatibles have a timer, which executes interrupt 8 approximately 18 times a second. Our multitasking system uses this interrupt to switch tasks. To do this, we will use the same procedure as used by the TSR in Chapter 3; however, we must be careful because interrupt 8 cannot be rerouted until at least one task is ready to run.

After each task is initialized, multitasking can begin. To start tasking requires three steps. First, interrupt 8 is rerouted so that it executes the scheduler. Once interrupt 8 is rerouted to the scheduler (called **int8 _ task _ switch( )**), multitasking begins with the next timer interrupt. The address of the original interrupt service routine associated with interrupt 8 is stored in **old _ int8** for later use. Second, the stack pointer and stack segment of the program are saved into two global variables. These values are used to return to the program when tasking stops. Finally, the stack is reset to point to the stack of the first task whose ID is specified in the global variable, **tswitch**. The function that starts up the multitasking system is called **multitask( )** and is shown here:

```
/* Start up multitasking, */
void interrupt multitask(void)
{
  disable();
    /* reset interrupt 8 */
    old_int8 = getvect(8);
    setvect(8, int8_task_switch);

    /* save original stack segment and pointer */
    oldss = _SS;
    oldsp = _SP;

    /* reroute stack to first task */
    _SS = tasks[tswitch].ss;
    _SP = tasks[tswitch].sp;
  enable();
  /* task will begin running upon return */
}
```

Even though this function is not executed via an interrupt it still must be declared as an **interrupt** function because it must restore all registers upon its return in order to start the first task.

The Scheduler

The dual-task scheduler hardly warrants being called a scheduler because it is so limited. All it does is switch execution back and forth between two tasks each time the timer causes interrupt 8 to be executed. The scheduler, called **int8_task_switch( )**, is shown here:

```
/* This intercepts timer interrupt 8 and performs
   a task switch.
*/
void interrupt int8_task_switch(void)
{

  (*old_int8)(); /* call old int8 function */

  tasks[tswitch].ss = _SS;   /* save old task stack */
  tasks[tswitch].sp = _SP;

  tswitch = !tswitch;   /* switch tasks */

  _SS = tasks[tswitch].ss;   /* set up stack of new task */
  _SP = tasks[tswitch].sp;

  if(!tasking) { /* stop tasking */
    disable();
      _SS = oldss;
      _SP = oldsp;
      setvect(8, old_int8);
      free(tasks[0].stck);
      free(tasks[1].stck);
    enable();
  }
}
```

The first thing that **int8_task_switch( )** does is to call the original routine associated with interrupt 8. *This is very important: if you fail to call the original routine, your system will crash.* The next two lines of code save the current task's stack pointer and segment registers. These values will be used again when the task is resumed. Next, the global variable **tswitch**, used to index **tasks**, is switched to the next task, and the SP and SS registers are loaded so that they point to the new task's stack. Assuming that tasking is still active, the function returns and the new task begins executing. A task can stop the multitasking system by setting the global variable **tasking** to zero. This causes the original program stack to be restored and interrupt 8 to be reset.

The Entire Dual-Tasking Model

The entire dual-tasking subsystem is shown here along with two very simple tasks. The tasks are functions **f1( )** and **f2( )**. The **f1( )** task increments the global variable **i** and prints the values of **i** and **j**. The **f2( )** task simply increments the global variable **j**. Do not use **printf( )** or any other standard output function in **f2( )** because these functions are not generally reentrant.

Note: Before continuing on to the next section, you should make sure that you understand how this simple multitasker operates. Keep one fact clearly in mind: the dual-task scheduler assumes that both tasks have been created. Don't try running it with only one task defined.

```c
/* A minimal two-task kernel for DOS. */
#include "stdio.h"
#include "dos.h"
#include "alloc.h"

typedef struct int_regs {
  unsigned bp;
  unsigned di;
  unsigned si;
  unsigned ds;
  unsigned es;
  unsigned dx;
  unsigned cx;
  unsigned bx;
  unsigned ax;
  unsigned ip;
  unsigned cs;
  unsigned flags;
} ;

struct task_struct {
  unsigned sp;
```

```
    unsigned ss;
    unsigned char *stck;
} tasks[2];

typedef int (far *task_type) (void);

void interrupt multitask(void);
void interrupt int8_task_switch(void);
void interrupt (*old_int8)(void);
void make_task(task_type task, unsigned stck, unsigned id);
void f2(void), f1(void);

unsigned oldss, oldsp;
int tswitch = 0;
char tasking = 1;

int i=0, j=0;

main()
{
  /* Initialize the tasks */
  make_task((task_type) f1, 1024, 0);
  make_task((task_type) f2, 1024, 1);

  /* start multitasking */
  multitask();
  printf("\ndone\n");
  printf("%d %d", i, j);
}

/* This intercepts timer interrupt 8 and performs
   a task switch.
*/
void interrupt int8_task_switch(void)
{

  (*old_int8)(); /* call old int8 function */

  tasks[tswitch].ss = _SS;  /* save old task stack */
  tasks[tswitch].sp = _SP;

  tswitch = !tswitch;  /* switch tasks */
```

```
  _SS = tasks[tswitch].ss;   /* set up stack of new task */
  _SP = tasks[tswitch].sp;

  if(!tasking) { /* stop tasking */
    disable();
      _SS = oldss;
      _SP = oldsp;
      setvect(8, old_int8);
      free(tasks[0].stck);
      free(tasks[1].stck);
    enable();
  }
}

/* Define a new task. */
void make_task(task_type task, unsigned stck_size,
               unsigned id)
{
  struct int_regs *r;

  disable();
    tasks[id].stck = malloc(stck_size +
                      sizeof(struct int_regs));

    r = (struct int_regs *) tasks[id].stck +
        stck_size - sizeof(struct int_regs);

    /* initialize task stack */
    tasks[id].sp = FP_OFF((struct int_regs far *) r);
    tasks[id].ss = FP_SEG((struct int_regs far *) r);

    /* set up task code segment and IP */
    r->cs = FP_SEG(task);
    r->ip = FP_OFF(task);

    /* set up DS and ES segments */
    r->ds = _DS;
    r->es = _ES;

    /* enable interrupts - see text */
    r->flags = r->flags | 0x200;
  enable();
}
```

```
/* Start up the multitasking kernel. */

void interrupt multitask(void)
{
  disable();
    /* reset interrupt 8 */
    old_int8 = getvect(8);
    setvect(8, int8_task_switch);

    /* save original stack segment and pointer */
    oldss = _SS;
    oldsp = _SP;

    /* reroute stack to first task */
    _SS = tasks[tswitch].ss;
    _SP = tasks[tswitch].sp;
  enable();
  /* task will begin running upon return */
}

/* Task 1 */
void f1(void)
{
  for(;;i++) {
    if(!(i%10)) printf("%d %d\n", i, j);
    if(i==1000) tasking = 0;
  }
}

/* Task 2 */
void f2(void)
{
  for(;;j++) ;
}
```

CREATING A FULL-FEATURED MULTITASKING KERNEL

Now that the necessary theory has been discussed, we can begin developing a full-featured multitasking kernel. This subsystem will embody all of the concepts presented in this chapter. You will be able to use it to create actual applications that multitask various parts of themselves.

Task States

Although the "bare-bones" dual-tasking model is simple and effectively illustrates how task switching takes place, it omits several items that all real multitasking systems will need. For example, it assumes that both tasks are always ready to run. However, in a real situation, a task may be prevented from executing because a resource that it needs is unavailable. In a multitasking system a *resource* is anything that a task may need, including things like memory, access to a library routine, or input from the user. In addition, a real multitasking system must recognize when a task ends and stop executing it. Finally, a task may simply want to suspend its execution for a specific number of clock cycles and then resume execution. There must be some mechanism to accommodate these situations.

As the preceding paragraph implies, a task can be in one of a variety of states. The state of the task determines what the scheduler will do with it. To fully implement a multitasking system, the following task states need to be provided for: running, ready-to-run, suspended, blocked (waiting for a resource), sleeping, and dead (terminated or non-existent). When a task is currently executing, it is in a state of running. When a task is not currently executing but is able to run as soon as it gets its time slice, it is in a "ready-to-run" state. A task can be suspended by itself or another task. When suspended, it will not execute. A suspended task can only be resumed if another task explicitly requests it. If a task is waiting for a resource, then it is blocked. It will resume execution when that resource becomes available. A task that is sleeping will not execute until a specific number of ticks have occurred. Finally, a dead state means that the task has terminated (or was never started). The multitasking kernel uses these states to manage tasking.

Expanding the Task Control Structure

Since the dual-tasking example was simply a model, we need to expand the information held in the task control structure to accommodate the additional features we will be adding. The expanded **task_struct** type is shown here along with some necessary definitions.

```
#define NUM_TASKS  5

enum task_state {RUNNING, READY, BLOCKED, SLEEPING,
                 SUSPENDED, DEAD };

struct task_struct {
  unsigned sp;
  unsigned ss;
  enum task_state status;  /* task state */
  unsigned *pending;       /* semaphore waiting for */
  int sleep;               /* number of ticks to sleep */
  unsigned char *stck;     /* stack */
} tasks[NUM_TASKS];
```

The task states are defined by the enumeration **task_state**. When a task is **DEAD** it is not executed and is considered to be removed from the system. If a task is waiting on a resource, then the address of a variable controlling access to that resource will be pointed to by **pending**. (Variables that control access to resources are called *semaphores*; they will be discussed shortly.) If a task is sleeping, the number of ticks to sleep is held in **sleep**. A nonsleeping task will have a **sleep** value of zero.

The maximum number of tasks is determined by the macro **NUM_TASKS**. As defined here, the maximum is five. The most tasks you will probably want to run on a PC is about 20. However, for the best performance, you should specify only the number of tasks that your application will actually use. If you specify too many tasks, the scheduler may not complete its work before the next timer interrupt occurs. If this happens, your system will crash.

From a practical point of view, system performance degrades very noticeably when running more than a few active tasks, so, in reality, you will want to limit the tasks to a small number.

Expanding **make_task( )**

Since each task will have a state associated with it, it is necessary to change **make_task( )** so that it initializes the state of each task properly, as shown here:

```
/* Make_task() returns false if the task cannot be added
   to the task queue.  Otherwise, it returns true.
*/
make_task(taskptr task, unsigned stck, unsigned id)
{
  struct int_regs *r;

  if(id>=NUM_TASKS || id<0) return 0;

  disable();
    /* allocate space for the task */
    tasks[id].stck = malloc(stck + sizeof(struct int_regs));
    r = (struct int_regs *) tasks[id].stck +
        stck - sizeof(struct int_regs);

    /* initialize task stack */
    tasks[id].sp = FP_OFF((struct int_regs far *) r);
    tasks[id].ss = FP_SEG((struct int_regs far *) r);

    /* set up new task's CS and IP registers */
    r->cs = FP_SEG(task);
    r->ip = FP_OFF(task);

    /* set up DS and ES */
    r->ds = _DS;
    r->es = _DS;

    /* enable interrupts */
    r->flags = 0x200;

    /* initialize as ready-to-run */
    tasks[id].status = READY;
  enable();
  return 1;
}
```

Expanding the Scheduler

To accommodate the various states that a task may be in, the scheduler must be greatly expanded over the simple version shown in the dual-task model. The new version of **int8_task_switch( )** is shown here:

```
/* Timer interrupt task scheduler. */
void interrupt int8_task_switch(void)
{
  (*old_int8)();  /* call original int8 routine */

  if(single_task) return;  /* if single tasking is
                              on, then return without
                              a task switch */

  tasks[tswitch].ss = _SS;  /* save current task's stack */
  tasks[tswitch].sp = _SP;

  /* if current task was running when interrupted, then
     change its state to READY
*/
  if(tasks[tswitch].status==RUNNING)
    tasks[tswitch].status = READY;

  /* see if any sleepers need to wake up */
  check_sleepers();
  /* See if all tasks are dead; if so, stop tasking */
  if(all_dead()) tasking = 0;

  if(!tasking) { /* stop tasking */
    disable();
      _SS = oldss;
      _SP = oldsp;
      setvect(8, old_int8);
      free_all();
    enable();
    return;
  }

  /* find new task */
  tswitch++;
  if(tswitch==NUM_TASKS) tswitch = 0;

  while(tasks[tswitch].status!=READY) {
    tswitch++;
    if(tswitch==NUM_TASKS) tswitch = 0;
```

```
      }

      _SS = tasks[tswitch].ss;  /* switch stack to new task */
      _SP = tasks[tswitch].sp;
      tasks[tswitch].status = RUNNING; /* state is running */

}
```

Let's look at this new version in detail.

The first addition is the test of the **single_task** flag. The multitasking kernel allows a task to monopolize the CPU's time by setting this flag to true. In this case, the scheduler performs no task switching. This can be useful if a task must perform a time-critical function that cannot be interrupted. In general, you should disable task switching with care, because it prevents all other tasks from receiving any CPU time.

After the stack of the current task is saved, the state of the current task is set to **READY** if it previously had been **RUNNING**. At first you might think that the current task must always be in the **RUNNING** state when **int8_task_switch( )** is executed; however, this is not necessarily the case. For example, a task may have just gone to sleep when its time slice expired. In cases like this, it must not be reset to **READY**.

Next, the function **check_sleepers( )** is called. This function scans the array **tasks**, looking for any tasks that are asleep. When it finds one it decrements its **sleep** field. If the field becomes zero, then the task's state is changed to **READY**, and it will resume execution with its next time slice.

The function **all_dead( )** scans the **tasks** array to see if any tasks are ready to run. If none are, it returns true; otherwise, it returns false. Although this test is not technically necessary, it is included as an important safety feature: it prevents *deadlock* from locking up the computer when no tasks are ready to run. Deadlock describes a situation in which no task can run because each is waiting for something only another task can give it. Since all tasks are waiting on another, the system effectively locks up. Remember, if no tasks can be run, the scheduler has no task to switch to. If no tasks can run, multitasking stops.

Manual Task Switching

As you will see, there are times when the multitasking kernel needs to force a task switch before a timer interrupt occurs. To accomplish this, the **task_switch( )** function is included. This function is similar to

int8_task_switch( ) except that it does not update any sleepers because a clock tick has not actually occurred. The function is defined using the **interrupt** type modifier because it must save and restore all registers, just the way **int8_task_switch( )** does. However, **task_switch( )** is executed only via a call from other C code, not from an interrupt. The function is shown here:

```
/* This is the manual task switcher which your program
   can call to force a task switch.  It does not
   decrement any sleeper's sleep counter because a clock
   tick has not occurred.
*/
void interrupt task_switch(void)
{
    if(single_task) return;

  disable();
    tasks[tswitch].ss = _SS;
    tasks[tswitch].sp = _SP;
    if(tasks[tswitch].status==RUNNING)
      tasks[tswitch].status = READY;

    if(all_dead()) tasking = 0;

    if(!tasking) {
      disable();
        _SS = oldss;
        _SP = oldsp;
        setvect(8, old_int8);
        free_all();
      enable();
      return;
    }

    /* find new task */
    tswitch++;
    if(tswitch==NUM_TASKS) tswitch = 0;

    while(tasks[tswitch].status!=READY) {
      tswitch++;
      if(tswitch==NUM_TASKS) tswitch = 0;
    }
```

```
    _SS = tasks[tswitch].ss;
    _SP = tasks[tswitch].sp;
    tasks[tswitch].status = RUNNING;
  enable();
}
```

Sleeping and Suspending

You can put a task to sleep for a specific number of clock ticks using **msleep( )**. This function causes the task that calls it to sleep. You can suspend any task in the system using **suspend( )**. Both of these functions make use of **task_switch( )** to switch tasks. To restart a suspended task, call **resume( )**. These functions are shown here:

```
/* Stop execution of a task for a specified
   number of clock cycles.
*/
void msleep(int ticks)
{
  disable();
    tasks[tswitch].status = SLEEPING;
    tasks[tswitch].sleep = ticks;
  enable();
  task_switch();
}

/* Suspend a task until resumed by another
   task.
*/
void suspend(int id)
{
  if(id<0 || id>=NUM_TASKS) return;
  tasks[id].status = SUSPENDED;
  task_switch();
}

/* Restart a previously suspended task. */
void resume(int id)
```

```
{
  if(id<0 || id>=NUM_TASKS) return;
  tasks[id].status = READY;
}
```

Killing a Task

You can remove a task from the system by calling **kill _ task( )**, which sets the specified task's state to **DEAD,** frees the stack region, and then executes **task _ switch( )** to force execution of another task to resume. The **kill _ task( )** function is shown here:

```
/* Kill a task. (i.e., make its state DEAD.) */
void kill_task(int id)
{
  disable();
    tasks[id].status = DEAD;
    free(tasks[id].stck);
    tasks[id].stck = NULL;
  enable();
  task_switch();
}
```

The **kill _ task( )** function is actually extremely important because it provides a way to terminate a task. The function that forms the entry point to a task must *never be allowed to terminate.* Instead, to end the function, call **kill _ task( )**. Remember, when a function ends, it executes a return. But if that function is the entry point to a task, the multitasking system won't know where to return to since the task's stack will be empty. This will cause the program to run wild.

Semaphores

As mentioned earlier, DOS and many C library functions are not reentrant. This means that access to them must be controlled, making sure that one—and only one—task uses a non-reentrant function at a time. The process of controlling access to a resource is called *serialization*. As the following discussion will explain, serialization of resources is not a trivial matter.

The Serialization Problem

The multitasking kernel must provide special services that allow access to a shared resource to be serialized because, without help from the multitasking kernel, there is no way for one task to know that it has sole access to a resource. To understand this fact, imagine that you are writing programs for a multitasking system that does *not* provide any serialization support. Further imagine that you have two simultaneously executing tasks, *A* and *B*, both of which occasionally require access to some resource *R* (such as a DOS function) that must only be accessed by one task at a time. As a means of preventing one task from accessing *R* while the other is using it, try the following solution. First, establish a variable called **flag**, that can be accessed by both tasks, and initialize **flag** to 0. Next, before accessing *R*, each task waits for the flag to be cleared (0). Once cleared, the task sets the flag, accesses *R*, and finally clears the flag—that is, before either program accesses *R*, it executes this piece of code:

```
while(flag)  ; /* wait for flag to be zero */
flag = 1;      /* set flag so another process knows
                  that you are using R
               */

*/ access resource R */

flag = 0;
```

The idea behind this code is that neither process will access *R* if **flag** is set. Conceptually, this approach is in the spirit of the correct solution. However, in actual fact, it leaves much to be desired because of one simple reason: it won't always work! Let's see why.

Using the code just given, it is possible for both tasks to access *R* at the same time. The **while** loop is, in essence, performing repeated load and compare instructions on **flag** or, in other words, testing **flag**'s value. The next line of code sets the **flag**'s value. The trouble is that it is possible for these two operations to be performed in two separate time slices. Between the two time slices, the value of **flag** might be changed by a different task, thus allowing R to be accessed by both processes at the same time. To understand this, imagine that task A enters the **while** loop and finds that **flag** is 0, which is the green light to access R. However, before it can set **flag** to 1, its time slice expires and task B resumes execution. If B executes its **while**, it too will find that **flag** is not set and will assume that it is safe to access R. However, when A resumes, it will also begin accessing R. The crucial point of the problem is that the testing of **flag** and the setting of **flag** do not comprise one, uninterruptable operation. Rather, as just illustrated, they can be separated by a time slice of the other task. No matter how you try, there is no way that you can absolutely guarantee that one—and only one—process will access R at a time using this approach.

The solution to the serialization problem is as elegant as it is simple: the multitasking kernel provides a routine that in one, uninterruptable operation, tests and, if possible, sets a flag. In the language of operating systems engineers, this is called a *Test-and-Set* operation. For historical reasons, the flags used to control serialization are called semaphores. The multitasking kernel services that allow you to use them are discussed in the next section.

The Semaphore Services

The multitasking kernel provides two semaphore services: **set_semaphore( )** and **clear_semaphore( )**. These functions allow separate tasks to synchronize their activity. As described in the previous section, one important use of semaphores is to control access to a shared resource. However, they have other uses, such as allowing one task to signal another that an event has occurred.

One of the first things you learn about the semaphore functions is that the semaphore routines work in conjunction with each other—you can't use just one!

For the multitasking kernel developed in this chapter, a semaphore is a global **unsigned** variable that must be initialized to 0 before it is used. This variable must be accessible to all functions that wish to use it.

To set a semaphore, use **set_semaphore( )**, which is shown here:

```
/* Wait for a semaphore. */
void set_semaphore(unsigned *sem)
```

Robert Ward
Publisher: C User's Journal

Few people have done more to advance the general acceptance of the C language than Robert Ward, the founder of R&D Publications, which operates the C User's Group and publishes the *C User's Journal*. He first discovered C when he formed a company to design a retrofit kit to upgrade the electronics in existing photo-typesetters. Needing a language that would handle the real-time constraints involved in managing a typesetting system, Robert chose Leor Zolman's BDS C running under CP/M for the project. As Robert puts it, "I needed an efficient, compiled, systems language with a simple assembly language interface. I wanted a structured language, but not one as confining as Pascal."

I asked Robert what his favorite C construct was. "More than a single construct, I like the expressiveness of the operators and the near equivalence between statements and expressions. I think C's greater freedom of expression makes it easier for a good programmer to write a program that is isomorphic to his or her conceptual solution. For example,

```
while ((*dest++ = *source++) != '\0') ;
```

is (at the lowest level of abstraction) exactly the way I understand string copy; that is, copy each character, and quit when you've copied the end-of-string marker. You can write the same code in Pascal, for example, but it is not as pure."

Robert believes that there are two common misconceptions about C. "First, some programmers think learning C will be like learning any other programming language. It isn't, because C is open ended—you never finish learning it. Unlike Pascal, which insulates the user from the details of the system, C deliberately makes the underlying system available and, thus, makes it part of what you must understand to expertly use the language. Second, C doesn't offer the run-time guarantees that some other languages do. Trivial errors can go undetected for thousands of lines and become "untraceable." Learning C means learning new debugging techniques."

Robert Ward lives in Lawrence, Kansas and is currently editor and publisher of the *C User's Journal*. He is a private pilot and enjoys flying in his spare time.

```
{
  disable();
    while(*sem) {
      semblock(tswitch, sem);
      task_switch();
      disable();  /* task switch will enable
                     interrupts, so they need to be
                     turned off again */
    }
    *sem = 1;
  enable();
}
```

In this function **sem** is a pointer to the variable that is the semaphore. The first thing the function does is disable interrupts. With interrupts disabled, no task switch will occur because the timer interrupt is temporarily blocked. Next, as long as the semaphore requested is in use (that is, already set to a non-zero value) the requesting task is put into a blocked state and a manual task switch is forced by calling **task_switch( )**. The **task_switch( )** function automatically enables interrupts, so it is necessary to disable them again before the loop repeats. Once the semaphore is clear, it is set to 1, interrupts are enabled, and the function returns, thus allowing the calling task access to the resource serialized by the specified semaphore.

The function **semblock( )** puts a task into a blocked state and stores the address of the semaphore that it is waiting for. It is shown here:

```
/* Set task to BLOCKED.  This is an
   internal function not to be called by
   your program.
*/
void semblock(int id, unsigned *sem)
{
  tasks[id].status = BLOCKED;
  tasks[id].pending = sem;
}
```

To clear a semaphore, use **clear_semaphore( )**, shown here along with its support function **restart( )**.

```
/* Release a semaphore. */
void clear_semaphore(unsigned *sem)
{
  disable();
    tasks[tswitch].pending = NULL;
    *sem = 0;
    restart(sem);
    task_switch();
  enable();
}


/* Restart a task  that is waiting for the
   specified semaphore.   This is an internal
   function not to be called by your
   program.
*/
void restart(unsigned *sem)
{
  register int i;

  for(i=0; i<NUM_TASKS; i++)
    if(tasks[i].pending == sem) {
      tasks[i].pending = NULL;
      if(tasks[i].status == BLOCKED)
        tasks[i].status = READY;
      return;
    }
}
```

The **clear‗semaphore( )** function clears the specified semaphore and then calls **restart( )**, which checks to see if any tasks are waiting for this semaphore. The **restart( )** function finds the first task (if any) that is waiting for the semaphore, clears its **pending** field in the task control structure, and sets its state to **READY**. This means that the next time it comes up for execution, it can proceed to access the resource serialized by the specified semaphore.

The following code fragment shows how to use the semaphore functions to control access to a function called **R( )**.

```
unsigned sem = 0;

/* first task */
```

```
f1()
{
  set_semaphore(&sem);
  R();
  clear_semaphore(&sem);
}

/* second task */
f2()
{
  set_semaphore(&sem);
  R();
  clear_semaphore(&sem);
}
```

Some Miscellaneous Functions

In addition to those already discussed, the multitasking kernel includes the functions shown here. These functions are necessary because **tasking** and **single_task** are declared as **static** variables, which means that they can only be accessed by functions within the same file. Your application code needs some way to interrogate or alter them there.

```
/* Stop tasking. */
void stop_tasking(void)
{
  tasking = 0;
  task_switch();
}

/* Execute only one task. */
void mono_task(void)
{
  disable();
    single_task = 1;
  enable();
}

/* Resume multitasking all tasks.  (Use to
    restart tasking after a call to mono_task().) */
```

```
void resume_tasking(void)
{
  single_task = 0;
}


/* Display the state of all tasks. This function must
   NOT be called while multitasking is in effect. */
void task_status(void)
{
  register int i;

  if(tasking) return;   /* cannot be used while
                           multitasking */
  printf("\n");
  for(i=0; i<NUM_TASKS; i++) {
    printf("Task %d: ", i);
    switch(tasks[i].status) {
      case READY: printf("READY\n");
        break;
      case RUNNING: printf("RUNNING\n");
        break;
      case BLOCKED: printf("BLOCKED\n");
        break;
      case SUSPENDED: printf("SUSPENDED\n");
        break;
      case SLEEPING: printf("SLEEPING\n");
        break;
      case DEAD: printf("DEAD\n");
    }
  }
}
```

The use for **task_status( )** is debugging. It can tell you the status of each task in the system. It can only be called when the multitasking is off. (You might find it an interesting project to convert it so that it can be used while task switching is active.)

A Small I/O Library

As stated earlier, many C library functions will not be reentrant because they make use of DOS. This includes most of the I/O system; however, this does not mean that these functions cannot be used by a task. It *does* mean, however, that access to these functions must be serialized to prevent a second, simultaneous activation by another task. There are two ways to approach serialization of C's I/O functions. First, you can surround each call to an I/O with calls to **set_semaphore( )** and **clear_semaphore( )**. However, if your program calls very many I/O functions, this makes for a lot of extra code. A better way to accomplish serialization is to create interface functions that serialize access to I/O via a single semaphore. This function, for example, serializes access to **puts( )**.

```
unsigned io_out=0;   /* i/o semaphore */

/* Serialized version of puts(). */
void mputs(char *s)
{
  set_semaphore(&io_out);
  puts(s);
  clear_semaphore(&io_out);
}
```

Instead of calling **puts( )** directly, your program calls **mputs( )**. All other I/O interface functions most also use the **io_out** semaphore. In this way, only one I/O request can be active at a single time. Here are two more I/O functions that use this concept.

```
/* Output a number. */
void mputnum(int num)
{
  set_semaphore(&io_out);
  printf("%d ", num);
  clear_semaphore(&io_out);
}

/* Serialized version of getche(). */
char mgetche(void)
{
  char ch;

  set_semaphore(&io_out);
  ch = getch();
```

```
   clear_semaphore(&io_out);
   return ch;
}
```

You can add whatever I/O functions, including disk functions, your program needs, as long as you serialize access to them using this approach.

The main disadvantage to serializing access to all I/O functions is that it can effectively turn your multitasking programs into single-tasking ones if all tasks perform numerous I/O requests. To help alleviate this problem, you can create your own reentrant versions of certain I/O functions. The easiest ones, of course, are the screen I/O functions because you can bypass DOS (and BIOS) altogether and simply write to the video RAM. (This process was described in Chapter 3 in reference to TSRs; refer there for details.) For example, here are reentrant functions similar to **putchar( )** and **puts( )**, along with two necessary initialization functions.

```
char far *vid_mem;

/* Output a string at specified X,Y coordinates.
   This function IS reentrant and may be called
   by any task at any time.
*/
void mxyputs(int x, int y, char *str)
{
   while(*str moutchar(x++, y, *str++));
}

/* Output a character at specified X,Y coordinates.
   This function IS reentrant and may be called
   by any task at any time.
*/

void moutchar(int x, int y, char ch)
{
   char far *y;

   v = vid_mem;

   v += (y*160)  + x*2;  /* compute char loc */
   *v++ = ch;     /* write the character */
   *v = 7;        /* normal character */
}
```

```
/*****************************************************
Initialize the video subsystem.
*****************************************************/

/* Returns the current video mode. */
video_mode(void)
{
  union REGS r;

  r.h.ah = 15; /* get video mode */
  return int86(0x10, &r, &r & 255;
}


/* Set the vid_mem pointer to the start of video
   memory.
*/
void set_vid_mem(void)
{
  int vmode;

  vmode = video_mode();
  if((vmode!=2) && (vmode!=3) && (vmode!=7)) {
    printf("video must be in 80 column text mode");
    exit(1);
  }
  /* set proper address of video RAM */
  if(vmode==7) vid_mem = (char far *) MK_FP(0xB000, 0000);
  else vid_mem = (char far *) MK_FP(0xB800, 0000);
}
```

THE ENTIRE MULTITASKING KERNEL

The entire multitasking kernel is shown here along with a small set of reentrant or serialized library functions. You should put all of this code into one file and then simply link it with any program you wish to multitask.

```
/* A multitasking kernel for DOS. */
```

```c
#include "stdio.h"
#include "dos.h"
#include "alloc.h"
#include "stdlib.h"
#include "conio.h"

#define NUM_TASKS  5

enum task_state {RUNNING, READY, BLOCKED, SLEEPING,
                 SUSPENDED, DEAD };

typedef struct int_regs {
  unsigned bp;
  unsigned di;
  unsigned si;
  unsigned ds;
  unsigned es;
  unsigned dx;
  unsigned cx;
  unsigned bx;
  unsigned ax;
  unsigned ip;
  unsigned cs;
  unsigned flags;
} ;

struct task_struct {
  unsigned sp;
  unsigned ss;
  enum task_state status; /* task state */
  unsigned *pending;      /* semaphore waiting for */
  int sleep;              /* number of ticks to sleep */
  unsigned char *stck;    /* stack */
} tasks[NUM_TASKS];

typedef int (far *taskptr) (void);

int make_task(taskptr task, unsigned stck,
              unsigned id);
void interrupt multitask(void), init_tasks(void);
void kill_task(int id);
void interrupt int8_task_switch(void);
void interrupt task_switch(void);
```

```
void interrupt (*old_int8)(void);
void set_semaphore(unsigned *sem), mono_task(void);
void clear_semaphore(unsigned *sem);
void resume_tasking(void);
void semblock(int id, unsigned *sem);
void restart(unsigned *sem), check_sleepers(void);
void stop_tasking(void), msleep(int ticks);
void suspend(int id), resume(int id);
void task_status(void), free_all(void);
int all_dead(void);

void mputnum(int num), mputs(char *s);
char mgetche(void);
void moutchar(int x, int y, char ch);
void mxyputs(int x, int y, char *str);
void set_vid_mem(void);

int video_mode(void);

static unsigned oldss, oldsp;

static int tswitch = 0;       /* task index */
static char tasking = 1;      /* tasking system enabled */
static char single_task = 0; /* single task flag off */

char far *vid_mem;   /* pointer to video memory */

/* Timer interrupt task scheduler. */
void interrupt int8_task_switch(void)
{
  (*old_int8)();   /* call original int8 routine */

  if(single_task) return;   /* if single tasking is
                               on, then return without
                               a task switch */

  tasks[tswitch].ss = _SS;   /* save current task's stack */
  tasks[tswitch].sp = _SP;

  /* if current task was running when interrupted, then
     change its state to READY
  */
  if(tasks[tswitch].status==RUNNING)
```

```
    tasks[tswitch].status = READY;

  /* see if any sleepers need to wake up */
  check_sleepers();

  /* See if all tasks are dead; if so, stop tasking */
  if(all_dead()) tasking = 0;

  if(!tasking) { /* stop tasking */
    disable();
      _SS = oldss;
      _SP = oldsp;
      setvect(8, old_int8);
      free_all();
    enable();
    return;
  }

  /* find new task */
  tswitch++;
  if(tswitch==NUM_TASKS) tswitch = 0;

  while(tasks[tswitch].status!=READY) {
    tswitch++;
    if(tswitch==NUM_TASKS) tswitch = 0;
  }

  _SS = tasks[tswitch].ss;  /* switch task to new task */
  _SP = tasks[tswitch].sp;
  tasks[tswitch].status = RUNNING; /* state is running */

}


/* This is the manual task switcher which your program
   can call to force a task switch.  It does not
   decrement any sleeper's sleep counter because a clock
   tick has not occurred.
*/
void interrupt task_switch(void)
{
    if(single_task) return;

  disable();
```

```
      tasks[tswitch].ss = _SS;
      tasks[tswitch].sp = _SP;
      if(tasks[tswitch].status==RUNNING)
        tasks[tswitch].status = READY;

      if(all_dead()) tasking = 0;

      if(!tasking) {
        disable();
          _SS = oldss;
          _SP = oldsp;
          setvect(8, old_int8);
          free_all();
        enable();
        return;
      }

      /* find new task */
      tswitch++;
      if(tswitch==NUM_TASKS) tswitch = 0;

      while(tasks[tswitch].status!=READY) {
        tswitch++;
        if(tswitch==NUM_TASKS) tswitch = 0;
      }

      _SS = tasks[tswitch].ss;
      _SP = tasks[tswitch].sp;
      tasks[tswitch].status = RUNNING;
    enable();
}

/* Return 1 if no tasks are ready to run; 0 if
   at least one task is READY.
*/
all_dead(void)
{
  register int i;

  for(i=0; i<NUM_TASKS; i++)
    if(tasks[i].status==READY) return 0;
  return 1;
}
```

```
/* Decrement the sleep count of any sleeping tasks. */
void check_sleepers(void)
{
  register int i;

  for(i=0; i<NUM_TASKS; i++) {
    if(tasks[i].status==SLEEPING) {
      tasks[i].sleep--;
      if(!tasks[i].sleep) tasks[i].status = READY;
    }
  }
}


/* Free all stack space. This function should
   not be called by your program.  */
void free_all(void)
{
  register int i;

  for(i=0; i<NUM_TASKS; i++) {
    if(tasks[i].stck) {
      free(tasks[i].stck);
      tasks[i].stck = NULL;
    }
  }
}


/* Make_task() returns false if the task cannot be added
   to the task queue.  Otherwise, it returns true.
*/
make_task(taskptr task, unsigned stck, unsigned id)
{
  struct int_regs *r;

  if(id>=NUM_TASKS || id<0) return 0;

  disable();
    /* allocate space for the task */
    tasks[id].stck = malloc(stck + sizeof(struct int_regs));
    r = (struct int_regs *) tasks[id].stck +
        stck - sizeof(struct int_regs);
```

```
     /* initialize task stack */
     tasks[id].sp = FP_OFF((struct int_regs far *) r);
     tasks[id].ss = FP_SEG((struct int_regs far *) r);

     /* set up new task's CS and IP registers */
     r->cs = FP_SEG(task);
     r->ip = FP_OFF(task);

     /* set up DS and ES */
     r->ds = _DS;
     r->es = _DS;

     /* enable interrupts */
     r->flags = 0x200;

     tasks[id].status = READY;
   enable();
   return 1;
}

/* Start up the multitasking kernel. */
void interrupt multitask(void)
{
   disable();

     /* Switch in the timer-based scheduler */
     old_int8 = getvect(8);
     setvect(8, int8_task_switch);

     /* Save the program's stack pointer and segment
        so that when tasking ends, execution can continue
        where it left off in the program.
     */
     oldss = _SS;
     oldsp = _SP;

     /* set stack to first task's stack */
     _SS = tasks[tswitch].ss;
     _SP = tasks[tswitch].sp;
   enable();
}

/* Kill a task. (i.e., make its state DEAD.) */
```

```
void kill_task(int id)
{
  disable();
    tasks[id].status = DEAD;
    free(tasks[id].stck);
    tasks[id].stck = NULL;
  enable();
  task_switch();
}

/* Initialize the task control structures. */
void init_tasks(void)
{
  register int i;

  for(i=0; i<NUM_TASKS; i++) {
    tasks[i].status = DEAD;
    tasks[i].pending = NULL;
    tasks[i].sleep = 0;
    tasks[i].stck = NULL;
  }
  set_vid_mem();
}

/* Stop tasking. */
void stop_tasking(void)
{
  tasking = 0;
  task_switch();
}

/* Execute only one task. */
void mono_task(void)
{
  disable();
    single_task = 1;
  enable();
}

/* Resume multitasking all tasks.  (Use to
   restart tasking after a call to mono_task().) */
void resume_tasking(void)
{
```

```
   single_task = 0;
}

/* Stop execution of a task for a specified
   number of clock cycles.
*/
void msleep(int ticks)
{
  disable();
    tasks[tswitch].status = SLEEPING;
    tasks[tswitch].sleep = ticks;
  enable();
  task_switch();
}

/* Suspend a task until resumed by another
   task.
*/
void suspend(int id)
{
  if(id<0 || id>=NUM_TASKS) return;
  tasks[id].status = SUSPENDED;
  task_switch();
}

/* Restart a previously suspended task. */
void resume(int id)
{
  if(id<0 || id>=NUM_TASKS) return;
  tasks[id].status = READY;
}

/* Wait for a semaphore. */
void set_semaphore(unsigned *sem)
{
  disable();
    while(*sem) {
      semblock(tswitch, sem);
      task_switch();
      disable();  /* task switch will enable
                     interrupts, so they need to be
                     turned off again */
    }
```

```
    *sem = 1;
  enable();
}

/* Release a semaphore. */
void clear_semaphore(unsigned *sem)
{
  disable();
    tasks[tswitch].pending = NULL;
    *sem = 0;
    restart(sem);
    task_switch();
  enable();
}

/* Set task to BLOCKED.  This is an
   internal function not to be called by
   your program.
*/
void semblock(int id, unsigned *sem)
{
  tasks[id].status = BLOCKED;
  tasks[id].pending = sem;
}

/* Restart a task that is waiting for the
   specified semaphore. This is an internal
   function not to be called by your
   program.
*/
void restart(unsigned *sem)
{
  register int i;

  for(i=0; i<NUM_TASKS; i++)
    if(tasks[i].pending == sem) {
      tasks[i].pending = NULL;
      if(tasks[i].status == BLOCKED)
        tasks[i].status = READY;
      return;
    }
}
```

```c
/* Display the state of all tasks. This function must
   NOT be called while multitasking is in effect. */
void task_status(void)
{
  register int i;

  if(tasking) return;   /* cannot be used while
                           multitasking */
  printf("\n");
  for(i=0; i<NUM_TASKS; i++) {
    printf("Task %d: ", i);
    switch(tasks[i].status) {
      case READY: printf("READY\n");
        break;
      case RUNNING: printf("RUNNING\n");
        break;
      case BLOCKED: printf("BLOCKED\n");
        break;
      case SUSPENDED: printf("SUSPENDED\n");
        break;
      case SLEEPING: printf("SLEEPING\n");
        break;
      case DEAD: printf("DEAD\n");
    }
  }
}


/************************************************************
Serialized and Reentrant I/O functions for the Multitasker.
************************************************************/
unsigned io_out=0;   /* i/o semaphore */

/* Serialized version of puts(). */
void mputs(char *s)
{
  set_semaphore(&io_out);
  puts(s);
  clear_semaphore(&io_out);
}

/* Output a number. */
void mputnum(int num)
{
```

```
    set_semaphore(&io_out);
    printf("%d ", num);
    clear_semaphore(&io_out);
}


/* Serialized version of getche(). */
char mgetche(void)
{
    char ch;

    set_semaphore(&io_out);
    ch = getch();
    clear_semaphore(&io_out);
    return ch;
}

/* Output a string at specified X,Y coordinates.
   This function IS reentrant and may be called
   by any task at any time.
*/
void mxyputs(int x, int y, char *str)
{
    while(*str) moutchar(x++, y, *str++);
}


/* Output a character at specified X,Y coordinates.
   This function IS reentrant and may be called
   by any task at any time.
*/
void moutchar(int x, int y, char ch)
{
    char far *v;

    v = vid_mem;

    v += (y*160) + x*2;  /* compute char loc */
    *v++ = ch;  /* write the character */
    *v = 7;     /* normal character */
}


/*****************************************************
   Initialize the video subsystem.
*****************************************************/
```

```
/* Returns the current video mode. */
video_mode(void)
{
  union REGS r;

  r.h.ah = 15;  /* get video mode */
  return int86(0x10, &r, &r) & 255;
}


/* Set the vid_mem pointer to the start of video
   memory.
*/
void set_vid_mem(void)
{
  int vmode;

  vmode = video_mode();
  if((vmode!=2) && (vmode!=3) && (vmode!=7)) {
    printf("video must be in 80 column text mode");
    exit(1);
  }
  /* set proper address of video RAM */
  if(vmode==7) vid_mem = (char far *) MK_FP(0xB000, 0000);
  else vid_mem = (char far *) MK_FP(0xB800, 0000);
}
```

A DEMONSTRATION PROGRAM

The following program demonstrates the use of the multitasking kernel
and several of its functions. The best way to learn about the multitasking
kernel is to write several sample programs on which to try each multitasking function.

```
/* A sample multitasking program. */

#include "stdio.h"

/**********************************************************
   Include these definitions in any file that
   uses the multitasking kernel.  You may want to
   put these into a header file which you simply include.
**********************************************************/
```

```
typedef int (far *taskptr) (void);

int make_task(taskptr task, unsigned stck,
              unsigned id);
void interrupt multitask(void), init_tasks(void);
void kill_task(int id);
void interrupt task_switch(void);
void set_semaphore(unsigned *sem), mono_task(void);
void clear_semaphore(unsigned *sem);
void semblock(int id, unsigned *sem);
void stop_tasking(void), msleep(int ticks);
void suspend(int id), resume(int id);
void task_status(void), resume_tasking(void);

void mputnum(int num), mputs(char *s);
char mgetche(void);
void moutchar(int x, int y, char ch);
void mxyputs(int x, int y, char *str);


/*************************************************/

void f2(void), f1(void), f3(void);
void f4(void), f5(void);

int i=0, j=0, k=0, l=0, m=0;

main()
{
  init_tasks();

  make_task((taskptr) f1, 1024, 0);
  make_task((taskptr) f2, 1024, 1);
  make_task((taskptr) f3, 1024, 2);
  make_task((taskptr) f4, 1024, 3);
  make_task((taskptr) f5, 1024, 4);

  multitask();
  printf("done\n");
  printf("counters: %d %d %d %d %d", i, j, k, l, m);
  task_status();
}

void f1(void)
```

```
{
  mxyputs(20, 0, "starting task 0");
  for(;;i++) {
    mputnum(i);
  }
}

void f2(void)
{
  char ch;

  mxyputs(20, 1, "starting task 1");
  for(;;j++) {
    mputs("type a key ('q' to quit)");
    ch = mgetche();
    if(ch=='q') kill_task(1);
    mputnum(ch);
  }
}

void f3(void)
{
  mxyputs(20, 2, "starting task 2");
  for(; k<30000; k++) {
    moutchar(k%24, k%24, 'A'+(k%26));
  }
  kill_task(2);
}

void f4(void)
{
  mxyputs(20, 3, "starting task 3");
  for(; l<30000; l++) {
    moutchar(79-l%24, l%24, 'A'+(l%26));
  }
  kill_task(3);
}

void f5(void)
{
  mxyputs(20, 4, "starting task 4");
  msleep(200);
  m++;
```

```
  kill_task(0);
  kill_task(4);
}
```

SOME THINGS TO TRY

As stated earlier, multitasking ends if no task is ready to run. This makes experimentation easier because it generally prevents deadlocked tasks from killing the system. This means that when all tasks are blocked, suspended, sleeping, or dead, multitasking terminates. But, technically, a sleeping task is not dead. The trouble is that if the only tasks still alive in the system are sleeping, then the scheduler still has no task to switch to. You can prevent the termination of multitasking when all tasks are asleep in two ways. First, you can create a dummy task that executes continuously. With this approach, the scheduler always has a task to run. You can prevent this task from using much CPU time by simply making it execute a loop such as this:

```
for(;;) task_switch();
```

A more elegant approach is to make the scheduler a task in itself. Using this approach, the code executed inside the timer ISR simply switches to the scheduler; the scheduler then selects the next task. Therefore, when nothing else can run, the scheduler will simply continue to loop until something else is able to run. You might find it interesting to modify the multitasking kernel so that it operates this way.

As stated earlier, if you try to run too many tasks (more than about 20 to 30), it is possible that the scheduler will still be processing a task switch when the next timer interrupt occurs, causing a system crash. The time-consuming portions of the scheduler are the updating of all sleeping tasks and checking to see if all tasks are **DEAD**. If you don't need a task to sleep and/or know that a task will always be able to run, then you can take these checks out of the scheduler. Doing this will allow you to run approximately 100 tasks. Also, if you move the scheduler out of the timer interrupt and make it a separate task, you can run a virtually unlimited number of tasks.

As previously stated, the multitasking kernel uses a "round-robin" time-slice scheduler. You might find it fun to modify the code so that it uses a priority-based scheduler instead. You will need to add a priority field to the task control structure.

CHAPTER FIVE

A Screen-Editor Subsystem

With so many different text editors available for any major operating system, you might wonder why yet another one is developed in this chapter. First, many common programming projects require a text-editor subsystem. A database manager, for example, needs an editor to allow the user to create complex queries. Some modem programs need an editor to support the creation of complex "scripts," which are then executed automatically. Also, a great many different types of programs offer the user small "notepads" on which notes and memos can be kept. Second (and less practical but more interesting), I have met few programmers who loved everything about the text editor they used! If you fall into this category and have ever wished you could create an editor that worked *exactly* the way *you* wanted, the subsystem developed here is an excellent starting point. Whatever the reasons, text-editor subsystems are enjoyable programming tasks.

The text editor developed in this chapter is screen based and is commonly referred to as a *screen editor*. The earliest text editors were line oriented. One common example of a line editor is EDLIN, the standard

Thomas Plum
Chairman of Plum Hall, Inc.

Thomas Plum is well-known in the C world. He coauthored (with Ralph Ryan) the ANSI C conformance tests in the Plum Hall Validation Suite for C. He has also written five textbooks and has been actively teaching C and structured design principles since the mid 1970s. He holds a B.A. in mathematics from Rice University and a Ph.D. in Computer and Communication Science from the University of Michigan.

I asked Tom what single element contributes most to the design of an elegant program. "Creative connections—that magic that connects two apparently separate and distinct entities. For example," he continued, "in the 1960s, we were conditioned to thinking of files as rather complicated, special-purpose entities. Then UNIX appeared, with files that were simplified enough to connect every command with every other command."

"Or take an example from C, itself. Ritchie saw the connection between the syntax of declarations and expressions, and completed the scheme with the elegant complementary use of the asterisk. In declarations it means 'pointer'; in expressions it means 'indirect'—creative connection."

"Most of my ideas come in collaboration with Joan Hall, my partner in everything. She complements my expertise with her intuitive rapport—she connects with the human side of our work."

Tom describes his own design philosophy as a "combination of structured design, structured analysis, and data-structure analysis. When I need to do a detailed design, I draw the BNF structure of it. This not only forces me to think through the program carefully, but gives me the outline of it as well."

Tom came to C in 1976 when he was teaching structured design at Yourdon, Inc., after P.J. Plauger installed a UNIX system there. Tom recalls, "I first used C because I had to! But I soon discovered its power and economy. I saw that by using C, applications that previously had required big machines could be executed on small ones, like the 8080."

Thomas Plum lives in New Jersey. When he is not programming or writing, he enjoys good food and Cable Network News.

(although little used) DOS editor. When you're using a line-oriented editor, the screen of the computer does not look exactly like your file. However, a screen editor displays the text as it occurs in the file.

The screen editor that we will create supports a small, yet adequate, number of operations. They are

- enter characters

- delete characters

- delete a line

- move a line

- scroll down

- scroll up

- page down

- page up

- go to the top of the file

- go to the end of the file

- find a string

- global search and replace

You will find it easy to add commands to the editor if needed.

The editor shown in this chapter is designed for use in a DOS environment. However, most of the code is portable, and you should have little trouble adapting it. As the code is shown, it can be compiled using Turbo C or Microsoft C. However, because it must bypass C's standard input functions and actually read the 16-bit scan codes generated by the PC keyboard, there is one compiler sensitivity. As you saw in Chapter 2, Turbo C's function to read 16-bit keyboard information is called **bioskey( )**. Microsoft calls theirs **_bios_keybrd( )**. At the top of the file, you must **#define** either **TURBOC** or **MICROSOFTC** so that the correct function is compiled. If you are using a different compiler, please consult your user manual.

SOME SCREEN-EDITOR THEORY

Although a screen editor is not an extremely difficult piece of software to write, it still presents some interesting challenges. Let's look at a few of these.

Current Locations

Perhaps the hardest single thing about writing a screen editor is keeping the file and the screen synchronized. When creating a screen editor, it is necessary to maintain two linked, but physically separate, concepts of the *current location*. For lack of a better term, the current location is the point at which the next action will take place. Relative to the file, the current location is a pointer into the file; relative to the screen, the current location is a coordinate pair that specifies the cursor's position. Assuming that these two frames of reference are correctly linked, the screen's current location corresponds to the expected point in the file. The first thing that complicates the linkage between the screen's current location and the file's current location is the fact that a file is linear and the screen is two-dimensional. The second problem is that, while the entire file is available at all times, the screen can generally only hold a portion of the file. Its contents are often changed. This means that there is not a one-to-one correspondence between a specific X,Y location on the screen and its related character in the file. Instead, it is a one-to-many relationship. For these reasons, linking the current locations of the screen and file requires considerable effort, as you will see.

Inserting and Deleting Characters

There are several different approaches one can take to creating an editor. The one we will use is very straightforward. All text editors revolve around two basic actions: character insertion and character deletion. In our editor, all text is stored in a linear buffer. Each time the user types a character, the text at and below the current position moves down, and the character is inserted. When a character is deleted, the text starting one character below and extending to the end of the buffer moves up, thus removing the character. Each time a character is inserted or deleted, the screen is updated to reflect the state of the file.

Boundary Conditions

The text being edited is contained in a buffer. This buffer has a beginning and an end. As you will see, there is significant code in the editor dedicated to preventing the current location from backing up over the beginning or moving past the end of the buffer. The file also has a beginning and an end. The user must not be allowed to move past these boundaries either. (Of course, text can be added on to the end of the file.) Much of the "clerical" code in the editor is concerned with maintaining these boundaries. In fact, errors can creep in quite easily unless you're very careful with boundary conditions any time you add features to the editor. (Alternative approaches to the construction of a screen editor can mask or hide this code, but it cannot be eliminated.)

THE EDITOR MAIN LOOP

Like most editors, the screen editor developed in this chapter is driven by a main loop that performs two basic functions. First, it inputs keystrokes and, second, it takes appropriate action based on what the user has typed. There are two general categories of keystrokes: those that are characters to be entered into the file and those that are commands to the editor. The editor recognizes the following as command keys:

Key	Meaning
LEFT ARROW	Move left one character
RIGHT ARROW	Move right one character
UP ARROW	Move up one line
DOWN ARROW	Move down one line
PGUP	Move up one screen
PGDN	Move down one screen
HOME	Go to top of file
END	Go to end of file
DEL	Delete character at cursor location

BACKSPACE	Delete character to left of cursor
F1	Save the file
F2	Load a file
F3	Find a string
F4	Global search and replace
CTRL-K	Delete a line
CTRL-Y	Restore the last deleted line
CTRL-Z	Quit the editor

The editor's main loop is contained in its entry function **edit( )**, which is shown here:

```
#define TURBOC
/* If you use Microsoft C, #define MICROSOFTC
   instead of TURBOC.   If you have a different
   C compiler, see the text.
*/

#define BUF_SIZE 32000
#define LINE_LEN 79
#define MAX_LINES 24
#define KILL_BUF_SIZE 4*LINE_LEN

char buf[BUF_SIZE];
char *curloc, *endloc;
int scrnx, scrny;
char killbuf[KILL_BUF_SIZE];


/*  This is the editor's entry function and contains
    its main loop.

    Call it with the name of the file you want to edit.
*/
void edit(char *fname)
{
  union k {
    char ch[2];
    unsigned i;
  } key;
  char name[80];
```

```
/* try to load the file */
if(!load(fname)) curloc = endloc = buf;
strcpy(name, fname);

clrscr();  /* clear the screen */

/* set initial values to X,Y coordinate vars */
scrnx = scrny = 0;

/* display a screen full of text */
display_scrn(0, 0, curloc);

help();  /* print the help line */
gotoxy(0, 0);

/* editor main loop */
do {
#ifdef TURBOC
    key.i = bioskey(0);  /* read 16-bit key code */
#endif
#ifdef MICROSOFTC
    key.i = _bios_keybrd(0);
#endif
    if(!key.ch[0]) { /* is a command */
      switch(key.ch[1]) {
        case 59: /* F1: save file */
          save(name);
          break;
        case 60: /* F2: load file */
          clrline(MAX_LINES);
          gotoxy(0, MAX_LINES);
          printf("enter filename: ");
          edit_gets(name);
          if(*name) load(name);
          clrscr();
          help();
          display_scrn(0, 0, curloc);
          scrnx = scrny = 0;
          break;
        case 61: /* F3: search */
          search();
          break;
        case 62: /* F4: replace */
```

```
          replace();
          break;
      case 71: /* home */
          home();
          break;
      case 79: /* end */
          gotoend();
          break;
      case 75: /* left */
          left();
          break;
      case 77: /* right */
          right();
          break;
      case 72: /* up  */
          upline();
          break;
      case 80: /* down */
          downline();
          break;
      case 73: /* page up */
          pageup();
          break;
      case 81: /* page down */
          pagedown();
          break;
      case 83: /* Del */
          if(curloc<endloc) delete_char();
          break;
    }
    if(curloc < buf) {
      scrnx = scrny = 0;
      curloc = buf;
    }
    gotoxy(scrnx, scrny); /* position cursor */
  }
  else {
    switch(key.ch[0]) {
      case '\r':  /* carriage return */
        /* see if buffer is full */
        if(endloc==buf+BUF_SIZE-2) break;

        /* move contents of file below current
```

```
          location down one byte to make room
          for the RETURN
      */
      memmove(curloc+1, curloc, endloc-curloc+1);

      *curloc = key.ch[0]; /* put RETURN in file */
      curloc++;

      /* clear rest of line */
      edit_clr_eol(scrnx, scrny);
      scrnx = 0;
      scrny++;

      /* move text on screen down */
      if(scrny==MAX_LINES) {  /* at bottom of page */
        scrny = MAX_LINES-1;
        scrollup(0, 0, LINE_LEN, scrny);
      }
      else scrolldn(scrnx, scrny);

      gotoxy(scrnx, scrny);
      printline(curloc); /* display the line */
      endloc++;  /* advance the end of file pointer */
      break;
    case '\b':  /* backspace */
      if(curloc==buf) break;
      left();
      delete_char();
      break;
    case 11: /* control-K: kill line */
      kill_line();
      break;
    case 25: /* control-Y: yank kill buffer */
      yank();
      break;
    default: /* enter keystroke into file */
      /* see if buffer is full */
      if(endloc==buf+BUF_SIZE-2) break;

      /* can't type past end of line */
      if(scrnx==LINE_LEN) break;

      /* move contents of file below current
```

```
            location down one byte to make room
            for the character
        */
        memmove(curloc+1, curloc, endloc-curloc+1);
        *curloc = key.ch[0];  /* put keystroke in file */
        putch(*curloc);  /* display the key on the screen */
        scrnx++;  /* advance X */
        gotoxy(scrnx, scrny);
        printline(curloc+1); /* display the line */
        curloc++;  /* advance the current location */
        endloc++;  /* advance the end of file pointer */
      }
      gotoxy(scrnx, scrny);
    }
  } while(key.ch[0]!=26);  /* control-Z quits the editor */
}
```

Let's take a close look at this function.

Notice that the macros **LINE_LEN** and **MAX_LINES** are defined as 79 and 24, respectively. These macros are used to specify the length of a line and the number of lines on the screen. These values are correct for a 25-line monitor using 80 characters per line. If your display accommodates more lines, you will want to change these.

The global variable **buf** holds the file while it is being edited. The pointer **curloc** points to the current location in **buf**. The pointer **endloc** points to the end of the file. The variables **scrnx** and **scrny** contain the coordinates of the cursor on the screen. The array **killbuf** is used to hold a deleted line so that it can be retrieved later.

When **edit( )** begins executing, it first tries to load the file specified by its **fname** parameter. If the file exists, it is loaded into the main editor buffer **buf**, the pointers **curloc** and **endloc** are set appropriately, and a screen full of text is displayed. If the file does not exist, **curloc** and **endloc** are set to the start of the buffer. Either way, the cursor is located at the upper left corner of the screen and a help line is shown at the bottom of the screen.

After the initialization, the main loop begins. At each pass it waits for a keypress and then processes the keystroke. As you read in Chapter 2, the PC generates 16-bit values each time a key is pressed. For the normal keys, the low-order byte contains the ASCII character code for the key and the high-order byte contains a position code. However, for the arrow keys, function keys, and END, HOME, DEL, PGUP, and PGDN keys, no ASCII code exists, so the low-order byte is 0. This is the reason that these keys are treated separately from the others, using their own **switch** statement. Each time one of these keys is pressed, the corresponding function is called.

When a normal key is pressed, the **default** case of the second **switch** statement executes. First, the program checks to see if there is room in the buffer and room on the line for another character. As the editor is written, it will not let you type past the rightmost column of the screen, although lines may be longer than the width of the screen. The main reason for this mild restriction is that it prevents text from wrapping around to the next line and thus makes it easier to manage the screen. Next, the contents of the buffer at the current location are moved down one character and the keystroke is entered into the file. The value of **scrnx** is incremented and the remainder of the line is reprinted using a call to **printline( )**. The reprinting of the line is necessary in order for the screen to reflect the current state of the file. The **printline( )** function displays one line starting at the current location. As defined here, a line is terminated by a carriage return or the end of the file—not by a null character. Finally, the values of **curloc** and **endloc** are incremented.

When the user enters a carriage return, a somewhat more complicated sequence of actions occurs. After the carriage return is put in the file, the editor clears any text remaining on the line after the carriage return using a call to **edit_clr_eol( )**. This function clears the line beginning at the specified location to the first carriage return (after the one just entered) or the end of the file. That is, it does *not* necessarily clear the entire physical line, but rather the logical (carriage-return-terminated) line. This makes the editor faster and gives it a snappier feel. Once this is done, the screen is scrolled. If the carriage return is entered in the middle of the screen, the text below it is scrolled down. However, if the carriage return is pressed at the bottom of the screen, the entire display is scrolled up. (Scrolling of the screen is accomplished through a call to BIOS, and will be discussed later.)

One important point: The editor does *not* insert a linefeed character into the file after each carriage return. The reason for this is that, relative to the editor, they are not needed. However, linefeeds are added when the file is saved. They are also automatically deleted when a file is loaded.

If the user presses BACKSPACE or DEL, a character is removed from the file and the screen is refreshed to reflect this. Pressing BACKSPACE removes the character to the immediate left of the original cursor position. Pressing DEL removes the character the cursor is currently on. (Actually, the function delete_char( ) is what removes a character from a file. We will look at this function later.) The editing process continues until the user presses CTRL-Z, which terminates **edit( )**.

Now that you have seen the main loop, let's look at the support functions, which actually do most of the work.

MOVING THE CURSOR LEFT AND RIGHT

To move the cursor left, the editor calls the **left( )** function, shown here:

```
/* Move current location left. */
void left(void)
{
  if(curloc==buf) return; /* can't go left */
  scrnx--;
  if(scrnx < 0) { /* at beginning of a line */
    scrnx = 0;
    upline();   /* go up to next line */

    /* find end of line */
    while(*curloc!='\r') {
      curloc++;
      scrnx++;
    }
  }
  else curloc--;
}
```

If the current location is at the start of the file, the function does nothing because there is no character to the left of the first one; otherwise, it decrements **scrnx**. If **scrnx** is less than zero, the user has moved left at the beginning of a line, so the cursor must be moved up one line. This is accomplished through a call to **upline( )**, which will be discussed in the next section. Finally, the function advances the cursor and the current location to the end of the line.

To move the cursor to the right, the editor calls **right( )**, which is shown in the following.

```
/* Move current position right. */
void right(void)
{
  /* can't move right */
  if(curloc+1 > endloc) return;

  scrnx++;

  /* if at end of line, go to next one */
  if(scrnx > LINE_LEN || *curloc=='\r') {
    scrnx = 0;
    scrny++;
    if(scrny==MAX_LINES) { /* at end of screen */
      scrny = MAX_LINES-1;
      downline();  /* get next line */

      /* move cursor and current loc to start of
         new line */
      curloc--;
      while(*curloc!='\r') curloc--;
      curloc++;
      scrnx = 0;
    }
    else curloc++;
  }
  else curloc++;
}
```

If the current location is at the end of the file, the function does nothing; otherwise, it increments **scrnx** and checks to see if it is at the end of a line. If so, it increments **scrny** and checks further to see if it is also at the bottom of the screen. If this is the case, it calls **downline( )**, discussed next, to move down one line.

MOVING UP AND DOWN ONE LINE

To move up one line, the editor calls **upline( )**, shown here:

```
/* Move up one line.  If possible, keep scrnx same
   as in previous line.
*/
```

```
void upline(void)
{
  register int i;
  char *p;

  if(curloc==buf) return;  /* at first byte in buffer */

  p = curloc;

  if(*p=='\r') p--; /* if at end of line, back up */

  /* back up locator to start of current line */
  for(; *p!='\r' && p>buf; p--) ;
  if(*p!='\r') return;  /* at first line, cannot go up */
  curloc = p;
  curloc--;  /* skip past CR */
  i = scrnx;  /* save X coordinate */

  /* find start of next line */
  while(*curloc!='\r' && curloc>=buf) curloc--;
  scrny--; scrnx = 0;
  curloc++;

  /* at top of screen, must scroll down */
  if(scrny<0) {
    scrolldn(0, 0);
    scrny = 0;
    gotoxy(0, 0);
    printline(curloc);
  }

  /* position the cursor and current location at
     same scrnx position as previous line if possible */
  while(i && *curloc!='\r') {
    curloc++;
    scrnx++;
    i--;
  }
}
```

The **upline( )** function works like this: If not at the top line of the file, it first backs up the current location to the start of the current line and saves the current value of **scrnx**. It then finds the start of the next line up. Finally, it advances both **curloc** and **scrnx** to the same X coordinate position in the new line, if possible. For example, if the X coordinate of the old cursor position was 10, then the **upline( )** function will position the cursor at X location 10 if the new line is long enough. Since moving up a line may mean moving off the screen, the function scrolls the screen down automatically if this occurs.

To move down one line, the editor calls **downline( )**, shown here:

```
/*  Move down one line.  Keep previous scrnx
    location if possible.
*/
void downline(void)
{
  register int i;
  char *p;

  i = scrnx;
  p = curloc;

  /* advance current location to start of next line */
  while(*p!='\r' && p<endloc) p++;
  if(p==endloc) return;  /* can't go down */
  p++;  /* skip past CR */
  curloc = p;
  scrny++; scrnx = 0;

  /* if moving down past the bottom of the screen */
  if(scrny==MAX_LINES) {
    scrny = MAX_LINES-1;
    scrollup(0, 0, LINE_LEN, MAX_LINES-1);
    gotoxy(scrnx, scrny);
    printline(curloc);
  }

  /* advance to corresponding character in next line */
  while(i && *curloc!='\r' && curloc<endloc) {
    curloc++;
    scrnx++;
    i--;
  }
}
```

The **downline( )** function works much like **upline( )**, except in the opposite direction. It finds the end of the current line, saves the value of **scrnx**, and advances the current location to the same X coordinate in the next line, if possible. If at the bottom of the screen, it calls **scrollup( )** to scroll the screen.

DELETING CHARACTERS AND LINES

To delete a single character, the editor calls **delete_char( )**, which is shown here:

```
/* Delete character at the current location. */
void delete_char(void)
{
  gotoxy(scrnx, scrny);

  if(*curloc=='\r') { /* RETURN, scroll display */
    scrollup(0, scrny+1, LINE_LEN, MAX_LINES-1);
    memmove(curloc, curloc+1, endloc-curloc);
    endloc--;
    display_scrn(scrnx, scrny, curloc);
    help();
  }
  else {
    memmove(curloc, curloc+1, endloc-curloc);
    endloc--;
    printline(curloc); printf(" ");
  }
}
```

The operation of **delete_char( )** is straightforward. If the deleted character is a carriage return, then the display must be scrolled up one line beginning at that point and the screen redisplayed. If the character is in the middle of the line, the line must be redisplayed. In either case, the text below the deleted character is moved up, thus removing the character from the file.

To delete an entire line, the editor calls **kill_line( )**, shown here:

```
/* Delete the line at the current location. */
void kill_line(void)
```

```
{
  register int i;
  char *p, *killbufptr;

  if(*curloc=='\r') {
    delete_char();
    return;
  }

  edit_clr_eol(scrnx, scrny);  /* clear to CR */

  /* find out how many characters are in the line */
  p = curloc;
  i = 0;
  killbufptr = killbuf;
  while(*p!='\r' && p<endloc) {
    i++;
    *killbufptr = *p;  /* put in kill buffer */
    p++;
    if(killbufptr<killbuf+KILL_BUF_SIZE-2) killbufptr++;
  }
  *killbufptr = '\0';

  /* remove the line */
  memmove(curloc, curloc+i, endloc-curloc);
  endloc -= i;
}
```

The **kill_line( )** function works in one of two ways. If the current location holds a carriage return, then that carriage return (and no other text) is deleted, and the function returns. Otherwise, all text from the current location to the end of the line (up to, but not including, the carriage return) is removed from the file. This removes the text, but leaves a blank line. To remove the blank line, press CTRL-K again; this removes the carriage return.

When a line is removed, its contents are copied into a buffer called **killbuf**. The contents of this buffer can be added back into the file at any point using the **yank( )** function, shown here:

```
/* Insert previously killed line. */
void yank(void)
{
```

```
  char *p;

  p = killbuf;
  while(*p) {
    memmove(curloc+1, curloc, endloc-curloc+1);
    *curloc = *p;  /* put character in file */
    if(scrnx<LINE_LEN) {
      putch(*curloc);  /* display char on the screen */
      scrnx++;
    }
    curloc++;
    endloc++;
    p++;
  }
  printline(curloc);
}
```

The **yank( )** function works by inserting each character from **killbuf** into the file and incrementing **curloc**, **endloc**, and **scrnx**. Once this is done, the line is redisplayed.

FINDING A STRING

To find a string in the file, the editor uses **search( )**, shown here:

```
/* Find a string. */
void search(void)
{
  char str[80];
  register char *p;
  int len, i;

  clrline(MAX_LINES);  /* clear message line */
  gotoxy(0, MAX_LINES);
  printf("search string: ");
  edit_gets(str);
  if(!*str) return;

  p = curloc;
  len = strlen(str);

  /* search for the string */
```

```
   while(*p && strncmp(str, p, len)) p++;
   if(!*p) return;  /* not found */

   /* back up to start of line */
   i = 0;
   while(p>buf && *p!='\r') {
     p--;
     i++;
   }
   p++;
   i--;

   /* reposition current location to start of match */
   curloc = p+i;
   scrnx = i;
   scrny = 0;

   /* display screen of text at location of match */
   clrscr();
   display_scrn(0, 0, p);
   help();
}
```

The **search( )** function works like this: First, it clears the bottom line of the
screen and prompts the user to input the string for which to search.
Instead of calling something like **gets( )** to input the string, however, it
calls **edit _ gets( )**. The **edit _ gets( )** function is a simple version of **gets( )**
with one important difference—it does not echo the carriage return.
Because input is occurring at the bottom of the screen, a carriage return
would scroll the entire screen, which is not what we want. The
edit _ gets( ) function is shown here:

```
/* Read a string from the keyboard, but do not
   scroll the display when a RETURN is entered.
*/
void edit_gets(char *str)
{
  char *p;

  p = str;

  for(;;) {
```

```
      *str = getch();
      if(*str=='\r') { /* return when RETURN entered */
        *str = '\0';   /* NULL terminate */
        return;
      }

      if(*str=='\b') {  /* backspace */
        if(str>p) {
          str--;
          putch('\b');
          putch(' ');
          putch('\b');
        }
      }
      else {
        putch(*str);
        str++;
      }
    }
  }
}
```

Once the search string has been entered, the file is searched from the current location to the end. The standard function **strncmp( )** is used to check for the match. If a match is found, the appropriate variables are updated, and a screen of text is displayed, beginning with the line in which the match is found. The cursor and **curloc** will be located at the beginning of the matching string.

GLOBAL SEARCH AND REPLACE

To change all occurrences of one string to another string, the editor calls **replace( )**, which is shown here:

```
/* Global search and replace. */
void replace(void)
{
  register int len1;
  char str1[80], str2[80];
  char *p, *p2;

  clrline(MAX_LINES);
```

```c
gotoxy(0, MAX_LINES);
printf("enter string to replace: ");
edit_gets(str1);

clrline(MAX_LINES);
gotoxy(0, MAX_LINES);
printf("enter replacement: ");
edit_gets(str2);

p = curloc;
len1 = strlen(str1);

while(*str1) {
  /* search for the string */
  while(*p && strncmp(str1, p, len1)) p++;
  if(!*p) break;   /* not found */

  /* remove old string */
  memmove(p, p+len1, endloc-p);
  endloc -= len1;

  /* insert new string */
  p2 = str2;
  while(*p2) {
    memmove(p+1, p, endloc-p+1);
    *p = *p2;
    p++;
    endloc++;
    p2++;
  }
}
clrscr();

/* find location of top of screen */
p = curloc;
for(len1 = scrny; len1>=0 && p>buf; ) {
  p--;
  if(*p=='\r') len1--;
}
if(*p=='\r') p++;

/* redisplay current screen */
display_scrn(0, 0, p);
help();
}
```

P. J. Plauger
Founder of Whitesmiths, Ltd. and Noted Writer

P. J. Plauger is one of the most respected names in the C arena. He is the founder of Whitesmiths, Ltd., one of the first firms to specialize in C compilers. Whitesmiths was instrumental in popularizing C in the small computer environment. Dr. Plauger personally created C code generators for the PDP-11, the VAX, the 8080/Z80, the 68000, and the 8086. He is an active participant in the ANSI C standardization committee and author of several books and many articles. (He currently writes a column for *Computer Language, C User's Journal,* and *Embedded Systems Programming* magazines.)

Because the art of programming is so young, P. J. Plauger, like many others, was not initially educated as a programmer. In fact, he holds a Ph.D. in nuclear physics from Michigan State University. However, it is in the realm of software engineering that Dr. Plauger has left his mark.

How Dr. Plauger came to C is the stuff that legends are made of. "I was experimenting with S.I.L.s for the PDP-11 at Bell Labs at the same time that Dennis Ritchie was developing C. I first learned C to keep up with the competition (Ritchie). However, I soon saw that it was better than any of my designs. I also found that I could lure old-line assembly language programmers to C by showing them that rewriting in C gave them readability with little cost in performance." In fact, P. J. Plauger was one of the first programmers to recognize the importance of C as a replacement for assembly language.

As one of the early proponents of C, Dr. Plauger had to dispel several misconceptions non-C programmers had about it. "Most misconceptions fall into three categories: that it is easier to write buggy programs in C than in a language like Pascal or Ada; that it's simply PDP-11 assembler (the processor on which C was developed) made portable, and that it's hard to read." Asked what elements he believes contribute to the creation of masterwork C programs, Dr. Plauger responded, "You need the perfect balance of elegance (that is, minimal complexity), readability, portability, and efficiency." Dr. Plauger elaborates further: "Keep rewriting each chunk of code until it's unabashedly elegant and readable—no matter what its supposed importance. Think about portability and efficiency from the start, but make no sacrifices for either until testing shows you must."

P. J. Plauger lives in Massachusetts and is currently a Chief Engineer at Intermetrics, Inc.

The **replace( )** function first prompts for the original string and then the replacement. Next, it searches for matches of the original string. When it finds one, it removes it from the file and inserts the replacement. This process continues until the end of the file is reached. Finally, the screen is redrawn so that any replacements will be shown correctly.

SCROLLING THE SCREEN USING BIOS

BIOS contains two functions that provide very fast scrolling of the screen. These functions are accessed through interrupt 16, functions 6 and 7. To scroll the screen down, use function 7. Put the Y coordinate of the upper left corner of the region to scroll in CH and the upper left X coordinate in CL. The X coordinate of the lower right corner of the region must be loaded into DL and the Y coordinate into DH. The attribute of the space scrolled in is specified in BH. A value of 7 specifies a normal space—that is, a blank line. To scroll the screen up, use function 6; all the other parameters are the same as function 7.

The **scrollup( )** and **scrolldn( )** functions are shown here. Notice that **scrolldn( )** only allows you to specify the upper left corner. As it is used by the editor, the end of the region to be scrolled is always the same. If you want to generalize this function, you will need to change it so that it has four parameters, as does **scrollup( )**. (If you are not using a PC, then you will need to rewrite these functions for your environment.)

```
/* Scroll down the screen. This function scrolls
   all but the bottom line. */
void scrolldn(int x, int y)
{
  union REGS r;

  r.h.ah = 7;
  r.h.al = 1;
  r.h.ch = y;
  r.h.cl = x;
  r.h.dh = MAX_LINES-1;
  r.h.dl = LINE_LEN;
  r.h.bh = 7;
  int86(0x10, &r, &r);
}
```

```
/* Scroll up the screen using the specified
   coordinates. */
void scrollup(int topx, int topy, int endx, int endy)
{
  union REGS r;

  r.h.ah = 6;
  r.h.al = 1;
  r.h.ch = topy;
  r.h.cl = topx;
  r.h.dh = endy;
  r.h.dl = endx;
  r.h.bh = 7;
  int86(0x10, &r, &r);
}
```

THE ENTIRE SCREEN-EDITOR SUBSYSTEM

The entire code for the screen-editor subsystem is shown here along with a **main( )** function, which calls it. However, remember to remove the **main( )** function when you use the editor as a part of another project.

```
/* A Screen Editor Subsystem. */

#define TURBOC
/* If you use Microsoft C, #define MICROSOFTC
   instead of TURBOC.   If you have a different
   C compiler, see the text.
*/

#include "stdio.h"
#include "dos.h"
#include "string.h"
#include "bios.h"
#include "conio.h"

#define BUF_SIZE 32000
#define LINE_LEN 79
#define MAX_LINES 24
#define KILL_BUF_SIZE 4*LINE_LEN
```

```
char buf[BUF_SIZE];
char *curloc, *endloc;
int scrnx, scrny;
char killbuf[KILL_BUF_SIZE];

char *helpline =
  "F1: save  F2: load  F3: find  F4: replace\
   ^K: Kill line  ^Y: Yank  ^Z: quit";

void edit(char *fname), help(void);
void gotoxy(int x, int y), clrline(int y);
void edit_clr_eol(int x, int y), clrscr(void);
void printline(char *p), delete_char(void);
void search(void), kill_line(void);
void upline(void);
void downline(void), left(void),  right(void);
void scrolldn(int x, int y);
void scrollup(int topx, int topy, int endx, int endy);
void display_scrn(int x, int y, char *p);
void pagedown(void), pageup(void), replace(void);
void home(void), gotoend(void), yank(void);
int load(char *fname), save(char *fname);
void edit_gets(char *str);

main(int argc, char *argv[])
{
  if(argc==2) edit(argv[1]);
  clrscr();
}

/*  This is the editor's entry function and contains
    its main loop.

    Call it with the name of the file you want to edit.
*/
void edit(char *fname)
{
  union k {
    char ch[2];
    unsigned i;
  } key;
  char name[80];
```

```
    /* try to load the file */
    if(!load(fname)) curloc = endloc = buf;
    strcpy(name, fname);

    clrscr();

    /* set initial values to X,Y coordinate vars */
    scrnx = scrny = 0;

    /* display a screen full of text */
    display_scrn(0, 0, curloc);
    help();  /* print the help line */
    gotoxy(0, 0);

    /* editor main loop */
    do {
#ifdef TURBOC
      key.i = bioskey(0);  /* read 16-bit key code */
#endif
#ifdef MICROSOFTC
      key.i = _bios_keybrd(0);
#endif
      if(!key.ch[0]) { /* is a command */
        switch(key.ch[1]) {
          case 59: /* F1: save file */
            save(name);
            break;
          case 60: /* F2: load file */
            clrline(MAX_LINES);
            gotoxy(0, MAX_LINES);
            printf("enter filename: ");
            edit_gets(name);
            if(*name) load(name);
            help();
            display_scrn(0, 0, curloc);
            scrnx = scrny = 0;
            break;
          case 61: /* F3: search */
            search();
            break;
          case 62: /* F4: replace */
            replace();
```

```
          break;
      case 71: /* home */
        home();
        break;
      case 79: /* end */
        gotoend();
        break;
      case 75: /* left */
        left();
        break;
      case 77: /* right */
        right();
        break;
      case 72: /* up  */
        upline();
        break;
      case 80: /* down */
        downline();
        break;
      case 73: /* page up */
        pageup();
        break;
      case 81: /* page down */
        pagedown();
        break;
      case 83: /* Del */
        if(curloc<endloc) delete_char();
        break;
    }
    if(curloc < buf) {
      scrnx = scrny = 0;
      curloc = buf;
    }
    gotoxy(scrnx, scrny); /* position cursor */
  }
  else { /* enter keystroke into file */
    switch(key.ch[0]) {
      case '\r':  /* carriage return */
        /* see if buffer is full */
        if(endloc==buf+BUF_SIZE-2) break;

        /* move contents of file below current
           location down one byte to make room
```

```
        for the RETURN
*/
memmove(curloc+1, curloc, endloc-curloc+1);

*curloc = key.ch[0]; /* put RETURN in file */
curloc++;

/* clear rest of line */
edit_clr_eol(scrnx, scrny);
scrnx = 0;
scrny++;

/* move text on screen down */
if(scrny==MAX_LINES) {   /* at bottom of page */
  scrny = MAX_LINES-1;
  scrollup(0, 0, LINE_LEN, scrny);
}
else scrolldn(scrnx, scrny);

gotoxy(scrnx, scrny);
printline(curloc); /* display the line */
endloc++;   /* advance the end of file pointer */
break;
case '\b':   /* backspace */
  if(curloc==buf) break;
  left();
  delete_char();
  break;
case 11: /* control-K: kill line */
  kill_line();
  break;
case 25: /* control-Y: yank kill buffer */
  yank();
  break;
default:
  /* see if buffer is full */
  if(endloc==buf+BUF_SIZE-2) break;

  /* can't type past end of line */
  if(scrnx==LINE_LEN) break;

  /* move contents of file below current
     location down one byte to make room
```

```
              for the character
           */
           memmove(curloc+1, curloc, endloc-curloc+1);
           *curloc = key.ch[0];   /* put keystroke in file */
           putch(*curloc);  /* display key on the screen */
           scrnx++;  /* advance X */
           gotoxy(scrnx, scrny);
           printline(curloc+1); /* display the line */
           curloc++;  /* advance the current location */
           endloc++;  /* advance the end of file pointer */
        }
        gotoxy(scrnx, scrny);
     }
   } while(key.ch[0]!=26);  /* control-Z quits the editor */
}


/* Display a line pointed to by p.  This function
   stops when it hits a carriage return or the
   end of the file.
*/
void printline(register char *p)
{
  register int i;

  i = scrnx;
  while(*p!='\r' && *p && i<LINE_LEN) {
    putch(*p);
    p++;
    i++;
  }
}


/* Insert previously killed line. */
void yank(void)
{
  char *p;

  p = killbuf;
  while(*p) {
    memmove(curloc+1, curloc, endloc-curloc+1);
    *curloc = *p;  /* put keystroke in file */
    if(scrnx<LINE_LEN) {
      putch(*curloc);  /* display the key on the screen */
```

```
        scrnx++;
      }
    curloc++;
    endloc++;
    p++;
  }
  printline(curloc);
}

/* Delete the line at the current location. */
void kill_line(void)
{
  register int i;
  char *p, *killbufptr;

  if(*curloc=='\r') {
    delete_char();
    return;
  }

  edit_clr_eol(scrnx, scrny);   /* clear to CR */

  /* find out how many characters are in the line */
  p = curloc;
  i = 0;
  killbufptr = killbuf;
  while(*p!='\r' && p<endloc) {
    i++;
    *killbufptr = *p;   /* put in kill buffer */
    p++;
    if(killbufptr<killbuf+KILL_BUF_SIZE-2) killbufptr++;
  }
  *killbufptr = '\0';

  /* remove the line */
  memmove(curloc, curloc+i, endloc-curloc);
  endloc -= i;
}

/* Global search and replace. */
void replace(void)
{
  register int len1;
```

```
char str1[80], str2[80];
char *p, *p2;

clrline(MAX_LINES);
gotoxy(0, MAX_LINES);
printf("enter string to replace: ");
edit_gets(str1);

clrline(MAX_LINES);
gotoxy(0, MAX_LINES);
printf("enter replacement: ");
edit_gets(str2);

p = curloc;
len1 = strlen(str1);

while(*str1) {
  /* search for the string */
  while(*p && strncmp(str1, p, len1)) p++;
  if(!*p) break;  /* not found */

  /* remove old string */
  memmove(p, p+len1, endloc-p);
  endloc -= len1;

  /* insert new string */
  p2 = str2;
  while(*p2) {
    memmove(p+1, p, endloc-p+1);
    *p = *p2;
    p++;
    endloc++;
    p2++;
  }
}
clrscr();

/* find location of top of screen */
p = curloc;
for(len1 = scrny; len1>=0 && p>buf; ) {
  p--;
  if(*p=='\r') len1--;
}
```

```
  if(*p=='\r') p++;

  /* redisplay current screen */
  display_scrn(0, 0, p);
  help();
}

/* Delete character at the current location. */
void delete_char(void)
{
  gotoxy(scrnx, scrny);

  if(*curloc=='\r') { /* RETURN, scroll display */
    scrollup(0, scrny+1, LINE_LEN, MAX_LINES-1);
    memmove(curloc, curloc+1, endloc-curloc);
    endloc--;
    display_scrn(scrnx, scrny, curloc);
    help();
  }
  else {
    memmove(curloc, curloc+1, endloc-curloc);
    endloc--;
    printline(curloc); printf(" ");
  }
}

/* Display help line.  You might want to expand on
   this idea.
*/
void help(void)
{
  gotoxy(0, MAX_LINES);
  printf(helpline);
}

/* Move current location left. */
void left(void)
{
  if(curloc==buf) return; /* can't go left */
  scrnx--;
  if(scrnx < 0) { /* at beginning of a line */
    scrnx = 0;
    upline();  /* go up to next line */
```

```c
    /* find end of line */
    while(*curloc!='\r') {
      curloc++;
      scrnx++;
    }
  }
  else curloc--;
}

/* Move current position right. */
void right(void)
{
  /* can't move right */
  if(curloc+1 > endloc) return;

  scrnx++;

  /* if at end of line, go to next one */
  if(scrnx > LINE_LEN || *curloc=='\r') {
    scrnx = 0;
    scrny++;
    if(scrny==MAX_LINES) { /* at end of screen */
      scrny = MAX_LINES-1;
      downline();  /* get next line */

      /* move cursor and current loc to start of
         new line */
      curloc--;
      while(*curloc!='\r') curloc--;
      curloc++;
      scrnx = 0;
    }
    else curloc++;
  }
  else curloc++;
}

/* Find a string. */
void search(void)
{
  char str[80];
  register char *p;
```

```
  int len, i;

  clrline(MAX_LINES);   /* clear message line */
  gotoxy(0, MAX_LINES);
  printf("search string: ");
  edit_gets(str);
  if(!*str) return;

  p = curloc;
  len = strlen(str);

  /* search for the string */
  while(*p && strncmp(str, p, len)) p++;
  if(!*p) return;   /* not found */

  /* back up to start of line */
  i = 0;
  while(p>buf && *p!='\r') {
    p--;
    i++;
  }
  p++;
  i--;

  /* reposition current location to start of match */
  curloc = p+i;
  scrnx = i;
  scrny = 0;

  /* display screen of text at location of match */
  clrscr();
  display_scrn(0, 0, p);
  help();
}

/* Move up one line.  If possible, keep scrnx same
   as in previous line.
*/
void upline(void)
{
  register int i;
  char *p;
```

```
   if(curloc==buf) return;   /* at first byte in buffer */

   p = curloc;

   if(*p=='\r') p--; /* if at end of line, back up */

   /* back up locator to start of current line */
   for(; *p!='\r' && p>buf; p--) ;
   if(*p!='\r') return;   /* at first line, cannot go up */
   curloc = p;
   curloc--;   /* skip past CR */
   i = scrnx;   /* save X coordinate */

   /* find start of next line */
   while(*curloc!='\r' && curloc>=buf) curloc--;
   scrny--; scrnx = 0;
   curloc++;

   /* at top of screen, must scroll up */
   if(scrny<0) {
     scrolldn(0, 0);
     scrny = 0;
     gotoxy(0, 0);
     printline(curloc);
   }

   /* position the cursor and current location at
      same scrnx position as previous line if possible */
   while(i && *curloc!='\r') {
     curloc++;
     scrnx++;
     i--;
   }
}

/*  Move down one line.  Keep previous scrnx
    location if possible.
*/
void downline(void)
{
   register int i;
   char *p;
```

```
  i = scrnx;
  p = curloc;

  /* advance current location to start of next line */
  while(*p!='\r' && p<endloc) p++;
  if(p==endloc) return;   /* can't go down */
  p++;   /* skip past CR */
  curloc = p;
  scrny++; scrnx = 0;

  /* if moving down past the bottom of the screen */
  if(scrny==MAX_LINES) {
    scrny = MAX_LINES-1;
    scrollup(0, 0, LINE_LEN, MAX_LINES-1);
    gotoxy(scrnx, scrny);
    printline(curloc);
  }

  /* advance to corresponding character in next line */
  while(i && *curloc!='\r' && curloc<endloc) {
    curloc++;
    scrnx++;
    i--;
  }
}

/* Display a screen full of text (up to 24 lines)
   starting at the specified location.
*/
void display_scrn(int x, int y, char *p)
{
  register int i;
  gotoxy(x, y);

  i = 0;
  while(y<MAX_LINES && *p) {
    switch(*p) {
      case '\r': printf("\n");
        y++;
        i = 0;
        break;
      default: if(i<LINE_LEN) putch(*p);
        i++;
```

```
    }
    p++;
  }
}

/* Page down MAX_LINES lines. */
void pagedown(void)
{
  register int i;

  clrscr();

  /* count down MAX_LINES lines */
  for(i=0; i<MAX_LINES && curloc<endloc; ) {
    if(*curloc=='\r') i++;
    curloc++;
  }
  help();
  scrnx=0; scrny=0;
  display_scrn(0, 0, curloc);
}

/* Page up MAX_LINES lines. */
void pageup(void)
{
  register int i;

  clrscr();
  /* if current location points to a CR,
     move current location back on position */
  if(*curloc=='\r' && curloc>buf) curloc--;

  /* go back MAX_LINES in buffer */
  for(i=0; i<MAX_LINES+1 && curloc>buf; ) {
    if(*curloc=='\r') i++;
    curloc--;
  }

  /* if not at the top line, increment the
     current location pointer past the CR */
  if(i==MAX_LINES+1) curloc += 2;

  help();
```

```
  scrnx=0; scrny=0;
  display_scrn(0, 0, curloc);
}

/* Go to the top of the file. */
void home(void)
{
  clrscr();
  curloc = buf;
  scrnx = scrny = 0;
  display_scrn(0, 0, curloc);
  help();
}

/* Go to the end of the file. */
void gotoend(void)
{
  clrscr();
  curloc = endloc;
  pageup();
}

/* Load a file. */
load(char *fname)
{
  FILE *fp;
  char ch, *p;

  if((fp = fopen(fname, "rb"))==NULL)
    return 0;

  p = buf;
  while(!feof(fp) && p!=buf+BUF_SIZE-2) {
    ch = getc(fp);
    if(ch!='\n' && ch!=EOF) {
      *p = ch;
      p++;
    }
  }
  *p = '\0';
  fclose(fp);
  curloc = buf;
  endloc = p;
```

```
    return 1;
}

/* Save a file. */
save(char *fname)
{
  FILE *fp;
  char *p, name[80];

  if(!*fname) {
    printf("filename: ");
    gets(name);
  }
  else strcpy(name, fname);

  if((fp = fopen(name, "wb"))==NULL)
    return 0;

  p = buf;
  while(p!=endloc) {
    if(*p!='\r')
      putc(*p, fp);
    else {
      putc('\r', fp);
      putc('\n', fp);
    }
    p++;
  }
  fclose(fp);
  return 1;
}

/* Read a string from the keyboard, but do not
   scroll the display when a RETURN is entered.
*/
void edit_gets(char *str)
{
  char *p;

  p = str;

  for(;;) {
    *str = getch();
```

```
    if(*str=='\r') { /* return when RETURN entered */
      *str = '\0';  /* NULL terminate */
      return;
    }

    if(*str=='\b') {  /* backspace */
      if(str>p) {
        str--;
        putch('\b');
        putch(' ');
        putch('\b');
      }
    }
    else {
      putch(*str);
      str++;
    }
  }
}

/* Read and save cursor coordinates. */
void cursor_pos(void)
{
  union REGS i, o;

  i.h.bh = 0;
  i.h.ah = 3;
  int86(16, &i, &o);
}

/* Send cursor to specified X,Y (0,0 is upper
   left corner). */
void gotoxy(int x, int y)
{
  union REGS i;

  i.h.dh = y;
  i.h.dl = x;
  i.h.ah = 2;
  i.h.bh = 0;
  int86(16, &i, &i);
}
```

```c
/* Clear entire line given its Y coordinate. */
void clrline(int y)
{
  register int i;

  gotoxy(0, y);
  for(i=0; i<LINE_LEN; i++) putch(' ');
}

/* Clear to end of specified line.  This function
   is for use with the editor only because it clears
   a line up to a carriage return. */
void edit_clr_eol(int x, int y)
{
  char *p;

  p = curloc;
  gotoxy(x, y);
  for(; x<LINE_LEN && *p!='\r' && *p; x++, p++) {
    printf(" ");
  }
}

/* Clear the screen. */
void clrscr(void)
{
  union REGS r;

  r.h.ah = 6;
  r.h.al = 0;
  r.h.ch = 0;
  r.h.cl = 0;
  r.h.dh = MAX_LINES;
  r.h.dl = LINE_LEN;
  r.h.bh = 7;
  int86(0x10, &r, &r);
}

/* Scroll down the screen. This function scrolls
   all but the bottom line. */
void scrolldn(int x, int y)
{
  union REGS r;
```

```
  r.h.ah = 7;
  r.h.al = 1;
  r.h.ch = y;
  r.h.cl = x;
  r.h.dh = MAX_LINES-1;
  r.h.dl = LINE_LEN;
  r.h.bh = 7;
  int86(0x10, &r, &r);
}


/* Scroll up the screen using the specified
   coordinates. */
void scrollup(int topx, int topy, int endx, int endy)
{
  union REGS r;

  r.h.ah = 6;
  r.h.al = 1;
  r.h.ch = topy;
  r.h.cl = topx;
  r.h.dh = endy;
  r.h.dl = endx;
  r.h.bh = 7;
  int86(0x10, &r, &r);
}
```

SOME THINGS TO TRY

As the screen editor stands, it is sufficient for use as an adjunct editor to a larger application. However, there are several features that you might want to add to it on your own. First, the editor does not recognize the tab character. This might be important to your application. You might want to make the editor capable of using multiple buffers to allow the simultaneous editing of multiple files. You may also want to add more editor commands, such as block moves, search and replace with query, and the like. If you study the operation of the commands currently recognized by the editor, these additions should be no trouble.

As stated in Chapter 1, you might find it fun to integrate the editor with the Little C interpreter. This will give you an integrated development environment.

One last idea: If you are really ambitious, try using the multitasking kernel from Chapter 4 to allow some concurrent operations.

CHAPTER SIX

A Database Subsystem

Database managers are one of the "big four" computer applications. (The others are word processing, accounting, and spreadsheets.) Database managers are interesting because there are so many different types and approaches. One might be a full-featured, flexible, relational database, such as dBASE or Paradox, and another might be a dedicated application, like a mailing list. The advent of the personal computer encouraged the creation of a new genre of database that can be called a *personal database*. A personal database is designed to be used by one person to store information relevant to that person alone. For example, you might use a personal database to store a list of clients or books. A personal database does not generally support a query language, but uses a menu-driven interface.

In this chapter, you will develop a database subsystem that allows the user to dynamically define the form of a database. The subsystem contains all the basic routines necessary for the creation and use of a database program. This subsystem is then used to construct a menu-driven, personal database that demonstrates the database subsystem. You can use the database subsystem to create a database with as much power and flexibility as you need.

Donald Killen
Creator of the Greenleaf Functions

Donald Killen's name may not be familiar, but his creation will almost certainly be: the Greenleaf Functions. The Greenleaf Functions was one of the first major third-party function libraries to cater to the PC C marketplace. It provided extensive support for PC interfacing, graphics, sound, and interrupts. The emergence of third-party libraries contributed to the dominance of C in the PC programming environment.

When I asked Don what advice he would give someone who wanted to create a top-of-the-line product in C, he responded in a way that reflects the view of many C programmers. "First, you must have a vision of what you want. A clear vision is more important than anything else because good software is not designed by committee. It is designed by one person who knows what the end result will be." Don, like many others, believes that truly great products are created by individuals and that the spark of insight is the key that unlocks genius.

Don also has some practical guidelines to software development. His basic approach is "First, make it work. Then, make it work right. Finally, make it work fast!" As a caution, Don adds, "I see too much emphasis on speed too early in projects. I have seen much effort wasted optimizing code that was later discarded!" Not surprisingly, considering his company's product line, Don adds, "Give me quality, reliable libraries, and I'm a leg up on anyone working from scratch." Given the success of Don's company, there is evidently truth in this statement.

Since Don has been involved in programming for several years, I asked him what he thought about some other computer languages. "Thinking back, I always hated FORTRAN, probably more than COBOL!"—a comment most C programmers will agree with. "SmallTalk is interesting. So are languages like Prolog. But, I don't think Prolog is general enough in scope to become a mainstream language." Echoing the view of many C programmers, he says, "I used to think Pascal was OK—but that was before I discovered C. I never could get used to Pascal's strong typing. I always saw it as too constraining. Training wheels are for kids, to prevent accidents. They have no place in professional software engineering."

Don Killen lives with his wife near Dallas, Texas. In his spare time (what little he has) he enjoys photography and writing articles about society and the environment.

Although the database subsystem is useful on its own, its main purpose is to serve as a user amenity attached to a larger application. For example, a TSR pop-up utility may provide a database as one of its features, or a modem program may provide a database to store frequently called numbers.

Because of some DOS-specific console and printer functions, the code in this chapter is designed to be run under a DOS environment. However, if you are using a different system, you should have little trouble making the appropriate changes. Also, the code makes use of the **int86( )** function to access operating system routines. This function is not defined by ANSI, but is found in most PC-based C compilers. (The **int86( )** function is discussed in Chapter 2.)

The database created here will compile correctly using Microsoft C and Turbo C. However, as is the case with many of the programs in this book, you must define either **TURBOC** or **MICROSOFTC** at the top of the program because of slight differences between the two compilers. If you have a different compiler, you must consult your user manual; you may need to rename one or more functions.

THE DATABASE SPECIFICATION

The database subsystem we develop supports the following operations:

- define the database
- enter information
- browse the database
- search the database
- modify a record
- delete a record
- print the database
- save the database
- load the database

The database subsystem allows you to dynamically define the structure of the data, specifying the number of fields, the length of each field, the name of each field, and the placement of each field on the screen. The structure of the database is saved when the database is saved and is loaded when a database is loaded. This means that the database subsystem can maintain several different types of databases without recompiling.

All information is stored in its ASCII string form, not converted into any internal format. However, the database subsystem does allow you to specify what type of data a field will hold. Although this information is not used by the code in this chapter, feel free to use it in your real applications.

The data is stored using a doubly linked list. As you probably know, there are many different ways that data can be stored, including linked lists, trees, and hashing schemes. The doubly linked list is used here for two main reasons. First, it is simple to implement, maintain, and understand. Second, it allows the database to be easily traversed in both the forward and backward directions. This makes it especially useful when browsing through the database. You are free to use any type of storage mechanism you like. (For very large applications, you may need to use a tree-structured approach, for example.)

Note: For a detailed discussion of linked list functions and other storage approaches, see *Advanced C* (Berkeley, Ca.: Osborne/McGraw-Hill, 1988).

TWO DEFINITIONS

Before beginning, it is necessary to define two terms. The first is *record*. As it is applied to databases, the word record refers to one complete unit of information as defined by the database. Each record consists of one or more *fields*. A field is an individual piece of information. For example, a mailing list database may contain these five fields: name, street, city, state, and ZIP code. Each complete address (that is, all five fields together) forms one record.

DEFINING THE DATABASE

Because the form of the data is defined dynamically, during run time, it is not possible to create a structure to hold each record as you might if you were designing a dedicated database application, such as a mailing list. However, there must be a structure that describes the nature of each field forming the record. This structure holds the following pieces of information: the position of each field within the record, the name of the field, the type of data being stored by the field, the length of the field (in bytes), and the screen location of the field. The **descriptor** structure, shown here, accomplishes this:

```
#define MAX_FIELDS 10
#define NAME_SIZE  40

enum field_type {STRING, DOUBLE, INT, CHAR};

struct descriptor {
  int position;  /* position of field in record */
  enum field_type type; /* type of field */
  char name[NAME_SIZE]; /* name of field */
  int size;  /* size of field in bytes */
  int x, y;  /* location on screen */
} fields[MAX_FIELDS];
```

The value of **MAX_FIELDS** is arbitrary; you will probably want to increase it.

Although the actual data being stored in the database is held in a dynamic object, we still need a fixed structure to help manage it. The one shown here, called **db_type**, holds a pointer to the data associated with each record. The database will use a doubly linked list to store the data. Therefore, the **db_type** structure contains pointers to the previous and following structures in the list.

```
/* This structure manages the database information */
struct db_type {
  char *data;  /* pointer to data */
  struct db_type *prior; /* pointer to previous record */
  struct db_type *next;  /* pointer to next record */
} *first, *last, *cur_rec;
```

Each record will have one **db_type** structure associated with it. Therefore, the database will appear, conceptually, like the one shown in Figure 6-1. The pointer **first** will point to the start of the list, **last** to the end of the list, and **cur_rec** to the record last accessed by the user.

Figure 6-1

How the database will appear in memory

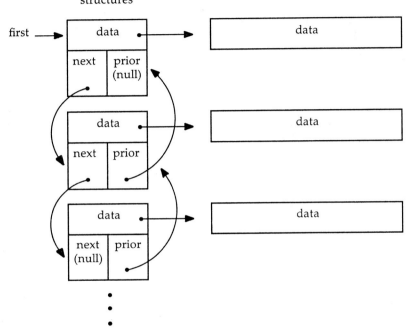

Although the data associated with each record may contain many different fields, they are all contained within one contiguous piece of memory, which is dynamically allocated.

The function that defines the database, **define( )**, is shown here:

```
#define MAX_FIELDS 10
#define NAME_SIZE  40
#define MAX_LINES  24
#define LINE_LEN   79
#define FNAME_SIZE  8

enum field_type {STRING, DOUBLE, INT, CHAR};
```

```
struct descriptor {
  int position;  /* position of field in record */
  enum field_type type; /* type of field */
  char name[NAME_SIZE]; /* name of field */
  int size;  /* size of field in bytes */
  int x, y;  /* location on screen */
} fields[MAX_FIELDS];

int num_fields;  /* number of fields in a record */
int record_size; /* record size in bytes */
int sort_field;  /* number of field to sort on */
int num_recs;     /* number of records in file */

/* This structure manages the database information */
struct db_type {
  char *data;  /* pointer to data */
  struct db_type *prior; /* pointer to previous record */
  struct db_type *next;  /* pointer to next record */
} *first, *last, *cur_rec;

/* Define the structure of the database. */
void define(void)
{
  char ch;
  int i;
  struct db_type *temp;

  clrscr();

  /* free any previously allocated memory */
  while(first) {
    temp = first->next;
    free(temp->data);  /* free the data */
    free(temp);        /* free the control structure */
    first = temp;
  }
  init();

  record_size = 0;

  do {
    gotoxy(0, 0);
```

```
      printf("number of fields (1-%d) (0 to skip): ", MAX_FIELDS);
      scanf("%d%*c", &num_fields);
      if(!num_fields) return;
   } while (num_fields<0 || num_fields>MAX_FIELDS);

   for(i=0; i<num_fields; i++) {
     clrscr();
     gotoxy(0, 0);
     fields[i].position = record_size;
     printf("Enter name of field %d (1-40 chars): ", i+1);
     db_gets(fields[i].name, 40);

     /* The field type is not used by any code in this
        example, but it may be needed by your applications.
     */
     printf("\nField types are: (S)tring, (D)ouble, (I)nt");
     printf(" and (C)har\n");
     do {
       printf("Enter field type (use first letter): ");
       ch = getche();
       ch = tolower(ch);
     }while(!strchr("sdic", ch));
     switch(ch) {
       case 's': fields[i].type = STRING;
         break;
       case 'd': fields[i].type = DOUBLE;
         break;
       case 'i': fields[i].type = INT;
         break;
       case 'c': fields[i].type = CHAR;
         break;
     }
     printf("\n");

     do {
       printf("enter length of field: ");
       scanf("%d%*c", &fields[i].size);
     } while(fields[i].size<0 || fields[i].size>LINE_LEN);
     fields[i].size++; /* make room for null terminator */

     do {
       printf("enter X,Y coordinates of field: ");
       scanf("%d%d%*c", &fields[i].x, &fields[i].y);
```

```
  } while(fields[i].x<0 ||
          fields[i].x+fields[i].size>=LINE_LEN
          || fields[i].y<0 || fields[i].y>=MAX_LINES);

  printf("Is this field defined OK? (Y/N): ");
  ch = getche();
  if(tolower(ch)!='y')
    i--; /* reenter */
  else
    record_size += fields[i].size;
}
printf("\nPress a key to see fields and screen layout");
getch();
clrscr();
display_fields();
sort_field = select_field("Select field to sort on");
}
```

Let's look at how it works. Because a database may have already been in use, the function first frees any memory that may have been allocated to it. The **init( )** function resets the global variables; the **record_size** variable is reset to 0. As the size of each field is determined, it will be added to **record_size**. Thus, when you have finished defining the structure of the database, you will know the size of the block of memory needed to hold a specific record. Next, you are prompted for the number of fields in each record, and the actual definition of each field begins.

You are prompted for the name of each field, then asked to specify the type of field being defined. As stated earlier, the example personal database in this chapter does not make use of the type information; however, your application may need to. Keep in mind one important point: Even though you can describe a field as something other than a string, all information stored in the database is in ASCII string form. This means that all numbers are stored using their string equivalents, not an internal format. If your application needs to manipulate numeric values, you will have to convert the numeric strings into numbers using functions such as **atoi( )**.

The final piece of information you need to define is the location of the field on the screen. As the program is written, the bottom line of the screen is reserved for prompting messages. You will not be able to position any field on that line.

Figure 6-2

How position specifies the location of each field in a record

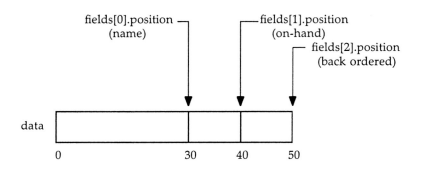

Once all the fields have been defined, they are positioned on the screen; you are then prompted to select one field to be used for sorting the data. To make a selection, use the up arrow and down arrow keys to position the cursor on the field you want to sort and press ENTER.

Because each field of a record is held in a single, dynamically allocated block of memory, it is necessary to know where in that memory each field begins. This is the purpose of the **position** field in the **descriptor** structure. For example, assume that we have defined a simple inventory database in such a way that it contains the name of each item, the number on hand, and the number back-ordered. Further assume that the name field is 30 bytes and the on-hand and back-ordered fields are 10 bytes each. Using these assumptions, Figure 6-2 illustrates how the **position** field is used to access the correct part of each record for each field.

ENTERING DATA

Once the structure of the database has been defined, you can enter information into it using the **enter( )** function, shown here:

```
/* Enter information into the database. */
enter(void)
```

```
{
  register int i, field;
  char ch;
  struct db_type *p;

  for(;;) {
    /* allocate memory for control structure */
    p = malloc(sizeof(struct db_type));
    if(!p) {
      printf("out of memory\n");
      return 0;
    }
    /* allocate memory for actual data */
    p->data = malloc(record_size);
    if(!p->data) {
      printf("out of memory\n");
      return 0;
    }

    clrscr();
    display_fields();   /* display blank fields */

    /* input the data */
    for(i=0; i<num_fields; i++) {
      gotoxy(fields[i].x+strlen(fields[i].name)+1, fields[i].y);
      db_gets(&(p->data)[fields[i].position], fields[i].size-1);
      if(!(*p->data+fields[0].position)) return 1;
    }
    num_recs++;

    prompt("Entry OK? (Y/N): ");
    ch = getche();
    ch = tolower(ch);
    while(ch!='y') {
      field = select_field("Select field to modify");
      change(p->data, field);  /* change field */
      prompt("Entry OK? (Y/N): ");
      ch = getche();
      ch = tolower(ch);
    }
    dls_store(p, &first, &last); /* store it */
  }
}
```

The **enter( )** function works in the following way. First, memory is allocated for the **db_type** control structure. Memory that will actually hold the data is allocated, and a pointer to this region is put in the **data** field of the control structure. Next, a blank template of the fields is displayed on the screen using **display_fields( )**, and the cursor is positioned at the start of the first field. The length of each field is shown using periods after the field's name. Input is actually performed by the **db_gets( )** function, which is similar to the standard **gets( )** function with three exceptions:

1. It does not echo a carriage return—outputting a carriage return would cause the screen layout to be overwritten.

2. It only inputs up to the number of characters specified by its second argument.

3. When BACKSPACE is pressed, a period is displayed, not a space. This preserves the appearance of the data-entry field.

The **db_gets( )** function is shown here:

```
/* Read a string from the keyboard, but do not
   scroll the display when a RETURN is entered.
*/
void db_gets(char *str, int maxlen)
{
  char *p;
  int i;

  p = str;

  for(i=0; ; ) {
    *str = getch();
    if(*str=='\r') { /* return when RETURN entered */
      *str = '\0';   /* NULL terminate */
      return;
    }

    if(*str=='\b') {  /* backspace */
      if(str>p) {
        str--;
        putch('\b');
        putch('.');
        putch('\b');
```

```
        i--;
      }
    }
    else if(i<maxlen) {
      putch(*str);
      str++;
      i++;
    }
  }
}
```

If you make a mistake while entering the data, you can change it. (The **change( )** function that performs this task will be discussed later.) Once the entry is correct, it is stored in order based on the sort field in the database using **dls _ store( )**, discussed in the next section.

As you can see, Figure 6-3 shows a sample data-entry screen for an order-entry database.

THE **dls _ store( )** FUNCTION

The function that enters data into a doubly linked list is called **dls _ store( )** and is shown here:

```
/* Create a doubly linked list in sorted order.
*/
void dls_store(
  struct db_type *i,    /* new element */
  struct db_type **first, /* first element in list */
  struct db_type **last /* last element in list */
)
{
  struct db_type *old, *p;

  if(*last==NULL) {  /* first element in list */
    i->next = NULL;
    i->prior = NULL;
    *last = i;
    *first = i;
    return;
  }
```

```
  p = *first; /* start at top of list */

  old = NULL;
  while(p) { /* find location to insert record */
    if(strcmp(p->data+fields[sort_field].position,
            i->data+fields[sort_field].position)<0) {
      old = p;
      p = p->next;
    }
    else {
      if(p->prior) { /* goes in middle of list */
        p->prior->next = i;
        i->next = p;
        i->prior = p->prior;
        p->prior = i;
        return;
      }
      i->next = p; /* new first element */
      i->prior = NULL;
      p->prior = i;
      *first = i;
      return;
    }
  }
  old->next = i; /* put on end */
  i->next = NULL;
  i->prior = old;
  *last = i;
}
```

This is how the function works. If the entry being stored is the first entry into the list, both its **next** and **prior** fields are set to **NULL**, and **first** and **last** are set to point to the first entry. Otherwise, the entry is inserted into the list at its appropriate point, based on the value of the sort field. This is accomplished by sequentially scanning the list until either the end of the list is reached or a field lexicographically greater than the new entry's sort field is found.

An entry may be put into the list at the start, in the middle, or at the end of the list. Each of these is handled by **dls_store( )**. Pay special attention to how each of the links is rearranged in each situation.

Figure 6-3

A sample data-entry screen

```
Name:   ......................................................
Street: ......................................................
City:   ........................ .         State:  ....
ZIP:    ............
Product: .....................................................
Cost:   ..............
```

SEARCHING THE DATABASE

The database can be searched using the **search( )** function, which is shown here along with its support function **find( )**:

```c
/* Look for a record in the list and return
   a pointer to the last match found. */
struct db_type *search(void)
{
  int field;
  char key[80], ch;
  struct db_type *info, *temp;

  clrscr();
  display_fields();
  field = select_field("Select field to search on");
  prompt("Enter key: "); /* search string */
  db_gets(key, fields[field].size);

  ch = '\0';

  /* find first match, if any */
  info = find(key, first, field);
  while(info && ch != 'q') {
    /* save pointer in case no other matches are found */
    temp = info;
    display_rec(info->data);
```

```
  /* find next match, if any */
  info = find(key, info->next, field);

  /* tell user if more matches exist */
  if(info) printf("\nmore, ");
  else printf("\nNo more matches, ");
  printf("press a key ('q' to quit): ");
  ch = getch();
  ch = tolower(ch);
}
return temp; /* return pointer to last match */
}


/* Find an entry and return a pointer to it. */
struct db_type *find(char *key, struct db_type *from,
                     int field)
{
  struct db_type *info;

  info = from;
  while(info) {
    if(!strcmp(key, info->data+
              fields[field].position)) return info;
    info = info->next;  /* get next db_type */
  }
  return NULL;  /* not found */
}
```

The **search( )** function operates in the following way. When the fields are displayed, use the up arrow and down arrow keys to position the cursor on the field you want to select; then, press ENTER. Next, you are prompted for the string you are searching for. The function then calls **find( )** to actually find the first match. The **find( )** function returns a pointer to the matching record if one is found or to a null pointer if no match is found. The **find( )** function begins looking for a match with the record pointed to by **from**. By advancing **from** after each match, **search( )** can be used to find multiple matches.

Each time a match is found, **search( )** displays the record on the screen. Notice that **search( )** has already called **find( )** to find the next match (if any) before the previous match is displayed. This way, **search( )** can tell you if more matches exist.

BROWSING IN THE DATABASE

You can browse through the database using the **browse( )** function, shown here. Because it uses the PC's arrow keys, this function uses **bioskey( )** or **_bios_keybrd( )**, neither of which is defined by ANSI. If you are using a compiler that does not support one of these functions, or if you are using a different operating system, consult your user's manual for the appropriate function to use.

```c
/* Browse through the list and return pointer
   to the last record examined. */
struct db_type *browse(void)
{
  union key {
    int i;
    char ch[2];
  } k;
  struct db_type *info;

  clrscr();
  clr_eol(0, MAX_LINES);
  gotoxy(0, MAX_LINES);
  printf("Down Arrow: forward   Up Arrow: backward");
  printf("   Home: beginning   End: end");

  /* If a current location has been defined,
     start at that point; otherwise, start at
     the top of the file.
  */
  if(cur_rec) info = cur_rec;
  else info = first;

  while(info) {
    display_rec(info->data); /* display record */

#ifdef TURBOC
    k.i = bioskey(0);
#endif
#ifdef MICROSOFTC
    k.i = _bios_keybrd(0);
#endif
```

```
    if(!k.ch[0])
      switch(k.ch[1]) {
        case 71: /* Home */
          info = first;
          break;
        case 72: /* up */
          if(info->prior)
            info = info->prior;   /* get previous rec */
          break;
        case 79: /* End */
          info = last;
          break;
        case 80: /* down */
          if(info->next)
            info = info->next;   /* get next rec */
          break;
      }
    else
      return info;  /* return current location */
  }
  return NULL;
}
```

Because the list is doubly linked, you can browse through the file in either direction. Each time you press DOWN ARROW, the next record, if one exists, is displayed. Pressing UP ARROW displays the previous record, if it exists. You can move to the beginning or end of the file by pressing HOME or END. Pressing any other key terminates the **browse( )** function.

Each record is displayed using the **display_rec( )** function, shown here:

```
/* Display one record's information. */
void display_rec(char *p)
{
  register int i;

  display_fields();
  for(i=0; i<num_fields; i++) {
    gotoxy(fields[i].x+strlen(fields[i].name)+1, fields[i].y);
    printf("%s", p+fields[i].position);
  }
}
```

This function must be called using a pointer to the data to be displayed as an argument. Notice how the **position** field of the **descriptor** structure is used to index the data.

MODIFYING A RECORD

To change the contents of a record in the database, use the **modify( )** function, shown here along with its support function, **change( )**.

```
/* Modify a record in the list and return
   a pointer to that record. */
struct db_type *modify(void)
{
  struct db_type *info;
  char key[80], ch;
  register int field;

  clrscr();

  /* find field to use for searching */
  display_fields();
  field = select_field("Select field");

  /* find record to search for */
  prompt("Enter key: ");
  db_gets(key, fields[field].size);

  /* find first match, if any */
  info = find(key, first, field);
  while(info) {
    display_rec(info->data);
    prompt("Modify this record? (Y/N): ");
    ch = getche();
    ch = tolower(ch);
    if(ch!='y') /* find next match, if any */
      info = find(key, info->next, field);
    else break;
  }
  if(!info) return NULL; /* not found */
```

```
/* which field to modify? */
field = select_field("Select field to modify");
change(info->data, field); /* change data */
return info;  /* return current location */
}

/* Change the specified record and field. */
void change(char *data, int field)
{
  int i;

  display_rec(data);
  prompt("Enter new data");

  /* display record, position cursor at beginning
     of the field, and input new data
 */
  gotoxy(fields[field].x, fields[field].y);
  printf("%s ", fields[field].name);
  for(i=0; i<fields[field].size-1; i++) putch('.');
  i = strlen(fields[field].name)+1;
  gotoxy(fields[field].x+i, fields[field].y);
  db_gets(data+fields[field].position, fields[field].size-1);
}
```

The **modify( )** function works this way. The user selects the field that will be used in searching the database for the proper record to change. Then the user is prompted to look for a specific string. The part of the code that searches for the record works exactly like the similar piece of code in the previously discussed **search( )** function. Once the proper record has been found, the user selects the field to modify and then enters the new value using the **change( )** function. The purpose of **change( )** is to allow the user to change the field at its current location on the screen.

DELETING A RECORD

To delete a record, use the **delete( )** function, shown here:

```
/* Remove an element from the list. */
void delete(struct db_type **start, struct db_type **last)
```

```
{
  struct db_type *info;
  char key[80], ch;
  int field;

  clrscr();
  display_fields();
  field = select_field("Select field");
  prompt("Enter key: ");
  db_gets(key, fields[field].size);

  info = find(key, first, field);
  while(info) {
    display_rec(info->data);
    prompt("Delete this record? (Y/N): ");
    ch = getche();
    ch = tolower(ch);
    if(ch!='y')
      info = find(key, info->next, field);
    else break;
  }
  if(!info) return; /* not found */

  /* if deleting current rec, set cur_rec to NULL */
  if(cur_rec==info) cur_rec = NULL;

  num_recs--;

  if(*start==info) { /* deleting first record */
    *start=info->next;
    if(*start) (*start)->prior = NULL;
    else *last = NULL;
  }
  else {
    info->prior->next = info->next;
    if(info!=*last)   /* deleting from middle */
      info->next->prior = info->prior;
    else
      *last = info->prior; /* deleting last record */
  }
  free(info->data); /* free data */
  free(info);   /* free control structure */
}
```

The **delete( )** function works much like **modify( )**, except that when the proper record is found, it is deleted from the list, and the memory allocated to it is freed. There are three places in which a record can be deleted from the list: from the start, from the middle, and from the end. Pay special attention to the rearrangement of the links in each case.

PRINTING THE LIST

To print the list requires the use of some functions not defined by the ANSI C standard. This is because the ANSI C standard does not define any functions that direct output to the printer. The function **print( )**, shown here, uses a BIOS routine found on PCs. This BIOS function is accessed using the special functions **biosprint( )** (when using Turbo C) or **_bios_printer( )** (when using Microsoft C). If you have a different compiler or environment, consult your compiler's user's manual.

```
/* Print the file either selectively or in full.

     NOTE: This function works only with PCs, so
     you may need to change it for other environments.

*/
void print(void)
{
  register int i, j, field;
  int blank_lines;
  struct db_type *info;
  char *p, selective, key[80], s[80], ch;

  clrscr();
  prompt("Selective search? (Y/N): ");
  ch = getche();
  if(tolower(ch)=='y') {
    display_fields();
    field = select_field("Select field");
    prompt("Enter key: ");
    db_gets(key, fields[field].size);
    selective = 1;
  }
  else selective = 0;
```

```
   /* Number of blank lines between records */
   prompt("Enter number of blank lines: ");
   db_gets(s, 20);
   blank_lines = atoi(s);

   prompt("Printing...");

   if(selective)
     info = find(key, first, field);
   else
     info = first;

   while(info) {
     /* display each record as it prints */
     display_rec(info->data);

     for(i=0; i<num_fields; i++) {
       p = info->data+fields[i].position;
       /* print the field */
       while(*p) {
#ifdef TURBOC
         biosprint(0, *p, 0);
#endif
#ifdef MICROSOFTC
         _bios_printer(0, 0, *p);
#endif
         p++;
       }
       /* output a CR-LF */
#ifdef TURBOC
       biosprint(0, '\r', 0);
       biosprint(0, '\n', 0);
#endif
#ifdef MICROSOFTC
       _bios_printer(0, 0, '\r');
       _bios_printer(0, 0, '\n');
#endif
     }
     /* output blank lines between records */
     for(j=0; j<blank_lines; j++) {
#ifdef TURBOC
       biosprint(0, '\r', 0);
```

```
      biosprint(0, '\n', 0);
#endif
#ifdef MICROSOFTC
      _bios_printer(0, 0, '\r');
      _bios_printer(0, 0, '\n');
#endif
    }

    /* get next record */
    if(selective)
      info = find(key, info->next, field);
    else
      info = info->next;
  }
#ifdef TURBOC
  biosprint(0, '\f', 0); /* form feed */
#endif
#ifdef MICROSOFTC
  _bios_printer(0, 0, '\f');
#endif
}
```

The **print( )** function lets you print either the entire file or only those records that match the field you specify. Also, it lets you determine how many blank lines are printed between each record. When a record is printed, it is simply displayed with each field on its own line. You will probably want to enhance the **print( )** function so that its output fits your specific needs. (You could also let the user decide dynamically the layout of what is printed.)

If the user chooses a selective print, then he or she is prompted for the field to search and the string to match. Any records that match the string will be printed.

The prototypes for **biosprint( )** and **_bios_printer( )** are shown here:

```
int biosprint(int function, int value, int port);

unsigned _bios_printer(unsigned function, unsigned port,
                       unsigned value);
```

For both functions, when *function* is 0, then the value in *port* is output to the printer specified by *port*. If *port* is 0, then LPT1 is used; if *port* is 1, then

LPT2 is used, and so on. If you are using a compiler other than Microsoft C or Turbo C, consult your user's manual for the equivalent function.

SAVING AND LOADING THE DATABASE

To save the database to a disk file, use the **save( )** function, shown here. It automatically saves both the field definitions and the database.

```c
/* Save both data and description to disk. */
save(char *fname)
{
  struct db_type *info;
  register int i;
  FILE *fp;
  char name[80];

  strcpy(name, fname);
  strcat(name, ".dat");
  fp = fopen(name, "wb");
  if(!fp) {
    printf("cannot open data file\n");
    return 0;
  }
  prompt("saving data");

  info = first;
  while(info) { /* save each record */
    fwrite(info->data, record_size, 1, fp);
    info = info->next;   /* get next db_type */
    if(ferror(fp)) {
      printf("error writing file\n");
      fclose(fp);
      return 0;
    }
  }
  fclose(fp);

  strcpy(name, fname);
  strcat(name, ".def");
  fp = fopen(name, "wb");
```

```
  if(!fp) {
    printf("cannot open definition file\n");
    fclose(fp);
    return 0;
  }

  putw(record_size, fp);
  putw(num_fields, fp);
  putw(sort_field, fp);

  for(i=0; i<num_fields; i++) {
    fwrite(&fields[i], sizeof(fields[i]), 1, fp);
    if(ferror(fp)) {
      printf("error writing file\n");
      fclose(fp);
      return 0;
    }
  }
  fclose(fp);
  return 1;
}
```

The **save( )** function must be called with the name of the file that will
receive the data. Do not use an extension. The data is stored in a .DAT
file. The field descriptions, number of fields, record sizes, and sort fields
are saved into a .DEF file.

   The **load( )** function loads a database given its filename (without extension). It first reads the appropriate .DEF file to determine the size of each
record. It then loads the data using **dls_store( )** to insert each item into
the linked list. The **load( )** function follows:

```
/* Load the data and definition files. */
load(char *fname)
{
  struct db_type *info;
  FILE *fp, *fp2;
  register int i;
  char name[80];

  strcpy(name, fname);
  strcat(name, ".dat");
  fp = fopen(name, "rb");
```

```
if(!fp) {
  printf("cannot open file\n");
  return 0;
}

strcpy(name, fname);
strcat(name, ".def");
fp2 = fopen(name, "rb");
if(!fp2) {
  printf("cannot open file\n");
  fclose(fp);
  return 0;
}

/* free any previously allocated memory */
while(first) {
  info = first->next;
  free(info->data); /* free the data */
  free(info);  /* free the control structure */
  first = info;
}

/* reset top and bottom pointers */
first = last = cur_rec = NULL;
num_recs = 0;

prompt("loading file");

/* load DEF file first */
record_size = getw(fp2);
num_fields = getw(fp2);
sort_field = getw(fp2);
for(i=0; i<num_fields; i++) {
  if(1!=fread(&fields[i], sizeof(fields[i]), 1, fp2)) {
    printf("error reading definition file\n");
    fclose(fp); fclose(fp2); getch();
    return 0;
  }
}
fclose(fp2);

while(!feof(fp)) {
  /* allocate memory for control structure */
```

```
    info = malloc(sizeof(struct db_type));
    if(!info) {
      printf("out of memory");
      fclose(fp);
      return 0;
    }
    /* allocate memory for actual data */
    info->data = malloc(record_size);
    if(!info->data) {
      printf("out of memory");
      fclose(fp);
      return 0;
    }
    /* read records */
    if(1!=fread(info->data, record_size, 1, fp)) {
      if(ferror(fp)) {
        printf("error reading data file\n");
        fclose(fp);
        return 0;
      }
      fclose(fp);
      cur_rec = first;
      return 1;
    }
    dls_store(info, &first, &last);
    num_recs++;
  }
  fclose(fp);
  cur_rec = first;
  return 0;
}
```

USING THE SUBSYSTEM TO CREATE A PERSONAL DATABASE

To demonstrate the database subsystem, a simple personal database is developed. As stated earlier, this database is menu driven. The main loop for the database is contained in the **db( )** function, shown here:

```c
/* Database subsystem entry function.  You can delete this
   function and substitute your own, if you like.
*/
void db(void)
{
  int choice;
  char fname[80];

  clrscr();
  init();  /* initialize */

  do {
    choice = menu();
    switch(choice) {
      case 1: /* define structure of database */
        define();
        break;
      case 2: /* enter info */
        enter();
        break;
      case 3: /* browse in the file */
        cur_rec = browse();
        break;
      case 4: /* search */
        cur_rec = search();
        break;
      case 5: /* modify */
        cur_rec = modify();
        break;
      case 6: /* delete */
        delete(&first, &last);
        break;
      case 7: /* print */
        print();
        break;
      case 8: /* save data */
        prompt("Enter file to save (ENTER to skip): ");
        db_gets(fname, FNAME_SIZE);
        if(*fname) save(fname);
        break;
```

```
      case 9: /* load data */
        prompt("Enter file to load (ENTER to skip): ");
        db_gets(fname, FNAME_SIZE);
        if(*fname) load(fname);
        break;
    }
  } while(choice!=0);
}
```

The **menu( )** function, which follows, is used to input the user's selection. Its operation should be clear.

```
/* Prompt the user for selection. */
menu(void)
{
  char ch;

  clrscr();
  gotoxy(0, 0);
  printf("0. quit\n");
  printf("1. Define database\n");
  printf("2. Enter information\n");
  printf("3. Browse\n");
  printf("4: Search\n");
  printf("5: Modify\n");
  printf("6: Delete\n");
  printf("7: Print\n");
  printf("8: Save database\n");
  printf("9: Load database\n");
  printf("(%d records in file)", num_recs);
  do {
    gotoxy(0, 12);
    printf("Enter number of your choice: ");
    ch = getche();
  } while(ch <'0' || ch >'9');
  return ch - '0';
}
```

THE ENTIRE MENU-DRIVEN PERSONAL DATABASE

The entire menu-driven, personal database is shown here:

```
/* A database subsystem. */
```

```
#define TURBOC
/* If you use Microsoft C, #define MICROSOFTC
   instead of TURBOC.   If you have a different
   C compiler, see the text.
*/

#include "stdio.h"
#include "ctype.h"
#include "dos.h"
#include "conio.h"
#include "string.h"
#include "stdlib.h"
#include "bios.h"

#define MAX_FIELDS 10
#define NAME_SIZE  40
#define MAX_LINES  24
#define LINE_LEN   79
#define FNAME_SIZE  8

enum field_type {STRING, DOUBLE, INT, CHAR};

struct descriptor {
  int position;  /* position of field in record */
  enum field_type type; /* type of field */
  char name[NAME_SIZE]; /* name of field */
  int size;  /* size of field in bytes */
  int x, y;  /* location on screen */
} fields[MAX_FIELDS];

int num_fields;  /* number of fields in a record */
int record_size; /* record size in bytes */
int sort_field;  /* number of field to sort on */
int num_recs;    /* number of records in file */

/* This structure manages the database information */
struct db_type {
  char *data;  /* pointer to data */
  struct db_type *prior; /* pointer to previous record */
  struct db_type *next;  /* pointer to next record */
} *first, *last, *cur_rec;

void db(void);
```

```
void db_gets(char *str, int maxlen), gotoxy(int x, int y);
void clr_eol(int x, int y);
void clrscr(void), define(void), display_rec(char *p);
void init(void), display_fields(void);
void dls_store(struct db_type *i, struct db_type **first,
               struct db_type **last);
void delete(struct db_type **start, struct db_type **last);
void prompt(char *s), print(void);
void change(char *data, int field);
int save(char *fname), load(char *fname);
int menu(void), enter(void), select_field(char *str);
struct db_type *find( char *key,
                      struct db_type *from, int field);
struct db_type *search(void), *modify(void);
struct db_type *browse(void);

main()
{
  db();
}

/* Database subsystem entry function.  You can delete this
   function and substitute your own, if you like.
*/
void db(void)
{
  int choice;
  char fname[80];

  clrscr();
  init();   /* initialize */

  do {
    choice = menu();
    switch(choice) {
      case 1: /* define structure of database */
        define();
        break;
      case 2: /* enter info */
        enter();
        break;
      case 3: /* browse in the file */
        cur_rec = browse();
```

```
            break;
        case 4: /* search */
          cur_rec = search();
          break;
        case 5: /* modify */
          cur_rec = modify();
          break;
        case 6: /* delete */
          delete(&first, &last);
          break;
        case 7: /* print */
          print();
          break;
        case 8: /* save data */
          prompt("Enter file to save (ENTER to skip): ");
          db_gets(fname, FNAME_SIZE);
          if(*fname) save(fname);
          break;
        case 9: /* load data */
          prompt("Enter file to load (ENTER to skip): ");
          db_gets(fname, FNAME_SIZE);
          if(*fname) load(fname);
          break;
      }
  } while(choice!=0);
}

/* Initialize */
void init(void)
{
  num_fields = 0;
  num_recs = 0;
  sort_field = 0;
  first = cur_rec = last = NULL;
}

/* Prompt the user for selection. */
menu(void)
{
  char ch;

  clrscr();
  gotoxy(0, 0);
```

```
    printf("0. quit\n");
    printf("1. Define database\n");
    printf("2. Enter information\n");
    printf("3. Browse\n");
    printf("4: Search\n");
    printf("5: Modify\n");
    printf("6: Delete\n");
    printf("7: Print\n");
    printf("8: Save database\n");
    printf("9: Load database\n");
    printf("(%d records in file)", num_recs);
    do {
      gotoxy(0, 12);
      printf("Enter number of your choice: ");
      ch = getche();
    } while(ch <'0' || ch >'9');
    return ch - '0';
}

/* Define the structure of the database. */
void define(void)
{
  char ch;
  int i;
  struct db_type *temp;
  clrscr();

  /* free any previously allocated memory */
  while(first) {
    temp = first->next;
    free(temp->data);   /* free the data */
    free(temp);         /* free the control structure */
    first = temp;
  }
  init();

  record_size = 0;

  do {
    gotoxy(0, 0);
    printf("number of fields (1-%d) (0 to skip): ", MAX_FIELDS);
    scanf("%d%*c", &num_fields);
    if(!num_fields) return;
```

```
} while (num_fields<0 || num_fields>MAX_FIELDS);

for(i=0; i<num_fields; i++) {
  clrscr();
  gotoxy(0, 0);
  fields[i].position = record_size;
  printf("Enter name of field %d (1-40 chars): ", i+1);
  db_gets(fields[i].name, 40);

  /* The field type is not used by any code in this
     example, but it may be needed by your applications.
  */
  printf("\nField types are: (S)tring, (D)ouble, (I)nt");
  printf(" and (C)har\n");
  do {
    printf("Enter field type (use first letter): ");
    ch = getche();
    ch = tolower(ch);
  }while(!strchr("sdic", ch));
  switch(ch) {
    case 's': fields[i].type = STRING;
      break;
    case 'd': fields[i].type = DOUBLE;
      break;
    case 'i': fields[i].type = INT;
      break;
    case 'c': fields[i].type = CHAR;
      break;
  }
  printf("\n");

  do {
    printf("enter length of field: ");
    scanf("%d%*c", &fields[i].size);
  } while(fields[i].size<0 || fields[i].size>LINE_LEN);
  fields[i].size++; /* make room for null terminator */

  do {
    printf("enter X,Y coordinates of field: ");
    scanf("%d%d%*c", &fields[i].x, &fields[i].y);
  } while(fields[i].x<0 ||
        fields[i].x+fields[i].size>=LINE_LEN
        || fields[i].y<0 || fields[i].y>=MAX_LINES);
```

```
    printf("Is this field defined OK? (Y/N): ");
    ch = getche();
    if(tolower(ch)!='y')
      i--; /* reenter */
    else
      record_size += fields[i].size;
  }
  printf("\nPress a key to see fields and screen layout");
  getch();
  clrscr();
  display_fields();
  sort_field = select_field("Select field to sort on");
}

/* Enter information into the database. */
enter(void)
{
  register int i, field;
  char ch;
  struct db_type *p;

  for(;;) {
    /* allocate memory for control structure */
    p = malloc(sizeof(struct db_type));
    if(!p) {
      printf("out of memory\n");
      return 0;
    }
    /* allocate memory for actual data */
    p->data = malloc(record_size);
    if(!p->data) {
      printf("out of memory\n");
      return 0;
    }

    clrscr();
    display_fields();

    /* input the data */
    for(i=0; i<num_fields; i++) {
      gotoxy(fields[i].x+strlen(fields[i].name)+1, fields[i].y);
      db_gets(&(p->data)[fields[i].position], fields[i].size-1);
```

```
      if(!(*p->data+fields[0].position)) return 1;
    }
    num_recs++;

    prompt("Entry OK? (Y/N): ");
    ch = getche();
    ch = tolower(ch);
    while(ch!='y') {
      field = select_field("Select field to modify");
      change(p->data, field);  /* change field */
      prompt("Entry OK? (Y/N): ");
      ch = getche();
      ch = tolower(ch);
    }
    dls_store(p, &first, &last); /* store it */
  }
}


/* Display the database fields. */
void display_fields(void)
{
  register int i, j;

  for(i=0; i<num_fields; i++) {
    gotoxy(fields[i].x, fields[i].y);
    printf("%s ", fields[i].name);
    for(j=0; j<fields[i].size-1; j++) putch('.');
  }
}


/* Display one record's information. */
void display_rec(char *p)
{
  register int i;

  display_fields();
  for(i=0; i<num_fields; i++) {
    gotoxy(fields[i].x+strlen(fields[i].name)+1, fields[i].y);
    printf("%s", p+fields[i].position);
  }
}
```

```
/* Return the number of the field the user selects
   using the arrow keys.
*/
select_field(char *str)
{
  union key {
    int i;
    char ch[2];
  } k;
  register int i, len;

  prompt(str); /* display prompting message */

  for(i=0;;) {
    /* position cursor at start of each field */
    len = strlen(fields[i].name) + 1;
    gotoxy(fields[i].x+len, fields[i].y);

#ifdef TURBOC
    k.i = bioskey(0);
#endif
#ifdef MICROSOFTC
    k.i = _bios_keybrd(0);
#endif

    if(!k.ch[0])
      switch(k.ch[1]) {
        case 72: /* up */
          if(i) i--;
          break;
        case 80: /* down */
          if(i<num_fields-1) i++;
          break;
      }
    else
      if(k.ch[0]=='\r') return i;
  }
}

/* Save both data and description to disk. */
save(char *fname)
{
  struct db_type *info;
```

```
register int i;
FILE *fp;
char name[80];

strcpy(name, fname);
strcat(name, ".dat");
fp = fopen(name, "wb");
if(!fp) {
  printf("cannot open data file\n");
  return 0;
}
prompt("saving data");

info = first;
while(info) { /* save each record */
  fwrite(info->data, record_size, 1, fp);
  info = info->next;  /* get next db_type */
  if(ferror(fp)) {
    printf("error writing file\n");
    fclose(fp);
    return 0;
  }
}
fclose(fp);

strcpy(name, fname);
strcat(name, ".def");
fp = fopen(name, "wb");
if(!fp) {
  printf("cannot open definition file\n");
  fclose(fp);
  return 0;
}

putw(record_size, fp);
putw(num_fields, fp);
putw(sort_field, fp);

for(i=0; i<num_fields; i++) {
  fwrite(&fields[i], sizeof(fields[i]), 1, fp);
  if(ferror(fp)) {
    printf("error writing file\n");
    fclose(fp);
```

```
      return 0;
    }
  }
  fclose(fp);
  return 1;
}

/* Load the data and definition files. */
load(char *fname)
{
  struct db_type *info;
  FILE *fp, *fp2;
  register int i;
  char name[80];

  strcpy(name, fname);
  strcat(name, ".dat");
  fp = fopen(name, "rb");
  if(!fp) {
    printf("cannot open file\n");
    return 0;
  }

  strcpy(name, fname);
  strcat(name, ".def");
  fp2 = fopen(name, "rb");
  if(!fp2) {
    printf("cannot open file\n");
    fclose(fp);
    return 0;
  }

  /* free any previously allocated memory */
  while(first) {
    info = first->next;
    free(info->data); /* free the data */
    free(info);   /* free the control structure */
    first = info;
  }

  /* reset top and bottom pointers */
  first = last = cur_rec = NULL;
  num_recs = 0;
```

```
prompt("loading file");

/* load DEF file first */
record_size = getw(fp2);
num_fields = getw(fp2);
sort_field = getw(fp2);
for(i=0; i<num_fields; i++) {
  if(1!=fread(&fields[i], sizeof(fields[i]), 1, fp2)) {
    printf("error reading definition file\n");
    fclose(fp); fclose(fp2); getch();
    return 0;
  }
}
fclose(fp2);

while(!feof(fp)) {
  /* allocate memory for control structure */
  info = malloc(sizeof(struct db_type));
  if(!info) {
    printf("out of memory");
    fclose(fp);
    return 0;
  }
  /* allocate memory for actual data */
  info->data = malloc(record_size);
  if(!info->data) {
    printf("out of memory");
    fclose(fp);
    return 0;
  }
  /* read records */
  if(1!=fread(info->data, record_size, 1, fp)) {
    if(ferror(fp)) {
      printf("error reading data file\n");
      fclose(fp);
      return 0;
    }
    fclose(fp);
    cur_rec = first;
    return 1;
  }
  dls_store(info, &first, &last);
```

```
    num_recs++;
  }
  fclose(fp);
  cur_rec = first;
  return 0;
}

/* Modify a record in the list and return
   a pointer to that record. */
struct db_type *modify(void)
{
  struct db_type *info;
  char key[80], ch;
  register int field;

  clrscr();

  /* find field to use for searching */
  display_fields();
  field = select_field("Select field");

  /* find record to search for */
  prompt("Enter key: ");
  db_gets(key, fields[field].size);

  /* find first match, if any */
  info = find(key, first, field);
  while(info) {
    display_rec(info->data);
    prompt("Modify this record? (Y/N): ");
    ch = getche();
    ch = tolower(ch);
    if(ch!='y') /* find next match, if any */
      info = find(key, info->next, field);
    else break;
  }
  if(!info) return NULL; /* not found */

  /* which field to modify? */
  field = select_field("Select field to modify");
  change(info->data, field); /* change data */
  return info;  /* return current location */
}
```

```
/* Change the specified record and field. */
void change(char *data, int field)
{
  int i;

  display_rec(data);
  prompt("Enter new data");

  /* display record, position cursor at beginning
     of the field, and input new data
  */
  gotoxy(fields[field].x, fields[field].y);
  printf("%s ", fields[field].name);
  for(i=0; i<fields[field].size-1; i++) putch('.');
  i = strlen(fields[field].name)+1;
  gotoxy(fields[field].x+i, fields[field].y);
  db_gets(data+fields[field].position, fields[field].size-1);
}

/* Browse through the list and return pointer
   to the last record examined. */
struct db_type *browse(void)
{
  union key {
    int i;
    char ch[2];
  } k;
  struct db_type *info;

  clrscr();
  clr_eol(0, MAX_LINES);
  gotoxy(0, MAX_LINES);
  printf("Down Arrow: forward   Up Arrow: backward");
  printf("   Home: beginning   End: end");

  /* If a current location has been defined,
     start at that point; otherwise, start at
     the top of the file.
  */
  if(cur_rec) info = cur_rec;
  else info = first;

  while(info) {
```

```
        display_rec(info->data); /* display record */

#ifdef TURBOC
    k.i = bioskey(0);
#endif
#ifdef MICROSOFTC
    k.i = _bios_keybrd(0);
#endif

    if(!k.ch[0])
      switch(k.ch[1]) {
        case 71: /* Home */
          info = first;
          break;
        case 72: /* up */
          if(info->prior)
            info = info->prior;  /* get previous rec */
          break;
        case 79: /* End */
          info = last;
          break;
        case 80: /* down */
          if(info->next)
            info = info->next;  /* get next rec */
          break;
      }
    else
      return info;  /* return current location */
  }
  return NULL;
}

/* Find an entry and return a pointer to it. */
struct db_type *find(char *key, struct db_type *from,
                     int field)
{
  struct db_type *info;

  info = from;
  while(info) {
    if(!strcmp(key, info->data+
               fields[field].position)) return info;
    info = info->next;  /* get next db_type */
```

```
  }
  return NULL;  /* not found */
}

/* Look for a record in the list and return
   a pointer to the last match found. */
struct db_type *search(void)
{
  int field;
  char key[80], ch;
  struct db_type *info, *temp;

  clrscr();
  display_fields();
  field = select_field("Select field to search on");
  prompt("Enter key: "); /* search string */
  db_gets(key, fields[field].size);

  ch = '\0';

  /* find first match, if any */
  info = find(key, first, field);
  while(info && ch != 'q') {
    /* save pointer in case no other matches are found */
    temp = info;

    display_rec(info->data);

    /* find next match, if any */
    info = find(key, info->next, field);

    /* tell user if more matches exist */
    if(info) printf("\nmore, ");
    else printf("\nNo more matches, ");
    printf("press a key ('q' to quit): ");
    ch = getch();
    ch = tolower(ch);
  }
  return temp; /* return pointer to last match */
}

/* Print the file either selectively or in full.
```

```
    NOTE: This function works only with DOS, so
    you may need to change it for other environments.

*/
void print(void)
{
  register int i, j, field;
  int blank_lines;
  struct db_type *info;
  char *p, selective, key[80], s[80], ch;

  clrscr();
  prompt("Selective search? (Y/N): ");
  ch = getche();
  if(tolower(ch)=='y') {
    display_fields();
    field = select_field("Select field");
    prompt("Enter key: ");
    db_gets(key, fields[field].size);
    selective = 1;
  }
  else selective = 0;

  /* Number of blank lines between records */
  prompt("Enter number of blank lines: ");
  db_gets(s, 20);
  blank_lines = atoi(s);

  prompt("Printing...");

  if(selective)
    info = find(key, first, field);
  else
    info = first;

  while(info) {
    /* display each record as it prints */
    display_rec(info->data);

    for(i=0; i<num_fields; i++) {
      p = info->data+fields[i].position;
      /* print the field */
      while(*p) {
```

```
#ifdef TURBOC
        biosprint(0, *p, 0);
#endif
#ifdef MICROSOFTC
        _bios_printer(0, 0, *p);
#endif
        p++;
      }
      /* output a CR-LF */
#ifdef TURBOC
      biosprint(0, '\r', 0);
      biosprint(0, '\n', 0);
#endif
#ifdef MICROSOFTC
      _bios_printer(0, 0, '\r');
      _bios_printer(0, 0, '\n');
#endif
    }
    /* output blank lines between records */
    for(j=0; j<blank_lines; j++) {
#ifdef TURBOC
      biosprint(0, '\r', 0);
      biosprint(0, '\n', 0);
#endif
#ifdef MICROSOFTC
      _bios_printer(0, 0, '\r');
      _bios_printer(0, 0, '\n');
#endif
    }

    /* get next record */
    if(selective)
      info = find(key, info->next, field);
    else
      info = info->next;
  }
#ifdef TURBOC
  biosprint(0, '\f', 0); /* form feed */
#endif
#ifdef MICROSOFTC
  _bios_printer(0, 0, '\f');
#endif
}
```

```
/*****************************************************
 Doubly Linked List Routines.
*****************************************************/

/* Create a doubly linked list in sorted order.
*/
void dls_store(
  struct db_type *i,     /* new element */
  struct db_type **first, /* first element in list */
  struct db_type **last /* last element in list */
)
{
  struct db_type *old, *p;

  if(*last==NULL) {   /* first element in list */
    i->next = NULL;
    i->prior = NULL;
    *last = i;
    *first = i;
    return;
   }

  p = *first; /* first at top of list */

  old = NULL;
  while(p) { /* find location to insert record */
    if(strcmp(p->data+fields[sort_field].position,
              i->data+fields[sort_field].position)<0) {
      old = p;
      p = p->next;
    }
    else {
      if(p->prior) {/* goes in middle of list */
        p->prior->next = i;
        i->next = p;
        i->prior = p->prior;
        p->prior = i;
        return;
      }
      i->next = p; /* new first element */
      i->prior = NULL;
      p->prior = i;
```

```
        *first = i;
        return;
      }
    }
  old->next = i; /* put on end */
  i->next = NULL;
  i->prior = old;
  *last = i;
}

/* Remove an element from the list. */
void delete(struct db_type **start, struct db_type **last)
{
  struct db_type *info;
  char key[80], ch;
  int field;

  clrscr();
  display_fields();
  field = select_field("Select field");
  prompt("Enter key: ");
  db_gets(key, fields[field].size);

  info = find(key, first, field);
  while(info) {
    display_rec(info->data);
    prompt("Delete this record? (Y/N): ");
    ch = getche();
    ch = tolower(ch);
    if(ch!='y')
      info = find(key, info->next, field);
    else break;
  }
  if(!info) return; /* not found */

  /* if deleting current rec, set cur_rec to NULL */
  if(cur_rec==info) cur_rec = NULL;

  num_recs--;

  if(*start==info) { /* deleting first record */
    *start=info->next;
    if(*start) (*start)->prior = NULL;
```

```
      else *last = NULL;
    }
    else {
      info->prior->next = info->next;
      if(info!=*last)  /* deleting from middle */
        info->next->prior = info->prior;
      else
        *last = info->prior; /* deleting last record */
    }
    free(info->data); /* free data */
    free(info);  /* free control structure */
}


/****************************************************
Miscellaneous support functions.
****************************************************/

/* Display a message on the bottom line of the screen. */
void prompt(char *s)
{
  clr_eol(0, MAX_LINES);
  gotoxy(0, MAX_LINES);
  printf(s);
}

/* Read a string from the keyboard, but do not
   scroll the display when a RETURN is entered.
*/
void db_gets(char *str, int maxlen)
{
  char *p;
  int i;

  p = str;

  for(i=0; ; ) {
    *str = getch();
    if(*str=='\r') { /* return when RETURN entered */
      *str = '\0';  /* NULL terminate */
      return;
    }

    if(*str=='\b') {  /* backspace */
```

```
      if(str>p) {
        str--;
        putch('\b');
        putch('.');
        putch('\b');
        i--;
      }
    }
    else if(i<maxlen) {
      putch(*str);
      str++;
      i++;
    }
  }
}

/* Send cursor to specified X,Y (0,0 is upper
   left corner). */
void gotoxy(int x, int y)
{
  union REGS i;

  i.h.dh = y;
  i.h.dl = x;
  i.h.ah = 2;
  i.h.bh = 0;
  int86(16, &i, &i);
}

/* Clear to end of specified line. */
void clr_eol(int x, int y)
{
  gotoxy(x, y);
  for(; x<LINE_LEN; x++) {
    printf(" ");
  }
}

#define MAX_LINES 24
#define LINE_LEN  79
/* Clear the screen. */
void clrscr(void)
{
```

```
    union REGS r;

    r.h.ah = 6;
    r.h.al = 0;
    r.h.ch = 0;
    r.h.cl = 0;
    r.h.dh = MAX_LINES;
    r.h.dl = LINE_LEN;
    r.h.bh = 7;
    int86(0x10, &r, &r);
}
```

SOME THINGS TO TRY

You may want to try linking the database subsystem with the multitasking kernel in Chapter 4. For example, you could make printing the list a separate task, so that the user would not have to wait for printing to finish to continue using the database. Also, you might want to let the user sort the database on any field at any time.

For a real challenge, try linking the database to the screen editor from Chapter 5 and then adapting the interpreter technology described in Chapter 1, so that it interprets a database query language. You could then add complex queries to the database.

CHAPTER SEVEN

Creating Custom Character Fonts

Something that has interested me for some time is creating custom character fonts. The term *font* describes a complete set of characters of a single type. For example, common typewriter fonts include pica, elite, and sans serif. What makes custom fonts exciting is that they can add variety and interest to your programs by making important pieces of text stand out on the screen.

This chapter develops a font editor to create character fonts and a small display subsystem that can display text in the custom font using a graphics mode. The code for the font editor and the display subsystem is designed for use on a PC that has graphics capabilities and it uses EGA/VGA graphics mode 16 (16 colors, 640×350). You can change the graphics mode if you desire.

As with many of the programs in this book, you must define either **TURBOC** or **MICROSOFTC** at the top of the program because of slight differences between the two compilers. If you have a different compiler, consult your user manual. You may need to rename one or more functions.

Jeff Betts
President of Creative Programming

Jeff Betts is the creator of the popular Vitamin C, a C language windowing interface library. Vitamin C was one of the first of many third-party libraries that contributed to the success of the C language in the microcomputer environment. The creation of Vitamin C is an interesting story, as related by Jeff. "We started with a mere $2,500, which was barely enough to cover the packaging of a few units and a couple of classified ads. We believed in our product, but had no idea what type of response we would get." Fortunately for Jeff and the C world, those ads worked.

Jeff came to C in 1982. He had been working in a CP/M environment using dBASE and CBASIC. But, as he explains, these languages were insufficient. "I kept wanting to do things that were impossible or too slow with those other languages—and I sure didn't want to resort to assembler."

Jeff's approach to programming reflects that of many C programmers. To write great programs, you must "Experiment. Take chances. Don't be afraid to crash your machine. Push yourself to your limits of understanding. Write code. Rewrite code. Rewrite your rewrites." He also stresses the importance of understanding how C works internally. "Know what happens when you call a function. Know how the stack is used. Also, understand how C bugs work and then understand how to kill them."

One of Jeff's favorite C constructs is the pointer. "It's so versatile," he says. "It allows programs to be incredibly dynamic. It also plays an important role in the modularity and generalization of functions. The function pointer is one of C's most important and innovative features, allowing extremely fast and flexible code."

Like many C programmers, Jeff drives himself hard. "I have recently become involved with amateur radio, which, by law, cannot be used for commercial purposes. I've had other hobbies, such as music and photography, but I turned them into money-making ventures. Without a good stress outlet, it is hard to do good creative programming. Amateur radio is my outlet."

Jeff Betts currently lives in Carrollton, Texas.

THE FONT EDITOR

Fortunately, the character font editor program can be derived from the icon editor developed in Chapter 2. The most noticeable change is that the font editor is designed to edit the full 127-character ASCII set while the icon editor only edits one icon at a time.

Representing the Characters

When characters are displayed on the screen, a certain number of pixels is allowed for the height of the character and a certain number for its width. This area is sometimes called the *character matrix*.

There are two basic types of character fonts: *proportional* and *fixed-spaced.* In a proportional font, each character is allocated only the room it needs. For example, an *i* needs less space than a *w*. This means that for a proportional font, the size of the character matrix changes from character to character. By contrast, each character's matrix in a fixed-space font is the same size. The font editor and display subsystem developed here use the fixed-space approach because it greatly simplifies both the font editor and the display subsystem. However, you might want to try experimenting with a proportional font on your own.

The font is held in the array **font**, shown here:

```
#define XDIM        7    /* change these to change dimensions */
#define YDIM        9    /* of the font you want to use */
#define NUM_CHARS 127    /* number of chars in a font */

unsigned char font[NUM_CHARS][XDIM][YDIM];  /* font */
```

As noted in the comments, you are free to change the size of the matrix. The 7×9 size is adequate for simple fonts. However, more complex ones may require a larger matrix. The reason that there are 127 characters in the font is that there are 127 ASCII characters. However, if you want to define some special characters, you can increase this number to 255.

The **edit_char( )** Function

The function that you use to create a character, called **edit_char( )**, is shown here. This function is derived from the **edit_icon( )** function found in Chapter 2.

```
/* Edit a character.  This function displays a large
   grid to make editing easy.  It also displays the
   normal size version of the char being edited. */
void edit_char(char chr)
{
  register int x, y;
  char ch, pen, temp;

  clr_eol(0, 0);
  gotoxy(0, 0);
  printf("F1: pen down  F2: pen up  F3: erase  F4: done");

  x = IX; y = IY;   /* set x,y to upper left corner */
  pen = BCK_GND;
  gotoxy(0, 23);
  printf("pen up  ");   /* tell user pen is up */

  display_char(chr, 0, IY);
  display_grid(chr);
  clr_eol(0, 22);
  gotoxy(0, 22);
  printf("editing character: %c", chr);

  do {
    /* write pixel to grid */
    putpoint(x+((x-IX)*XPAND), y+((y-IY)*XPAND), pen, 0);

    /* save pixel color in char, use
       blank background */
    if(pen==BCK_GND)
      font[chr][x-IX][y-IY] = BLANK;
    else font[chr][x-IX][y-IY] = FORE_GND;

    /* write pixel to char */
    putpoint(x-IX, y, font[chr][x-IX][y-IY], 0);

    /* This code displays a dot that indicates the current
       position, waits for a keystroke and then replaces
       the original value.
    */
    temp = getpoint(x+((x-IX)*XPAND), y+((y-IY)*XPAND));
    putpoint(x+((x-IX)*XPAND), y+((y-IY)*XPAND),
             HIGHLIGHT, 0);
```

```
ch = getkey();
putpoint(x+((x-IX)*XPAND), y+((y-IY)*XPAND), temp, 0);

switch(ch) {
  case 75: /* left */
    x--;
    break;
  case 77: /* right */
    x++;
    break;
  case 72: /* up */
    y--;
    break;
  case 80: /* down */
    y++;
    break;
  case 71: /* up left */
    x--; y--;
    break;
  case 73: /* up right */
    x++; y--;
    break;
  case 79: /* down left*/
    x--; y++;
    break;
  case 81: /* down right */
    x++; y++;
    break;
  case 59: /* F1 - pen down */
    pen = FORE_GND;
    gotoxy(0, 23);
    printf("pen down");
    break;
  case 60: /* F2 - pen up */
    pen = BCK_GND;
    gotoxy(0, 23);
    printf("pen up   ");
    break;
  case 61: /* F3 - erase */
    init_char(chr);
    display_char(chr, 0, IY);
    display_grid(chr);
    break;
```

```
    }
    if(x < IX) x++;   if(x > IX+XDIM-1) x--;
    if(y < IY) y++;   if(y > IY+YDIM-1) y--;

  } while(ch != 62); /* F4 - quit */
  clr_eol(0, 22);
  clr_eol(0, 23);
  return;
}
```

The character to be created or modified is passed to the function. Notice that **chr** is used to index the **font** array directly. Because the ASCII character set is defined to start at zero, the value of the character you wish to edit can also be used as the index of the array location that will hold the character's image. When the function first begins, an expanded image of the character being edited is shown in the middle of the screen and a regular-size version is shown to the right. A highlight (in red) shows the pixel that is currently active.

A character is created by moving through the matrix via the arrow keys. When the pen is up, any pixel you pass through is set to the background color. When the pen is down, any pixel you pass through is set to the foreground color. To put the pen down, press F1. To raise the pen, press F2. To erase the entire character, press F3. To stop editing that character, press F4.

The **main( )** Loop

The font editor is driven by a loop inside the **main( )** function. This loop first calls **menu( )**, which returns a user's selection; this may be used to edit a character, save the font, load the font, or exit. Then, **main( )** takes appropriate action based on the user's request. The **main( )** and **menu( )** functions are shown here:

```
char far *egabase;

void main(int argc, char *argv[])
{
  char ch, choice;
  mode(16);
```

```
#ifdef TURBOC
  egabase = (char far *) MK_FP(0xA000, 0000);
#endif
#ifdef MICROSOFTC
  egabase = (char far *) 0xA0000000;
#endif

  clear_chars();

  if(argc==2) load_font(argv[1]);

  do {
    choice = menu();
    switch(choice) {
      case 'e':  /* edit a character */
        clr_eol(0, 0);
        gotoxy(0, 0);
        printf("enter character to edit: ");
        ch = getch(); printf("%c", ch);
        edit_char(ch);
        break;
      case 's': /* save */
        save_font();
        break;
      case 'l': /* load */
        load_font("");
        break;
    }
  } while(choice!='q'); /* quit */
  mode(2);
}

/* Get user's selection. */
char menu(void)
{
  char ch;

  clr_eol(0, 0);
  gotoxy(0, 0);

  printf("(E)dit character, (S)ave fonts, ");
  printf("(L)oad fonts, (Q)uit\");
  do {
```

```
    clr_eol(0, 1);
    gotoxy(0, 1);
    printf("Enter letter of choice: ");
    ch = getche();
  } while(!strchr("eslq", tolower(ch)));

  return tolower(ch);
}
```

The Entire Font Editor

The code for the entire font editor is shown here. (The function **put-point( )**, which actually draws one pixel on the screen, was developed in Chapter 2. Refer to page 87 for details of its operation.) Figure 7-1 shows an example of the editing screen.

Figure 7-1

An example of the font editor

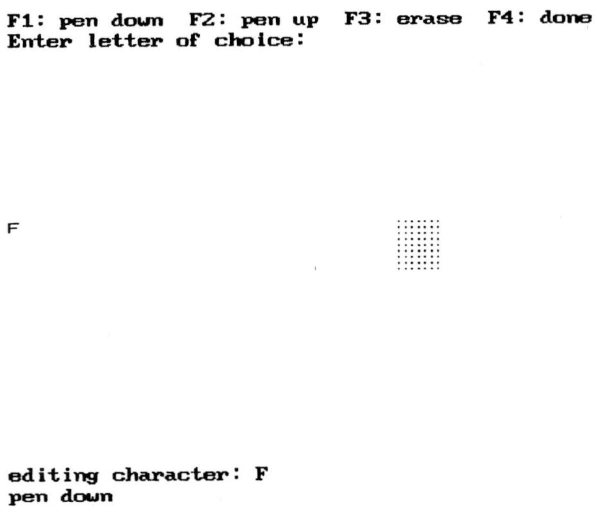

F1: pen down F2: pen up F3: erase F4: done
Enter letter of choice:

F

editing character: F
pen down

```
/* Font Editor Program. */

#define TURBOC
/* If you use Microsoft C, define MICROSOFTC instead
   of TURBOC.
*/

#include "stdio.h"
#include "dos.h"
#include "conio.h"
#include "bios.h"
#include "string.h"
#include "ctype.h"

#define IY          144
#define IX          240

#define XDIM          7    /* change these to change dimensions */
#define YDIM          9    /* of the font you want to use */
#define NUM_CHARS   127    /* number of chars in a font */

#define XPAND         3

#define MAX_LINES    24
#define LINE_LEN     79

#define BLANK         0
#define BCK_GND       9
#define FORE_GND     15
#define HIGHLIGHT    13

char getpoint(int x, int y), getkey(void);
void mode(int mode_code), gotoxy(int x, int y);
void clr_eol(int x, int y), clrscr(void);
void display_grid(char chr),  edit_char(char chr);
void display_char(char chr, int x, int y);
void init_char(char chr), clear_chars(void);
int save_font(void), load_font(char *fname);
void putpoint(int x, int y, int color, int how);
char menu(void);

unsigned char font[NUM_CHARS][XDIM][YDIM];  /* fonts */
```

```
char far *egabase;

void main(int argc, char *argv[])
{
  char ch, choice;
  mode(16);

#ifdef TURBOC
  egabase = (char far *) MK_FP(0xA000, 0000);
#endif
#ifdef MICROSOFTC
  egabase = (char far *) 0xA0000000;
#endif

  clear_chars();

  if(argc==2) load_font(argv[1]);

  do {
    choice = menu();
    switch(choice) {
      case 'e':  /* edit a character */
        clr_eol(0, 0);
        gotoxy(0, 0);
        printf("enter character to edit: ");
        ch = getch(); printf("%c", ch);
        edit_char(ch);
        break;
      case 's': /* save */
        save_font();
        break;
      case 'l': /* load */
        load_font("");
        break;
    }
  } while(choice!='q'); /* quit */
  mode(2);
}

/* Get user's selection. */
char menu(void)
{
  char ch;
```

```
    clr_eol(0, 0);
    gotoxy(0, 0);

    printf("(E)dit character, (S)ave fonts, ");
    printf("(L)oad fonts, (Q)uit\"");
    do {
      clr_eol(0, 1);
      gotoxy(0, 1);
      printf("Enter letter of choice: ");
      ch = getche();
    } while(!strchr("eslq", tolower(ch)));

    return tolower(ch);
}

/* Display the expanded grid. */
void display_grid(char chr)
{
  register int x, y;

  for(y = IY; y<(IY+YDIM); y++)
    for(x = IX; x<(IX+XDIM); x++) {
      if(font[chr][x-IX][y-IY] == BLANK)
        putpoint(x+((x-IX)*XPAND), y+((y-IY)*XPAND),
                 BCK_GND, 0);
      else
        putpoint(x+((x-IX)*XPAND), y+((y-IY)*XPAND),
                 font[chr][x-IX][y-IY], 0);
    }
}

/* Edit a character.  This function displays a large
   grid to make editing easy.  It also displays the
   normal size version of the char being edited. */
void edit_char(char chr)
{
  register int x, y;
  char ch, pen, temp;

  clr_eol(0, 0);
  gotoxy(0, 0);
  printf("F1: pen down  F2: pen up  F3: erase  F4: done");
```

```
x = IX; y = IY;   /* set x,y to upper left corner */
pen = BCK_GND;
gotoxy(0, 23);
printf("pen up  ");   /* tell user pen is up */

display_char(chr, 0, IY);
display_grid(chr);
clr_eol(0, 22);
gotoxy(0, 22);
printf("editing character: %c", chr);

do {
  /* write pixel to grid */
  putpoint(x+((x-IX)*XPAND), y+((y-IY)*XPAND), pen, 0);


  /* save pixel color in char, use
     blank background */
  if(pen==BCK_GND)
    font[chr][x-IX][y-IY] = BLANK;
  else font[chr][x-IX][y-IY] = FORE_GND;

  /* write pixel to char */
  putpoint(x-IX, y, font[chr][x-IX][y-IY], 0);

  /* This code displays a dot that indicates the current
     position, waits for a keystroke and then replaces
     the original value.
  */
  temp = getpoint(x+((x-IX)*XPAND), y+((y-IY)*XPAND));
  putpoint(x+((x-IX)*XPAND), y+((y-IY)*XPAND),
           HIGHLIGHT, 0);
  ch = getkey();
  putpoint(x+((x-IX)*XPAND), y+((y-IY)*XPAND), temp, 0);

  switch(ch) {
    case 75: /* left */
      x--;
      break;
    case 77: /* right */
      x++;
      break;
    case 72: /* up */
```

```
            y--;
            break;
        case 80: /* down */
            y++;
            break;
        case 71: /* up left */
            x--; y--;
            break;
        case 73: /* up right */
            x++; y--;
            break;
        case 79: /* down left*/
            x--; y++;
            break;
        case 81: /* down right */
            x++; y++;
            break;
        case 59: /* F1 - pen down */
            pen = FORE_GND;
            gotoxy(0, 23);
            printf("pen down");
            break;
        case 60: /* F2 - pen up */
            pen = BCK_GND;
            gotoxy(0, 23);
            printf("pen up   ");
            break;
        case 61: /* F3 - erase */
            init_char(chr);
            display_char(chr, 0, IY);
            display_grid(chr);
            break;
        }
        if(x < IX) x++;   if(x > IX+XDIM-1) x--;
        if(y < IY) y++;   if(y > IY+YDIM-1) y--;

    } while(ch != 62); /* F4 - quit */
    clr_eol(0, 22);
    clr_eol(0, 23);
    return;
}

/* Displays the char at specified X,Y. */
```

```c
void display_char(char chr, int startx, int starty)
{
  register int x, y;

  for(y = starty; y<starty+YDIM; y++)
    for(x = startx; x<startx+XDIM; x++)
      putpoint(x, y, font[chr][x-startx][y-starty], 0);
}

/* Initialize all characters. */
void clear_chars(void)
{
  register int i;

  for(i=0; i<NUM_CHARS; i++)
    init_char(i);
}

/* Initializes the character. */
void init_char(char chr)
{
  register int x, y;

  for(x= 0; x<XDIM; x++)
    for(y=0; y<YDIM; y++)
      font[chr][x][y] = BLANK;
}

/* Saves the font. */
save_font(void)
{
  FILE *fp;
  char fname[80];
  int result;

  gotoxy(0, 22);
  printf("save to: ");
  gets(fname);

  if((fp = fopen(fname, "wb"))==NULL) {
    printf("cannot open file");
    return 0;
  }
```

```
  fwrite(font, sizeof font, 1, fp);

  if(ferror(fp)) result = 0;
  else result = 1;
  fclose(fp);
  clr_eol(0, 22);
  return result;
}

/* Loads the font. */
load_font(char *name)
{
  FILE *fp;
  char fname[80];
  int result;

  if(!*name) {
    clr_eol(0, 22);
    gotoxy(0, 22);
    printf("load from: ");
    gets(fname);
  }
  else strcpy(fname, name);

  if((fp = fopen(fname, "rb"))==NULL) {
    printf("cannot open file");
    return 0;
  }

  fread(font, sizeof font, 1, fp);

  if(ferror(fp)) result = 0;
  else result = 1;
  fclose(fp);
  clr_eol(0, 22);
  return result;
}

/* Return the scan code of the key pressed.
   This function is compatible with Turbo C and
   Microsoft C (be sure to #define the appropriate
   symbol).  If you use a different compiler, consult
   your user's manual.
```

```
*/
char getkey(void)
{
  union key {
    int i;
    char ch[2];
  } k;

#ifdef TURBOC
  k.i = bioskey(0);
#endif
#ifdef MICROSOFTC
  k.i = _bios_keybrd(0);
#endif
  return k.ch[l];
}

/* Set the video mode. */
void mode(int mode_code)
{
  union REGS r;

  r.h.al = mode_code;
  r.h.ah = 0;
  int86(0x10, &r, &r);
}

/* Send the cursor to x,y. */
void gotoxy(int x, int y)
{
  union REGS r;

  r.h.ah = 2; /* cursor addressing function */
  r.h.dl = x; /* column coordinate */
  r.h.dh = y; /* row coordinate */
  r.h.bh = 0; /* video page */
  int86(0x10, &r, &r);
}

/* Clears to end of line. */
void clr_eol(int x, int y)
{
    for(; x<80; x++) {
```

```
      gotoxy(x, y);
      printf(" ");
   }
}

/* Returns the value at the specified pixel. */
char getpoint(int x, int y)
{
  union REGS r;

  r.h.ah = 13;
  r.x.dx = y;
  r.x.cx = x;
  r.h.bh = 0;
  int86(16, &r, &r);
  return r.h.al;
}


/* This version of putpoint will work for all video
   adapters but is incredibly slow!
*/
/*
void putpoint(int x, int y, int color, int how)
{
  union REGS r;

  if(how==0x18) color = color | 128;
  r.h.bh = 0;
  r.h.ah = 12;
  r.h.al = color;
  r.x.dx = y;
  r.x.cx = x;
  int86(16, &r, &r);
}
*/

/* Clear the screen. */
void clrscr(void)
{
  union REGS r;

  r.h.ah = 6;
  r.h.al = 0;
```

```
  r.h.ch = 0;
  r.h.cl = 0;
  r.h.dh = MAX_LINES;
  r.h.dl = LINE_LEN;
  r.h.bh = 7;
  int86(0x10, &r, &r);

}

 * This function sets the specified pixel to the
   specified color using an EGA/VGA video adapter.
   The value of the parameter "how" may be one of
   these:

   action         value

   overwrite       0
   XOR             0x18
   AND             8
   OR              0x10

*/
#define ENABLE 0x0F
#define INDEXREG 0x3CE
#define VALREG 0x3CF

/* Note: Borland does not document outp(), but it is
   in the library of Turbo C 2.0.  The documented function
   is called outport(), but it runs much slower.  However,
   in future versions you may need to use it instead.
   For this reason, the following conditional compilation
   directives have been included.
*/
#ifdef TURBOC
#define OUTINDEX(index, val) outp((INDEXREG), (index));\
                             outp((VALREG), (val));

#endif
#ifdef MICROSOFTC
#define OUTINDEX(index, val) outp((INDEXREG), (index));\
                             outp((VALREG), (val));

#endif

#define WIDTH 80L
```

```
/* These range values assume EGA mode 16 */
#define XMAX 639
#define YMAX 349
#define XMIN 0
#define YMIN 0

void putpoint(int x, int y, int color, int how)
{
  register unsigned char mask = 0x80;
  register char far *base;
  unsigned dummy;
```

9   /* if you want range checking at this point, activate
       this line of code. It will slow down the function
       however.
    */

```
  /*if(x<XMIN || x>XMAX || y<YMIN || y>YMAX) return;*/

  base = (char far *) (egabase
          + ( (long) y * WIDTH + (long) x/8L ));

  mask >>= x % 8;

  /* This causes the memory READ necessary to
     load the EGA/VGA's internal registers.
  */

  dummy = *base;

  OUTINDEX(0, color);
  OUTINDEX(1, ENABLE);
  OUTINDEX(3, how);
  OUTINDEX(8, mask);

  *base = 1;

  OUTINDEX(0, 0);
  OUTINDEX(1, 0);
  OUTINDEX(3, 0);
  OUTINDEX(8, 0xff);
}
```

A CUSTOM-FONT-DISPLAY SUBSYSTEM

Once you have created your custom fonts, you need some way to use them. Toward this end, a small but effective custom-font-display subsystem will be developed. This subsystem will support the following functions:

- Display a character at the current location.
- Display a string beginning at the current location.
- Scale each character to the desired height and width.
- Determine the color of the character.
- Set the current location.

Let's see how these functions are implemented.

Displaying a Character

The lowest-level function simply writes a character to the screen. This is called **display_char( )** and is shown here with its necessary global data:

```
int xscale=1, yscale=1;
int fontx=0, fonty=0;
int color=FORE_GND;

/* Displays the character at current X,Y. */
void display_char(char chr)
{
  register int x, y, i, j, clr;

  /* is a carriage return */
  if(chr=='\n') {
    fontx = 0;
    fonty += YDIM*yscale + 1;
    return;
  }

  for(y = 0; y<YDIM; y++)
```

```
    for(x = 0; x<XDIM; x++) {
      for(i=0; i<xscale; i++)
        for(j=0; j<yscale; j++) {
          if(font[chr][x][y]==FORE_GND) clr = color;
          else clr = BCK_GND;
          putpoint(x*xscale+fontx+i,
                  y*yscale+fonty+j, clr, 0);
        }
    }
    fontx += XDIM*xscale + 1;
}
```

This function performs four main tasks. First, it determines the color of the character from the value of the global variable **color**. Second, it scales the size of the character according to the values of **xscale** and **yscale**, which must be positive. If **xscale** and **yscale** are 1, then the character prints in normal size. Otherwise, the character is displayed as a multiple of its size. Third, it increases **fontx** to the next character position. If the character is a newline, then it resets **fontx** to 0 and increases **fonty** to the next character location. Finally, it outputs the character at the current location specified by **fontx** and **fonty**.

Writing a String of Characters

The function **font_puts( )**, shown here, outputs a string of characters at the current X, Y location.

```
/* Display a string. */
void font_puts(char *str)
{
  while(*str) {
    display_char(*str);
    str++;
  }
}
```

Setting the Current Location, Scale, and Color

To change the current location, use **font_xy( )** to provide new values for **fontx** and **fonty**. The default color is white. To set the color to something else, use **setcolor( )**. The new color stays in effect until you change it. By default, the scale factors are set to 1. Use **setscale( )** to provide new values for **xscale** and **yscale**. The new scale factors stay in effect until you reset them. These functions are shown here:

```c
/* Position the font cursor to the specified X,Y */
void font_xy(int x, int y)
{
  if(x<0 || x>XMAX) return;
  if(y<0 || y>YMAX) return;
  fontx = x;
  fonty = y;
}

/* Set the scale factors. */
void setscale(int x, int y)
{
  if(x<0 || y<0) return;

  xscale = x;
  yscale = y;
}

/* Set the foreground color. */
void setcolor(int c)
{
  if(c<0) return;
  color = c;
}
```

The Display Subsystem with a Sample Program

The entire font-display subsystem is shown here, along with a short demonstration of the **main( )** function. Figure 7-2 shows a sample output of this program. Be sure to specify the name of the font file (created by the font editor) on the command line.

```c
/* Font-display subsystem and test program. */

#define TURBOC
```

Figure 7-2

Sample output from the font-display program

ABCDEFGHIJKLMNOPQRSTUVWXYZ$.!abcdefghijklmnopqrstuvwxyz

This is an example
line of text.

This is a bigger line of text.

This is even bigger!

```
/*  If you use Microsoft C, define MICROSOFTC instead
    of TURBOC.
*/

#include "stdio.h"
#include "dos.h"
#include "conio.h"
#include "bios.h"
#include "string.h"
#include "stdlib.h"

#define IY          144
#define IX          240
#define XDIM          7
#define YDIM          9
#define NUM_CHARS   127
#define XPAND         3
```

```
#define XMAX      639
#define YMAX      349

#define BCK_GND    0
#define FORE_GND  15

void mode(int mode_code);
void display_char(char chr);
int  load_font(char *fname);
void putpoint(int x, int y, int color, int how);
void font_puts(char *str);
void font_xy(int x, int y);
void setscale(int x, int y);
void setcolor(int color);

unsigned char font[NUM_CHARS][XDIM][YDIM];  /* fonts */

char far *egabase;
int xscale=1, yscale=1;
int fontx=0, fonty=0;
int color=FORE_GND;

/* A simple main() to demonstrate the font routines */
void main(int argc, char *argv[])
{
  mode(16);

#ifdef TURBOC
  egabase = (char far *) MK_FP(0xA000, 0000);
#endif
#ifdef MICROSOFTC
  egabase = (char far *) 0xA0000000;
#endif

  if(argc==2) {
    if(!load_font(argv[1])) exit(1);
  }
  else exit(1);

  font_xy(0, 0);
  font_puts("ABCDEFGHIJKLMNOPQRSTUVWXYZ$.!");
  font_puts("abcdefghijklmnopqrstuvwxyz");
```

```
    font_xy(0, 100);
    setcolor(12);
    font_puts("This is an example\nline of text.");

    setcolor(14);
    setscale(2, 3);
    font_xy(0, 200);
    font_puts("This is a bigger line of text.");

    setscale(3, 4);
    font_xy(0, 300);
    font_puts("This is even bigger!");

    getch();
    mode(2);
}

/* Display a string. */
void font_puts(char *str)
{
  while(*str) {
    display_char(*str);
    str++;
  }
}

/* Position the font cursor to the specified X,Y */
void font_xy(int x, int y)
{
  if(x<0 || x>XMAX) return;
  if(y<0 || y>YMAX) return;
  fontx = x;
  fonty = y;
}

/* Set the scale factors. */
void setscale(int x, int y)
{
  if(x<0 || y<0) return;

  xscale = x;
  yscale = y;
}
```

```
/* Set the foreground color. */
void setcolor(int c)
{
  if(c<0) return;
  color = c;
}

/* Displays the character at current X,Y. */
void display_char(char chr)
{
  register int x, y, i, j, clr;

  /* is a carriage return */
  if(chr=='\n') {
    fontx = 0;
    fonty += YDIM*yscale + 1;
    return;
  }

  for(y = 0; y<YDIM; y++)
    for(x = 0; x<XDIM; x++) {
      for(i=0; i<xscale; i++)
        for(j=0; j<yscale; j++) {
          if(font[chr][x][y]==FORE_GND) clr = color;
          else clr = BCK_GND;
          putpoint(x*xscale+fontx+i,
                   y*yscale+fonty+j, clr, 0);
        }
    }
    fontx += XDIM*xscale + 1;
}

/* Loads the font. */
load_font(char *fname)
{
  FILE *fp;
  int result;

  if((fp = fopen(fname, "rb"))==NULL) {
    printf("cannot open font file");
    return 0;
  }
```

```
   fread(font, sizeof font, 1, fp);

   if(ferror(fp)) result = 0;
   else result = 1;
   fclose(fp);
   return result;
}

/* Set the video mode. */
void mode(int mode_code)
{
   union REGS r;

   r.h.al = mode_code;
   r.h.ah = 0;
   int86(0x10, &r, &r);
}

/* This version of putpoint will work for all video
   adapters but is incredibly slow!
*/
/*
void putpoint(int x, int y, int color, int how)
{
   union REGS r;

   if(how==0x18) color = color | 128;
   r.h.bh = 0;
   r.h.ah = 12;
   r.h.al = color;
   r.x.dx = y;
   r.x.cx = x;
   int86(16, &r, &r);
}
*/


/* This function sets the specified pixel to the
   specified color using an EGA/VGA video adapter.
   The value of how may be one of these:
```

```
   action          value

   overwrite       0
   XOR             0x18
   AND             8
   OR              0x10
*/
#define ENABLE 0x0F
#define INDEXREG 0x3CE
#define VALREG 0x3CF

/* Note: Borland does not document outp(), but it is
   in the library of Turbo C 2.0.  The documented function
   is called outport(), but it runs much slower.  However,
   in future versions you may need to use it instead.
   For this reason, the following conditional compilation
   directives have been included.
*/
#ifdef TURBOC
#define OUTINDEX(index, val) outp((INDEXREG), (index));\
                             outp((VALREG), (val));

#endif
#ifdef MICROSOFTC
#define OUTINDEX(index, val) outp((INDEXREG), (index));\
                             outp((VALREG), (val));

#endif

#define WIDTH 80L

/* These range values assume EGA mode 16 */
#define XMAX 639
#define YMAX 349
#define XMIN 0
#define YMIN 0

void putpoint(int x, int y, int color, int how)
{
  register unsigned char mask = 0x80;
  register char far *base;
  unsigned dummy;

  /* if you want range checking at this point, activate
     this line of code.  It will slow down the function
     however.
  */
```

```
/*if(x<XMIN || x>XMAX || y<YMIN || y>YMAX) return;*/

base = (char far *) (egabase
       + ( (long) y * WIDTH + (long) x/8L ));

mask >>= x % 8;

/* This causes the memory READ necessary to
   load the EGA/VGA's internal registers.
*/
dummy = *base;

OUTINDEX(0, color);
OUTINDEX(1, ENABLE);
OUTINDEX(3, how);
OUTINDEX(8, mask);

*base = 1;

OUTINDEX(0, 0);
OUTINDEX(1, 0);
OUTINDEX(3, 0);
OUTINDEX(8, 0xff);
}
```

CHAPTER EIGHT

Object Animation and Mouse Interfacing

In this chapter two interesting topics are examined: animation and mouse interfacing. This chapter develops an animation editor and display subsystem which can be used to create small objects and interactively define the paths of motion they will follow. It also contains the code to a complete animation-display subsystem, which can be included with your own application programs. The display subsystem allows you to use animation with other applications.

Mouse support is included in the animation editor because the mouse is an excellent input device when *dragging* an image about the screen. This is especially true when fluid, curved motions are required. Part of the animation editor is used to define the motion of an object. This process is performed interactively by dragging the object across the screen along the desired path while each location the object passes through is being recorded for later playback. In fact, you can think of this process as *training* the object. If you don't have a mouse, don't worry—you can remove the mouse references from the code and use the arrow keys.

Dennis Saunders
Cofounder of Mix Software, Inc., and
Developer of Mix Power C

As cofounder of Mix Software, Inc., and developer of Mix Power C, Dennis Saunders has established himself as a leading proponent of C. Before learning C, Dennis had been writing software for several years in other languages. This is how he came to adopt C as his language of choice: "I began hearing more and more about the C language. I initially became interested in C because of its portability. A C compiler was available for almost any computer you could name, and most followed the guidelines specified in *The C Programming Language* by Kernighan and Ritchie. Unlike Pascal and most other languages, C didn't impose any restrictions on what you (or your program) could do. That sounded wonderful because hardware was changing ever more rapidly, and I did not relish the thought of rewriting all of my software each time I changed machines."

I asked Dennis how he defines a top quality C program. "A quality program begins with a well thought out design. That applies to C as it does to any other language. Any program of substance should be designed in a modular fashion. What makes C special is its suitability to modular programming." In his opinion, each module should perform a specific task and each module should be kept as isolated as possible from other modules. He thinks that this approach not only makes programs more reliable but also makes them easier to maintain.

Dennis takes great care in the construction of his programs. As he explains, "Before I start programming, I spend a great deal of time just thinking about the problem the program is supposed to solve. I also think about the people who will use the program, and, perhaps more important, *how* they will use it." Once he has a clear picture of the program in mind, Dennis typically uses a top-down design approach. "I like to start with a main module and then work my way down to the lower level functions. I usually have to do some bottom-up and middle-out design before I'm finished, though," Dennis adds, jokingly. "However, if I've planned the project well, the final outcome doesn't vary much from the original plan."

According to Dennis, his favorite C construct is one of the least used, yet most powerful, features of the C language: the function pointer. "One feature of C that I really appreciate is the ability to declare pointers to functions. By using pointers to functions, you can easily create many variations of a particular function. The C standard library functions **printf( )**, **vprintf( )**, **qsort( )**, and **bsearch( )** are good examples."

Dennis lives in Richardson, Texas.

There are several types and brands of mice, and some function differently from others. The routines in this chapter use the Microsoft two-button mouse, which is functionally identical to the IBM PS/2 mouse. In order to interface to the Microsoft mouse in a DOS environment you must have the *Microsoft Mouse Programmer's Reference Guide* and companion disk (part number 000-098-158). The disk contains a special library, called MOUSE.LIB, that provides the low-level support functions for the mouse. We will be using these functions as a basis for the mouse routines developed here. Keep in mind that your compiler must be capable of linking library routines from a Microsoft-compatible library. (Most PC compilers can.) Also required is the device driver MOUSE.SYS or MOUSE.COM, which is supplied with your mouse.

The programs in this chapter require a graphics video adapter for operation. Further, the examples are written for a DOS environment with an EGA or VGA video adapter, using graphics mode 16. If you have different hardware or another operating environment, you will need to make a few changes.

As is the case with many of the programs in this book, you must define either **TURBOC** or **MICROSOFTC** at the top of the program because of slight differences between the two compilers. If you have a different compiler, consult your user's manual. You may need to rename one or more functions. Also, if you are using OS/2, then you will want to use its built-in mouse API services, which loosely parallel those provided in MOUSE.LIB.

Before going into the details of animation, a brief overview of the mouse is necessary since it is used by the animation editor.

SOME MOUSE BASICS

Before the mouse can be used, its device driver must be installed. For the Microsoft mouse, the way to do this is to place this line of code in the CONFIG.SYS file.

```
device=mouse.sys
```

For the IBM mouse, the program MOUSE.COM is executed instead. Place this line in the AUTOEXEC.BAT file.

mouse

Either way, the device driver is installed.

Once the mouse driver is in place, any time you move the mouse or press a button an interrupt 33H is generated. The mouse driver processes the interrupt, setting the appropriate internal variables and returns. Because an interrupt is generated only when the mouse changes state, an idle mouse has no effect on the performance of the computer.

Just as there is a cursor associated with the keyboard, there is a cursor associated with the mouse. The routines in the MOUSE library from Microsoft define a default cursor whose shape is an arrow in the graphics modes and a solid block in the text modes. The cursor shows the current mouse position on the screen. Like the keyboard cursor, the mouse cursor can be turned on or off. Generally, it is only on when the mouse is actually in use. Otherwise it is off, so that it does not interfere with the application.

Although they are physically separate, the mouse seems to be linked to the screen because the mouse driver automatically maintains counters that indicate where the mouse cursor is currently located. As you move the mouse, the cursor will automatically move across the screen in the same direction as the mouse.

The distance traveled by the mouse is measured in *mickeys*. One mickey equals about 1/200th of an inch. For the most part, however, you will not need to know the actual distance moved by the mouse.

THE VIRTUAL VERSUS ACTUAL SCREEN

The Microsoft mouse library routines operate on a *virtual screen* with pixel dimensions that may be different than the actual physical screen. As the mouse is moved, the cursor location counters are updated. When the cursor is displayed on the screen the virtual cursor coordinates are mapped onto the actual screen coordinates. In video modes 6, 14, 15, and 16 this is a one-to-one mapping. In modes 4 and 5, however, only every *other* point of the virtual horizontal positions are mapped to the actual screen.

THE MOUSE LIBRARY FUNCTIONS

The MOUSE.LIB routines are accessed through a single function using the number of the specific mouse function you wish to call. This is somewhat similar to the way you access DOS functions through interrupt 21H using the number of the specific function desired. The actual name of this mouse function varies, depending upon the memory model with which you are compiling. Use **cmouses( )** for the small model, **cmousec( )** for the compact model, **cmousem( )** for the medium model, and **cmousel( )** for both the large and huge models. There is no support for the tiny memory model. The examples in this chapter use the small model, but you can change that if you like.

The general form of the **cmouses( )** function is

void cmouses(int *fnum, int *arg2, int *arg3, int *arg4);

As indicated, *fnum* points to the number of the mouse function you want to call. The other parameters point to whatever information is required by the specific function. Notice that pointers to the arguments — not the actual arguments themselves — are passed. The **cmouses( )** function returns results in these parameters and, therefore, needs the addresses.

There are 30 mouse functions defined by Microsoft, but we will only use a few of them. They are discussed next.

Resetting and Status

Function 0 resets the mouse. It places the mouse in the center of the screen with the cursor turned off and returns the number of buttons the mouse has in *arg2*. Upon return, *fnum* will be 0 if the mouse and software are not installed; *fnum* will be −1 otherwise.

Displaying Cursor

Function 1 causes the mouse cursor to be displayed. There are no return values.

Removing Cursor

Function 2 removes the mouse cursor from the screen. There are no return values.

Reading Button Status and Cursor Position

Function 3 returns the status of the buttons in *arg2*, using bits 0 and 1. When bit 0 is set, the left button is being pressed. If bit 1 is set, the right button is being pressed. When either bit is off, its associated button is not being pressed. The virtual horizontal cursor position is in *arg3* and the virtual vertical cursor position is in *arg4*.

Setting Cursor Location

Function 4 sets the mouse cursor location. The value pointed to by *arg3* determines the horizontal position and the value pointed to by *arg4* sets the vertical position. Be sure to use only valid values within the range of the virtual screen.

Motion Indication

Function 11 returns the change in vertical and horizontal mickey counts since the last call to function 11 in *arg3* and *arg4*, respectively. It also resets its internal counting registers to 0. This means that if the mouse has not been moved since the last call, both the horizontal and vertical counts will be zero. If either or both are not zero, the mouse has moved.

A positive vertical mickey count means that the mouse has moved downward; a negative count indicates that the mouse has moved upward. A positive horizontal count means that the mouse has moved to the right; a negative count indicates that the mouse has moved to the left.

Setting the Mickey Ratio

By default, the mouse must move 8 mickeys on the desk to move 8 pixels in the horizontal direction and 16 mickeys on the desk to move 8 pixels in the vertical direction. The ratio between the number of mickeys the mouse moves on the desk to the number of pixels the cursor moves on the screen can be called the *mickey ratio*. Although not affected by the programs in this chapter, it is sometimes useful to change this ratio, for example, to give a more deliberate feel to a drawing program. To do this, use function 15. The number of mickeys the mouse must move for the pointer to move 8 pixels in the horizontal direction is pointed to by *arg3* and the number of mickeys the mouse must move for the pointer to move 8 pixels in the vertical direction is pointed to by *arg4*. For example, if *arg3* is 24, then the mouse must move 24 mickeys in order for the pointer to move 8 pixels horizontally.

THE HIGH-LEVEL MOUSE FUNCTIONS

Using the **cmouses( )** function, it is possible to construct a set of high-level C routines that make programming for the mouse much easier. The animation editor and training program will use these functions, so let's look at them now.

Resetting the Mouse

A simple function to start with, **mouse_reset( )**, is used to reset the mouse.

```
/* Reset the mouse. */
void mouse_reset(void)
{
  int fnum, arg2, arg3, arg4;

  fnum = 0; /* reset the mouse */
  cmouses(&fnum, &arg2, &arg3, &arg4);
  if(fnum!=-1) {
    printf("mouse hardware or software not installed");
    exit(1);
  }
  if(arg2!=2) {
   printf("two-button mouse required");
   exit(1);
  }
}
```

Notice that it confirms that the proper hardware and software are present and that a two-button mouse is installed.

Displaying and Removing the Mouse Cursor

The companion functions **cursor_on( )** and **cursor_off( )** are used to activate and deactivate the visual mouse cursor. The two functions are shown here:

```
/* Turn on the mouse cursor. */
void cursor_on(void)
{
  int fnum;

  fnum = 1; /* show the cursor */
  cmouses(&fnum, &fnum, &fnum, &fnum);
}

/* Turn off the mouse cursor. */
void cursor_off(void)
{
  int fnum;

  fnum = 2; /* erase the cursor */
  cmouses(&fnum, &fnum, &fnum, &fnum);
}
```

Determining If a Button Is Pressed

Another pair of companion functions is **rightb_pressed( )** and **leftb_pressed( )**. Each returns true if its button is pressed.

```
/* Return true if right button is pressed;
   false otherwise. */
rightb_pressed(void)
{
  int fnum, arg2, arg3, arg4;
```

```
  fnum = 3; /* get position and button status */
  cmouses(&fnum, &arg2, &arg3, &arg4);
  return arg2 & 2;
}


/* Return true if left button is pressed;
   false otherwise. */
leftb_pressed(void)
{
  int fnum, arg2, arg3, arg4;

  fnum = 3; /* get position and button status */
  cmouses(&fnum, &arg2, &arg3, &arg4);
  return arg2 & 1;
}
```

Detecting Motion

You can use function 11, which returns the change in the mickey count
since the last call, to detect mouse motion. The **mouse_motion( )** function, shown here, returns the directions of travel, horizontal and vertical,
in variables pointed to by its arguments. If both **deltax** and **deltay** are
zero, then no motion has occurred.

```
/* Return the direction of travel. */
void mouse_motion(char *deltax, char *deltay)
{
  int fnum, arg2, arg3, arg4;

  fnum = 11; /* get direction of motion */
  cmouses(&fnum, &arg2, &arg3, &arg4);
  if(arg3>0) *deltax = RIGHT;
  else if(arg3<0) *deltax = LEFT;
  else *deltax = NOT_MOVED;

  if(arg4>0) *deltay = DOWN;
  else if(arg4<0) *deltay = UP;
  else *deltay = NOT_MOVED;
```

The macros **RIGHT, LEFT, UP, DOWN,** and **NOT‗MOVED** are defined this way:

```
#define NOT_MOVED 0
#define RIGHT     1
#define LEFT      2
#define UP        3
#define DOWN      4
```

Reading and Setting the Cursor Position

The functions **set‗mouse‗position( )** and **mouse‗position( )**, shown here, are used to set and read the current position of the mouse:

```
/* Set mouse cursor coordinates. */
void set_mouse_position(int x, int y)
{
  int fnum, arg2;

  fnum = 4; /* set position */
  cmouses(&fnum, &arg2, &x, &y);
}

/* Return mouse cursor coordinates. */
void mouse_position(int *x, int *y)
{
  int fnum, arg2, arg3, arg4;

  fnum = 3; /* get position and button status */
  cmouses(&fnum, &arg2, &arg3, &arg4);
  *x = arg3;
  *y = arg4;
}
```

Setting the Mickey Ratio

To change the mickey ratio, use **mickey‗ratio( )**, shown here. The greater the ratio, the farther on the desk the mouse must move in order for it to advance the mouse cursor to the next pixel.

```
/* Set mickey ratio. */
void mickey_ratio(int xratio, int yratio)
{
  int fnum, arg2;

  fnum = 15;

  cmouses(&fnum, &arg2, &xratio, &yratio);
}
```

HOW ANIMATION IS ACCOMPLISHED

This chapter is concerned with the animation of small objects, which we will refer to as *symbols*. There are two basic components to symbolic animation: motion of the symbol relative to the screen, which we will refer to as *screen-relative animation*, and motion within the symbol, which we will call *symbol-relative animation*. For example, imagine that you are animating the image of a dog running across the screen from left to right. First the symbol of the dog must be moved across the screen. This is the screen-relative part of the animation process. However, for the motion to look lifelike, the legs of the dog (and possibly the head and tail) must be moving to give the appearance of running. This is the symbol-relative part of the animation. Let's see how these two animation techniques are accomplished.

A symbol is moved against a stationary background (the screen) by drawing it in one location, erasing it, and redrawing it in the neighboring location, and so on. By far the fastest way to accomplish the draw-erase operation is to display the symbol on the screen using the XOR write mode. Using this approach, each pixel in the symbol is XORed with the corresponding pixel on the screen. This makes the symbol visible regardless of the background color. To erase the symbol, it is simply XORed onto the screen again, thus returning that part of the screen to its original condition. As long as the distance from one position to the next is not too great, the symbol will appear to move smoothly across the screen.

Animating parts of a symbol relative to itself requires that each symbol consist of one or more *images*. Each image is slightly different than the others. Continuing with the dog example, a running dog symbol may consist of 3 slightly different images, each having the legs in different positions. Each time the dog is moved, a different image is displayed in round-robin fashion. Therefore, as the dog moves relative to the screen, its legs will appear to move relative to the symbol (see Figure 8-1).

The animation system developed in this chapter supports both screen-relative and symbol-relative animation.

THE ANIMATION EDITOR AND TRAINING PROGRAM

The animation editor consists of two main parts: the system that creates each image of a symbol and the system that trains the symbol to move the way you want it to. The system that creates each image is a modification of the icon editor presented in Chapter 2, so we won't spend much time discussing it. Most of the emphasis here will be on the training of the object and how the mouse is interfaced to the system.

The Symbol Structure

Each symbol in the animation system is defined by the structure shown on the next page.

Figure 8-1

Screen- and symbol-relative animation of a dog

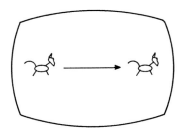

Screen-relative motion

Symbol-relative motion

image 1   image 2   image 3

```
#define MAX_POS 500   /* number of different positions that
                         can be recorded for any one symbol */

#define XDIM        21    /* change these to change dimensions */
#define YDIM        27    /* of the symbol you want to use */

#define MAX_IMG      5    /* number of images in symbol */

struct symbol_type {
  unsigned char image[MAX_IMG][XDIM][YDIM];  /* symbol */
  int x[MAX_POS], y[MAX_POS]; /* X,Y coordinates */
  int last_pos;  /* current coordinate position */
  int delay;  /* delay factor */
  int num_images; /* number of separate images in symbol */
} symbol;
```

Each image of the symbol is held in the **image** array. The size of each image, in pixels, is determined by **XDIM** and **YDIM**. Although you can make these as large as you want, the larger the symbol, the longer it takes to draw it, thus slowing the animation. Each symbol can be animated through as many as **MAX _ POS** locations on the screen. The value shown here is 500. For most purposes, 500 animation locations are more than enough, but you can change this if you like. The coordinates of each position are held in **x** and **y**. The animation sequence begins with **x[0]**, **y[0]**. The index of the last position is held in **last _ pos**; thus the last coordinates of the animation sequence are **x[last _ pos]**, **y[last _ pos]**. The value of **delay** determines a delay factor, which is used to slow the animation of a symbol. The value of **delay** must be small (0−10). You will see how it is used later. Finally, the number of images that actually make up the symbol is specified in **num _ images**. As shown here, a symbol can have up to five different images, but most symbols will probably use only two or three.

The Animation Editor Top-Level Menu

When the animation editor begins execution it presents a menu of options and waits for the user to select one. The options are

- edit a symbol

- start a new symbol

- load a symbol

- save a symbol

- train a symbol

- animate a symbol

- quit

An option can be selected either by using the keyboard and typing the first letter of the option or by pressing the left mouse button while the pointer is on the menu item you want to activate. The menu is supported by two functions called **menu( )** and **mouse _ menu( )**, shown here:

```
/* Microsoft C cannot initialize local arrays */
#ifdef MICROSOFTC
  char options[][20] = {
    "(E)dit", "(N)ew", "(S)ave", "(L)oad",
    "(T)rain", "(A)nimate", "(Q)uit", ""
  };
  char ret_codes[] = "ensltaq";
#endif
/* Get user's selection. */
char menu(void)
{
  int i;
  char ch;

#ifdef TURBOC
  char options[][20] = {
    "(E)dit", "(N)ew", "(S)ave", "(L)oad",
    "(T)rain", "(A)nimate", "(Q)uit", ""
  };
  char ret_codes[] = "ensltaq";
#endif

  clr_eol(0, 0);
  gotoxy(0, 0);
  /* display options in menu */
  for(i=0; *options[i]; i++) {
    printf("%s", options[i]);
    if(*options[i+1]) printf(", ");
```

```
    }

    clr_eol(0, 1);
    gotoxy(0, 1);
    printf("Enter letter of choice: ");
    cursor_on();
    ch = 26;
    do {
      if(kbhit()) ch = getche();

      /* if left button is pressed, user is making
         a menu selection using the mouse
      */
      if(leftb_pressed())
        ch = mouse_menu(options, ret_codes, 0, 0);
    } while(!strchr(ret_codes, tolower(ch)));
    cursor_off();
    clrscr();

    return tolower(ch);
}


/* Process a mouse selection.   Call this function
   with a pointer to the options list, a pointer to
   the characters to be returned with each selection,
   and the X,Y location that the menu starts at.
*/
mouse_menu(char opts[][20], char *codes,
           int startx, int starty)
{
  int x, y, i, start, end;

  mouse_position(&x, &y);

  /* if in correct row */
  if(y >= starty*CHAR_HEIGHT &&
     y <= starty * CHAR_HEIGHT + CHAR_HEIGHT) {

    /* see if on a menu option */
    start = startx; end = startx;
    for(i=0; *opts[i]; i++) {
      end = end + strlen(opts[i]) * CHAR_WIDTH;
      if(x>=start && x<=end) {
```

```
        return codes[i];
      }
      end += 2 * CHAR_WIDTH;
      start = end;
    }
  }
  return -1;
}
```

Let's take a close look at these now.

The **menu( )** function creates an array of strings that will be used for the menu prompt. These strings are held in the array **options**. The **ret_codes** array holds the characters that are associated with each option. The characters in **ret_codes** are those the user would type when selecting options with the keyboard. Next, the options are displayed on one line using a comma-separated list. The **menu( )** function then enters its main loop, which waits for either a keypress or for the left mouse button to be pressed. If a key is pressed, the value of the keystroke is checked against the list of return codes. If a match is found, that option is returned by the function to the calling routine. If the mouse button is pressed, the **mouse_menu( )** function is called. The **mouse_menu( )** function determines if the mouse pointer is on a menu item. If it is, it returns that item's return code to the calling routine. Let's see how this works.

The **mouse_menu( )** function determines if the mouse pointer is resting on a menu item by checking to see if the current X,Y position of the mouse pointer is within a rectangle defined by a menu entry. Each menu entry is one character tall and one or more characters wide. (The mouse coordinates are in terms of pixels, however, so we need to know how tall and wide each character is. These values are defined by **CHAR_HEIGHT** and **CHAR_WIDTH**. For mode 16 graphics, each character is 12 pixels tall and 8 pixels wide. This may vary somewhat between systems, so some experimentation may be necessary.) Thus, if the mouse cursor is inside the rectangle described by a menu entry, then the **mouse_menu( )** function returns the corresponding code to **menu( )**, which is, in turn, returned to the calling routine.

The Main Loop

The animation editor has its main loop located inside the **main( )** function, which is shown here. It is this loop that calls the **menu( )** function described in the previous section.

```
void main(int argc, char *argv[])
{
  char choice, str[80];
  register int i;

  mode(16);   /* ega mode 16 - use another if you like */

#ifdef TURBOC
  egabase = (char far *) MK_FP(0xA000, 0000);
#endif
#ifdef MICROSOFTC
  egabase = (char far *) 0xA0000000;
#endif

  /* initialize the images */
  for(i=0; i<MAX_IMG; i++) init_symbol(i);

  mouse_reset(); /* reset the mouse */

  if(argc==2) {
    if(!load_symbol(argv[1])) {
      printf("cannot load file");
      exit(1);
    }
    new_sym = 0;
  }

  do {
    choice = menu();   /* get user's request */
    switch(choice) {
      case 'n': /* edit a new symbol */
        new_sym = 1;
        for(i=0; i<MAX_IMG; i++) init_symbol(i);
        /* drop through to edit */
      case 'e':  /* edit a symbol */
        clr_eol(0, 0);
        gotoxy(0, 0);

        /* if new symbol, how many images does
           this symbol have? */
        if(new_sym) do {
          printf("How many images (1-%d)? ", MAX_IMG);
          gets(str);
```

```
            symbol.num_images = atoi(str);
          } while (symbol.num_images<1 ||
                   symbol.num_images>MAX_IMG);
          clrscr();

          /* create/edit each image in the symbol */
          for(i=0; i<symbol.num_images; i++) {
            edit_image(i);
            /* copy first image into second, etc., to
               make slight changes easier */
            if(i+1<symbol.num_images && new_sym)
              copyimage(i, i+1);
          }
          new_sym = 0; /* symbol now exists */

          /* request delay factor */
          do {
            gotoxy(0, 22);
            printf("enter delay factor (0-10): ");
            gets(str);
            symbol.delay = atoi(str);
          } while (symbol.delay<0 || symbol.delay>10);
          break;
        case 's': /* save the symbol */
          save_symbol();
          break;
        case 'l': /* load a symbol */
          if(load_symbol("")) new_sym = 0;
          break;
        case 't': /* train */
          train();
          break;
        case 'a': /* animate (after it is trained) */
          animate();
          break;
      }
  } while(choice!='q'); /* quit */
  mode(2);
}
```

Let's take a brief look at each of the menu options now.

Editing an Image

To create or modify an image, select the **Edit** option. If you are editing a new symbol, the global variable **new_sym** will be equal to 1, and you will be prompted to enter the number of images associated with the symbol. Next, the **edit_image( )** function, shown here, will be called repeatedly so that each image can be created. Remember, to achieve symbol-relative animation, you must define two or more slightly different images of the same symbol. The **edit_image( )** function edits the image specified by its argument. If you are simply modifying an image of a symbol that already exists, then **edit_image( )** will redisplay each image and allow you to change it.

```
/* Edit an image.  This function displays a large
   grid to make editing easy.  It also displays the
   normal size version of the image being edited. */
void edit_image(char i)
{
  register int x, y;
  char ch, pen, temp;
  int xl, yl;

  clr_eol(0, 0);
  gotoxy(0, 0);
  printf("F1: pen down  F2: pen up  F3: erase  F4: done");
  gotoxy(0, 1);
  printf("left button toggles pen, right button erases, ");
  printf("both buttons terminate");

  x = IX; y = IY;  /* set x,y to upper left corner */

  pen = BCK_GND;
  gotoxy(0, 23);
  printf("pen up  ");  /* tell user pen is up */

  display_image(i, 0, IY);
  display_grid(i);
  clr_eol(0, 22);
  gotoxy(0, 22);
  printf("editing image: %c", i+'0');

  do {
```

```
/* write pixel to grid */
putpoint(x+((x-IX)*XPAND), y+((y-IY)*XPAND), pen, 0);

/* save pixel color in image, use
   blank background */
if(pen==BCK_GND)
  symbol.image[i][x-IX][y-IY] = BLANK;
else symbol.image[i][x-IX][y-IY] = FORE_GND;

/* write pixel to image */
putpoint(x-IX, y, symbol.image[i][x-IX][y-IY], 0);

/* This code displays a dot that indicates the current
   position, waits for a keystroke and then replaces
   the original value.
*/
temp = getpoint(x+((x-IX)*XPAND), y+((y-IY)*XPAND));
putpoint(x+((x-IX)*XPAND), y+((y-IY)*XPAND),
         HIGHLIGHT, 0);

/* wait for either mouse or keyboard input */
ch = 0;
x1 = y1 = NOT_MOVED;
while(!x1 && !y1) {  /* while mouse has not moved */
  mouse_motion(&x1, &y1);  /* see if moved */

  /* if both left and right buttons pushed, terminate */
  if(leftb_pressed() && rightb_pressed()) {
    ch = 62; /* F4's scan code */

    /* wait for buttons to clear */
    while(leftb_pressed() || rightb_pressed()) ;
    break;
  }

  /* if left button pressed, pen up/down toggle */
  if(leftb_pressed()) {
    if(pen==BCK_GND)
      ch = 59;  /* F1's scan code */
    else ch = 60;

    /* wait for user to release button */
    while(leftb_pressed()) ;
```

```
      break;
   }

   /* if right button pressed, erase image */
   if(rightb_pressed()) {
     ch = 61; /* F3's scan code */

     /* wait for user to release button */
     while(rightb_pressed()) ;
     break;
   }

   if(kbhit()) {  /* otherwise, process key input */
     ch = getkey();
     break;
   }
}
putpoint(x+((x-IX)*XPAND), y+((y-IY)*XPAND), temp, 0);

/* process mouse motion */
if(xl==LEFT) x --;
else if(xl==RIGHT) x ++;
if(yl==UP) y --;
else if(yl==DOWN) y ++;
else
switch(ch) {
   case 75: /* left */
     x--;
     break;
   case 77: /* right */
     x++;
     break;
   case 72: /* up */
     y--;
     break;
   case 80: /* down */
     y++;
     break;
   case 71: /* up left */
     x--; y--;
     break;
   case 73: /* up right */
     x++; y--;
```

```
          break;
      case 79: /* down left*/
        x--; y++;
        break;
      case 81: /* down right */
        x++; y++;
        break;
      case 59: /* F1 - pen down */
        pen = FORE_GND;
        gotoxy(0, 23);
        printf("pen down");
        break;
      case 60: /* F2 - pen up */
        pen = BCK_GND;
        gotoxy(0, 23);
        printf("pen up  ");
        break;
      case 61: /* F3 - erase */
        init_symbol(i);
        display_image(i, 0, IY);
        display_grid(i);
        break;
    }
    if(x < IX) x++;  if(x > IX+XDIM-1) x--;
    if(y < IY) y++;  if(y > IY+YDIM-1) y--;

  } while(ch != 62); /* F4 - quit */
  clr_eol(0, 22);
  clr_eol(0, 23);
  /* give symbol default beginning coordinates */
  symbol.x[0] = 0;
  symbol.y[0] = 0;

  return;
}
```

As stated earlier, **edit_image( )** is a modification of the icon editor described in Chapter 2, so we won't spend too much time on it, but let's take a close look at how the mouse is interfaced to it.

The mouse is used by **edit_image( )** a little differently than it is by the **mouse_menu( )** function and many other applications. In **edit_image( )**, the actual position of the mouse is irrelevant. Instead, only its relative motion, as obtained through calls to **mouse_motion( )**, is used. If the mouse moves left, the value of **x** is decremented; if it moves right, the value of **x** is incremented. The same thing applies to the vertical directions: if the mouse moves up, **y** is decremented; if it moves down, **y** is incremented.

When you move the highlight shown in the expanded view of the symbol, it will leave a trail if the pen is down, but not if the pen is up. To lower the pen, press either F1 or the left mouse button. To raise the pen, press either F2 or the left mouse button a second time—the left mouse button acts as a toggle. To erase the image and start over, press either F3 or the right mouse button. To stop editing, press either F4 or both mouse buttons simultaneously.

The **edit_image( )** function can be operated using either the mouse or the arrow keys. Unfortunately, the keyboard and the mouse are not easily combined, and the code to handle them tends to become somewhat "dirty." (From the user's perspective, however, the mouse and the keyboard interact fluidly.) To accomplish this, the following code fragment is used:

```
/* wait for either mouse or keyboard input */
ch = 0;
xl = yl = NOT_MOVED;
while(!xl && !yl) {   /* while mouse has not moved */
  mouse_motion(&xl, &yl);   /* see if moved */

  /* if both left and right buttons pushed, terminate */
  if(leftb_pressed() && rightb_pressed()) {
    ch = 62; /* F4's scan code */

    /* wait for buttons to clear */
    while(leftb_pressed() || rightb_pressed()) ;
    break;
  }

  /* if left button pressed, pen up/down toggle */
  if(leftb_pressed()) {
   if(pen==BCK_GND)
     ch = 59;   /* F1's scan code */
   else ch = 60;

   /* wait for user to release button */
```

```
      while(leftb_pressed()) ;
      break;
  }

  /* if right button pressed, erase image */
  if(rightb_pressed()) {
    ch = 61; /* F3's scan code */

    /* wait for user to release button */
    while(rightb_pressed()) ;
    break;
  }

  if(kbhit()) {  /* otherwise, process key input */
    ch = getkey();
    break;
  }
}
putpoint(x+((x-IX)*XPAND), y+((y-IY)*XPAND), temp, 0);

/* process mouse motion */
if(xl==LEFT) x --;
else if(xl==RIGHT) x ++;
if(yl==UP) y --;
else if(yl==DOWN) y ++;
```

This code fragment waits until either the user presses a key, the mouse is moved, or a mouse button is pressed, then takes the appropriate action. Notice that when a button is pressed, the code waits until the button is released before taking any further action. The reason for this is simple: the computer is so much faster than a person that multiple triggerings will occur before the button can be released.

Once all the images have been edited, you will be asked to specify a delay factor. For some symbols, it may be necessary to slow down their animation in order to make them appear natural. You will have to experiment with different delay values to see what works best for your system and application.

One final point about **Edit**—if the symbol being edited is new, the preceding image is automatically copied into the next. The copying of an image is performed by the **copyimage( )** function. This makes it easier to make the small changes necessary to achieve symbol-relative animation.

Starting a New Symbol

If you have finished editing one symbol and want to work on another, select the **New** option from the menu. This option reinitializes each image and sets **new_sym** to 1, signaling that a new symbol is being created. The **case** statement then "drops through" to the **Edit** option and the new symbol can be created.

Saving and Loading a Symbol

To save a symbol once it has been created, select the **Save** option. To load an existing symbol, select the **Load** option or specify the symbol's file on the command line when you begin the animation editor. The **save_symbol( )** and **load_symbol( )** functions are shown here:

```c
/* Saves the symbol. */
save_symbol(void)
{
  FILE *fp;
  char fname[80];
  int result;

  gotoxy(0, 22);
  printf("save to: ");
  gets(fname);

  if((fp = fopen(fname, "wb"))==NULL) {
    printf("cannot open file");
    return 0;
  }

  fwrite(&symbol, sizeof symbol, 1, fp);

  if(ferror(fp)) result = 0;
  else result = 1;
  fclose(fp);
  clr_eol(0, 22);
  return result;
}
```

```
/* Loads the symbol. */
load_symbol(char *name)
{
  FILE *fp;
  char fname[80];
  int result;

  if(!*name) {
    clr_eol(0, 22);
    gotoxy(0, 22);
    printf("load from: ");
    gets(fname);
  }
  else strcpy(fname, name);

  if((fp = fopen(fname, "rb"))==NULL) {
    printf("cannot open file");
    return 0;
  }

  fread(&symbol, sizeof symbol, 1, fp);

  if(ferror(fp)) result = 0;
  else result = 1;
  fclose(fp);
  clr_eol(0, 22);
  return result;
}
```

Defining a Symbol's Movement

After you have defined all the images of a symbol, you can define the movement of the symbol by selecting the **Train** option, which executes the **train( )** function. The **train( )** function allows you to guide the symbol through the path you wish it to travel. For straight-line movement you can use the arrow keys, and for fluid curves you can use the mouse. You can think of this process as training the symbol. During the training process, each location the symbol moves through is recorded in its **x** and **y** arrays. As the symbol moves, each image is displayed in a round-robin fashion, thus creating the illusion of motion relative to the screen as well as relative to the symbol.

The **train( )** function is shown here:

```
/* Train the symbol using the mouse or arrow keys.
   Each movement you make will be recorded for later
   playback.
*/
void train()
{
  int x, y, xl, yl;
  char ch;
  unsigned k;

  symbol.last_pos = 0;

  getstartpos(); /* get starting position */

  x = symbol.x[0];  /* load starting coordinates */
  y = symbol.y[0];

  clrscr();
  gotoxy(0, 23);
  printf("Use arrow keys or press left button to use mouse");
  gotoxy(0, 24);
  printf("F1 or right button to stop");

  k = 0;

  for(;;) {
    ch = 0;
    record(x, y);  /* record each position */

    display_symbol(symbol, k % symbol.num_images,
                   symbol.last_pos); /* display image */

    xl = yl = NOT_MOVED;
    /* while mouse has not moved */
    while(!xl && !yl || !leftb_pressed()) {
      mouse_motion(&xl, &yl);  /* see if moved */
      if(kbhit()) {  /* otherwise, process key input */
        ch = getkey();
        break;
      }
    }
```

```
/* stop when right button pressed */
if(rightb_pressed()) {
  ch = 59; /* Fl's scan code */
  break;
}
}

display_symbol(symbol, k % symbol.num_images,
                symbol.last_pos); /* erase image */

/* process mouse motion */
if(xl==LEFT) x -= 5;
else if(xl==RIGHT) x += 5;
if(yl==UP) y -= 5;
else if(yl==DOWN) y += 5;

if(ch)   /* if key input, process */
  switch(ch) {
    case 75: /* left */
      x -=5;
      break;
    case 77: /* right */
      x +=5;
      break;
    case 72: /* up */
      y -= 5;
      break;
    case 80: /* down */
      y +=5;
      break;
    case 71: /* left up */
      y -= 5;   x -= 5;
      break;
    case 73: /* right up */
      y -= 5;   x += 5;
      break;
    case 79: /* left down */
      y += 5;   x -= 5;
      break;
    case 81: /* right down */
      y += 5;   x += 5;
      break;
    case 59: /* stop training on Fl */
```

```
        return;
    }

    /* increase last_pos */
    if(symbol.last_pos<MAX_POS-1) symbol.last_pos++;
    else putch(7); /* ring bell if out of space */

    k++;
  }
}
```

The **train( )** function works like this. First, it initializes **last _ pos** to 0, which effectively removes any old training. Next, it calls **getstartpos( )**. The **getstartpos( )** function is used to position the symbol at its initial location. (Its general operation is similar in principle to **train( )** and will not be discussed separately, but you should examine it in the complete animation editor listing.) Once the symbol is at its starting location, you can move it by pressing the arrow keys or using the mouse. The mouse will only affect the symbol when the left button is depressed — that is, to move the symbol, press and hold the left button and move the mouse. The symbol will move in the same direction as the mouse. When you have finished training, press either Fl or the right mouse button.

As you can see by examining the **train( )** function, the symbol is moved in increments of 5. Experimentation showed this to be a good distance between locations in order for the animation to appear natural. Feel free to try other increments that may better suit your own needs.

Each time the symbol is moved, its new position is recorded in the symbol's **x** and **y** arrays using a call to **record( )**, shown here, and the value of **last _ pos** is incremented.

```
/* Record the motion entered by the user. */
void record(int x, int y)
{
  symbol.x[symbol.last_pos] = x;
  symbol.y[symbol.last_pos] = y;
}
```

Animating the Symbol

Once the symbol has been trained, it can be animated by selecting the **Animate** option, which executes the **animate( )** function. The **animate( )**

function repeatedly draws, erases, and redraws the symbol in the locations held in the **x** and **y** arrays. In essence, it replays what it was taught during the training session. In the process, it automatically cycles through the various images associated with the symbol. The **animate( )** function is shown here:

```
/* Replay the animation sequence. */
void animate(void)
{
  register int i, j;
  int delay;

  /* for number of positions recorded */
  for(i=0; i<symbol.last_pos; i++ ) {
    /* display images */
    for(j=0; j<symbol.num_images; j++) {
      display_symbol(symbol, j, i);
      /* delay x 1000 */
      for(delay=0; delay<symbol.delay*1000; delay++) ;
      display_symbol(symbol, j, i);
      i++;
    }
  }
}
```

As you can see, the value of **delay** is multiplied by 1000, and this value is used as the target of a time-delay **for** loop. On faster computers, you may need to increase this value to slow the animation down to appear natural. On slower computers you may need to decrease it to make the object move faster.

The Entire Animation Editor

The code for the entire animation editor is shown here. It includes all of the high-level mouse interface functions, even though some are not actually used by this program. The reason they are included is to make it easier for you to expand or modify the mouse interface, if you choose.

```
/* Animation editor and training program. This program
   uses the mouse, but if you don't have a mouse, simply
   delete the mouse code and use the arrow keys.
*/

#define TURBOC
/*  If you use Microsoft C, define MICROSOFTC instead
    of TURBOC.
*/

#include "stdio.h"
#include "dos.h"
#include "conio.h"
#include "bios.h"
#include "string.h"
#include "ctype.h"
#include "stdlib.h"

#define IY          144
#define IX          240

#define XDIM        21   /* change these to change dimensions */
#define YDIM        27   /* of the symbol you want to use */


#define MAX_IMG      5   /* number of images in symbol */

#define XPAND        3   /* editor grid expansion ratio */

/* mouse motion macros */
#define NOT_MOVED 0
#define RIGHT      1
#define LEFT       2
#define UP         3
#define DOWN       4

#define MAX_POS 500   /* number of different positions that
                         can be recorded for any one symbol */

#define MAX_LINES  24
#define LINE_LEN   79

#define CHAR_HEIGHT 12  /* height of graphics character */
```

```
#define CHAR_WIDTH   8  /* width of graphics character */

#define BLANK       0
#define BCK_GND     9
#define FORE_GND   15
#define HIGHLIGHT  13

char getpoint(int x, int y), getkey(void);
void mode(int mode_code), gotoxy(int x, int y);
void clr_eol(int x, int y), clrscr(void);
void display_grid(char i),  edit_image(char i);
void display_image(char i, int x, int y);
void init_symbol(char i);
void copyimage(int i, int j);
void train(void);
void getstartpos(void);
void putpoint(int x, int y, int color, int how);
int save_symbol(void), load_symbol(char *fname);
char menu(void);

void mouse_position(int *x, int *y);
void set_mouse_position(int x, int y);
void mouse_motion(int *deltax, int *deltay);
void cursor_on(void), cursor_off(void), mouse_reset(void);
void mouse_direction(int *deltax, int *deltay);
int rightb_pressed(void), leftb_pressed(void);
void mickey_ratio(int xratio, int yratio);

void cmouses(int *a, int *b, int *c, int *d);
void record(int x, int y);
void animate(void);
mouse_menu(char opts[][20], char *codes,
           int startx, int starty);

struct symbol_type {
  unsigned char image[MAX_IMG][XDIM][YDIM];  /* symbol */
  int x[MAX_POS], y[MAX_POS]; /* X,Y coordinates */
  int last_pos;  /* current coordinate position */
  int delay;  /* delay factor */
  int num_images; /* number of separate images in symbol */
} symbol;

void display_symbol(struct symbol_type symbol, int img,
```

```
                        int pos);

char new_sym = 1;   /* when new symbol is being edited, this
                          is 1; otherwise, 0 */

char far *egabase;

void main(int argc, char *argv[])
{
  char choice, str[80];
  register int i;

  mode(16);   /* ega mode 16 - use another if you like */

#ifdef TURBOC
  egabase = (char far *) MK_FP(0xA000, 0000);
#endif
#ifdef MICROSOFTC
  egabase = (char far *) 0xA0000000;
#endif

  /* initialize the images */
  for(i=0; i<MAX_IMG; i++) init_symbol(i);

  mouse_reset(); /* reset the mouse */

  if(argc==2) {
    if(!load_symbol(argv[1])) {
      printf("cannot load file");
      exit(1);
    }
    new_sym = 0;
  }

  do {
    choice = menu();   /* get user's request */
    switch(choice) {
      case 'n': /* edit a new symbol */
        new_sym = 1;
        for(i=0; i<MAX_IMG; i++) init_symbol(i);
        /* drop through to edit */
      case 'e':  /* edit a symbol */
        clr_eol(0, 0);
```

```
  gotoxy(0, 0);

  /* if new symbol, how many images does
     this symbol have? */
  if(new_sym) do {
    printf("How many images (1-%d)? ", MAX_IMG);
    gets(str);
    symbol.num_images = atoi(str);
  } while (symbol.num_images<1 ||
          symbol.num_images>MAX_IMG);
  clrscr();

  /* create/edit each image in the symbol */
  for(i=0; i<symbol.num_images; i++) {
    edit_image(i);
    /* copy first image into second, etc., to
       make slight changes easier */
    if(i+1<symbol.num_images && new_sym)
      copyimage(i, i+1);
  }
  new_sym = 0; /* symbol now exists */

  /* request delay factor */
  do {
    gotoxy(0, 22);
    printf("enter delay factor (0-10): ");
    gets(str);
    symbol.delay = atoi(str);
  } while (symbol.delay<0 || symbol.delay>10);
  break;
case 's': /* save the symbol */
  save_symbol();
  break;
case 'l': /* load a symbol */
  if(load_symbol("")) new_sym = 0;
  break;
case 't': /* train */
  train();
  break;
case 'a': /* animate (after it is trained) */
  animate();
  break;
}
```

```
  } while(choice!='q'); /* quit */
  mode(2);
}

/* Microsoft C cannot initialize local arrays */
#ifdef MICROSOFTC
  char options[][20] = {
    "(E)dit", "(N)ew", "(S)ave", "(L)oad",
    "(T)rain", "(A)nimate", "(Q)uit", ""
  };
  char ret_codes[] = "ensltaq";
#endif
/* Get user's selection. */
char menu(void)
{
  int i;
  char ch;

#ifdef TURBOC
  char options[][20] = {
    "(E)dit", "(N)ew", "(S)ave", "(L)oad",
    "(T)rain", "(A)nimate", "(Q)uit", ""
  };
  char ret_codes[] = "ensltaq";
#endif

  clr_eol(0, 0);
  gotoxy(0, 0);
  /* display options in menu */
  for(i=0; *options[i]; i++) {
    printf("%s", options[i]);
    if(*options[i+1]) printf(", ");
  }

  clr_eol(0, 1);
  gotoxy(0, 1);
  printf("Enter letter of choice: ");
  cursor_on();
  ch = 26;
  set_mouse_position(0, 0);
  do {
    if(kbhit()) ch = getche();
```

```
      /* if left button is pressed, user is making
         a menu selection using the mouse
      */
      if(leftb_pressed())
        ch = mouse_menu(options, ret_codes, 0, 0);
  } while(!strchr(ret_codes, tolower(ch)));
  cursor_off();
  clrscr();

  return tolower(ch);
}


/* Process a mouse selection.   Call this function
   with a pointer to the options list, a pointer to
   the characters to be returned with each selection,
   and the X,Y location that the menu starts at.
*/
mouse_menu(char opts[][20], char *codes,
           int startx, int starty)
{
  int x, y, i, start, end;

  mouse_position(&x, &y);

  /* if in correct row */
  if(y >= starty*CHAR_HEIGHT &&
     y <= starty * CHAR_HEIGHT + CHAR_HEIGHT) {

    /* see if on a menu option */
    start = startx; end = startx;
    for(i=0; *opts[i]; i++) {
      end = end + strlen(opts[i]) * CHAR_WIDTH;
      if(x>=start && x<=end) {
        return codes[i];
      }
      end += 2 * CHAR_WIDTH;
      start = end;
    }
  }
  return -1;
}

/* Display the expanded symbol editor grid. */
```

```
void display_grid(char i)
{
  register int x, y;

  for(y = IY; y<(IY+YDIM); y++)
    for(x = IX; x<(IX+XDIM); x++) {
      if(symbol.image[i][x-IX][y-IY] == BLANK)
        putpoint(x+((x-IX)*XPAND), y+((y-IY)*XPAND),
                 BCK_GND, 0);
      else
        putpoint(x+((x-IX)*XPAND), y+((y-IY)*XPAND),
                 symbol.image[i][x-IX][y-IY], 0);
    }
}


/* Edit an image.  This function displays a large
   grid to make editing easy.  It also displays the
   normal size version of the image being edited. */
void edit_image(char i)
{
  register int x, y;
  char ch, pen, temp;
  int x1, y1;

  clr_eol(0, 0);
  gotoxy(0, 0);
  printf("F1: pen down  F2: pen up  F3: erase  F4: done");
  gotoxy(0, 1);
  printf("left button toggles pen, right button erases, ");
  printf("both buttons terminate");

  x = IX; y = IY;   /* set x,y to upper left corner */

  pen = BCK_GND;
  gotoxy(0, 23);
  printf("pen up  ");   /* tell user pen is up */

  display_image(i, 0, IY);
  display_grid(i);
  clr_eol(0, 22);
  gotoxy(0, 22);
  printf("editing image: %c", i+'0');
```

```
do {
  /* write pixel to grid */
  putpoint(x+((x-IX)*XPAND), y+((y-IY)*XPAND), pen, 0);

  /* save pixel color in image, use
     blank background */
  if(pen==BCK_GND)
    symbol.image[i][x-IX][y-IY] = BLANK;
  else symbol.image[i][x-IX][y-IY] = FORE_GND;

  /* write pixel to image */
  putpoint(x-IX, y, symbol.image[i][x-IX][y-IY], 0);

  /* This code displays a dot that indicates the current
     position, waits for a keystroke, and then replaces
     the original value.
  */
  temp = getpoint(x+((x-IX)*XPAND), y+((y-IY)*XPAND));
  putpoint(x+((x-IX)*XPAND), y+((y-IY)*XPAND),
           HIGHLIGHT, 0);

  /* wait for either mouse or keyboard input */
  ch = 0;
  xl = yl = NOT_MOVED;
  while(!xl && !yl) {  /* while mouse has not moved */
    mouse_motion(&xl, &yl);  /* see if moved */

    /* if both left and right buttons pushed, terminate */
    if(leftb_pressed() && rightb_pressed()) {
      ch = 62; /* F4's scan code */

      /* wait for buttons to clear */
      while(leftb_pressed() || rightb_pressed()) ;
      break;
    }

    /* if left button pressed, pen up/down toggle */
    if(leftb_pressed()) {
      if(pen==BCK_GND)
        ch = 59;  /* Fl's scan code */
      else ch = 60;

      /* wait for user to release button */
```

```
      while(leftb_pressed()) ;
      break;
   }

   /* if right button pressed, erase image */
   if(rightb_pressed()) {
     ch = 61; /* F3's scan code */

     /* wait for user to release button */
     while(rightb_pressed()) ;
     break;
   }

   if(kbhit()) {  /* otherwise, process key input */
     ch = getkey();
     break;
   }
}
putpoint(x+((x-IX)*XPAND), y+((y-IY)*XPAND), temp, 0);

/* process mouse motion */
if(x1==LEFT) x --;
else if(x1==RIGHT) x ++;
if(y1==UP) y --;
else if(y1==DOWN) y ++;
else
switch(ch) {
  case 75: /* left */
    x--;
    break;
  case 77: /* right */
    x++;
    break;
  case 72: /* up */
    y--;
    break;
  case 80: /* down */
    y++;
    break;
  case 71: /* up left */
    x--; y--;
    break;
  case 73: /* up right */
```

```
            x++; y--;
            break;
          case 79: /* down left*/
            x--; y++;
            break;
          case 81: /* down right */
            x++; y++;
            break;
          case 59: /* F1 - pen down */
            pen = FORE_GND;
            gotoxy(0, 23);
            printf("pen down");
            break;
          case 60: /* F2 - pen up */
            pen = BCK_GND;
            gotoxy(0, 23);
            printf("pen up   ");
            break;
          case 61: /* F3 - erase */
            init_symbol(i);
            display_image(i, 0, IY);
            display_grid(i);
            break;
      }
      if(x < IX) x++;  if(x > IX+XDIM-1) x--;
      if(y < IY) y++;  if(y > IY+YDIM-1) y--;

    } while(ch != 62); /* F4 - quit */
    clr_eol(0, 22);
    clr_eol(0, 23);
    /* give symbol default beginning coordinates */
    symbol.x[0] = 0;
    symbol.y[0] = 0;

    return;
}

/* Copy image from, to. */
void copyimage(int i, int j)
{
    register int x, y;

    for(x=0; x<XDIM; x++)
```

```
    for(y=0; y<YDIM; y++)
      symbol.image[j][x][y] = symbol.image[i][x][y];
}

/* Displays the image at specified X,Y. */
void display_image(char i, int startx, int starty)
{
  register int x, y;

  for(y = starty; y<starty+YDIM; y++)
    for(x = startx; x<startx+XDIM; x++)
      putpoint(x, y, symbol.image[i][x-startx][y-starty], 0);
}

/* Train the symbol using the mouse or arrow keys.
   Each movement you make will be recorded for later
   playback.
*/
void train()
{
  int x, y, x1, y1;
  char ch;
  unsigned k;

  symbol.last_pos = 0;

  getstartpos(); /* get starting position */

  x = symbol.x[0];  /* load starting coordinates */
  y = symbol.y[0];

  clrscr();
  gotoxy(0, 23);
  printf("Use arrow keys or press left button to use mouse");
  gotoxy(0, 24);
  printf("F1 or right button to stop");

  k = 0;

  for(;;) {
    ch = 0;
    record(x, y);  /* record each position */
```

```
    display_symbol(symbol, k % symbol.num_images,
                 symbol.last_pos); /* display image */

  x1 = y1 = NOT_MOVED;
  /* while mouse has not moved */
  while(!x1 && !y1 || !leftb_pressed()) {
    mouse_motion(&x1, &y1);  /* see if moved */
    if(kbhit()) {  /* otherwise, process key input */
      ch = getkey();
      break;
    }

    /* stop when right button pressed */
    if(rightb_pressed()) {
      ch = 59; /* F1's scan code */
      break;
    }
  }

  display_symbol(symbol, k % symbol.num_images,
                 symbol.last_pos); /* erase image */

  /* process mouse motion */
  if(x1==LEFT) x -= 5;
  else if(x1==RIGHT) x += 5;
  if(y1==UP) y -= 5;
  else if(y1==DOWN) y += 5;

  if(ch)  /* if key input, process */
    switch(ch) {
      case 75: /* left */
        x -=5;
        break;
      case 77: /* right */
        x +=5;
        break;
      case 72: /* up */
        y -= 5;
        break;
      case 80: /* down */
        y +=5;
        break;
      case 71: /* left up */
```

```
            y -= 5;   x -= 5;
            break;
        case 73: /* right up */
            y -= 5;   x += 5;
            break;
        case 79: /* left down */
            y += 5;   x -= 5;
            break;
        case 81: /* right down */
            y += 5;   x += 5;
            break;
        case 59: /* stop training on F1 */
            return;
      }

    /* increase last_pos */
    if(symbol.last_pos<MAX_POS-1) symbol.last_pos++;
    else putch(7); /* ring bell if out of space */

    k++;
  }
}

/* Set starting position for animation. */
void getstartpos(void)
{
  int x, y, x1, y1;
  char ch;
  unsigned k;

  clrscr();
  gotoxy(0, 23);
  printf("Use arrow keys or press left button to use mouse");
  gotoxy(0, 24);
  printf("press F1 or right button at starting position");

  symbol.x[0] = 0;   /* give symbol initial coordinates */
  symbol.y[0] = 0;
  x = 0; y =. 0;

  k = 0;
  do {
    ch = 0;
```

```
display_symbol(symbol, k % symbol.num_images,
               symbol.last_pos); /* display image */

x1 = y1 = NOT_MOVED;
/* while mouse has not moved */
while(!x1 && !y1 || !leftb_pressed()) {
  mouse_motion(&x1, &y1);  /* see if moved */
  if(kbhit()) {  /* otherwise, process key input */
    ch = getkey();
    break;
  }

  /* stop when right button pressed */
  if(rightb_pressed()) {
    ch = 59; /* F1's scan code */
    break;
  }
}

display_symbol(symbol, k % symbol.num_images,
               symbol.last_pos); /* erase image */

/* process mouse motion */
if(x1==LEFT) x -= 5;
else if(x1==RIGHT) x += 5;
if(y1==UP) y -= 5;
else if(y1==DOWN) y += 5;

if(ch)  /* if key input, process */
  switch(ch) {
    case 75: /* left */
      x -=5;
      break;
    case 77: /* right */
      x +=5;
      break;
    case 72: /* up */
      y -= 5;
      break;
    case 80: /* down */
      y +=5;
      break;
```

```
        case 71: /* left up */
          y -= 5;   x -= 5;
          break;
        case 73: /* right up */
          y -= 5;   x += 5;
          break;
        case 79: /* left down */
          y += 5;   x -= 5;
          break;
        case 81: /* right down */
          y += 5;   x += 5;
          break;
        case 59:  /* F1: abort */
          return;
      }

    k++;

    symbol.x[0] = x;   /* update starting position */
    symbol.y[0] = y;

  } while(ch!=59);   /* press F1 at starting position */
}

/* Record the motion entered by the user. */
void record(int x, int y)
{
  symbol.x[symbol.last_pos] = x;
  symbol.y[symbol.last_pos] = y;
}

/* Replay the animation sequence. */
void animate(void)
{
  register int i, j;
  int delay;

  /* for number of positions recorded */
  for(i=0; i<symbol.last_pos; i++ ) {
    /* display images */
    for(j=0; j<symbol.num_images; j++) {
      display_symbol(symbol, j, i);
      /* delay x 1000 */
```

```
        for(delay=0; delay<symbol.delay*1000; delay++) ;
        display_symbol(symbol, j, i);
        i++;
    }
  }
}

/* Display a symbol at its X,Y location. */
void display_symbol(struct symbol_type symbol,
                    int img, int pos)
{
  register int x, y;
  int xtemp, ytemp;

  ytemp = symbol.y[pos];
  xtemp = symbol.x[pos];

  for(y = ytemp; y<ytemp+YDIM; y++)
    for(x = xtemp; x<xtemp+XDIM; x++)
      if(symbol.image[img][x-xtemp][y-ytemp]==FORE_GND)
        putpoint(x, y,
                 symbol.image[img][x-xtemp][y-ytemp], 0x18);
}

/* Initializes the image. */
void init_symbol(char i)
{
  register int x, y;

  for(x= 0; x<XDIM; x++)
    for(y=0; y<YDIM; y++)
      symbol.image[i][x][y] = BLANK;
}

/* Saves the symbol. */
save_symbol(void)
{
  FILE *fp;
  char fname[80];
  int result;

  gotoxy(0, 22);
  printf("save to: ");
```

```
  gets(fname);

  if((fp = fopen(fname, "wb"))==NULL) {
    printf("cannot open file");
    return 0;
  }

  fwrite(&symbol, sizeof symbol, 1, fp);

  if(ferror(fp)) result = 0;
  else result = 1;
  fclose(fp);
  clr_eol(0, 22);
  return result;
}

/* Loads the symbol. */
load_symbol(char *name)
{
  FILE *fp;
  char fname[80];
  int result;

  if(!*name) {
    clr_eol(0, 22);
    gotoxy(0, 22);
    printf("load from: ");
    gets(fname);
  }
  else strcpy(fname, name);

  if((fp = fopen(fname, "rb"))==NULL) {
    printf("cannot open file");
    return 0;
  }

  fread(&symbol, sizeof symbol, 1, fp);

  if(ferror(fp)) result = 0;
  else result = 1;
  fclose(fp);
  clr_eol(0, 22);
  return result;
```

```
}

/***********************************************/
/* Mouse interface functions.                  */
/***********************************************/

/* Turn off the mouse cursor. */
void cursor_off(void)
{
  int fnum;

  fnum = 2; /* erase the cursor */
  cmouses(&fnum, &fnum, &fnum, &fnum);
}

/* Turn on the mouse cursor. */
void cursor_on(void)
{
  int fnum;

  fnum = 1; /* show the cursor */
  cmouses(&fnum, &fnum, &fnum, &fnum);
}

/* Return true if right button is pressed;
   false otherwise. */
rightb_pressed(void)
{
  int fnum, arg2, arg3, arg4;

  fnum = 3; /* get position and button status */
  cmouses(&fnum, &arg2, &arg3, &arg4);
  return arg2 & 2;
}

/* Return true if left button is pressed;
   false otherwise. */
leftb_pressed(void)
{
  int fnum, arg2, arg3, arg4;

  fnum = 3; /* get position and button status */
  cmouses(&fnum, &arg2, &arg3, &arg4);
```

```
    return arg2 & 1;
}


/* Set mouse cursor coordinates. */
void set_mouse_position(int x, int y)
{
   int fnum, arg2;

   fnum = 4; /* set position */
   cmouses(&fnum, &arg2, &x, &y);
}


/* Return mouse cursor coordinates. */
void mouse_position(int *x, int *y)
{
   int fnum, arg2, arg3, arg4;

   fnum = 3; /* get position and button status */
   cmouses(&fnum, &arg2, &arg3, &arg4);
   *x = arg3;
   *y = arg4;
}


/* Return the direction of travel. */
void mouse_motion(int *deltax, int *deltay)
{
   int fnum, arg2, arg3, arg4;

   fnum = 11; /* get direction of motion */
   cmouses(&fnum, &arg2, &arg3, &arg4);
   if(arg3>0) *deltax = RIGHT;
   else if(arg3<0) *deltax = LEFT;
   else *deltax = NOT_MOVED;

   if(arg4>0) *deltay = DOWN;
   else if(arg4<0) *deltay = UP;
   else *deltay = NOT_MOVED;
}

void mouse_direction(int *deltax, int *deltay)
{
   int fnum, arg2;
```

```
  cmouses(&fnum, &arg2, deltax, deltay);
}

/* Reset the mouse. */
void mouse_reset(void)
{
  int fnum, arg2, arg3, arg4;

  fnum = 0; /* reset the mouse */
  cmouses(&fnum, &arg2, &arg3, &arg4);
  if(fnum!=-1) {
    printf("mouse hardware or software not installed");
    exit(1);
  }
  if(arg2!=2) {
   printf("two-button mouse required");
   exit(1);
  }
}

/* Set mickey ratio. */
void mickey_ratio(int xratio, int yratio)
{
  int fnum, arg2;

  fnum = 15;

  cmouses(&fnum, &arg2, &xratio, &yratio);
}
/*****************************************************
 Console and keyboard functions.
 *****************************************************/

/* Return the scan code of the key pressed.
   This function is compatible with Turbo C and
   Microsoft C (be sure to #define the appropriate
   symbol).  If you use a different compiler, consult
   the text.
*/
char getkey(void)
{
  union key {
    int i;
```

```
    char ch[2];
  } k;

#ifdef TURBOC
  k.i = bioskey(0);
#endif
#ifdef MICROSOFTC
  k.i = _bios_keybrd(0);
#endif
  return k.ch[1];
}

/* Set the video mode. */
void mode(int mode_code)
{
  union REGS r;

  r.h.al = mode_code;
  r.h.ah = 0;
  int86(0x10, &r, &r);
}

/* Send the cursor to x,y. */
void gotoxy(int x, int y)
{
  union REGS r;

  r.h.ah = 2; /* cursor addressing function */
  r.h.dl = x; /* column coordinate */
  r.h.dh = y; /* row coordinate */
  r.h.bh = 0; /* video page */
  int86(0x10, &r, &r);
}

/* Clears to end of line. */
void clr_eol(int x, int y)
{
   for(; x<80; x++) {
     gotoxy(x, y);
     printf(" ");
   }
}
```

```
/* Returns the value at the specified pixel. */
char getpoint(int x, int y)
{
  union REGS r;

  r.h.ah = 13;
  r.x.dx = y;
  r.x.cx = x;
  r.h.bh = 0;
  int86(16, &r, &r);
  return r.h.al;
}

/* This version of putpoint will work for all video
   adapters but is incredibly slow!
*/
/*
void putpoint(int x, int y, int color, int how)
{
  union REGS r;

  if(how==0x18) color = color | 128;
  r.h.bh = 0;
  r.h.ah = 12;
  r.h.al = color;
  r.x.dx = y;
  r.x.cx = x;
  int86(16, &r, &r);
}
*/

/* Clear the screen. */
void clrscr(void)
{
  union REGS r;

  r.h.ah = 6;
  r.h.al = 0;
  r.h.ch = 0;
  r.h.cl = 0;
  r.h.dh = MAX_LINES;
  r.h.dl = LINE_LEN;
  r.h.bh = 0;
```

```
  int86(0x10, &r, &r);
}


/* This function sets the specified pixel to the
   specified color using an EGA/VGA video adapter.
   The value of how may be one of these:

   action          value

   overwrite       0
   XOR             0x18
   AND             8
   OR              0x10

*/
#define ENABLE 0x0F
#define INDEXREG 0x3CE
#define VALREG 0x3CF


/* Note: Borland does not document outp(), but it is
   in the library of Turbo C 2.0.  The documented function
   is called outport(), but it runs much slower.  However,
   in future versions you may need to use it instead.
   For this reason, the following conditional compilation
   directives have been included.
*/
#ifdef TURBOC
#define OUTINDEX(index, val) outp((INDEXREG), (index));\
                             outp((VALREG), (val));

#endif
#ifdef MICROSOFTC
#define OUTINDEX(index, val) outp((INDEXREG), (index));\
                             outp((VALREG), (val));

#endif

#define WIDTH 80L

/* These range values assume EGA mode 16 */
#define XMAX 639
#define YMAX 349
#define XMIN 0
#define YMIN 0
```

```
void putpoint(int x, int y, int color, int how)
{
  register unsigned char mask = 0x80;
  register char far *base;
  unsigned dummy;

  /* if you want range checking at this point, activate
     this line of code.  It will slow down the function
     however.
  */
  /*if(x<XMIN || x>XMAX || y<YMIN || y>YMAX) return;*/

  base = (char far *) (egabase
          + ( (long) y * WIDTH + (long) x/8L ));

  mask >>= x % 8;

  /* This causes the memory READ necessary to
     load the EGA/VGA's internal registers.
  */
  dummy = *base;

  OUTINDEX(0, color);
  OUTINDEX(1, ENABLE);
  OUTINDEX(3, how);
  OUTINDEX(8, mask);

  *base = 1;

  OUTINDEX(0, 0);
  OUTINDEX(1, 0);
  OUTINDEX(3, 0);
  OUTINDEX(8, 0xff);
}
```

THE ANIMATION-DISPLAY SUBSYSTEM

Once you have defined and trained one or more symbols, you can use it in your application program as long as you include the animation-display subsystem described in this section. Through the selective use of animation, you can give your programs an exciting and distinctive visual appearance. For example, a modem program might animate the symbol of a file across the screen, indicating a successful file transfer. Another good use of animation is in children's programs. For example, an addition drill program might "launch" a rocket each time the child gives the correct answer. The uses of animation are limited only by your imagination.

Since a program may need to animate more than one symbol, the symbols are held in an array of structures, as shown here:

```
struct symbol_type {
  unsigned char image[MAX_IMG][XDIM][YDIM]; /* symbol */
  int x[MAX_POS], y[MAX_POS]; /* X, Y coordinates */
  int last_pos; /* last position */
  int delay;  /* delay factor */
  int num_images; /* number of images in symbol */
} symbol[MAX_SYM];
```

where **MAX_SYM** must be defined to be equal to the number of symbols your program will be animating.

Animating One Symbol

To animate one symbol, use the **animate_one( )** function, shown here:

```
/* Replay the animation sequence. */
void animate_one(int sym)

{
  register int i, j, t;
  int delay;

  t = symbol[sym].last_pos;
  for(i=0; i<t; i++ ) {
    for(j=0; j<symbol[sym].num_images; j++) {
      symbol[sym].last_pos = i;
      display_symbol(symbol[sym], j, i); /* turn on */

      for(delay=0; delay<symbol[sym].delay*1000; delay++) ;
```

```
      display_symbol(symbol[sym], j, i); /* turn off */
      i++;
    }
  }
}
```

This function is called using the index of the symbol you wish to animate. Its operation is similar to the **animate( )** function found in the animation editor.

Animating All Symbols Simultaneously

At times you may wish to animate all symbols simultaneously. To do this, use the **animate _ all( )** function, shown here:

```
/* Replay all animation sequences. */
void animate_all(void)
{
  register int i, j;
  int delay[MAX_SYM], count[MAX_SYM], max_pos[MAX_SYM];
  char on[MAX_SYM];
  char active;

  /* initialize counters */
  for(i=0; i<num_syms; i++) {
    count[i] = 0;
    delay[i] = symbol[i].delay;
    max_pos[i] = symbol[i].last_pos;
    on[i] = 0;
  }

  active = 1;
  do {
    /* turn on images */
    for(i=0; i<num_syms; i++) {
      if(count[i] < max_pos[i] && !on[i]) {
        display_symbol(symbol[i],
            count[i] % symbol[i].num_images, count[i]);
        on[i] = 1;
```

```
      }
    }
    /* turn off images */
    for(i=0; i<num_syms; i++) {
      /* if delay active, don't turn off */
      if(count[i] < max_pos[i] && !delay[i]) {
        display_symbol(symbol[i],
            count[i] % symbol[i].num_images, count[i]);
        count[i]++;
        on[i] = 0;
      }

      /* update delay count */
      if(delay[i]==0) delay[i] = symbol[i].delay;
      if(delay[i]) delay[i]--;
    }
    active = 0;
    /* see if any symbols still active */
    for(j=0; j<num_syms; j++)
      if(count[j]<max_pos[j]) active = 1;
  } while(active); /* display while at least one active
                      symbol */
}
```

The **animate_all( )** function works likes this. After initializing some
counters, it begins executing its main animation loop. Inside this loop,
each symbol is displayed, then each symbol is erased, and the next
position of each symbol is displayed. If a symbol has a delay associated
with it, then it is not moved until its delay count equals zero. Each time a
delay count reaches zero, it is reset to its original value, and the delay
begins again.

Notice that the position count (used to index **x** and **y**) of each symbol
is stored independently in the array **count**. This way, you can animate
several objects even though they do not have animation sequences of the
same length. When the end of a symbol's sequence has been reached, it
simply disappears from the screen. The other symbols continue until they
have exhausted their own sequences.

The main loop terminates when all symbols have been animated
through their entire sequence. The function knows when this has occurred because the value of **count[j]** will equal **max_pos[j]** for each
symbol.

Although this approach to **animate‗all( )** will work in virtually any computing environment, an interesting improvement (and challenge), if you have a PC, is to use the multitasking subsystem developed in Chapter 4 to animate each figure, thus bypassing the manual "multitasking" present in **animate‗all( )**. You could define separate tasks for each symbol and then call **animate‗one( )** from each task. The task switching will handle the simultaneous animation of each symbol.

Animating Selected Symbols

By adding just a few lines of code to **animate‗all( )**, we can transform it into a function that animates a selected group of symbols. This function, called **animate‗some( )**, is shown here. The new lines have been marked.

```
/* Replay selected animation sequences. Call this
   function with a character array that contains
   a true value for each symbol to be animated and
   a false value for those that are not. */
void animate_some(char *syms)
{
  register int i, j;
  int delay[MAX_SYM], count[MAX_SYM], max_pos[MAX_SYM];
  char on[MAX_SYM];
  char active;

  /* initialize counters */
  for(i=0; i<num_syms; i++) {
    count[i] = 0;
    delay[i] = symbol[i].delay;
    max_pos[i] = symbol[i].last_pos;
    on[i] = 0;
  }

  active = 1;
  do {
    /* turn on images */
    for(i=0; i<num_syms; i++) {
/*new*/ if(!syms[i]) continue;  /* skip this symbol */
      if(count[i] < max_pos[i] && !on[i]) {
        display_symbol(symbol[i],
```

```
                    count[i] % symbol[i].num_images, count[i]);
                  on[i] = 1;
                }
            }
            /* turn off images */
            for(i=0; i<num_syms; i++) {
/*new*/       if(!syms[i]) continue;  /* skip this symbol */
                /* if delay active, don't turn off */
                if(count[i] < max_pos[i] && !delay[i]) {
                    display_symbol(symbol[i],
                        count[i] % symbol[i].num_images, count[i]);
                    count[i]++;
                    on[i] = 0;
                }

                /* update delay count */
                if(delay[i]==0) delay[i] = symbol[i].delay;
                if(delay[i]) delay[i]--;
            }
            active = 0;
            /* see if any symbols still active */
            for(j=0; j<num_syms; j++) {
/*new*/       if(!syms[j]) continue;  /* skip this symbol */
                if(count[j]<max_pos[j]) active = 1;
            }
        } while(active); /* display while at least one active
                            symbol */
}
```

To use **animate_some( )**, you first define a character array that is the same length as the number of symbols used by your program—that is, at least **MAX_SYM** characters long. Each element of this array will be used to determine whether its corresponding symbol is animated by **animate_some( )**. Initialize the array so that an element contains a true value if its corresponding symbol is to be animated and a false value otherwise. You will then use this array as an argument to **animate_some( )**. For example, using **syms**, the following definition will cause symbols 0, 2, and 4 to be animated.

```
char syms[MAX_SYM] = {1, 0, 1, 0, 1};

animate_some(syms);
```

To animate symbols 2 and 3, use this initialization.

```
char syms[MAX_SYM] = {0, 0, 1, 1, 0};

animate_some(syms);
```

The Entire Animation-Display Subsystem

The entire animation-display subsystem is shown here, along with a sample **main( )** function that demonstrates its use. The demonstration assumes that you have defined five symbols: a dog, a cat, a worm, a tree, and a bird. These symbols are in the files DOG.AN, CAT.AN, WORM.AN, TREE.AN, and BIRD.AN. (Of course, you can define other symbols.) A sample sequence is shown in Figure 8-2.

Figure 8-2

Sample output from the animation display subsystem

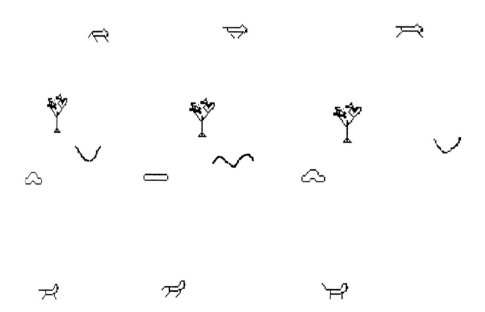

```
/* Animation subsystem and demonstration program. */

#define TURBOC
/*  If you use Microsoft C, define MICROSOFTC instead
    of TURBOC.
*/

#include "stdio.h"
#include "dos.h"
#include "conio.h"
#include "bios.h"
#include "string.h"
#include "ctype.h"
#include "stdlib.h"

#define XDIM        21    /* change these to change dimensions */
#define YDIM        27    /* of the symbol you want to use */

#define MAX_SYM      5    /* max number of separate symbols */
#define MAX_IMG      5    /* number of images in symbol */

#define MAX_POS 500   /* number of different positions that
                         can be recorded for any one symbol */

#define MAX_LINES   24
#define LINE_LEN    79

#define BLANK        0
#define BCK_GND      9
#define FORE_GND    15
#define HIGHLIGHT   13

void mode(int mode_code);
void clrscr(void);
void putpoint(int x, int y, int color, int how);
void animate_all(void), animate_one(int sym);
void animate_some(char *syms);
int load_symbols(void);

struct symbol_type {
  unsigned char image[MAX_IMG][XDIM][YDIM]; /* symbol */
```

```
  int x[MAX_POS], y[MAX_POS]; /* X, Y coordinates */
  int last_pos; /* last position */
  int delay;   /* delay factor */
  int num_images; /* number of images in symbol */
} symbol[MAX_SYM];

void display_symbol(struct symbol_type symbol, int img,
                    int pos);


char far *egabase;

/* array of filenames of animation files */
char files[][14] = {
  "dog.an",
  "bird.an",
  "cat.an",
  "tree.an",
  "worm.an",
  ""   /* terminate with a null name */
};

/* will hold number of symbols actually loaded */
int num_syms;

char syms[] = {1, 1, 0, 1, 0};

void main()
{
  register int i;

  mode(16);   /* ega mode 16 - use another if you like */

#ifdef TURBOC
  egabase = (char far *) MK_FP(0xA000, 0000);
#endif
#ifdef MICROSOFTC
  egabase = (char far *) 0xA0000000;
#endif

  if(!load_symbols()) {
      printf("cannot load file");
```

```
      exit(l);
  }

  /* individually animate the symbols */
  for(i=0; i<num_syms; i++)
    animate_one(i);

  animate_all();  /* animate all symbols */

  animate_some(syms); /* animate some symbols */

  getch();
  mode(2);
}

/* Replay all animation sequences. */
void animate_all(void)
{
  register int i, j;
  int delay[MAX_SYM], count[MAX_SYM], max_pos[MAX_SYM];
  char on[MAX_SYM];
  char active;

  /* initialize counters */
  for(i=0; i<num_syms; i++) {
    count[i] = 0;
    delay[i] = symbol[i].delay;
    max_pos[i] = symbol[i].last_pos;
    on[i] = 0;
  }

  active = l;
  do {
    /* turn on images */
    for(i=0; i<num_syms; i++) {
      if(count[i] < max_pos[i] && !on[i]) {
        display_symbol(symbol[i],
            count[i] % symbol[i].num_images, count[i]);
        on[i] = l;
      }
    }
    /* turn off images */
    for(i=0; i<num_syms; i++) {
```

```
      /* if delay active, don't turn off */
      if(count[i] < max_pos[i] && !delay[i]) {
        display_symbol(symbol[i],
            count[i] % symbol[i].num_images, count[i]);
        count[i]++;
        on[i] = 0;
      }

      /* update delay count */
      if(delay[i]==0) delay[i] = symbol[i].delay;
      if(delay[i]) delay[i]--;
    }
    active = 0;
    /* see if any symbols still active */
    for(j=0; j<num_syms; j++)
      if(count[j]<max_pos[j]) active = 1;
  } while(active); /* display while at least one active
                      symbol */
}

/* Replay selected animation sequences. */
void animate_some(char *syms)
{
  register int i, j;
  int delay[MAX_SYM], count[MAX_SYM], max_pos[MAX_SYM];
  char on[MAX_SYM];
  char active;

  /* initialize counters */
  for(i=0; i<num_syms; i++) {
    count[i] = 0;
    delay[i] = symbol[i].delay;
    max_pos[i] = symbol[i].last_pos;
    on[i] = 0;
  }

  active = 1;
  do {
    /* turn on images */
    for(i=0; i<num_syms; i++) {
      if(!syms[i]) continue;  /* skip this symbol */
      if(count[i] < max_pos[i] && !on[i]) {
        display_symbol(symbol[i],
```

```
            count[i] % symbol[i].num_images, count[i]);
        on[i] = 1;
      }
    }
    /* turn off images */
    for(i=0; i<num_syms; i++) {
      if(!syms[i]) continue;  /* skip this symbol */
      /* if delay active, don't turn off */
      if(count[i] < max_pos[i] && !delay[i]) {
        display_symbol(symbol[i],
            count[i] % symbol[i].num_images, count[i]);
        count[i]++;
        on[i] = 0;
      }

      /* update delay count */
      if(delay[i]==0) delay[i] = symbol[i].delay;
      if(delay[i]) delay[i]--;
    }
    active = 0;
    /* see if any symbols still active */
    for(j=0; j<num_syms; j++) {
      if(!syms[j]) continue;  /* skip this symbol */
      if(count[j]<max_pos[j]) active = 1;
    }
  } while(active); /* display while at least one active
                      symbol */
}

/* Replay the animation sequence. */
void animate_one(int sym)
{
  register int i, j, t;
  int delay;

  t = symbol[sym].last_pos;
  for(i=0; i<t; i++ ) {
    for(j=0; j<symbol[sym].num_images; j++) {
      symbol[sym].last_pos = i;
      display_symbol(symbol[sym], j, i); /* turn on */

      for(delay=0; delay<symbol[sym].delay*1000; delay++) ;
```

```
        display_symbol(symbol[sym], j, i); /* turn off */
        i++;
      }
    }
}

/* Display a symbol at its X,Y location. */
void display_symbol(struct symbol_type symbol,
                    int img, int pos)
{
  register int x, y;
  int xtemp, ytemp;

  ytemp = symbol.y[pos];
  xtemp = symbol.x[pos];

  for(y = ytemp; y<ytemp+YDIM; y++)
    for(x = xtemp; x<xtemp+XDIM; x++)
      if(symbol.image[img][x-xtemp][y-ytemp]==FORE_GND)
        putpoint(x, y,
                 symbol.image[img][x-xtemp][y-ytemp], 0x18);
}

/* Loads the symbols. */
load_symbols(void)
{
  FILE *fp;
  int result, i;

  for(i=0; *files[i]; i++) {
    if((fp = fopen(files[i], "rb"))==NULL) {
      printf("cannot open file %s", files[i]);
      return 0;
    }

    fread(&symbol[i], sizeof symbol, 1, fp);

    if(ferror(fp)) result = 0;
    else result = 1;
    fclose(fp);
  }
  num_syms = i;
  return result;
}
```

```
/*****************************************************
 Console functions.
*****************************************************/

/* Set the video mode. */
void mode(int mode_code)
{
  union REGS r;

  r.h.al = mode_code;
  r.h.ah = 0;
  int86(0x10, &r, &r);
}

/* This version of putpoint will work for all video
   adapters but is incredibly slow!
*/
/*
void putpoint(int x, int y, int color, int how)
{
  union REGS r;

  if(how==0x18) color = color | 128;
  r.h.bh = 0;
  r.h.ah = 12;
  r.h.al = color;
  r.x.dx = y;
  r.x.cx = x;
  int86(16, &r, &r);
}
*/

/* Clear the screen. */
void clrscr(void)
{
  union REGS r;

  r.h.ah = 6;
  r.h.al = 0;
  r.h.ch = 0;
  r.h.cl = 0;
```

```
   r.h.dh = MAX_LINES;
   r.h.dl = LINE_LEN;
   r.h.bh = 0;
   int86(0x10, &r, &r);
}


/* This function sets the specified pixel to the
   specified color using an EGA/VGA video adapter.
   The value of how may be one of these:

   action        value

   overwrite     0
   XOR           0x18
   AND           8
   OR            0x10

*/
#define ENABLE 0x0F
#define INDEXREG 0x3CE
#define VALREG 0x3CF

/* Note: Borland does not document outp(), but it is
   in the library of Turbo C 2.0.  The documented function
   is called outport(), but it runs much slower.  However,
   in future versions you may need to use it instead.
   For this reason, the following conditional compilation
   directives have been included.
*/
#ifdef TURBOC
#define OUTINDEX(index, val) outp((INDEXREG), (index));\
                             outp((VALREG), (val));

#endif
#ifdef MICROSOFTC
#define OUTINDEX(index, val) outp((INDEXREG), (index));\
                             outp((VALREG), (val));

#endif

#define WIDTH 80L

/* These range values assume EGA mode 16 */
#define XMAX 639
#define YMAX 349
```

```
#define XMIN 0
#define YMIN 0

void putpoint(int x, int y, int color, int how)
{
  register unsigned char mask = 0x80;
  register char far *base;
  unsigned dummy;

  /* if you want range checking at this point, activate
     this line of code.  It will slow down the function
     however.
  */
  /*if(x<XMIN || x>XMAX || y<YMIN || y>YMAX) return;*/

  base = (char far *) (egabase
        + ( (long) y * WIDTH + (long) x/8L ));

  mask >>= x % 8;

  /* This causes the memory READ necessary to
     load the EGA/VGA's internal registers.
  */
  dummy = *base;

  OUTINDEX(0, color);
  OUTINDEX(1, ENABLE);
  OUTINDEX(3, how);
  OUTINDEX(8, mask);

  *base = 1;

  OUTINDEX(0, 0);
  OUTINDEX(1, 0);
  OUTINDEX(3, 0);
  OUTINDEX(8, 0xff);
}
```

SOME THINGS TO TRY

As mentioned earlier, you might want to try using the multitasking
subsystem from Chapter 4 to animate objects. This way, your program can

continue processing information during the animation process. Another thing you might want to try is adding color to the symbols. Finally, you might find it fun to rotate each symbol automatically, relative to the direction it is moving. For example, if you animate a car, the car will always face in the direction of motion.

You might also find it interesting to add to the animation editor an option that lets you draw a background scene on which the animation will take place. You will want to save the background scene and display it whenever you animate an object.

One last thought—the animation sequences do not necessarily need to be trained; they can be computed instead. For example, if an object is to move in a circle, the coordinates for each move can be computed. It might be fun to use the **rand( )** random number generator to produce random motions.

CHAPTER NINE

Fancy Printer Control

Possibly the most underutilized part of the average computer system is the printer, which spends most of its time in its default configuration, printing text. However, most printers have many interesting features that can be used to enhance the printing of text or graphics images. In this chapter, we will explore several features of the most common family of printers: the Epson dot-matrix printers and compatibles.

The Epson line of dot-matrix printers has evolved and been enhanced over the years. The first popular version was the MX-80. However, the most common line began with the FX-80. At the time of this writing, the current version is the LX-800. Since virtually all Epson dot-matrix printers understand a common set of commands, the examples shown in this chapter will work with most Epson printers. Keep in mind that older printers may not support all the features discussed here — for example, the original MX-80 does not support graphics.

The features of the Epson printers can be divided into two categories: text and graphics. We will begin with the text-based options and conclude with the graphics commands. In the discussion of graphics, a print-screen

Richard Schwartz
Cocreator of Paradox and Chief Technical Officer
at Borland International

Richard Schwartz is a programmer with a long list of accomplishments. He holds B.S., M.S., and Ph.D. degrees in Computer Science from UCLA. He was a cofounder of Ansa Software (which later became part of Borland International) and cocreator of the relational database Paradox. In addition to his many accomplishments, he was a senior computer scientist at the Stanford Research Institute, a member of the Editorial Board for the *Journal of Computer Languages* and a Contributing Editor to *PC Tech Journal*.

Richard first came to C in 1981 when he began work on Paradox, which is coded in C. "Paradox development began on an S-100 8-bit computer using BDS-C. The assumption was that some unknown, later model computer would be the actual host for the product, so we needed a portable language. We chose C because it was available on a large number of machines, from a variety of vendors. Most C implementations are also efficient and provide excellent access to the machine and operating system."

Since Paradox is one of the most respected database products available on the PC market, I asked Richard for his design secrets. "Quality C programs take into account the style and level of sophistication of the intended user. However, these can never be completely anticipated at the outset, so it is critical to design the program to be flexible and general enough to evolve as requirements change. Avoid tricky coding. Remember, code changes hands many times and others will have to figure out what you have done. Perhaps more important, faster performance comes more often from clever algorithms than from ringing the last couple of CPU cycles out of an inferior approach."

Richard believes wholeheartedly in the saying "the customer is always right" and applies it to his work. "Design programs that solve the user's problems in the user's terms; try to find a simple, intuitive model that expresses everything that a person needs to use the product. Great programs all share one common feature: they are intuitively easy to use by their target users."

Richard believes in learning from and improving on the past. "The best programs borrow elements from the successful portions of other programs and innovate where previous programs have been less successful. The program then appeals to the familiarity that the user may have with the previous program, while solving its problems." His last comment summarizes his approach: "Make the program smarter at dealing with complexity so that the user won't have to deal with it." In Richard's view, this is what computers and software are all about.

subsystem will be created that can be called by an application program to print all or a portion of the screen anywhere on the page. You will also see how to construct a full-page image in RAM, bypassing the screen altogether, and how to print this image.

As is the case with many of the programs in this book, you must define either **TURBOC** or **MICROSOFTC** at the top of the programs because of slight differences between the two compilers. If you have a different compiler, consult your user manual. You may need to rename one or more functions.

SENDING COMMANDS TO THE PRINTER

The Epson printers have several different modes of operation. When the printer is turned on, it is, by default, in a text mode that uses six lines per inch and a ten-character-per-inch, pica type font. To access other features of the printer, you must change its mode of operation. This is accomplished by sending the printer a command. In general, a command is signaled by first sending the printer an Esc character (decimal value 27). Next, the actual command is sent. For example, to print in italics, send these two decimal values: **27 52**. Most commands consist of a single character, but a few take additional characters.

In general, sending the printer a command changes its mode of operation. The new mode stays in effect until the next command arrives. Some modes can be combined with others. For example, you can instruct the printer to print text in boldface using double-wide characters.

SENDING OUTPUT TO A PRINTER

Because C defines no standard library function to output a character to the printer, the method to accomplish this will vary between compilers. The following function, called **print( )**, will work for both Turbo C and Microsoft C (assuming you define the proper macro name).

```
/* Send a character to the printer. */
void print(char ch)
{
```

```
#ifdef TURBOC
  biosprint(0, ch, 0);
#endif
#ifdef MICROSOFTC
  _bios_printer(0, 0, ch);
#endif
}
```

The functions **biosprint( )** and **_bios_printer( )** were discussed in Chapter 6; refer there for details.

To send a string to the printer, use the **print_str( )** function, shown here:

```
/* Send a string to the printer */
void print_str(char *s)
{
  while(*s) {
    print(*s);
    s++;
  }
}
```

Simply call it with the string you wish to be printed.

THE TEXT COMMANDS

The text-based commands we will be using are summarized in Table 9-1. (Your printer will probably support other commands; see your user's manual.) We will use these commands to construct a set of functions that can be used to print text in various formats.

Condensed and Wide Characters

By default, when using the pica type font, the printer will print 10 characters per inch. If you use the condensed format, it will print 17 characters per inch. If you print a string using the double-wide format, it will print 5 characters per inch. No matter how many characters are

---

Table 9-1

Selected Text-Based Commands for the Epson Dot-Matrix Printers

Command Sequence	Effect
27 14	Print in wide characters
27 15	Print in condensed characters
18	Stop printing in condensed characters
20	Stop printing in wide characters
27 45 0	Stop underlining
27 45 1	Underline each character
27 48	Set 1/8″ line spacing
27 49	Set 7/72″ line spacing
27 50	Set 1/6″ line spacing (default)
27 65 n	Set n/72″ line spacing ($0 < n < 86$)
27 51 n	Set n/216″ line spacing ($0 < n < 256$)
27 52	Print in italics
27 53	Stop printing in italics
27 69	Print in emphasized characters
27 70	Stop printing in emphasized characters
27 71	Print in bold characters
27 72	Stop printing in bold characters
27 77	Print in elite type font
27 80	Print in pica type font (default)
27 83 0	Print superscript
27 83 1	Print subscript
27 84	Stop printing in super- or subscript
27 120 0	Print in draft mode
27 120 1	Print in near-letter-quality mode

---

printed per inch, the height of the characters remains unchanged. The functions **print_condensed( )** and **print_wide( )**, shown here, print their string arguments in the styles indicated.

```
/* Print a string in condensed format. */
void print_condensed(char *s)
```

```
{
  print(27); print(15);
  print_str(s);
  print(18);  /* cancel condensed */
}

/* Print a string in wide format. */
void print_wide(char *s)
{
  print(27); print(14);
  print_str(s);
  print(20);
}
```

Using Bold and Emphasized Characters

The Epson printers have two methods of producing darker characters: bold and emphasized. When a character is printed in boldface, each dot that comprises the character is printed twice, with the second one just below the first one. When a character is printed using emphasized format, each dot is printed twice, but the second one is just to the right of the first one. The functions **print_emphasized( )** and **print_bold( )** are shown here:

```
/* Print a string in emphasized type. */
void print_emphasized(char *s)
{
  print(27); print(69); /* enable emphasized */
  print_str(s);
  print(27); print(70); /* disable emphasized */
}

/* Print a string in bold. */
void print_bold(char *s)
{
  print(27); print(71); /* enable bold */
  print_str(s);
  print(27); print(72); /* disable bold */
}
```

Underlining and Italics

You can underline each character in a string using **print_underlined( )**. To display a string in italics, use **print_italic( )**. These functions are shown here:

```
/* Print an underlined string. */
void print_underlined(char *s)
{
  print(27); print(45); print(1); /* enable underlining */
  print_str(s);
  print(27); print(45); print(0); /* disable underlining */
}

/* Print a string in italics. */
void print_italic(char *s)
{
  print(27); print(52); /* enable italics */
  print_str(s);
  print(27); print(53); /* disable italics */
}
```

Using Superscripts and Subscripts

One particularly nice feature of the Epson printers is their ability to print superscripts and subscripts. This makes it easier to display mathematical formulas, for example. To output a superscripted string, use **print_super( )**. To output a subscripted string, use **print_sub( )**. These functions are shown here, along with **cancel_super_sub( )**, which terminates either mode.

```
/* Print a string in superscript. */
void print_super(char *s)
{
  select_superscript();
  print_str(s);
  cancel_super_sub();
}

/* Print a string in subscript. */
```

```
void print_sub(char *s)
{
  select_subscript();
  print_str(s);
  cancel_super_sub();
}

/* Cancel super- or subscript mode. */
void cancel_super_sub(void)
{
  print(27); print(84);
}
```

As you can infer from their command structures, superscript and subscript are mutually exclusive. You cannot, for example, subscript a superscripted character. (Watch for the functions **select_subscript( )** and **select_superscript( )**, which are shown later in this chapter.)

Selecting a Type Font

You can select either the pica or elite type using **select_pica( )** or **select_elite( )**, shown here:

```
/* Select elite type font. */
void select_elite(void)
{
  print(27); print(77);
}

/* Select pica type font. */
void select_pica(void)
{
  print(27); print(80);
}
```

The pica font is the default. The elite font is smaller, printing 12 characters per inch. When elite is used in the condensed print mode, it prints 20 characters per inch.

Altering the Line Spacing

By default, six lines are printed per inch. You can change the spacing between lines using one of the following functions: **select_8( )**, **select_6( )**, **select_7_72( )**, **select_72( )**, and **select_216( )**, all of which are shown here:

```
/* Select 8 lines per inch. */
void select_8(void)
{
  print(27); print(48);
}


/* Select 6 lines per inch (default). */
void select_6(void)
{
  print(27); print(50);
}


/* Select 7/72 line spacing. */
void select_7_72(void)
{
  print(27); print(49);
}


/* Select num/72 line spacing */
void select_72(char num)
{
  print(27); print(65), print(num);
}


/* Select num/216 line spacing. */
void select_216(char num)
{
  print(27); print(51); print(num);
}
```

The **select_8( )** function sets the line spacing to eight lines per inch. The **select_6( )** restores line spacing to the default six lines per inch. The **select_7_72( )** sets the distance between lines at 7/72 inch. This is about ten lines per inch. You can specify the space between lines in increments of 1/72 inch using **select_72( )**. Finally, you can specify the spacing between lines in increments of 1/216 inch using **select_216( )**.

Draft Versus Near-Letter-Quality Modes

Often, when you need printed output, speed is more important than print quality. By default, the Epson printers use what is called *draft mode.* In this mode of operation, each character is defined by an 11×9 matrix. However, if you want high-quality output, you can select near-letter-quality (NLQ) mode, which uses an 18×12 matrix. Although this mode produces better-looking characters, it takes about twice as long to print.

You can select the printing mode using the **select_style( )** function, shown here:

```
#define DRAFT 0
#define NLQ 1

/* If mode is 0, print in draft (fast printing) mode.
   If mode is 1, print in near-letter-quality (NLQ)
   style.
*/
void select_style(char mode)
{
  print(27); print(120); print(mode);
}
```

Resetting the Printer

You can reset the printer to its default mode using the **reset( )** function, shown here:

```
/* Reset the printer to defaults. */
void reset(void)
```

```
{
  print(27); print(64);
}
```

Combining Features

Some print features can be combined with others. If you wish to combine features, simply activate the ones you want, then use **print_str( )** to output text. To make this process a little easier, the following functions and macros are defined. To select superscripting, subscripting, or underlining, use **select_super( )**, **select_sub( )**, or **select_underlined( )**. To cancel super- or subscripting, use the **cancel_super_sub( )** function discussed earlier. To cancel underlining, use **cancel_underlined( )**. To activate or deactivate one (or more) of the other features, call **select_mode( )** using the appropriate macro.

These functions are shown here:

```
/* Various mode definitions */
#define WIDE            14
#define CONDENSED       15
#define KILL_CONDENSED  18
#define KILL_WIDE       20
#define EMPHASIZED      69
#define KILL_EMPHASIZED 70
#define BOLD            71
#define KILL_BOLD       72

/* Select underlining. */
void select_underlined(void)
{
  print(27); print(45); print(1); /* enable underlining */
}

/* Cancel underlining. */
void cancel_underlined(void)
{
  print(27); print(45); print(0); /* disable underlining */
}

/* Select superscript mode. */
```

```
void select_superscript(void)
{
  print(27); print(83); print(0);
}

/* Select subscript mode. */
void select_subscript(void)
{
  print(27); print(83); print(1);
}

/* Set a mode. */
void select_mode(unsigned char mode)
{
  print(27); print(mode);
}
```

A Text Features Demonstration Program

The following program contains all the text functions just described. The output from the program is shown in Figure 9-1.

```
/* Printer control subsystem for Epson dot-matrix
   printers (and compatibles): Text functions and
   demonstration program.
*/

#define TURBOC
/* If you use Microsoft C, define MICROSOFTC instead
   of TURBOC.  If you use a different C compiler, refer
   to the text.
*/

#include "stdio.h"
#include "stdlib.h"
#include "bios.h"

#define ON 1
#define OFF 0
#define DRAFT 0
#define NLQ 1
```

```
/* Various mode definitions */
#define WIDE                14
#define CONDENSED           15
#define KILL_CONDENSED      18
#define KILL_WIDE           20
#define EMPHASIZED          69
#define KILL_EMPHASIZED     70
#define BOLD                71
#define KILL_BOLD           72
```

Figure 9-1

The output from the text features demonstration program

```
This is normal.
This is condensed.
This is normal, again.
This is condensed, again.
This is wide.
This is italic.
This is emphasized.
This is in bold.
this is in elite
This is a test of superscripted subscripted text.
This is wide and bold.
Super- and subscripts make mathematical symbols easy: X² * N₁
This line is underlined
This line isn't underlined.
This is NLQ.
This is draft.
Six lines per inch:
x
x
x
x
x
x
8 lines per inch:
x
x
x
x
x
x
About 10 lines per inch:
x
x
x
x
x
About 20 lines per inch:
x
x
x
```

```
void print(char ch);
void print_condensed(char *s);
void print_wide(char *s), print_str(char *s);
void print_italic(char *s), print_emphasized(char *s);
void print_bold(char *s), print_underlined(char *s);
void print_super(char *s), print_sub(char *s);

void select_pica(void), select_elite(void);
void select_superscript(void), select_subscript(void);
void cancel_super_sub(void), select_style(char mode);
void select_6(void), select_8(void), select_72(char num);
void select_7_72(void), select_216(char num);
void select_underlined(void), cancel_underlined(void);
void select_mode(unsigned char mode);
void reset(void);

main()
{
  int i;

  print_str("This is normal.\n");
  print_condensed("This is condensed.\n");
  print_str("This is normal, again.\n");
  print_condensed("This is condensed, again.\n");
  print_wide("This is wide.\n");
  print_italic("This is italic.\n");
  print_emphasized("This is emphasized.\n");
  print_bold("This is in bold.\n");

  select_elite();
  print_str("this is in elite\n");
  select_pica();

  print_str("This is a test of ");
  select_superscript();
  print_str("superscripted");
  select_subscript();
  print_str("subscripted ");
  cancel_super_sub();
  print_str("text.\n");
```

```
   select_mode(WIDE);
   select_mode(BOLD);
   print_str("This is wide and bold.\n");
   select_mode(KILL_BOLD);
   select_mode(KILL_WIDE);

   print_str("Super- and subscripts make mathematical ");
   print_str("symbols easy: ");
   print_str("X");
   print_super("2");
   print_str(" * N");
   print_sub("i\n");

   print_underlined("This line is underlined\n");
   print_str("This line isn't underlined.\n");

   select_style(NLQ);
   print_str("This is NLQ.\n");
   select_style(DRAFT);
   print_str("This is draft.\n");

   select_6();
   print_str("Six lines per inch:\n");
   for(i=0; i<6; i++) print_str("x\n");

   select_8();
   print_str("8 lines per inch:\n");
   for(i=0; i<6; i++) print_str("x\n");

   select_7_72();
   print_str("About 10 lines per inch:\n");
   for(i=0; i<6; i++) print_str("x\n");

   print_str("About 20 lines per inch:\n");
   select_216(10);
   for(i=0; i<6; i++) print_str("x\n");
   reset();
}

/* Print a string in condensed format. */
void print_condensed(char *s)
{
  print(27); print(15);
```

```
  print_str(s);
  print(18);  /* cancel condensed */
}

/* Print a string in wide format. */
void print_wide(char *s)
{
  print(27); print(14);
  print_str(s);
  print(20);
}

/* Print a string in italics. */
void print_italic(char *s)
{
  print(27); print(52); /* enable italics */
  print_str(s);
  print(27); print(53); /* disable italics */
}

/* Print a string in emphasized type. */
void print_emphasized(char *s)
{
  print(27); print(69); /* enable emphasized */
  print_str(s);
  print(27); print(70); /* disable emphasized */
}

/* Print a string in bold. */
void print_bold(char *s)
{
  print(27); print(71); /* enable bold */
  print_str(s);
  print(27); print(72); /* disable bold */
}

/* Print an underlined string. */
void print_underlined(char *s)
{
  print(27); print(45); print(1); /* enable underlining */
  print_str(s);
  print(27); print(45); print(0); /* disable underlining */
}
```

```
/* Select underlining. */
void select_underlined(void)
{
  print(27); print(45); print(1); /* enable underlining */
}

/* Cancel underlining. */
void cancel_underlined(void)
{
  print(27); print(45); print(0); /* disable underlining */
}

/* Select elite type font. */
void select_elite(void)
{
  print(27); print(77);
}

/* Select pica type font. */
void select_pica(void)
{
  print(27); print(80);
}

/* Select superscript mode. */
void select_superscript(void)
{
  print(27); print(83); print(0);
}

/* Select subscript mode. */
void select_subscript(void)
{
  print(27); print(83); print(1);
}

/* Print a string in superscript. */
void print_super(char *s)
{
  select_superscript();
  print_str(s);
  cancel_super_sub();
```

```
}

/* Print a string in subscript. */
void print_sub(char *s)
{
  select_subscript();
  print_str(s);
  cancel_super_sub();
}

/* Cancel super- or subscript mode. */
void cancel_super_sub(void)
{
  print(27); print(84);
}

/* If mode is 0, print in draft (fast printing) mode.
   If mode is 1, print in near-letter-quality (NLQ)
   style.
*/
void select_style(char mode)
{
  print(27); print(120); print(mode);
}

/* Select 8 lines per inch. */
void select_8(void)
{
  print(27); print(48);
}

/* Select 6 lines per inch (default). */
void select_6(void)
{
  print(27); print(50);
}

/* Select 7/72 line spacing. */
void select_7_72(void)
{
  print(27); print(49);
}
```

```c
/* Select num/72 line spacing */
void select_72(char num)
{
  print(27); print(65), print(num);
}


/* Select num/216 line spacing. */
void select_216(char num)
{
  print(27); print(51); print(num);
}


/* Reset the printer to defaults. */
void reset(void)
{
  print(27); print(64);
}


/* Set a mode. */
void select_mode(unsigned char mode)
{
  print(27); print(mode);
}


/* Send a string to the printer */
void print_str(char *s)
{
  while(*s) {
    print(*s);
    s++;
  }
}


/* Send a character to the printer. */
void print(char ch)
{
#ifdef TURBOC
  biosprint(0, ch, 0);
#endif
#ifdef MICROSOFTC
  _bios_printer(0, 0, ch);
#endif
}
```

USING THE GRAPHICS MODES

The Epson line of dot-matrix printers allows the printing of graphics images. A graphics image is built dot-by-dot by sending special eight-bit codes. In the most common graphics modes, each bit in an eight-bit code corresponds to a pin on the print head. Thus, while in a graphics mode, each value sent to the printer effects a vertical, eight-dot column. To print a graphics image you send the printer a sequence of eight-bit values that correspond to the bit patterns used to construct an image.

Graphics images can be printed using three different horizontal densities. The lowest density prints 60 dots per inch. Double density prints 120 dots per inch, and quad density prints 240 dots per inch. The density you use is determined, in part, by the application. Remember that it takes twice as long to print a double-density image as it does a single-density one and four times as long to print a quad-density image. Therefore, it is to your advantage to use the lowest density that will meet your needs.

The graphics modes work a little differently than the text modes: when you select a graphics mode, you must tell the printer how many columns of information you will be sending it. (Each column is eight dots tall.) After you send the information, the printer *automatically reverts to text mode.* Therefore, to print a graphics image, you must continually reenter the desired graphics mode.

Once the graphics mode has been entered and the number of columns of graphics information specified, the next characters received are treated by the printer as graphics information, not characters, and the printer fires the pins of the print head according to the bit pattern of each byte. When a bit is set (1), the pin fires; if a bit is cleared (0), the pin is not fired. The lowest pin on the head corresponds to bit 0, the highest pin to bit 7. Therefore, when the printer receives the value 131, for example, it fires pins 0, 1, and 7, producing a column that looks like this:

```
pin 7 *
    6
    5
    4
    3
    2
    1 *
    0 *
```

In single-density graphics, there are 480 columns per page, assuming an eight-inch page. In double-density graphics, there are 960 columns per page; in quad-density graphics there are 1920 columns per page. When activating a graphics mode, you must specify the number of columns to be printed as graphics. Since this number may exceed 255, you will need to send the printer an integer. However, you can only send the printer eight bits at a time, so the integer must be sent in two pieces, with the low-order byte first and the high-order byte last.

The command sequence to set the printer to a graphics mode is shown here:

Sequence	Mode
27 75 *arg1 arg2*	single-density graphics
27 76 *arg1 arg2*	double-density graphics
27 90 *arg1 arg2*	quad-density graphics

Here, *arg1* is the low-order byte of the number of columns and *arg2* is the high-order byte.

Before you can use a graphics mode to print an image, you will need to change the line spacing to 8/72 inch. By default, the printer leaves a gap between lines. This is obviously undesirable for graphics images. The pins on the print head are 1/72 inch apart, so an eight-pin column occupies 8/72 inch. By setting the line spacing to 8/72 inch, you can print a graphics image that has no breaks in it. Keep in mind one point: to advance to a new line, you must issue a carriage-return/linefeed sequence. A carriage-return/linefeed sequence is not automatically performed at the end of a row of graphics output.

The functions **select_single_graphics( )**, **select_double_graphics( )**, and **select_quad_graphics( )**, shown here, activate the indicated graphics modes.

```
/* Select single-density graphics.  Specify number of
   columns in cols. */
void set_single_graphics(int cols)
{
  union {
    unsigned char c[2];
    unsigned int i;
  } u;
```

```
  u.i = cols;

  print(27); print(65); print(8); /* 8/72 line spacing */
  print(27); print(75); print(u.c[0]); print(u.c[1]);
}

/* Select double-density graphics.  Specify
   number of columns in cols. */
void set_double_graphics(int cols)
{
  union {
    unsigned char c[2];
    unsigned int i;
  } u;

  u.i = cols;

  print(27); print(65); print(8); /* 8/72 line spacing */
  print(27); print(76); print(u.c[0]); print(u.c[1]);
}

/* Select quad-density graphics.  Specify
   number of columns in cols.
*/
void set_quad_graphics(int cols)
{
  union {
    unsigned char c[2];
    unsigned int i;
  } u;

  u.i = cols;

  print(27); print(65); print(8); /* 8/72 line spacing */
  print(27); print(90); print(u.c[0]); print(u.c[1]);
}
```

Notice how a union is used to split the integer that specifies the number of graphics columns into two parts.

The following program demonstrates these functions by drawing a solid bar, 480 columns wide, in each of the graphics modes.

```
/* Printer Graphics functions for Epson dot-matrix
   printers.
*/

#define TURBOC
/* If you use Microsoft C, define MICROSOFTC instead
   of TURBOC.  If you use a different C compiler, refer
   to the text.
*/

#include "stdio.h"
#include "stdlib.h"
#include "bios.h"

void print(char ch);
void set_single_graphics(int cols);
void set_double_graphics(int cols);
void set_quad_graphics(int cols);
void reset(void);

main()
{
  int i;

  set_single_graphics(480);
  for(i=0; i<480; i++) print(255);

  /* draw two bars in double-density graphics */
  set_double_graphics(480);
  for(i=0; i<480; i++) print(255);
  print('\n');
  reset();
  set_double_graphics(480);
  for(i=0; i<480; i++) print(255);
  print('\n');

  set_quad_graphics(480);
  for(i=0; i<480; i++) print(255);
  print('\n');
  reset();
}

/* Select single-density graphics.  Specify number of
```

```
   columns in cols. */
void set_single_graphics(int cols)
{
  union {
    unsigned char c[2];
    unsigned int i;
  } u;

  u.i = cols;

  print(27); print(65); print(8); /* 8/72 line spacing */
  print(27); print(75); print(u.c[0]); print(u.c[1]);
}

/* Select double-density graphics.  Specify
   number of columns in cols. */
void set_double_graphics(int cols)
{
  union {
    unsigned char c[2];
    unsigned int i;
  } u;

  u.i = cols;

  print(27); print(65); print(8); /* 8/72 line spacing */
  print(27); print(76); print(u.c[0]); print(u.c[1]);
}

/* Select quad-density graphics.  Specify
   number of columns in cols.
*/
void set_quad_graphics(int cols)
{
  union {
    unsigned char c[2];
    unsigned int i;
  } u;

  u.i = cols;

  print(27); print(65); print(8); /* 8/72 line spacing */
  print(27); print(90); print(u.c[0]); print(u.c[1]);
```

```
}

/* Reset the printer to defaults. */
void reset(void)
{
  print(27); print(64);
}

/* Send a character to the printer. */
void print(char ch)
{
#ifdef TURBOC
  biosprint(0, ch, 0);
#endif
#ifdef MICROSOFTC
  _bios_printer(0, 0, ch);
#endif
}
```

CREATING A CUSTOM PRINT-SCREEN UTILITY

You will have numerous occasions when you want an application program to print a graphics image that is on the screen. Although it is possible to execute an INT 5 instruction (which calls the DOS print-screen function) from within a program, this solution is often unsatisfactory for three important reasons. First, for the DOS print-screen feature to work properly with a graphics image, the GRAPHICS command must have been issued previously by the user. (There is no easy way to know if this command has been issued.) Second, the DOS print-screen function prints the entire screen; however, you may want to print only a portion of the screen. Finally, you may want to print a screen image at a specific location on the page. The solution to these problems is to create your own print-screen utility. As you will see, this is really quite easy.

Printing the screen requires that each pixel be read from the screen, and if that pixel is lit, a corresponding dot is printed on the page. If the pixel is off, the dot is not printed. This approach prints black and white images as they appear on the screen, or transforms a color image into black and white for printing. Since the printer needs to be sent graphics information in eight-dot columns, you must read eight pixels at a time from the screen.

The **print_scr( )** function, shown here, prints the portion of the screen specified by the first four parameters. It prints the image on the page beginning at the location specified by **pagex** and **pagey**. This location is specified in terms of characters by lines. For example, if you want to start printing the image on the fourteenth line, 20 characters from the left margin, you would specify **20, 14** for **pagex, pagey**. Finally, **print_scr( )** uses the graphics mode specified in **density**. You should use the macros **SINGLE**, **DOUBLE**, and **QUAD** as values for **density**.

```
#define SINGLE 0
#define DOUBLE 1
#define QUAD   2

/* This function prints the specified screen region at the
   specified page location.

   Startx,starty are the coordinates of the upper left
   corner of the region of the screen to print; endx,endy
   specify the lower right corner.

   The starting location of the page to print the image
   is specified by pagex,pagey. The horizontal page
   location is in characters; the vertical is in lines
   (1/6"). Upper left corner of page is 0, 0.

   The graphics density is specified by the density
   parameter.
*/
void print_scr(int startx, int starty, int endx, int endy,
               int pagex, int pagey, int density)
{
  register int i, x, y, px;
  int cols, color, sum;

  endx++;  endy++;
  cols = endx - startx;

  for(; pagey>=0; pagey--) print('\n');

  for(y = starty; y<endy; y+=8) {
    for(px=0; px<pagex; px++) print(' ');
    set_graphics(cols, density);
```

```
   for(x = startx; x<endx; x++) {
     sum = 0;
     for(i=0; i<8; i++) {
       if(y+i < endy) {
         color = getpoint(x, y+i);
         if(color) sum += 1<<(7-i);
       }
     }
     print(sum);
   }
   print('\n');
 }
}
```

It is important to understand that **print_scr( )** does not check to see if the image you want printed will fit on the page at the location you specify. You must ensure this prior to calling it. (There is no reliable way for the function to know where the print head is actually located. Your program must keep track of this manually.)

The **set_graphics( )** function activates the specified density. It is shown here:

```
/* Set the graphics density as specified. */
void set_graphics(int cols, int density)
{
  union {
    unsigned char c[2];
    unsigned int i;
  } u;
  char den_code;

  u.i = cols;

  switch(density) {
    case SINGLE: den_code = 75;
      break;
    case DOUBLE: den_code = 76;
      break;
    case QUAD: den_code = 90;
      break;
  }
```

```
  print(27); print(65); print(8); /* 8/72 line spacing */
  print(27); print(den_code); print(u.c[0]); print(u.c[1]);
}
```

If you know that you will always be using the same graphics density, you can use one of the other functions developed earlier and eliminate the overhead of the **density** parameter to **print_scr( )**.

The following demonstration program draws several boxes on the screen, then prints a portion of the screen using each graphics density. The output of this program is shown in Figure 9-2. This program uses video mode 16, which requires an EGA or VGA video adapter. You can use a different mode if you like, but you may have to adjust the size of the boxes and the region being printed if you use a lower-resolution mode.

```
/* A print-screen utility that can be called from
   your application programs.  (Shown here with
   a main() function for demonstration purposes.)

   It also allows you to specify the graphics density
   you desire.
*/

#define TURBOC
/*  If you use Microsoft C, define MICROSOFTC instead
    of TURBOC.  If you use a different C compiler, refer
    to the text.
*/

#include "stdio.h"
#include "stdlib.h"
#include "bios.h"
#include "dos.h"

/* These values work for video graphics mode 16;
   you may need to change them for other modes.
*/
#define RED 12
#define GREEN 10
#define WHITE 15

/* These definitions are mode 16 graphics only */
#define XDIM 639
```

Figure 9-2

Output from the print screen sample program

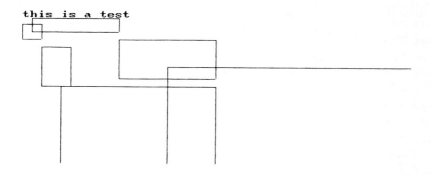

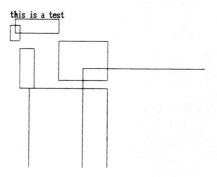

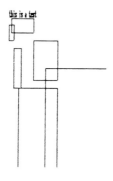

```
#define YDIM 349

#define SINGLE 0
#define DOUBLE 1
#define QUAD   2

void print(char ch);
void set_graphics(int cols, int density);
void reset(void);

void print_scr(int startx, int starty, int endx, int endy,
               int pagex, int pagey, int density);

void mode(int mode_code);
void putpoint(int x, int y, int color, int how);
char getpoint(int x, int y);
char getkey(void);

void box(int startx, int starty,
         int endx, int endy, int color, int how);

char far *egabase;

main()
{
#ifdef TURBOC
  egabase = (char far *) MK_FP(0xA000, 0000);
#endif
#ifdef MICROSOFTC
  egabase = (char far *) 0xA0000000;
#endif

  mode(16);

  printf("this is a test");
  box(0, 20, 20, 40, WHITE, 0);
  box(20, 50, 50, 100, WHITE, 0);
  box(10, 12, 100, 30, WHITE, 0);
  box(40, 100, 200, 300, WHITE, 0);
  box(100, 40, 200, 90, WHITE, 0);
  box(150, 75, 500, 250, WHITE, 0);

  print_scr(0, 0, 400, 200, 0, 5, SINGLE);
```

```
    print_scr(0, 0, 400, 200, 40, 5, DOUBLE);
    print_scr(0, 0, 400, 200, 20, 5, QUAD);
    reset();
    mode(3);
}


/* This function prints the specified screen region at the
   specified page location.

   Startx,starty are the coordinates of the upper left
   corner of the region of the screen to print; endx,endy
   specify the lower right corner.

   The starting location of the page to print the image
   is specified by pagex,pagey. The horizontal page
   location is in characters; the vertical is in lines
   (1/6"). Upper left corner of page is 0, 0.

   The graphics density is specified by the density
   parameter.
*/
void print_scr(int startx, int starty, int endx, int endy,
               int pagex, int pagey, int density)
{
    register int i, x, y, px;
    int cols, color, sum;

    endx++;  endy++;
    cols = endx - startx;

    for(; pagey>=0; pagey--) print('\n');

    for(y = starty; y<endy; y+=8) {
      for(px=0; px<pagex; px++) print(' ');
      set_graphics(cols, density);
      for(x = startx; x<endx; x++) {
        sum = 0;
        for(i=0; i<8; i++) {
          if(y+i < endy) {
            color = getpoint(x, y+i);
            if(color) sum += 1<<(7-i);
          }
        }
```

```
      print(sum);
    }
    print('\n');
  }
}

/* Set the graphics density as specified. */
void set_graphics(int cols, int density)
{
  union {
    unsigned char c[2];
    unsigned int i;
  } u;
  char den_code;

  u.i = cols;

  switch(density) {
    case SINGLE: den_code = 75;
      break;
    case DOUBLE: den_code = 76;
      break;
    case QUAD: den_code = 90;
      break;
  }

  print(27); print(65); print(8); /* 8/72 line spacing */
  print(27); print(den_code); print(u.c[0]); print(u.c[1]);
}

/* Reset the printer to defaults. */
void reset(void)
{
  print(27); print(64);
}

/* Send a character to the printer. */
void print(char ch)
{
#ifdef TURBOC
  biosprint(0, ch, 0);
#endif
#ifdef MICROSOFTC
```

```
  _bios_printer(0, 0, ch);
#endif
}


/**************************************************
 Video functions
**************************************************/

/* Set the video mode. */
void mode(int mode_code)
{
  union REGS r;

  r.h.al = mode_code;
  r.h.ah = 0;
  int86(0x10, &r, &r);
}


/* Returns the value at the specified pixel. */
char getpoint(int x, int y)
{
  union REGS r;

  r.h.ah = 13;
  r.x.dx = y;
  r.x.cx = x;
  r.h.bh = 0;
  int86(16, &r, &r);
  return r.h.al;
}


/* This version of putpoint will work for all video
   adapters but is incredibly slow!
*/
/*
void putpoint(int x, int y, int color, int how)
{
  union REGS r;

  if(how==0x18) color = color | 128;
  r.h.bh = 0;
  r.h.ah = 12;
  r.h.al = color;
```

```
  r.x.dx = y;
  r.x.cx = x;
  int86(16, &r, &r);
}
*/

/* This function sets the specified pixel to the
   specified color using an EGA/VGA video adapter.
   The value of how may be one of these:

   action          value

   overwrite        0
   XOR              0x18
   AND              8
   OR               0x10

*/
#define ENABLE 0x0F
#define INDEXREG 0x3CE
#define VALREG 0x3CF

/* Note: Borland does not document outp(), but it is
   in the library of Turbo C 2.0.  The documented function
   is called outport(), but it runs much slower.  However,
   in future versions you may need to use outport().
   For this reason, the following conditional compilation
   directives have been included.
*/
#ifdef TURBOC
#define OUTINDEX(index, val) outp((INDEXREG), (index));\
                             outp((VALREG), (val));
#endif
#ifdef MICROSOFTC
#define OUTINDEX(index, val) outp((INDEXREG), (index));\
                             outp((VALREG), (val));
#endif

#define WIDTH 80L

/* These range values assume EGA mode 16 */
#define XMAX 639
#define YMAX 349
```

```c
#define XMIN 0
#define YMIN 0

void putpoint(int x, int y, int color, int how)
{
  register unsigned char mask = 0x80;
  register char far *base;
  unsigned dummy;

  /* If you want range checking at this point, activate
     this line of code.  It will slow down the function,
     however.
  */
  /*if(x<XMIN || x>XMAX || y<YMIN || y>YMAX) return;*/

  base = (char far *) (egabase
        + ( (long) y * WIDTH + (long) x/8L ));

  mask >>= x % 8;

  /* This causes the memory READ necessary to
     load the EGA/VGA's internal registers.
  */
  dummy = *base;

  OUTINDEX(0, color);
  OUTINDEX(1, ENABLE);
  OUTINDEX(3, how);
  OUTINDEX(8, mask);

  *base = 1;

  OUTINDEX(0, 0);
  OUTINDEX(1, 0);
  OUTINDEX(3, 0);
  OUTINDEX(8, 0xff);
}

/* Draw a box in the foreground color. The
   how parameter determines how the box will
   be displayed on the screen.  See putpoint()
   for details.
*/
```

```
void box(int startx, int starty,
         int endx, int endy, int color, int how)
{
  register int x, y;

  for(x=startx; x<endx; x++)
    putpoint(x, endy, color, how);
  for(y=starty; y<endy; y++)
    putpoint(endx, y, color, how);
  for(x=startx; x<endx; x++)
    putpoint(x, starty, color, how);
  for(y=starty; y<endy; y++)
    putpoint(startx, y, color, how);
}

/* Return the scan code of the key pressed.
   This function is compatible with Turbo C and
   Microsoft C (be sure to #define the appropriate
   symbol).  If you use a different compiler, consult
   the text.
*/
char getkey(void)
{
  union key {
    int i;
    char ch[2];
  } k;

#ifdef TURBOC
  k.i = bioskey(0);
#endif
#ifdef MICROSOFTC
  k.i = _bios_keybrd(0);
#endif
  return k.ch[1];
}
```

You can tell by comparing what is on the screen to what is printed that the double-density graphics mode most accurately depicts the screen image in this example. The best graphics mode is determined by matching as closely as possible the resolution of the screen graphics mode with the resolution of the printer graphics mode.

Enhancing the Print-Screen Utility

We can increase the power of the print-screen utility by letting the user define interactively the rectangular region of the screen to be printed. To accomplish this, the user will define the upper left and lower right corners of the region by moving a small crosshairs-style locator about the screen with the arrow keys. Once the region is defined, the coordinates can be passed to **print_scr( )** for printing.

The function **def_region( )**, shown here, allows the user to define a region of the screen.

```
/* Interactively define a region using the arrow keys.
   When the locator is at the upper left corner of the
   region you want printed, press F1.  Next, move
   the locator to the lower right corner of the region
   and press F2.  By default, each time you press an arrow
   key, the locator moves 1 pixel.  However, by pressing
   F3, you can cause the locator to move in increments of
   5 pixels.  F3 acts as a toggle, switching between
   increments of 1 and 5 each time it is pressed.

   To print the region, press F4.
*/
void def_region(int *startx, int *starty,
                int *endx, int *endy)
{
  register int x, y;
  char ch;
  int inc;

  inc = 1;

  *startx = *starty = *endx = *endy = 0;
  x = 0; y = 0;
  do {
    /* show a box around the region selected for
       printing
    */
    box(*startx, *starty, *endx, *endy, RED, 0x18);
    locator(x, y, GREEN); /* display locator */
    ch = getkey();
    locator(x, y, GREEN); /* erase locator */
```

```
/* erase box */
box(*startx, *starty, *endx, *endy, RED, 0x18);

switch(ch) {
  case 75: /* left */
    x -= inc;
    break;
  case 77: /* right */
    x += inc;
    break;
  case 72: /* up */
    y -= inc;
    break;
  case 80: /* down */
    y += inc;
    break;
  case 71: /* up left */
    x -= inc; y -= inc;
    break;
  case 73: /* up right */
    x += inc; y -= inc;
    break;
  case 79: /* down left*/
    x -= inc; y += inc;
    break;
  case 81: /* down right */
    x += inc; y += inc;
    break;
  case 59: /* F1 define upper right corner */
    *startx = x;
    *starty = y;
    break;
  case 60: /* F2 - define lower left corner */
    *endx = x;
    *endy = y;
    break;
  case 61: /* F3 - fast/slow */
    if(inc==1) inc = 5;
    else inc = 1;
    break;
}
if(x < 0) x++;  if(x > XDIM-1) x--;
if(y < 0) y++;  if(y > YDIM-1) y--;
```

```
} while(ch != 62); /* F4 - quit */
}
```

The function works like this. The function is passed pointers to four variables, which will receive the coordinate values after the user has defined the region. After various initializations are performed, the function prints a small locator on the screen at the current location by calling **locator( )** and waits for keyboard intput. Each time an arrow key is pressed, the locator is moved in the direction of the arrow key. By default each keypress moves the locator one pixel. This can be quite slow when defining large regions, so, by pressing F3, you can cause the locator to move in increments of five pixels. F3 works as a toggle, so you can return to one-pixel increments by pressing it a second time. When the locator is in the upper left corner of the region you want, press F1. Next, move the locator to the lower right corner, and press F2. You will see a red box drawn around the region you have defined. If this is not the region you want, change it using the procedure just described, and the box will reflect these changes. After the region is defined, press F4, and the region will be printed. (The box will be removed prior to printing.)

The locator consists of a small crosshairs and is generated using the **locator( )** function shown here. Notice that it uses the XOR write mode so that it can be moved about the screen without destroying the current contents of any location.

```
/* Display a small crosshairs-style locator
   using XOR mode. */
void locator(int x, int y, int color)
{
  putpoint(x, y, color, 0x18);
  putpoint(x+1, y, color, 0x18);
  putpoint(x-1, y, color, 0x18);
  putpoint(x, y+1, color, 0x18);
  putpoint(x, y-1, color, 0x18);
}
```

The entire improved print-screen program is shown here. It prints the defined region in all three densities, but you will probably want to use only one density for actual applications.

```
/* A refined print-screen utility that can be called from
   your application programs.  (Shown here with
   a main() function for demonstration purposes.)

   This version allows you to interactively specify
   a region of the screen to be printed by using
   the cursor keys.

   It also allows you to specify the graphics density
   you desire.
*/

#define TURBOC
/*  If you use Microsoft C, define MICROSOFTC instead
    of TURBOC.  If you use a different C compiler, refer
    to the text.
*/

#include "stdio.h"
#include "stdlib.h"
#include "bios.h"
#include "dos.h"

/* These values work for video graphics mode 16;
   you may need to change them for other modes.
*/
#define RED 12
#define GREEN 10
#define WHITE 15

/* these values are from mode 16 graphics only */
#define XDIM 639
#define YDIM 349

#define SINGLE_WIDTH 480
#define DOUBLE_WIDTH 960
#define QUAD_WIDTH   1920

#define SINGLE 0
#define DOUBLE 1
#define QUAD   2

void print(char ch);
```

```c
void set_graphics(int cols, int density);
void reset(void);

void print_scr(int startx, int starty, int endx, int endy,
               int pagex, int pagey, int density);

void mode(int mode_code);
void putpoint(int x, int y, int color, int how);
char getpoint(int x, int y);
char getkey(void);

void box(int startx, int starty,
         int endx, int endy, int color, int how);

void def_region(int *startx, int *starty,
                int *endx, int *endy);
void locator(int x, int y, int color);

char far *egabase;

main()
{
  int startx, starty, endx, endy;

#ifdef TURBOC
  egabase = (char far *) MK_FP(0xA000, 0000);
#endif
#ifdef MICROSOFTC
  egabase = (char far *) 0xA0000000;
#endif

  mode(16);

  printf("this is a test");
  box(0, 20, 20, 40, WHITE, 0);
  box(20, 50, 50, 100, WHITE, 0);
  box(10, 12, 100, 30, WHITE, 0);
  box(40, 100, 200, 300, WHITE, 0);
  box(100, 40, 200, 90, WHITE, 0);
  box(150, 75, 500, 250, WHITE, 0);

  def_region(&startx, &starty, &endx, &endy);
  print_scr(startx, starty, endx, endy, 0, 0, SINGLE);
```

```
  print_scr(startx, starty, endx, endy, 0, 0, DOUBLE);
  print_scr(startx, starty, endx, endy, 0, 0, QUAD);
  reset();
  mode(3);
}

/* This function prints the specified screen region at the
   specified page location.

   Startx,starty are the coordinates of the upper left
   corner of the region of the screen to print; endx,endy
   specify the lower right corner.

   The starting location of the page to print the image
   is specified by pagex,pagey. The horizontal page
   location is in characters; the vertical is in lines
   (1/6").  Upper left corner of page is 0, 0.

   The graphics density is specified by the density
   parameter.
*/
void print_scr(int startx, int starty, int endx, int endy,
               int pagex, int pagey, int density)
{
  register int i, x, y, px;
  int cols, color, sum;

  endx++;  endy++;
  cols = endx - startx;

  for(; pagey>=0; pagey--) print('\n');

  for(y = starty; y<endy; y+=8) {
    for(px=0; px<pagex; px++) print(' ');
    set_graphics(cols, density);
    for(x = startx; x<endx; x++) {
      sum = 0;
      for(i=0; i<8; i++) {
        if(y+i < endy) {
          color = getpoint(x, y+i);
          if(color) sum += 1<<(7-i);
        }
      }
```

```
      print(sum);
    }
    print('\n');
  }
}


/* Interactively define a region using the arrow keys.
   When the locator is at the upper left corner of the
   region you want printed, press F1.  Next, move
   the locator to the lower right corner of the region
   and press F2.  By default, each time you press an arrow
   key, the locator moves 1 pixel.  However, by pressing
   F3, you can cause the locator to move in increments of
   5 pixels.  F3 acts as a toggle, switching between
   increments of 1 and 5 each time it is pressed.

   To print the region, press F4.
*/
void def_region(int *startx, int *starty,
                int *endx, int *endy)
{
  register int x, y;
  char ch;
  int inc;

  inc = 1;

  *startx = *starty = *endx = *endy = 0;
  x = 0; y = 0;
  do {
    /* show a box around the region selected for
       printing
    */
    box(*startx, *starty, *endx, *endy, RED, 0x18);
    locator(x, y, GREEN); /* display locator */
    ch = getkey();
    locator(x, y, GREEN); /* erase locator */
    /* erase box */
    box(*startx, *starty, *endx, *endy, RED, 0x18);

    switch(ch) {
      case 75: /* left */
        x -= inc;
```

```
        break;
      case 77: /* right */
        x += inc;
        break;
      case 72: /* up */
        y -= inc;
        break;
      case 80: /* down */
        y += inc;
        break;
      case 71: /* up left */
        x -= inc; y -= inc;
        break;
      case 73: /* up right */
        x += inc; y -= inc;
        break;
      case 79: /* down left*/
        x -= inc; y += inc;
        break;
      case 81: /* down right */
        x += inc; y += inc;
        break;
      case 59: /* F1 define upper right corner */
        *startx = x;
        *starty = y;
        break;
      case 60: /* F2 - define lower left corner */
        *endx = x;
        *endy = y;
        break;
      case 61: /* F3 - fast/slow */
        if(inc==1) inc = 5;
        else inc = 1;
        break;
    }
    if(x < 0) x++;  if(x > XDIM-1) x--;
    if(y < 0) y++;  if(y > YDIM-1) y--;

  } while(ch != 62); /* F4 - quit */
}

/* Display a small crosshairs-style locator
   using XOR mode. */
```

```
void locator(int x, int y, int color)
{
  putpoint(x, y, color, 0x18);
  putpoint(x+1, y, color, 0x18);
  putpoint(x-1, y, color, 0x18);
  putpoint(x, y+1, color, 0x18);
  putpoint(x, y-1, color, 0x18);
}

/* Set the graphics density as specified. */
void set_graphics(int cols, int density)
{
  union {
    unsigned char c[2];
    unsigned int i;
  } u;
  char den_code;

  u.i = cols;

  switch(density) {
    case SINGLE: den_code = 75;
      break;
    case DOUBLE: den_code = 76;
      break;
    case QUAD: den_code = 90;
      break;
  }

  print(27); print(65); print(8); /* 8/72 line spacing */
  print(27); print(den_code); print(u.c[0]); print(u.c[1]);
}

/* Reset the printer to defaults. */
void reset(void)
{
  print(27); print(64);
}

/* Send a character to the printer. */
void print(char ch)
{
#ifdef TURBOC
```

```
  biosprint(0, ch, 0);
#endif
#ifdef MICROSOFTC
  _bios_printer(0, 0, ch);
#endif
}


/***************************************************
 Video functions
***************************************************/

/* Set the video mode. */
void mode(int mode_code)
{
  union REGS r;

  r.h.al = mode_code;
  r.h.ah = 0;
  int86(0x10, &r, &r);
}

/* Returns the value at the specified pixel. */
char getpoint(int x, int y)
{
  union REGS r;

  r.h.ah = 13;
  r.x.dx = y;
  r.x.cx = x;
  r.h.bh = 0;
  int86(16, &r, &r);
  return r.h.al;
}

/* This version of putpoint will work for all video
   adapters but is incredibly slow!
*/
/*
void putpoint(int x, int y, int color, int how)
{
  union REGS r;

  if(how==0x18) color = color | 128;
```

```
   r.h.bh = 0;
   r.h.ah = 12;
   r.h.al = color;
   r.x.dx = y;
   r.x.cx = x;
   int86(16, &r, &r);
}
*/

/* This function sets the specified pixel to the
   specified color using an EGA/VGA video adapter.
   The value of how may be one of these:

   action          value

   overwrite       0
   XOR             0x18
   AND             8
   OR              0x10

*/
#define ENABLE 0x0F
#define INDEXREG 0x3CE
#define VALREG 0x3CF

/* Note: Borland does not document outp(), but it is
   in the library of Turbo C 2.0.  The documented function
   is called outport(), but it runs much slower.  However,
   in future versions you may need to use outport() instead.
   For this reason, the following conditional compilation
   directives have been included.
*/
#ifdef TURBOC
#define OUTINDEX(index, val) outp((INDEXREG), (index));\
                             outp((VALREG), (val));

#endif
#ifdef MICROSOFTC
#define OUTINDEX(index, val) outp((INDEXREG), (index));\
                             outp((VALREG), (val));

#endif

#define WIDTH 80L
```

```
/* These range values assume EGA mode 16 */
#define XMAX 639
#define YMAX 349
#define XMIN 0
#define YMIN 0

void putpoint(int x, int y, int color, int how)
{
  register unsigned char mask = 0x80;
  register char far *base;
  unsigned dummy;

  /* If you want range checking at this point, activate
     this line of code.  It will slow down the function,
     however.
  */
  /*if(x<XMIN || x>XMAX || y<YMIN || y>YMAX) return;*/

  base = (char far *) (egabase
          + ( (long) y * WIDTH + (long) x/8L ));

  mask >>= x % 8;

  /* This causes the memory READ necessary to
     load the EGA/VGA's internal registers.
  */
  dummy = *base;

  OUTINDEX(0, color);
  OUTINDEX(1, ENABLE);
  OUTINDEX(3, how);
  OUTINDEX(8, mask);

  *base = 1;

  OUTINDEX(0, 0);
  OUTINDEX(1, 0);
  OUTINDEX(3, 0);
  OUTINDEX(8, 0xff);
}
```

```
/* Draw a box in the foreground color. The
   how parameter determines how the box will
   be displayed on the screen.  See putpoint()
   for details.
*/
void box(int startx, int starty,
         int endx, int endy, int color, int how)
{
  register int x, y;

  for(x=startx; x<endx; x++)
    putpoint(x, endy, color, how);
  for(y=starty; y<endy; y++)
    putpoint(endx, y, color, how);
  for(x=startx; x<endx; x++)
    putpoint(x, starty, color, how);
  for(y=starty; y<endy; y++)
    putpoint(startx, y, color, how);
}


/* Return the scan code of the key pressed.
   This function is compatible with Turbo C and
   Microsoft C (be sure to #define the appropriate
   symbol).  If you use a different compiler, consult
   the text.
*/
char getkey(void)
{
  union key {
    int i;
    char ch[2];
  } k;

#ifdef TURBOC
  k.i = bioskey(0);
#endif
#ifdef MICROSOFTC
  k.i = _bios_keybrd(0);
#endif
  return k.ch[1];
}
```

CONSTRUCTING GRAPHICS IMAGES IN RAM

While it is very common to want to print a graphics screen image, there are applications in which you may want to construct a graphics image that will only be sent to the printer, never displayed on the screen. For example, you might want to print in its entirety something that fills the page, not just the part of it that can fit on a screen. With a few changes and a couple of additional functions, we can convert the print-screen utility into a print-buffer utility.

In order to construct a graphics image in RAM we will need to create a buffer large enough to hold one pageful of data. Since, as far as this chapter is concerned, all images are printed in black and white (no gray scale is supported), we can use a single bit to hold the value of one dot on the page. Therefore, there will be a one-to-one correspondence between the bits in the buffer and the dots on the page. In single-density graphics there are 480 dots per line. At a line spacing of 8/72 inch, approximately 792 dots fit vertically on a page. Since one byte can hold the values for eight dots, we will need $480 \times 792 / 8$ (or 47,520) bytes to store a complete-page image in single-density mode. The dimensions of the page in terms of dots are 480×792. For the higher-density modes, the number of bytes exceeds 64K, and you must use a large data memory model. For the example developed here, the single-density mode is used and the small memory model will still work. (For information on C's 8086-related memory models, refer to Appendix A.)

To allow an easy way to access the buffer, two special buffer functions are created. To write a dot into the buffer, use the **putbuf( )** function, shown here:

```
/* Write a value to the specified buffer
   at the specified location.
*/
void putbuf(char *buf, int x, int y, int val)
{
  /* compute correct byte */
  buf += y * 60;
  buf += x / 8;

  val &= 1;  /* zero all but the low-order bit */

  /* write correct bit within byte */
```

```
  if(val) *buf |= val << (x % 8); /* write a 1 */
  else *buf &= val << (x % 8); /* write a 0 */
}
```

This function determines the correct byte and bit within the byte to modify. All other bits of the affected byte remain unchanged. This function writes 1 if the value of **val** is 1 and 0 otherwise. If **val** has any other value, unpredictable results will occur. The buffer that the function uses is specified by the **buf** parameter, which must point to the start of the buffer. The parameters X and Y specify the coordinate of the bit to modify assuming a 480 x 792 matrix.

To read a bit from the buffer, use **getbuf( )**, shown here:

```
/* Read value from the specified buffer at the
   specified location.
*/
unsigned char getbuf(char *buf, int x, int y)
{
  unsigned char mask;

  mask = 1;

  /* compute correct byte */
  buf += y * 60;
  buf += x / 8;

  mask <<= x % 8;  /* set mask for proper bit */
  return (*buf & mask); /* return value */
}
```

This function returns the value of a bit at the specified location from the specified buffer.

To actually send the contents of the buffer to the printer, the **print_scr( )** function is modified to become the **print_buf( )** function, shown here:

```
/* This function prints the specified region of the
   specified buffer at the specified page location.

   Startx,starty are the coordinates of the upper left
   corner of the region of the buffer to print; endx,endy
   specify the lower right corner.
```

The starting location of the page to print the image
is specified by pagex,pagey. The horizontal page
location is in characters; the vertical is in
lines (1/6″). Upper left corner of the page is 0, 0.

The graphics density is specified by the density
parameter.

```
*/
void print_buf(char *buf,
               int startx, int starty, int endx, int endy,
               int pagex, int pagey, int density)
{
  register int i, x, y, px;
  int cols, color, sum;

  endx++;  endy++;
  cols = endx - startx;

  for(; pagey>=0; pagey--) print('\n');

  for(y = starty; y<endy; y+=8) {
    for(px=0; px<pagex; px++) print(' ');
    set_graphics(cols, density);
    for(x = startx; x<endx; x++) {
      sum = 0;
      for(i=0; i<8; i++) {
        if(y+i < endy) {
          color = getbuf(buf, x, y+i);
          if(color) sum += 1<<(7-i);
        }
      }
      print(sum);
    }
    print('\n');
  }
}
```

To see how these functions work, try this sample program, which
constructs several boxes in a buffer, then prints the contents of the buffer.

```
/* This program demonstrates how a graphics image
   can be built in RAM and then printed to the printer.
```

```
*/

#define TURBOC
/*  If you use Microsoft C, define MICROSOFTC instead
    of TURBOC.  If you use a different C compiler, refer
    to the text.
*/

#include "stdio.h"
#include "stdlib.h"
#include "bios.h"
#include "dos.h"

/* These values work for video graphics mode 16;
   you may need to change them for other modes.
*/
#define RED 12
#define GREEN 10
#define WHITE 15

#define XDIM 639
#define YDIM 349

#define SINGLE 0
#define DOUBLE 1
#define QUAD   2

void print(char ch);
void set_graphics(int cols, int density);
void reset(void);

void print_buf(char *buf,
               int startx, int starty, int endx, int endy,
               int pagex, int pagey, int density);

void rambox(char *buf, int startx, int starty,
            int endx, int endy, int color);

void putbuf(char *buf, int x, int y, int val);
unsigned char getbuf(char *buf, int x, int y);

char far *egabase;
```

```
char *buf;

main()
{
  unsigned int i;

#ifdef TURBOC
  egabase = (char far *) MK_FP(0xA000, 0000);
#endif
#ifdef MICROSOFTC
  egabase = (char far *) 0xA0000000;
#endif

  buf = malloc((unsigned)47520);
  if(!buf) exit(1);
  for(i=0; i<(unsigned)47520; i++) buf[i] = 0;

  rambox(buf, 0, 20, 20, 40, 1);
  rambox(buf, 20, 50, 50, 100, 1);
  rambox(buf, 10, 12, 100, 30, 1);
  rambox(buf, 40, 100, 200, 300, 1);
  rambox(buf, 400, 150, 450, 175, 1);
  rambox(buf, 100, 40, 200, 90, 1);
  rambox(buf, 150, 75, 200, 750, 1);

  printf("printing...");

  print_buf(buf, 0, 0, 479, 791, 0, 0, SINGLE);
  reset();
}

/* This function prints the specified region of the
   specified buffer at the specified page location.

   Startx,starty are the coordinates of the upper left
   corner of the region of the buffer to print; endx,endy
   specify the lower right corner.

   The starting location of the page to print the image
   is specified by pagex,pagey. The horizontal page
   location is in characters; the vertical is in
   lines (1/6"). Upper left corner of the page is 0, 0.
```

The graphics density is specified by the density
parameter.

```
*/
void print_buf(char *buf,
               int startx, int starty, int endx, int endy,
               int pagex, int pagey, int density)
{
  register int i, x, y, px;
  int cols, color, sum;

  endx++;   endy++;
  cols = endx - startx;

  for(; pagey>=0; pagey--) print('\n');

  for(y = starty; y<endy; y+=8) {
    for(px=0; px<pagex; px++) print(' ');
    set_graphics(cols, density);
    for(x = startx; x<endx; x++) {
      sum = 0;
      for(i=0; i<8; i++) {
        if(y+i < endy) {
          color = getbuf(buf, x, y+i);
          if(color) sum += 1<<(7-i);
        }
      }
      print(sum);
    }
    print('\n');
  }
}

/* Write a value to the specified buffer
   at the specified location.
*/
void putbuf(char *buf, int x, int y, int val)
{
  /* compute correct byte */
  buf += y * 60;
  buf += x / 8;

  val &= 1;
```

```
  /* write correct bit within byte */
  if(val) *buf |= val << (x % 8); /* write a 1 */
  else *buf &= val << (x%8); /* write a 0 */
}

/* Read value from the specified buffer at the
   specified location.
*/
unsigned char getbuf(char *buf, int x, int y)
{
  unsigned char mask;

  mask = 1;

  /* compute correct byte */
  buf += y * 60;
  buf += x / 8;

  mask <<= x % 8;  /* set mask for proper bit */
  return (*buf & mask); /* return value */
}

/* Set the graphics density as specified. */
void set_graphics(int cols, int density)
{
  union {
    unsigned char c[2];
    unsigned int i;
  } u;
  char den_code;

  u.i = cols;

  switch(density) {
    case SINGLE: den_code = 75;
      break;
    case DOUBLE: den_code = 76;
      break;
    case QUAD: den_code = 90;
      break;
  }
```

```
    print(27); print(65); print(8); /* 8/72 line spacing */
    print(27); print(den_code); print(u.c[0]); print(u.c[1]);
}

/* Reset the printer to defaults. */
void reset(void)
{
  print(27); print(64);
}

/* Send a character to the printer. */
void print(char ch)
{
#ifdef TURBOC
  biosprint(0, ch, 0);
#endif
#ifdef MICROSOFTC
  _bios_printer(0, 0, ch);
#endif
}

/* Construct a box in RAM.
*/
void rambox(char *buf, int startx, int starty,
            int endx, int endy, int color)
{
  register int x, y;

  for(x=startx; x<endx; x++)
    putbuf(buf, x, endy, color);
  for(y=starty; y<endy; y++)
    putbuf(buf, endx, y, color);
  for(x=startx; x<endx; x++)
    putbuf(buf, x, starty, color);
  for(y=starty; y<endy; y++)
    putbuf(buf, startx, y, color);
}
```

C's Memory Models

Memory models are among C's most confusing aspects when implemented for the 8086 family of processors. You can compile a C program using one of six different memory models defined by the 8086 family of processors. (C may not have this ability on other types of processors.) Each model organizes the memory of the computer differently and governs the size of the code or the data (or both) that your program can utilize. The purpose of this appendix is to familiarize you with the different memory models and their ramifications.

This appendix is specifically for C on the 8086 family of processors. Further, the discussion of the C memory models assumes that you understand loosely how the 8086 family of CPUs operates. If not, you can still understand the difference between the various memory models and their uses.

THE 8086 FAMILY OF PROCESSORS

Before you can understand how the various memory models work, you need to understand how the 8086 processors address memory. For the rest of this appendix, the CPU will be referred to as the 8086, but the information applies to all processors in this family including the 8088, 80186, 80286, and the 80386. (The 80286 and the 80386 have modes of operation that are not relevant to the discussion that follows. However, when running DOS, they operate in a mode to which the information presented here relates.)

The 8086 contains 14 *registers* (memory locations) into which information is placed for processing or for program control. The registers fall into the following categories:

- general-purpose registers
- base-pointer and index registers
- segment registers
- special-purpose registers

All the registers in the 8086 CPU are 16 bits (two bytes) wide.

The *general-purpose registers* are the "workhorse" registers of the CPU. It is in these registers that values are placed for the processing of arithmetic operations: adding or multiplying; comparisons, including equality, less than, greater than, and the like; and branch, or jump, instructions. Each general-purpose register may be accessed either as one 16-bit register or as two 8-bit registers.

The *base-pointer* and *index registers* are used to provide support for such things as relative addressing, the stack pointer, and block move instructions.

The *segment registers* are used to support the 8086's segmented-memory scheme. The CS register holds the current code segment, the DS holds the current data segment, the ES holds the extra segment, and the SS holds the stack segment. Segments will be discussed later.

Finally, the *special-purpose registers* are: the flag register, which holds the state of the CPU, and the instruction pointer, which points to the next instruction for the CPU to execute.

Figure A-1 shows the layout of the 8086 registers.

Figure A-1

The 8086 CPU registers

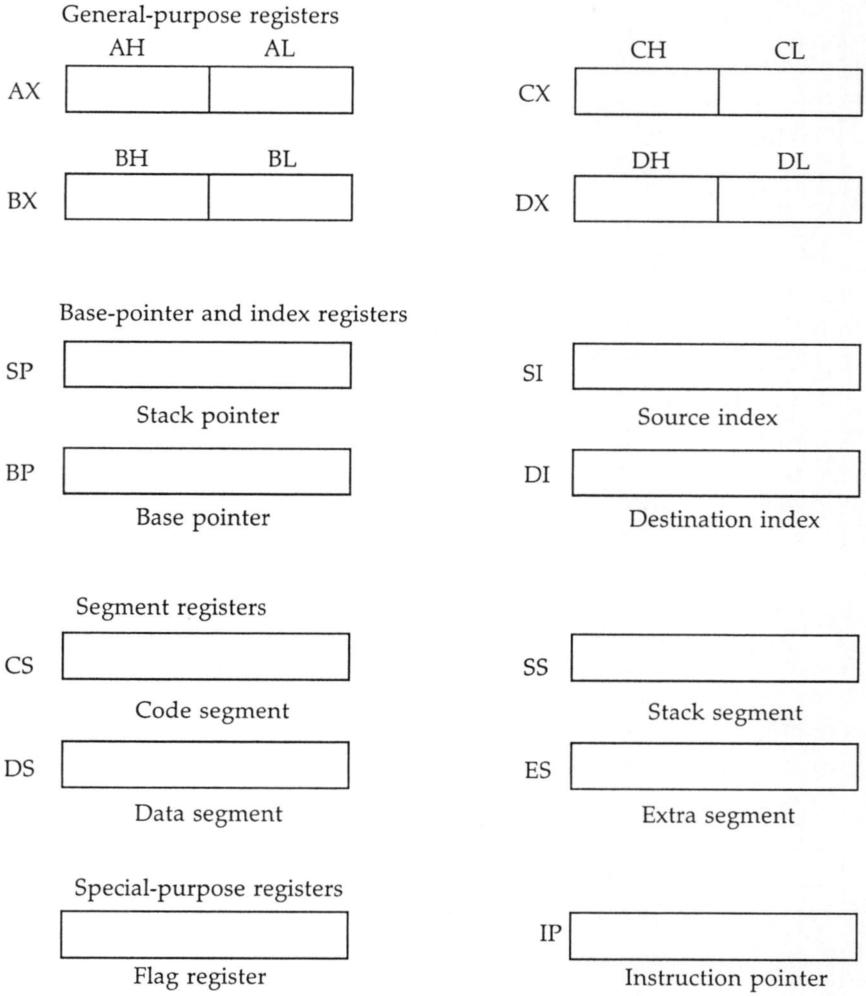

General-purpose registers

AH	AL
AX

CH	CL
CX

BH	BL
BX

DH	DL
DX

Base-pointer and index registers

SP

Stack pointer

SI

Source index

BP

Base pointer

DI

Destination index

Segment registers

CS

Code segment

SS

Stack segment

DS

Data segment

ES

Extra segment

Special-purpose registers

Flag register

IP

Instruction pointer

Address Calculation

The 8086 uses a segmented-memory architecture with a total address space of one megabyte, which is divided into 64K *segments*. The 8086 can directly access any byte within a segment and does so with a 16-bit register. Therefore, the address of any specific byte within the computer is the combination of the segment number and the 16-bit offset into the segment.

The 8086 uses four segments: one for code, one for data, one for the stack, and one extra segment. All segments start on addresses that are integer multiples of 16.

To calculate the actual byte referred to by the combination of the segment and the offset, you first shift the value in the segment register to the left by four bits and then add in the offset. This makes a 20-bit address. For example, if the segment register holds the value 10H and the offset 100H, then the following sequence shows how the actual address is derived:

```
segment register:               0 0 0 0  0 0 0 0  0 0 0 1  0 0 0 0
segment shifted:  0 0 0 0       0 0 0 0  0 0 0 1  0 0 0 0
offset:                         0 0 0 0  0 0 0 1  0 0 0 0  0 0 0 0
_ _ _ _ _ _ _ _ _ _ _ _ _ _ _ _ _ _ _ _ _ _ _ _ _ _ _ _ _ _ _ _
segment + offset  0 0 0 0       0 0 0 0  0 0 1 0  0 0 0 0  0 0 0 0
```

Most addresses are referred to in the 8086 in *segment:offset* form. The outcome of the example in this form is 0010:0100H. There are many segment:offsets that can describe the same byte because the segments may overlap each other. For example, 0000:0010 is the same as 0001:0000.

16- VERSUS 20-BIT POINTERS

As stated in the previous section, the 8086 only requires a 16-bit address to access memory within the segment already loaded into one of its segment registers. However, if you wish to access memory outside that segment, both the segment register and the offset must be loaded with the proper values. This means that a 20-bit address is required, and, since all registers in the 8086 are 16 bits long, the 20-bit address requires two registers, or 32 bits, to hold it. This is why you will sometimes see the phrase "32-bit address" used instead of the more accurate "20-bit adddress." The only difference between accessing memory within a current segment and accessing outside of it is that loading two 16-bit registers takes twice as long as loading one. Hence your programs run much more slowly. How they run more slowly is the subject of the next section.

MEMORY MODELS

Most C compilers implemented for the 8086 family of processors can compile your program in six different ways, and each organizes the computer's memory differently. The six models are called tiny, small, medium, compact, large, and huge. Let's look at each.

Tiny Model

The tiny model compiles a C program so that all the segment registers are set to the same value, and all addressing is done using 16 bits. This means that the code, data, and stack must all be within the same 64K segment. This method of compilation produces the smallest, fastest code.

Small Model

The small model is the default mode of compilation for many 8086-based C compilers and is useful for a wide variety of tasks. Although all addressing is done using only the 16-bit offset, the code segment is separate from the data, stack, and extra segments, which share a second segment. This means that the total size of a program compiled this way is 128K. The addressing time is the same for the tiny model, but the program can be twice as big. Most programs that you write will utilize this model.

Medium Model

The medium model is for large programs where the code exceeds the one-segment restriction of the small model. Here, the code may use multiple segments and requires 20-bit pointers, but the code, data, and extra segments share their own segment and use 16-bit addresses. This model works well for large programs that use little data.

Compact Model

The complement of the medium model is the compact model, in which the program code is restricted to one segment but the data may occupy several segments. This means that all accesses to data require 20-bit addressing but the code uses 16-bit addressing. This works well for programs with little code and large amounts of data.

Large Model

The large model allows both code and data to use multiple segments. However, each individual data item is limited to 64K. This model is used when you have both large code and large data requirements. It also runs much more slowly than any model except the huge model.

Huge Model

The huge model is the same as the large model except that in it a single item of data may exceed 64K. This makes run-time speed even slower, so it should not be used unless you need single data items to be larger than 64K.

Selecting a Model

Examine the size of your program and amount of data. Generally, you should use the small model unless there is a reason to do otherwise, as the table on page 515 illustrates.

Remember, both the large and huge models run substantially slower than the others.

Memory Models

	use if:	speed:
tiny	code, data, and stack are within 64K segment	fast
small	total program size is 128K or less	fast
medium	program code exceeds the one-segment restriction	moderate
compact	program code is one segment but data occupies several	moderate
large	both data and code use multiple segments, but each data item is 64K or less	slow
huge	single items of data exceed 64K	slow

OVERRIDING A MEMORY MODEL

You may think it unfortunate that even a single reference to data in another segment would require the slower compact model rather than the small model. Even though only an isolated part actually needs a 20-bit pointer, the entire program is slowed down. For example, as you have seen, it is necessary to use 20-bit addressing to access the video RAM to enable the graphics functions to write directly to it. These routines cannot afford to be slowed down by a larger memory model. To solve this and other related problems, the *segment override* type modifiers are added by many 8086-based C compilers. They are

near   far   huge

These modifiers may only be applied to pointers or functions. When applied to pointers they affect the way data is accessed. When applied to functions they affect the way in which a function is called and returned.

These modifiers follow the base type and precede the variable name. For example, this statement declares a **far** pointer called **f_pointer**.

```
char far *f_pointer;
```

Let's look at these now.

far

The most common model override is the **far** pointer. The reason for this is that it is very common to want to access some region of memory that may be outside the data segment. If the program is compiled for one of the larger data models, however, *all* access to data becomes very slow. The solution to this problem is to explicitly declare **far** pointers to the memory outside the current data segment. In this way, only references to objects actually far away will incur additional overhead.

The use of **far** functions is less common and is generally restricted to specialized programming situations in which a function may lie outside the current code segment (for example, in ROM). In these cases, the use of **far** ensures that the proper calling and returning sequences are used.

One very important thing about **far** pointers, as implemented by many 8086-based C compilers, is that pointer arithmetic only affects the offset. This means that if a **far** pointer with the value 0000:FFFF is incremented, its new value will be 0000:0000, not 1000:0000. Therefore, even though the pointer can access objects that are not in its own data segment, it may not access objects larger than 64K.

Two **far** pointers, as generally implemented, should not be used in a relational expression because only their offsets will be checked. As stated earlier, it is possible to have two different pointers actually contain the same physical address but have different segments and offsets. If you need to compare 20-bit pointers you must use **huge** pointers.

near

A **near** pointer is a 16-bit offset that uses the value of the appropriate segment to determine the actual memory location. The **near** modifier forces C to treat the pointer as a 16-bit offset to the segment contained in DS. You will use a **near** pointer when you have compiled a program using either the medium, large, or huge memory model.

Using **near** on a function causes that function to be treated as if it were compiled using the small code model. When a function is compiled using either the tiny, small, or compact model, all calls to the function place a 16-bit return address on the stack. If compiled with a large model, a 20-bit address is pushed on the stack. Therefore, in programs that are compiled for the large model, a highly recursive function should be declared as **near** to conserve stack space and speed execution time.

huge

The **huge** pointer is like the **far** pointer with two additions. First, its segment is normalized so that comparisons between **huge** pointers are meaningful. Second, a **huge** pointer may be incremented any number of times; it doesn't suffer from the "wraparound" problem as do **far** pointers.

AT®	International Business Machines Corporation
CBASIC®	Digital Research
dBASE™	Ashton-Tate Corporation
Epson®	Seiko Epson Corporation
Epson® FX-80™	Seiko Epson Corporation
Epson® LX-800™	Seiko Epson Corporation
Epson® MX-80™	Seiko Epson Corporation
Greenleaf Functions™	Greenleaf Software, Inc.
IBM®	International Business Machines Corporation
Intel®	Intel Corporation
Lattice® C	Lattice Corporation
Lisa®	Apple Computer, Inc.
Macintosh™	Apple Computer, Inc.
Microsoft® C	Microsoft Corporation
Microsoft Mouse™	Microsoft Corporation
Model 60™	International Business Machines Corporation
Paradox®	Ansa Software, a company of Borland International, Inc.
PDP-11™	Digital Equipment Corporation
Power C™	Mix Software
PS/2®	International Business Machines Corporation
Quattro®	Borland International, Inc.
QuickC™	Microsoft Corporation
Reflex: The Database Manager®	Borland International, Inc.
SideKick®	Borland International, Inc.

The manuscript for this book was prepared and submitted to
Osborne/McGraw-Hill in electronic form.
The acquisitions editor for this project was Jeffrey Pepper,
the technical reviewer was Tom Green,
and the project editor was Nancy Beckus.

Text design by Judy Wohlfrom, using Zaph for text body and for display.

Cover art by Stephen Black Design, Inc.
Color separation by Colour Image;
cover supplier, Phoenix Color Corporation.
Screens produced with InSet, from InSet Systems, Inc.
Book printed and bound by R.R. Donnelley & Sons Company,
Crawfordsville, Indiana.